THE MIDDLE AGES

AND THE EARLY MODERN PERIOD

FROM THE 5TH CENTURY TO THE 18TH CENTURY

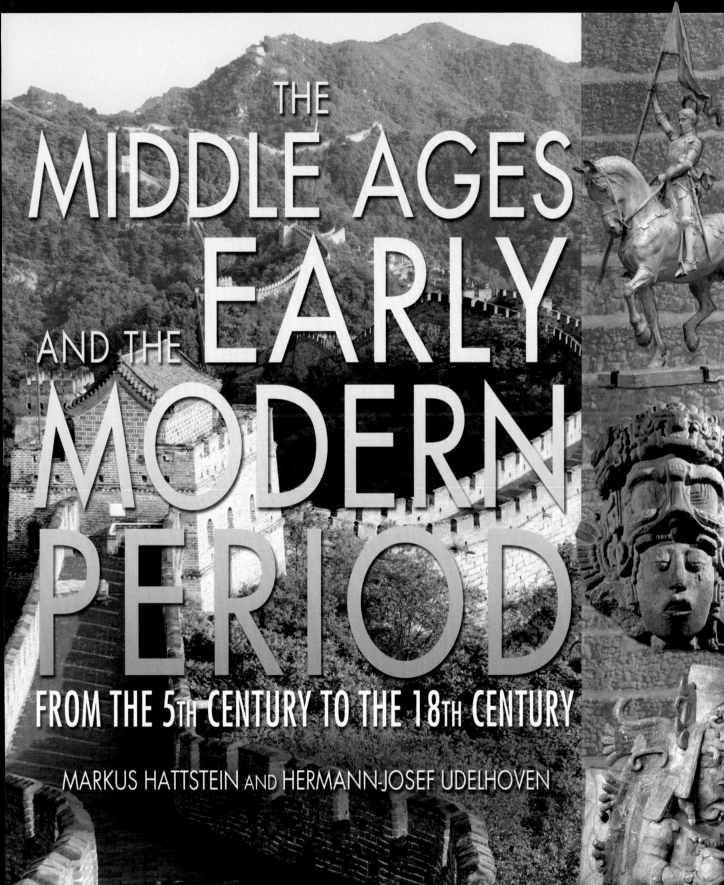

THE MIDDLE AGES AND THE EARLY MODERN PERIOD

FROM THE 5TH CENTURY TO THE 18TH CENTURY

MARKUS HATTSTEIN AND HERMANN-JOSEF UDELHOVEN

ROSEN
PUBLISHING

New York

This edition first published in 2013 by:

The Rosen Publishing Group, Inc.
29 East 21st Street
New York, NY 10010

Additional end matter copyright © 2013 by The Rosen Publishing Group, Inc.

Library of Congress Cataloging-in-Publication Data

Hattstein, Markus.
The Middle Ages and the early modern period: from the 5th century to the 18th century/Markus Hattstein, Hermann-Josef Udelhoven.
      p. cm.—(Witness to history—a visual chronicle of the world)
Includes bibliographical references and index.
ISBN 978-1-4488-7223-7 (library binding)
1. Middle Ages—Juvenile literature. 2. Civilization, Medieval—Juvenile literature. 3. Europe—History—476–1492—Juvenile literature. 4. Europe—History—1492–1648—Juvenile literature. 5. Europe—History—1648–1715—Juvenile literature. I. Udelhoven, Hermann-Josef. II. Title.
D117.H35 2012
940.1—dc23

                                                                                            2012010916

Manufactured in the United States of America

CPSIA Compliance Information: Batch #S12YA: For further information, contact Rosen Publishing, New York, New York, at 1-800-237-9932.

Copyright © 2005 Peter Delius Verlag, Berlin
Publisher: Peter Delius

All images from akg-images Berlin/London/Paris and from dpa Deutsche Presse Agentur, Hamburg. For detailed copyright information, please see *The Contemporary World: From 1945 to the 21st Century.*

The publishers would like to express their special gratitude to the team at akg-images Berlin/London/Paris who have made their incredible picture archive accessible and thus the extraordinary illustrations of this book possible.

Contents

Persecution: The prophet Muhammad hides from his enemies **p. 78**

Coronation: Charlemagne, king of the Franks, is crowned emperor **p. 17**

The architecture of the temples embodies the philosophy: Angkor Vat, Khmer temple, in the tropical jungle of Cambodia **p. 98**

8 The Middle Ages
5th–15th century

12 The Germanic Empires
14 The Kingdom of the Franks
18 The Holy Roman Empire in the High and Late Middle Ages
26 Switzerland
28 France in the High and Late Middle Ages
32 Burgundy and the Netherlands
34 England in the Middle Ages
40 Ireland and Scotland in the Middle Ages
42 Italy in the Middle Ages
50 Spain and Portugal in the Middle Ages
52 Northern Europe
54 Eastern Europe
58 Russia
62 The Byzantine Empire
66 Southeast Europe
70 The Crusades
76 *Key Ideas: Islam*
78 The Spread of Islam
88 The Mongolian Empire and Its Successors
92 India
94 China after the Han Dynasty
96 Japan
98 Southeast Asia
100 Sub-Saharan Africa
102 The Settlement and Early High Cultures of America

104 The Early Modern Period
16th–18th century

108 The German Empire: The Reformation and Its Consequences
112 The Thirty Years' War
116 The Holy Roman Empire under Enlightened Absolutism
122 France: From the Wars of Religion to the Eve of the Revolution
128 The Rise of England
134 The Netherlands: From the Struggle for Independence to the French Occupation
138 The Italy of Popes and Princes
142 Spain and Portugal
148 Eastern Europe and Scandinavia
152 Russia's Rise as a Great Power
154 The Ottoman Empire, the Great Power of the East
158 North Africa
160 Persia under the Safavids and Qajars
164 Mogul India and the European Trading Companies
168 China under the Ming and Manchu Emperors
172 Japan from the Muromachi Period to the Tokugawa Shogunate
176 Southeast Asia
178 Africa
180 The Ancient American Empires and the Conquest by Spain and Portugal
186 North America to the Founding of Canada and the United States

Conquest: Spanish soldiers invade the Mexican empire of the Aztecs **p. 181**

Reformation: Luther defends his ideas before Emperor Charles V **p. 108**

The Palace of Versailles: The bed-chamber of Louis XIV of France **p. 125**

190   Oceania and Australia to the Arrival of the
       Europeans
192   Glossary
194   For More Information
196   For Further Reading
197   Index

The Middle Ages
5th–15th century

T he upheaval that accompanied the migration of European peoples of late antiquity shattered the power of the Roman Empire and consequently the entire political order of Europe. Although Germanic kingdoms replaced Rome, the culture of late antiquity, especially Christianity, continued to have an effect and defined the early Middle Ages. Concurrent to the developments in the Christian West, in Arabia the Prophet Muhammad in the seventh century founded Islam, a new religion with immense political and military effectiveness. Within a very short time, great Islamic empires developed from the Iberian Peninsula and the Maghreb to India and Central Asia, with centers such as Córdoba, Cairo, Baghdad, and Samarkand.

The Cathedral Notre Dame de Reims, built in the 13th–14th century in the Gothic style; the cathedral served for many centuries as the location for the ceremonial coronation of the French king.

Tournament, book illustration, 15th century

Eltz castle on the Moselle, built 13th century

A Lord and his vassal, book illustration, 15th century

THE MIDDLE AGES

It was the humanists at the end of the 15th and beginning of the 16th centuries who gave the Middle Ages its name. They saw the Middle Ages merely as a "dark" time between the much-admired antiquity and their own modern times. However, our picture of this period is not shaped solely by this negative evaluation depicting intellectual decay, primitive customs, and lack of personal freedom. There also exist the images of the splendor of life at the royal courts, noble ❶ knights who would throw themselves into adventures for the honor of the king or the love of a lady, of huge ❷ stone castles, and of traveling troubadours and ❺ minstrels. We experience this world through the tales of the High Middle Ages—those of Chrétien de Troyes, Wolfram von Eschenbach, or Gottfried von Strassburg. These, however, as is known today, were idealized constructions of reality rather than its depiction. The literary reports that were passed down nurtured the ardor for the Middle Ages and its transfiguration by the German Romantics of the 19th century, whose sense of identity as a nation was fostered by the image of this supposedly glittering past.

A minstrel is given a wreath in return for his services, book illustration, beginning 14th century

Social Order

Society in the Middle Ages was a distinct class structure at whose head stood the nobility and the clergy. Underneath these, the third "estate" comprised the majority of the population, from the poorest beggars to the richest merchants. The discrete hierarchy was justified by the view that each estate had—like the limbs of a body—specific tasks to carry out for one another and the good of the whole. The association into social communities, as represented by the estates, was carried over into other areas of life, where the artisans formed guilds and believers organized into religious fraternities. In this, one sees not only the need for a sense of social security and belonging, but also the desire to find a place in the divine order.

Peasants work in the fields around Paris, which can be seen in the background, book illustration, ca. 16th c.

family of the vassal. If the vassal succeeded in making the fief hereditary in his family, he achieved a degree of independence, and his descendents had the chance to establish their own power base over time.

With investiture, however, a social relationship was also established: The vassal owed the ❸ lord loyalty and service, particularly in the case of war, while the lord on the other hand was obligated to provide loyalty and protection. The king stood at the top of this fiefdom pyramid, which encompassed all people from regional princes and high clergy to merchants and down to ❹ the peasants.

Living Conditions

In the Middle Ages, the working and living conditions, particularly of the simple population but also of the lower clergy and nobility, were relatively primitive—in comparison, for example, with those in the concurrently blossoming Islamic culture. Bad nutrition, miserable medical care, and wars and feuds provided insecure living conditions and a very low life expectancy. Mankind was powerless against epidemics such as the plague, or "Black Death," which in the middle of the 14th century took the lives of around 25 million people—a third of the total population—in Europe alone. It appears that movement by the Mongols and

Because agriculture was the most significant economic factor in the Middle Ages, the social order was strongly tied to the possession of land: Those who had land at their disposal had power and influence. Feudalism (from the Latin *feudum*, fief), which developed in France in the early Middle Ages, characterized this era in Europe. A fief was lent to a vassal by his lord. After the vassal's death, the land was returned to the lord, although later it often became hereditary in the

ca. 476	End of the Roman Empire	**800**	Charlemagne is crowned emperor	**1074–1122**	Investiture controversy
568	End of the Great Migration	**ca. 1031–1492**	Reconquista	**1096**	First crusades

6 Procession of flagellants, book illustration, 14th c.

7 Medieval bathing house, book illustration, ca. 1450

8 Lecture in theology at the Sorbonne, 15th century

merchant caravans brought the plague from Central Asia, where it had presumably already killed as many people, to the Middle East and Europe. Such epidemics made a huge impact on public consciousness, leading to a mood of impending doom and ❻ religious fanaticism, as well as a greed for ❼ life and pleasure.

Culture and Spiritual Life

The Church—and particularly its ❿ monasteries and convents, out of which internal church reforms were initiated—were the carriers and shapers of culture in the Middle Ages. Here, the knowledge of antiquity was preserved through the copying of texts, but also debate over them, and the creation of new religious and philosophical tracts, as well as

10 Parents bring their child to a convent school to be educated, book illustration, beginning 14th century

spiritual compositions for the Mass. The churches and monasteries were responsible not only for the preservation but also for the mediation of education and culture. Monastery and cathedral schools taught the *septem artes liberales* (seven liberal arts): grammar, rhetoric, dialectics, arithmetic, geometry, astronomy, and music. From these schools developed the first ❽ universities in the 12th century, initially as fraternities (*universitas*) of teachers and students. In addition to theology, law and medicine were the most important faculties.

It was also theologians who, through the philosophical discipline of scholasticism, set themselves the difficult task of unifying belief and knowledge, of combining theological dogma with scientific discoveries. As a reaction to the rational scholasticism, mystics such as Hildegard of Bingen and Meiseter Eckart sought an individualized internal experience of the divine. Lay movements such as the Beguines attempted, in non-monastic fraternities, to combine a new form of piety (*devotio moderna*) with everyday life. The institutionalized Inquisition (from the Latin for

"examination") was one of the innovations of the Church that strongly shaped the negative picture of the "dark Middle Ages." However, it was not only an instrument of repression, although its methods are infamous today; legally it constituted progress, in that it replaced the practice of "God's judgment," as the deciding factor in a trial, with examinations that had to follow certain rules. This opened the way for a modern criminal process trial.

9 Palazzo Comunale in Montepulciano, Tuscany, end of 14th c.

Transition to the Modern Era

The transition to the Modern Era took place in many fields, including philosophy, society, and the economy. With the emergence of the new international financial system and early capitalism after the 13th century, the possession of land became less important and the position of ❾ cities, where capital could be made through other means, primarily through international trade, became more powerful. The ⓫ "middle class" of society gained political influence in relation to the nobility and clergy, as they adapted quicker to these new paths to capital and wealth.

Especially in Flanders and Italy, with their many rich trading cities, the perception of mankind and the environment changed to a more worldly view that saw the here and now as increasingly important, which developed in the late Middle Ages in the wake of humanism and the emerging Renaissance. This was influenced by the rediscovery of texts from antiquity. Ultimately the demand of Catholic dogma for absolute interpretative authority broke up and made way for the scholarship of the Modern Era.

11 *Portrait of Giovanni Arnolfini and his Wife*, painting by Jan van Eyck, 1434

| 1209 | Franciscan Order founded | 1339–1453 | Hundred Years' War | 1492 | Columbus reaches the New World |
| 1231–32 | Inquisition centralized | 1453 | Ottomans conquer Constantinople | 1517 | Beginning of the Reformation |

1

THE GERMANIC EMPIRES 5TH CENTURY–774

The decline of the Roman Empire meant that the Germanic tribes were able to advance into its former territory. Although German peoples had been migrating through Europe since the second century, the large-scale westward advance of the Huns now put pressure on the Germanic tribes inhabiting Eastern Europe. They too moved further west, into Western and Southern Europe, where they founded generally short-lived kingdoms, such as the Ostrogoth empire of ❶ Theodoric the Great.

Tomb of Theodoric the Great in Ravenna, built ca. 520

Vandals, Burgundians, and Anglo-Saxons

In the fifth century, the Vandals, Burgundians, and Anglo-Saxons founded numerous states on the territory of the Western Roman Empire.

Moving from Eastern Europe through Spain, the Vandals arrived in North Africa in 429, and under their king ❷ Gaiseric, founded a kingdom with its capital at Carthage. They conquered the islands of the Western Mediterranean and in 455 ❸ plundered Rome in further campaigns. Later, the state was weakened by struggles over succession in the royal family and religious conflicts, particularly the persecution of Catholics by the Arian Vandals. By 535 the Byzantine general Belisarius had reconquered the Vandal kingdom for the emperor.

The Burgundians left Eastern Europe with the Vandals, but they only traveled as far as the Rhine-Main area, where they possibly made Worms their capital. In 437, this first Burgundian kingdom was destroyed by ❹ Hun mercenaries under the Roman general Flavius Aetius—an event described in the German epic story the "Nibelungenlied." In the following years, Aetius settled the rest of the tribe on Lake Geneva, where the Burgundians built up a second kingdom. In 534, they were defeated by the Merovingians and absorbed into the Frankish empire.

According to legend, the Angles, Saxons, and Jutes—under their leaders, the brothers ❺ Hengist and Horsa—had originally been called by the Britons themselves to help in internal disputes. The Germans settled permanently, however, and pushed the Celtic Britons into Wales and Cornwall. The Germans, who gradually merged to become the Anglo-Saxon people, founded numerous kingdoms, which were only gradually Christianized. One of these was the kingdom of Wessex, which initiated the unification of England in the ninth century.

2 GEISERICH.

Gaiseric, king of the Vandals, wood engraving, 1869

3

The Vandals loot Rome, wood engraving, 19th c.

4

The Burgundians defend themselves against the Huns, painting, 19th century

5 A king of the Celtic Britons greets Hengist and Horsa

"Nibelungenlied"

The medieval "Nibelungenlied" preserves the memory of the Great Migration of Peoples. In the second part, it describes the destruction of the Burgundian kingdom by the legendary king of the Huns, Etzel (Attila). The great heroic epic by an unknown author consists of 39 "adventures" and is based on various legendary cycles. It was not until the 18th century that the "Nibelungenlied" was rediscovered and elevated to the status of a German national epic.

Etzel or Attila, king of the Huns, and the daughter of the Burgundian king, book illustration, 15th c.

5th century | Creation of states by Vandals, Burgundians, and Anglo-Saxons
410 | Sack of Rome by Alaric
437 | Destruction of Burgundians by the Huns
455 | Plundering of Rome by Gaiseric
507 | Death of Alaric II

The Kingdoms of the Visigoths, Ostrogoths, and Lombards

The Visigoths created a kingdom in southern France in the fifth century, but were eventually driven into Spain by the Franks a century later. The kingdom of the Ostrogoths in Italy succumbed to the campaigns of the Byzantines. Eventually it was replaced by the kingdom of the Lombards.

6 Decorative cover of a Langobard bible, ca. 800

After the ⓫ Visigoths under Alaric had plundered Rome in 410, they eventually settled in south western France. Officially still under the sovereignty of the Roman emperor, they founded their own kingdom with Toulouse as its capital. In the second half of the fifth century, King Euric extended Visigoth rule all the way to Spain. His son ❼ Alaric II, however, fell in battle against the Franks in 507 when these breached the treaty made between the two empires a generation earlier. The Visigoths were then forced to withdraw to the Iberian Peninsula, where ⓬ Toledo became their new capital. There the Visigoths, who had previously practiced the Arian religion, converted to Catholicism in 568. This made assimilation into the local population possible. At the same time, the influence of the Church, which had allied itself with the higher ranks of the nobility, weakened the central authority within the kingdom. This facilitated rapid Arab subjugation of the Visigoths by 714–719; Christian rule continued only in the north of the Peninsula.

10 A Lombard, lithograph, 19th c.

The Ostrogoth king, ❾ Theodoric the Great, was raised as a hostage at the imperial court of Constantinople; his presence guaranteed Ostrogoth compliance with a treaty made between his father and the Byzantine Empire. As an ally of Eastern Rome, he marched to Italy and defeated Odoacer, the local ruler, and built up his own kingdom with ❽ Ravenna as capital. Theodoric unsuccessfully attempted to bind the German states together through dynastic marriages and so create a counterweight to the Eastern Roman Empire; he himself married the sister of the Frankish ruler Clovis I. After his death in 526 the Ostrogoth kingdom was weakened by the strict separation he had established between Arian Goths and Catholic Romans, as well as the resulting conflicts and unclear succession.

In 552, the Byzantine general Narses defeated the Ostrogoth king Totila, who had sought to restore the Gothic kingdom in Italy. For a short period Narses controlled Italy. However, the Byzantines were soon driven out by the ❻, ❿ Lombards under King Alboin. The Lombards settled in northern Italy in 568, in the area that came to be known as Lombardy, and later also in southern Italy. Only Ravenna, Rome, the southern tip of Italy, and Sicily remained Byzantine. These territories too were later partially conquered by the Lombards, while in central Italy the papacy gradually developed its own area of control that later became the Papal States. The Lombard kings in fact ruled only northwestern Italy from their capital Pavia, and several ruling dynasties reigned in rapid succession; there were other duchies only nominally subject to the king. Once the Franks under Charlemagne conquered northern Italy in 774, only the Lombard princes in the south remained independent.

7 Alarich II is defeated by Clovis I, lithograph, 19th century

8 Theodoric's palace in Ravenna, mosaic, ca. 500

9 Theodoric the Great welcomes delegates of Germanic tribes, wood engraving, 19th century

11 Visigoth kings, book illustration

12 The Old Town of Toledo with the cathedral on the left and the castle on the right

534 | Victory of the Franks over the Burgundians **552** | Victory of Narses over Totila **714** | Subjugation of the Visigoths by the Arabs

526 | Death of Theodoric the Great **535** | Defeat of the Vandal kingdom by Belisarius **568** | Arian Visigoths convert to Catholicism

1

THE KINGDOM OF THE FRANKS 486–843

Under Clovis I of the House of the Merovingians, the ❶ Franks gained supremacy in Western Europe. After his death, a dispute that would characterize the social and political history of the Middle Ages—that between a central monarch and local princes—began. The nobility had to be pacified with concessions before they would recognize the king. Frequent divisions of the kingdom under the legitimate heirs so weakened the Merovingians that they were ultimately forced to relinquish their power to the Carolingians, the former mayors of the palace. After a series of successful Carolingians came Charlemagne, the first emperor of the Holy Roman Empire.

The Frankish Empire in the age of the Merovingians and Carolingians, copperplate engraving, 17th c.

■ The Merovingians' Frankish Empire

Beginning with a small region south of the Rhine estuary, the Merovingians created the largest empire of the Germans of the early Middle Ages.

2

The death of Queen Brunhild in 613 following family intrigues, wood engraving, 19th century

4

Victory of Clovis I over Syagrius in the Battle of Soissons, embroidered tapestry, 15th century

The expansion of the Franks ❸ brought them into conflict with Syagrius, the last Roman governor of the region, who was defeated ❹ by the Merovingian Clovis I in 486. Clovis enlarged his domain considerably and, by the time of his death in 511, he ruled an area encompassing present-day France, Belgium, the Rhineland, and southwestern Germany. Clovis was baptized a Christian ❺ by Bishop Remigius of Reims, facilitated the merging of the Franks with the indigenous Gallo-Romans, and also allied the rulers of the Frankish kingdom, and later those of the Holy Roman Empire, with the papacy. In his legal code, the *Lex Salica*, Clovis excluded female accession to the throne. This established the continuity of the Merovingian line and that of their successors— the Carolingians and Capetians— into the 19th century, but also led to major conflicts such as the Hundred Years' War between France and England in the 14th century.

Despite this new regulation of succession, after his death, Clovis's empire was parceled out

among his four sons according to the old Frankish custom of drawing lots. Three new kingdoms thus came into being—Austrasia, Neustria, and Burgundy—whose respective rulers attempted to ❷ destroy each other. Chlotar II managed reunification a century later, but at great political cost. In order to gain the support of the nobility, he was forced to agree to the *Edictum Chlotharii* of 614, which stipulated that the royal officials—the counts—were to be chosen from among the property owners of the counties, strengthening the local nobility at the expense of central authority. Furthermore, the three kingdoms were each to have a "mayor of the

3

Frankish warrior armed for battle, wood engraving, 19th century

palace," who would represent the king and hold great authority. The last Merovingian to reign over a unified empire, from 629 to 639, was Dagobert I. ❻ Discord within the dynasty made possible the ascent of the Carolingians.

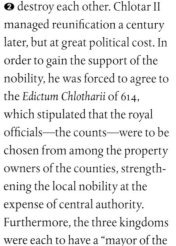

5

The baptism of Clovis I by Bishop Remigius, painting, 19th century

6

King Dagobert I builds the church of Saint-Denis, manuscript, 14th century

The Rise of the Carolingians

The Carolingian mayors of the palace seized power in the Frankish kingdom

In Dagobert I's Austrasia, the office of mayor of the palace was held by Pépin I, who founded the Carolingian ❾ line. While the Merovingians remained on the throne as puppet rulers, his grandson Pépin II acquired effective power throughout the Frankish kingdom after he defeated the mayor of the palace of Neustria at Tertry in 687.

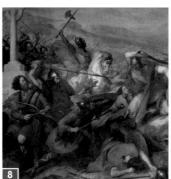

7 Charles Martel slays an Arab, bronze casting, 19th century

When Pépin II died in 714, his son, ❼ Charles Martel ("the Hammer"), came to power, though he also never laid claim to the crown. He defeated Germanic tribes such as the Thuringians, bound the Bavarians to the kingdom, and promoted the mission of St. Boniface ❿ in Germany. Most famously, he halted the advance of the Arabs into Western Europe, for which he was later celebrated as the "Savior of the West." In 732, Charles defeated an Arab army in battle ❽ at Tours, near Poitiers; seven years later, the Arabs were also driven out of Provence. Charles assembled a heavily armed mounted army—a military innovation that laid the foundation for the European feudal system and chivalry. To pay for their armor, the cavalry were allotted fiefs and had to swear an oath to serve their king when called upon.

In 747 Charles Martel's son, Pépin III, took over the post of mayor of the palace in Austrasia from his brother Carloman, who, after a bloody fight against the Alemanni, retired to a monastery. In 751, Pépin III ended the nominal rule of the Merovingians by exiling the last king to a monastery. He assumed the title of king, the first of the Carolingian dynasty, and three years later he had himself confirmed by Pope Stephen II.

Pépin III returned the favor by defending Rome ⓫ against the Lombard princes and offering their captured territories to the pope as the "Donation of Pépin". These territories later became the basis of the Papal States. Shortly before his death in 768, following the example of the Merovingians, Pépin divided the Frankish kingdom between his sons, Charlemagne and Carloman.

8 The Battle of Tours, near Poitiers, painting, 19th century

9 Pépin and Bega, first of the Carolingian line, painting by Rubens, 17th century

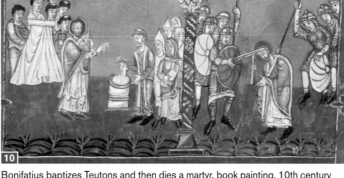

10 Bonifatius baptizes Teutons and then dies a martyr, book painting, 10th century

11 Pépin III and Pope Stephan II defeat the Lombards, copper engraving, 17th c.

The Mayors of the Palace

The mayor of the palace was initially responsible only for the running of the royal household. However, once they began to take on military tasks their political influence increased. The mayors of the palace were not only governors in their respective areas of the kingdom, but under weak kings became the true rulers of these territories. In the end, the Merovingian kings had a merely symbolic function until the Carolingian mayors of the palace finally took the throne for themselves, in name as well as in practice.

King Clovis III, a minor, with the mayor of the palace, Pippin II, wood engraving, 19th century

746 | "Canstatte Court Day" bloodbath against the Alemanni   751 | Pépin III becomes king   768 | Death of Pépin III and division of the Frankish empire

747 | Pépin III becomes mayor of the palace in Austrasia   754 | Donation of Pépin

Charlemagne's Wars

Charlemagne enlarged the Frankish kingdom by annexing numerous territories.

Pépin III's son, Carloman, died just three years after his father, in 771. His elder brother, ❶ Charlemagne, took Carloman's territories for himself and ignored the custom whereby the lands would be divided between the sons. Carloman's sons then fled to seek refuge in the court of the Lombards, who were at this time threatening the Papal State. When, in 772, ❺ Pope Hadrian I reminded Charlemagne of his duty as protector of Rome, Charlemagne came to his defense in 773–774. The Lombards were comprehensively defeated, and Charlemagne proclaimed himself their new king. Most of northern Italy was thereby incorporated into the Frankish kingdom.

1 Charlemagne riding, statue, ca. 870

Since 772 Charlemagne had also been attempting to conquer the Saxons. Initial military successes, attempts at Christianization, and even collaboration with the Saxon nobility were not enough to subjugate the free Saxon peasants, who fought against the Franks under ❸ the leadership of Wittekind. After they annihilated a Frankish army in 782, Charlemagne ordered a vengeful massacre. Thousands of captured Saxons were murdered at *Verden an der Aller*. In 785 Wittekind made peace with Charlemagne and was baptized. It still took a long time, however, until all the Saxons submitted to Charlemagne and were baptized as Christians. The Bavarians were particularly reticent and refused to pay taxes to the Church. In the course of his campaign of Christianization, Charlemagne established many new ❷ bishoprics among the Saxons. In Bavaria, which Charles Martel had already conquered, Duke Tassilo III threatened to ally himself with

2 St. Peter's Dome in Minden, seat of the bishopric founded ca. 800 by Charlemagne

3 Wittekind bows before Charlemagne, painting, 19th century

the Avars and secede from the kingdom. He was deposed for this disloyalty at the Diet of Ingelheim in 788.

Charlemagne then began to secure his borders by setting up margravates in which the royal administrators also held military authority. In 796, the Avarian margravate was founded after the Avars in present-day Hungary had been subdued. Further north, treaties with the Bohemians and the Slavic Sorbs regulated the flow of tribute payments, and in 811 Charlemagne made peace with the Danes on the northern border. His only defeats came against the Basques and ❻ the Arabs—the latter triumphing in ❹ the 778 Battle of Roncesvalles, which is described in the medieval "Song of Roland."

5 Pope Hadrian I greets Charlemagne as he arrives in Rome, illustrated manuscript, 13th century

Einhard

Einhard wrote the famous biography of Charlemagne called the Vita Caroli Magni. *He entered Charlemagne's palace school around 794 at the age of 25 and was soon employed in diplomatic work. Einhard counseled Charlemagne's son Louis the Pious in his church policies and was the abbot of Seligenstadt monastery until his death in 840.*

Einhard writing the life of Charlemagne, manuscript, 14 c.

4 Battle of Roncesvalles, stone relief, 12th century

6 Arabs dress as devils to frighten Charlegmagne's army, book illustration, 14th century

771	Death of Carloman	773–774	War against the Lombards	782	Saxons under Wittekind defeat the Franks	788	Deposition of Tassilo III
	772	Crusades against the Saxons	778	Battle of Roncesvalles	785	Peace between the Saxons and Franks	

The Empire of Charlemagne

Charlemagne modernized the administration and culture of his empire. Under his successors, however, the Frankish empire fell to ruin. Despite this, the reign of Charlemagne had a major bearing on the course of history in the Middle Ages.

7 Cupola of the Imperial Cathedral in Aachen, built 788–805

By the turn of the ninth century **8** Charlemagne's empire encompassed major portions of West and South Europe. The papacy wanted to secure the support of the powerful Frankish king for good, and so Pope Leo III crowned Charlemagne **10** emperor in 800 during the Christmas Mass at St. Peter's Basilica in Rome. The emperor of Byzantium, who considered himself to be the true heir of the Roman Empire, initially refused to accept this.

Only when Charlemagne relinquished territories on the Adriatic, under the Treaty of Aachen in 812, did Byzantium recognize the new empire. Charlemagne ruled his empire from Aachen and wanted to turn the city, his main residence, into a "new Rome." He had an imperial cathedral, with an **7**, **9** octagonal chapel built. Charlemagne sent *missi dominici*—agents—**11** to control the counts in whose hands the provinces were placed. As long as the laws of the subjugated peoples did not contradict those of Charlemagne, they were allowed to retain them.

When he died in 814, Charlemagne left his whole empire to his youngest son, Louis the Pious. Louis's sons, however—Louis the German,

9 Charlemagne's throne in the Octagonal chapel of Aachen Cathedral, marble, late 8th century

Charles II (the Bald), and Lothair I—later fought for the succession and ended up dividing the empire in the **12** Treaty of Verdun of 843. This division roughly established

8 Bust of Charlemagne, silver with gold-plating, 14th century

the future frontier between France and Germany. The border territory was named Lotharingia (later Lorraine) after Lothair II. Further divisions and disputes among the successors as well as attacks by the Normans and Magyars, saw the empire decline. The Carolingian line died out in the East Frankish empire— today's Germany—with the death of Louis III ("the Child") in 911. In the West Frankish territories— today's France— they ruled until 987.

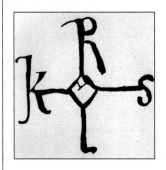

The "Carolingian Renaissance"

The "Carolingian Renaissance" of Charlemagne, who probably could not read or write himself but sought the restoration of the Roman Empire, aimed to fuse Christian, ancient, and Germanic cultures. Under the leadership of the Anglo-Saxon scholar and priest Alcuin, an educational campaign was set in motion and scholars were summoned from all over Europe. The centrally established palace school was emulated throughout the empire in the form of cathedral and monastery schools. In these, monks functioned as the leading disseminators of medieval culture. The Carolingian minuscule script forms the basis of today's Roman, or Antiqua, typefaces.

above: Charlemagne's signature, a monogram written in Carolingian minuscule script, which became the standard across most of Europe.

10 Pope Leo III crowns Charlemagne, illustrated manuscript, 15th century

11 Charlemagne dispatches messengers to the provinces of his empire, illustrated manuscript, 15th century

12 The signing of the Treaty of Verdun, wood engraving, 19th century

THE HOLY ROMAN EMPIRE IN THE HIGH AND LATE MIDDLE AGES 911–1519

The German High Middle Ages were marked by three successive ❶ imperial dynasties—the Saxon, the Salian, and the Hohenstaufen—that struggled for unity of the empire and the central authority of the ruler. While the Saxons leaned on the clergy, the Salians and the Hohenstaufens saw the enhanced status of the Church merely as further competition, added to that of the princes, for supremacy in the empire. Attempts to introduce a hereditary monarchy failed. In the Late Middle Ages, the particularism of the princes triumphed over the concept of a centralized state.

The crown of the Holy Roman Empire made of gold, silver and gemstones, tenth–eleventh century

The Beginnings of the Holy Roman Empire under the Saxons

The Holy Roman Empire developed out of the East Frankish empire. The duke of Saxony, Henry I, was chosen as king and consolidated the empire.

The Carolingians, descendants of the Frankish king Charles the Great and his son Louis, had quickly dismantled tribal duchies such as those of the Saxons, the Swabians, the Alemanni, the Thuringians, and the Bavarians in the east of their empire. However, they were reintroduced for the administration of the vast realm. Facing threats from the Magyars, Slavs, and Normans, the dukes appointed by the king were granted military authority, and with the decline in royal authority, they became increasingly autonomous. With the end of the East Frankish Carolingians in 911, at a great assembly the German princes chose Duke Conrad of Franconia as king. He was followed in 919 by ❹ Henry I of Saxony, known popularly as "Henry the Fowler." This procedure instituted the concept of a monarchy that was elective rather than hereditary.

Henry immediately signed a ❷ treaty with the West Frankish— that is, French—king, Charles III (the Simple), confirming the independence of the East Frankish or Holy Roman Empire. Henry brought the West Frankish Lorraine under his control in 925. In the Battle of Riade in Thuringia in 933, he was able to fend off the ❸ Magyars, who attacked the kingdom in plundering raids.

Henry's successors were remarkable for their energy. After Henry's death in 936, his son Otto I became the first German king to be crowned in Aachen, or Aix-la-Chapelle, thereby establishing a link to the tradition of Charlemagne. As a counterbalance to the nobility, Otto relied heavily on the ❺ Church for support. He increased the Church's possessions as well as the legal authority of its dignitaries. In return, the Church was obligated to provide the ruler with financial and military support. The celibacy of the clergy prohibited hereditary transmission of offices and fiefs, so after the death of each incumbent, these reverted to the crown. In order for this policy to work, investiture—that is, the filling of ecclesiastical offices—had to be an entitlement of the ruler, not the pope. This led to long-term disputes that resulted in the investiture controversy of the eleventh and twelfth centuries.

Henry I and Charles the Simple meet before signing the treaty in 921

Henry I's victory over the Magyars, wood engraving, 19th century

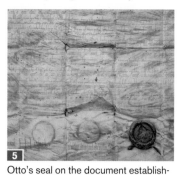

Otto's seal on the document establishing the bishopric of Brandenburg, 948

Quedlinburg in Saxony-Anhalt, view of the castle, home of the Saxons under Henry I, and later a convent founded by St. Matilda and Henry's son Otto

| 911 | Election of Conrad I as king | 925 | Incorporation of West Frankish Lorraine | 936 | Coronation of Otto I in Aachen | 955 | Battle of Lechfeld |
| 919 | Election of Henry I as king | 933 | Battle of Riade | 950 | Unterwerfung Böhmens |

The Ottonian Renaissance and the End of the Saxons

Otto I (the Great) prevailed in Italy and against the Slavs and was able to maintain his power. His successor, on the other hand, did not have time to consolidate his empire.

In order to control the fractious duchies, Otto I gave Bavaria to his brother Henry and Swabia, which had emerged out of the former Alemannia, to his eldest son Liudolf. Even they repeatedly challenged the authority of the king as did the other dukes.

Otto the Great was more successful in foreign affairs. In 950, he subjugated the Bohemians. He secured the border territories by erecting new marches and bishoprics for converting the

8 Henry II's tombstone, sculptures by Tilman Riemenschneider, 1513

Slavs. A plea for help from the widow of the king of Italy, Adelaide of Lombardy, took Otto across the Alps for the first time in 951. He married Adelaide and became king of Italy. In further campaigns, Otto was once again able to repulse the Magyars in 955 at ⓫ Lechfeld near Augsburg, defeated the Lombard princes, and prevailed against the Byzantines. In 962, he was crowned Holy Roman Emperor by the pope. From this event dates the tradition by which the king crowned at Aachen was entitled to be crowned Holy Roman Emperor at Rome. As a means of reconciliation with Byzantium, Otto's son, Otto II, married Theophano, the daughter of the Byzantine emperor.

Otto II reigned for only ten years, from 973 to 983. Within the empire, he had

to subdue his cousin Henry II (the Quarrelsome) of Bavaria. Otto's position in Italy was weakened in 982 by a defeat in Calabria at the hands of the Arabs, and the great Slavic uprising of 983 meant the loss of territories beyond the Elbe River.

Following the death of Otto II, Theophano and her mother-in-law Adelaide defended the reign of young ❾ Otto III against Henry the Quarrelsome. Otto later promoted the spread of Eastern missionary work through the founding of archbishoprics in Gniezno in Poland and Gran in Hungary. In Italy, he succeeded in having his cousin Bruno elected as ❼ Pope Gregory V—the first German pope—in 996. Roman ❿ patricians did not like the idea of a ❻ German empire being ruled from Rome, however, and drove Otto out of the city in 1001. The son of Henry the Quarrelsome, from the Bavarian line of Saxons,

7 Pope Gregory V, copper engraving, 16th century

9 Otto III between two clerical and two secular gentlemen, book illustration, late tenth century

took the throne as Emperor ❽ Henry II in 1002, but he died without issue, and the dynasty died with him.

6 The four parts of the Empire; Sclavinia (Eastern Europe), Germania (Germany), Gallia (France), and Roma (Italy) pay tribute, book illustration, tenth c.

Theophano

After the death of Otto II, Theophano, the Byzantine princess, took over the regency for the underage Otto III until her own death in 991. During this period, Byzantine culture gained greatly in influence, as she brought many artists with her from her homeland, along with the worship of Saint Nicholas. Her daughters, Adelaide and Sophia, became abbesses in Quedlinburg, Gandersheim, and Essen. These centers of medieval culture in Saxony remained autonomous principalities ruled over by the abbesses until 1803.

10 Otto III punishes the leader of a rebellion in 998 by gouging out his eyes and chopping off his hands, copper engraving, 17th century

11 Otto I's victory over the Magyars in the Battle of Lechfeld, book illustration, 15th century

Otto II, Theophano, and her son Otto III kneel before Christ, ivory carving in Byzantine style, ca. 983–84

The Prelude to the Investiture Controversy under the Salians

In their power struggle with the princes, Conrad II and Henry III looked to the cities, the reformed papacy, and the ministeriales for support.

In 1024 on the death of Henry II, ❶ Conrad II, a Franconian relative of the Ottonians, was elected king of Germany by the nobles and founded the ❺ Salian dynasty. A hereditary contract concluded under the Ottonians led to the annexation of the kingdom of Burgundy by Germany during his reign in 1033.

1 Seal depicting Holy Roman Emperor Conrad II

Though the king now controlled all the passes through the Alps, the cities of Burgundy were becoming more independent. As a counterbalance to the powerful princes, the Lombard cities had been granted privileges by the king, but they too had begun to oppose the royal claim to authority. The wealth of the metropolitan bishops and the higher nobility created conflict with the lesser gentry.

Conrad's son ❷ Henry III, who ascended the throne in 1039, intervened more directly in ecclesiastical affairs. He thought he could control the papacy by standing up for the Cluniac reform movement. He supported the reformers in their fight against marriage of the clergy and simony. Henry succeeded, despite the influence of the opposing Roman aristocracy, in having several ❸ reform-minded popes elected, among them Clement II and Leo IX. Although he was initially successful, his actions created great problems for the Holy Roman Empire in the long run, as the newly acquired self-confidence of the Church made it, in addition to the princes, a powerful opponent of the king—as the reign of his son Henry IV would show.

The German kings came to depend more and more on the *ministeriales*, whose rise to power had begun in the eleventh century. ❹ Ministeriales were originally servants working in the administration and the army who were provided with nonhereditary fiefs. This dependency on their lords made them trustworthy and so they were increasingly entrusted with court offices and the administration of royal property at the state level.

2 Henry III and his wife before the Virgin Mary, book illustration, 1050

3 Henry III designates Pope Clement II in 1046, wood engraving, 19th century

4 Ministers draw up documents, book illustration from the *Codex Manesse*, 14th century

5 Speyer Cathedral, built by Conrad II, where kings of the Salian dynasty are buried

The Cluniac Reform

The Cluniac reform movement was a religious model that initially sought to cleanse the Church of worldly influences. It developed out of the French Benedictine monastery founded in 910 in Cluny and owed its importance to the greatness of its abbots, who were pious and strong-willed. It insisted that the clergy must strictly observe celibacy and prohibited simony—the sale of Church offices. Pope Gregory VII gave the movement a political direction: The new moral superiority was to be reflected in temporal dominance. The popes thereafter claimed supremacy over monarchies and fought the investiture of clergy by the king, particularly in the German empire.

Model of the Benedictine abbey of Cluny, ca. 1900

| 1024 | Election of Conrad II as king | 1039 | Henry III becomes king | 1049–54 | Pontificate of Leo IX | 1073–85 | Pontificate of Gregory VII / Cluniac reforms |
| 1033 | Incorporation of Burgundy | | 1046 | Election of Pope Clement II | 1066 | Henry IV becomes king |

The Investiture Controversy and the End of the Salians

Henry IV struggled with the revitalized papacy for political supremacy, but no compromise was reached between the two powers until his son Henry V took the throne.

When ❻ Henry IV, the son of Henry III, assumed power in 1056, he sought support from the ministeriales, as well as from the increasingly important ❼ cities. In the cities, a self-confident middle class had emerged whose capital provided a counterbalance to the nobility's control over the countryside.

The reform papacy favored by his father had grown to be the chief opponent of Henry IV. ❾ Pope Gregory VII demanded the papacy's complete control over all interests of the Church, particularly over investiture—the right to appoint clergy to their offices. When Henry consequently declared the pope deposed at the Synod of Worms in January 1076, Gregory responded by excommunicating the king, freeing Henry's subjects as well as the princes from their loyalty oath to the king. An assembly of princes held at Tribur demanded Henry's abdication should the excommunication remain in effect. This conflict precipitated the breakup of the feudal system in the Empire and destroyed the sovereignty of the German monarchs. The nobles took advantage of the struggle between emperor and pope to enrich themselves with the wealth abandoned by the bishops.

In 1077 Henry went to see the pope at Canossa, where he regained his right of regency. This put him in a position in 1080 to defeat the rebellion of princes who had elected ❽ Rudolf of Swabia as their king in the meantime. Later, Pope Urban II repeated the ban on lay investiture at the Synod of Clermont in 1095, and even Henry's own children turned against him. Conrad, his oldest, disempowered him in Italy in the 1090s, aided by a rebellion of the Lombard cities. Henry, his second son, whom he had chosen as his successor, pressured by an uprising of the princes, forced his father to abdicate in 1105, becoming Henry V. Henry IV died the following year.

Following revolts, ⓫ Henry V brought about an agreement with the princes at the Diet of the Holy Roman Empire at Würzburg in 1121. The ❿ Concordat of Worms of 1122 finally brought an end to the investiture controversy: The Church would choose who would hold the offices of bishops and abbots, while the king would invest them with their temporal jurisdictions. The imperial Church could therefore not be used as an instrument of power.

The Journey to Canossa

Henry IV went to Canossa in northern Italy to meet Pope Gregory VII and have his excommunication rescinded. The pope is said to have made Henry wait barefoot in the snow and cold of January for three days and nights, as proof of penance. Although a "journey to Canossa" proverbially means to admit defeat, this was actually more of a victory for Henry IV, who regained his freedom to act with the blessing of the Church through the revocation of his excommunication.

above: Henry IV in Canossa in 1077, painting, 19th century

6 Emperor's seal of Henry IV with the inscription "Heinricus D(ei) Gra(tia) Rex" (Henry, king by the mercy of God)

7 View of Nuremberg, city of the Holy Roman Empire, founded in the 11th century, with the emperor's castle, wood engraving, late 15th century

9 Pope Gregory VII is liberated and dies in exile in 1085; Henry IV with the antipope Clement III, wood engraving, twelfth century

10 Cathedral of Worms, built in the 12th–13th century

8 Rudolf of Swabia is killed in battle in 1080, wood engraving, 19th century

11 Henry V captures Pope Paschal II, wood engraving, 19th century

◼ The Battle between the Welfs and the Hohenstaufens

Neither Conrad III nor Frederick I was able to achieve permanent supremacy over the papacy and the powerful princes of the empire.

The battle of Legnano, painting, 19th century

Tombs of Henry the Lion and his wife Maud of England in Brunswick, chalk-stone statues, before 1250

Henry V, the last Salian king, died in 1125, and the Saxon duke Lothair of Supplinburg was chosen as his successor. As emperor, Lothair II allied himself with the Welfs, who reigned over the duchy of Bavaria, to successfully oppose his rival, the Hohenstaufen Duke Conrad of Swabia. Lothair arranged the marriage of his daughter Gertrude to Henry the Proud, the son of the Welf duke. Henry thus inherited both his family's and Lothair's estates, thereby unifying Saxony and Bavaria and making the Welfs the most powerful princes of the empire.

Nevertheless, the princes chose Conrad as the new king to succeed Lothair in 1138. Conrad III deposed Henry and gave his duchy to loyal princes, and the conflict between the Welfs and the Hohenstaufens split the empire throughout the next century. Saxony was given to the Ascanian Albrecht the Bear, and Bavaria went to the Babenberg Henry Jasomirgott. However, Henry the Proud's son ❷ Henry the Lion—who was also the son-in-law of the powerful English king Henry II—regained Saxony only four years later.

To finally bring about a reconciliation, Conrad's nephew and successor Frederick I reinstated the Welfs in Bavaria in 1156, naming Henry Jasomirgott duke of Austria as compensation.

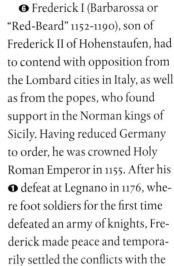

❸ Pope Adrian IV (1154–59), copper engraving, 16th century

❻ Frederick I (Barbarossa or "Red-Beard" 1152-1190), son of Frederick II of Hohenstaufen, had to contend with opposition from the Lombard cities in Italy, as well as from the popes, who found support in the Norman kings of Sicily. Having reduced Germany to order, he was crowned Holy Roman Emperor in 1155. After his ❶ defeat at Legnano in 1176, where foot soldiers for the first time defeated an army of knights, Frederick made peace and temporarily settled the conflicts with the Italian cities, the ❸ papacy, and Sicily.

During the battles in Italy, ❹ Henry the Lion, head of the House of Welf, contrary to his feudal oath, refused to assist the king. In a subsequent trial, Henry was denounced and lost his duchies; the Welfs were allowed to retain only their private estates. Bavaria was given to the House of Wittelsbach, and the greatly reduced Saxony once again went to the Ascanians. Many territories that had been dependencies of Bavaria or Saxony were placed directly under the emperor's authority. Thus the old tribal duchies were dissolved once and for all, and the path was then open for the emergence of smaller territorial states. Henry

Frederick I Barbarossa begs in vain for help from Henry the Lion for the war against the Lombard cities' league, sketch, 19th century

Frederick I drowns in 1190 in the Saleph, book illustration, 13th century

went to live in exile with his English relatives.

In 1189, Frederick handed over power to his eldest son, Henry, and took over the leadership of the Third Crusade, but after winning two great victories, he ❺ drowned under mysterious circumstances in the river Saleph in Asia Minor in 1190.

❻ Frederick I Barbarossa makes Henry II Jasomirgott Duke of Upper Austria and gives back Bavaria to Henry the Lion, painting, 19th century

| 1125 | Death of Henry V | 1142 | Henry the Lion reacquires Saxony | 1176 | Battle of Legnano | 1190 | Death of Frederick I, succeeded by Henry VI |
| 1138 | Election of King Conrad III | 1156 | Coronation of Frederick I as Holy Roman Emperor | 1189 | Frederick I leads the Third Crusade |

The Decline of the Hohenstaufens

The conflict between the Hohenstaufens and the Welfs irrevocably weakened the German monarchy. It continued until the Hohenstaufen line died out.

7

Dankwarderode Castle in Brunswick with dome and lion monument

The Norman kingdom of Sicily became a base for Hohenstaufen rule. ❿ Henry VI, who followed his father Frederick Barbarossa, as emperor in 1190, married ❾ Constance, heiress of Sicily. But Henry died before realizing his plans for a hereditary monarchy over Germany and Italy. His underage son Frederick succeeded him only in Sicily, while in the empire the struggle between the Hohenstaufens and the Welfs erupted once again.

In 1198, two rival kings were chosen: the Hohenstaufen Philip of Swabia, a brother of Henry VI, and the Welf Otto IV, a son of Henry the Lion. Pope Innocent III at first supported the Welfs, but when Otto, the sole monarch after the death of Philip in 1208, moved to appropriate Sicily, Innocent changed sides and accepted Frederick II as king of Germany. Otto, though supported by his English relatives, was defeated by Frederick and his ally, the French king Philip II Augustus, in 1214 at the ❽ Battle of Bouvines, near Lille. When Otto died in 1218, Frederick became the undisputed king, and in 1220 he was crowned Holy Roman Emperor.

⓫ Frederick II lived in ⓭ Southern Italy, founded the University of Bologna to train state officials and reigned over Germany primarily through the allocation of royal prerogatives, leaving the sovereign authority and imperial estates to the ecclesiastical and secular princes. This favored the division of the empire and the autonomy

8

The flight of the emperor's army after the Battle of Bouvines, book illustration

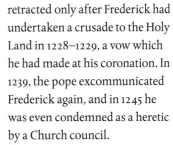

10 Henry VI, wood engraving, 19th century

of the sovereign princes. In 1226, Frederick tasked the German orders with the conquest and conversion of Prussia. A reconciliation with the Welfs took place in 1235, when Otto the Child, grandson of Henry the Lion, was named duke of ❼ Brunswick and Lunenburg. However, the power struggle with the popes continued and resulted in Frederick's excommunication in 1227, which was retracted only after Frederick had undertaken a crusade to the Holy Land in 1228–1229, a vow which he had made at his coronation. In 1239, the pope excommunicated Frederick again, and in 1245 he was even condemned as a heretic by a Church council.

When Frederick died in 1250, his son Conrad IV reigned only a short time before his own death in 1254. His son Conradin immediately had to defend Sicily against an invasion by Charles of Anjou, a brother of the French king. Conradin was defeated in 1268 at the Battle of Tagliacozza

9

Crown of Constance, heiress of Sicily, ca. 1200

11

Frederick II, marble sculpture, ca. 1240

12

Execution of Conradin in 1268 in Naples, quill lithograph, 19th century

and was handed over to Charles after having fled the battlefield and was ⓬ executed in Naples. He was the last of the Hohenstaufen dynasty.

13

Castel del Monte in Southern Italy, Frederick II's hunting lodge, built ca. 1240–50

| 1220 | Coronation of Frederick II as Holy Roman Emperor | 1227 and 1239 | First and second excommunication of Frederick II | 1268 | Battle of Tagliacozza |
| 1214 | Battle of Bouvines | 1228 | Start of the conquest and conversion of Prussia | 1250 | Death of Frederick II |

The Power Politics of the Houses of Habsburg, Luxembourg, and Wittelsbach

After the breakdown of centralized royal authority, local rulers fell back on their authority over their own lands. This led to conflicts of interests between the empire and the individual dynasties.

Following the end of the Hohenstaufen dynasty, a period known as the Interregnum set in. In 1257, a descendant of Philip of Swabia, the Spanish king Alfonso X of Castile, was elected Holy Roman

Rudolf I invests his sons with Austria and Styria in 1282, book illustration, 16th century

Emperor. However, he was just as incapable of gaining recognition as his rival, the English claimant, Richard, earl of Cornwall. The absence of both these foreign monarchs made it possible for the local clerical and secular princes to extend their own power.

Gradually, a group of the most important princes, the *Kurfürsten*, emerged and claimed the exclusive right to elect the king.

Following the death of Richard of Cornwall in 1273, the princes elected ❶ Count Rudolf of Habsburg as the new king. Although Rudolf came from a respected and wealthy family, he did not belong to the high nobility. The princes thought they could easily control him, but he energetically set to work eradicating irregularities in the kingdom, for example, by combating the ❷ robber barons. He also established a strong territorial power base for his family. Rudolf I defeated Otakar II of Bohemia in 1278 and ❹ invested his sons as the dukes of Austria and Styria, territories that had been occupied by the Bohemians after the extinction of the Babenbergs.

Following Rudolf's death in 1291 and the brief reign of Adolf of Nassau through 1298, Rudolf's son was elected King Albert I. He ruled only ten years, however, ❸ assassinated in 1308 by his own

Rudolf of Habsburg's tomb in Speyer

nephew, which shattered the Habsburgs' plans for a hereditary monarchy. The elector Baldwin of Trier succeeded in having his brother Henry VII of Luxembourg elected king. Henry's son ❺ John married the heiress of the kingdom of Bohemia, which from then on became the territorial base of Luxembourg power.

❻ Louis IV (the Bavarian), from the House of Wittelsbach, beat a rival Habsburg candidate in the next election, becoming king in 1314. He was ❼ crowned emperor by the people of Rome in 1328, despite having been excommunicated by Pope John XXII in 1324 for having supported an antipope. In 1338, the German electors finally forbade the popes from influencing the election of German kings at the Diet of Rense. Because Louis was too actively enlarging his power base, the princes chose Charles IV— the grandson of Henry VII and son of John of Bohemia from the House of Luxembourg—as rival king and Holy Roman Emperor in 1346. He also gained the crown of Lombardy in 1355. When Louis died in 1347, Charles became the sole ruler.

Looting of a village by robber barons, quill lithography, 15th century

Murder of Albert I of Habsburg, copper engraving, 17th century

Henry VII of Luxembourg invests his son John with Bohemia, after his marriage, wood engraving, 19th century

Louis IV the Bavarian is crowned emperor by layman Sciarra Colonna in Rome in 1328, painting, 19th century

Emperor Louis the Bavarian defeats the rival claimant of the throne, Frederick of Austria, book illustration, 14th century

| 1254–73 | Interregnum | 1278 | Victory over Otakar II of Bohemia | 1324 | Excommunication of Louis IV |
| 1273 | Coronation of Rudolf of Habsburg | 1291–98 | Reign of Adolf of Nassau | 1328 | Coronation of Louis IV as Holy Roman emperor |

The Rise of the Habsburgs

After the end of the Luxembourgs, the Habsburgs were able to establish themselves as the imperial dynasty until the end of the Holy Roman Empire in 1806. Their actual power, however, was based on the family estates, which they enlarged through a judicious marriage diplomacy.

In the ⓮ "Golden Bull" of 1356, Charles IV redefined the election process of the king, specifying three elector archbishops (Mainz, Trier, and Cologne) and four secular ❾ electors (Palatine of the Rhine, Saxony, Brandenburg, and Bohemia). Without the involvement of the pope, the king would be crowned in Aachen and thereby become emperor as well. The seven electors had influence on imperial policies as well as rights within their own territories.

through marriage. The wars against the Hussites in Bohemia, where he had succeeded his brother Wenceslas as king in 1419, distracted him from urgent domestic problems in the empire.

After the death of Sigismund in 1437, his son-in-law, the Habsburg ❽ Albert II of Austria, inherited Sigismund's lands. But due to

8   Albert II of Austria's seal

hereditary lands was Albert's cousin Emperor ⓬ Frederick III able, with great difficulty, to hold authority.

Frederick's son Maximilian I, called the "Last Knight," acquired sovereignty over the prosperous Netherlands through his marriage to Mary of Burgundy in 1477, which he was also able to defend successfully against French attacks. In the empire, where he succeeded his father in 1493, his reforms failed in the initial stages, but he was more successful in his marital diplomacy. The marriage of his son Philip the Handsome to the heiress of the Spanish kingdom and the double wedding of his grandchildren Ferdinand and Mary with the heirs of Hungary and Bohemia laid the foundation for the rise of the Habsburgs as a great power that would culminate in the world empire of Charles V, who became emperor in 1519 after the death of his grandfather Maximilian I.

9   The seven electors, book illustration, ca. 1350

Charles had his capital ⓫ Prague magnificently improved and founded the first university on German soil there in 1348.

Charles's son Wenceslas was deposed by the electors because of his lack of interest in the affairs of the empire. Wenceslas's brother ⓭ Sigismund, the German king from 1410, spent his energy in numerous conflicts. Although he was able to end the Great Schism of the papacy through his intervention at the ⓾ Council of Constance in 1414–1418, he was unable to defeat the Ottomans in Hungary, an area he had acquired

Albert's early death in 1439 and that of his son László V (Posthumus) in 1457, the Habsburgs lost both Bohemia and Hungary. Only in the empire and in the Austrian

Maximilian I with his family: his son Philip the Handsome of Castille and his wife Mary of Burgundy, first row; his grandsons, the future emperors Ferdinand I and Charles V, as well as Louis II of Hungary and Bohemia, painting, ca. 1515

10   Cardinals leaving the conclave after the election of Martin V at the Council of Constance, book illustration, 15th c.

11   The Charles Bridge in Prague with the Lesser Quarter Bridge Towers, built in the 13th–14th centuries

12 13 14   **left:** Frederick III, painting, 15th century **middle:** Sigismund of Luxembourg, painting by Pisanello, ca. 1433 **right:** first page of the "Golden Bull," the empire's constitutional law, enacted by Charles IV in 1356

| 1346 | Charles IV becomes anti-king | 1356 | Golden Bull | 1439-57 | Rule of László V | 1493 | Charles V takes power |
| 1328 | Charles IV becomes king upon death of Louis IV | 1410 | Election of King Sigismund | 1493 | Election of Maximilian I |

SWITZERLAND 1291–1848

In the 13th and 14th centuries, the ❶ Swiss Confederation developed out of the region's defensive struggles against foreign domination. In the 16th century, it became a center of the Reformation, although large areas remained Catholic. Switzerland gained full sovereignty in the 17th century. Despite great structural and religious differences between the individual cantons, freedom from foreign domination remained a common goal. Nevertheless, it was not until after the interlude of a Helvetic Republic during the Napoleonic era and the great constitutional crisis of the *Sonderbundskrieg* (Special Alliance civil war) in 1847 that a unified federal state was founded.

The Swiss defend themselves against the knights' army of Duke Leopold I of Austria in the Battle of Morgarten, book illustration, ca. 1450

From the Struggle for Independence to Neutrality

The Swiss Confederation developed out of local security alliances against the Habsburgs, Savoyards, and Burgundians.

In the High Middle Ages, today's Switzerland was part of the kingdom of Burgundy and—as part of the duchy of Swabia—of the kingdom of Germany. Many secular and ecclesiastical rulers held power, initially under the control of kings and dukes, but steadily increasing in autonomy. In the 13th century, the decline of the Hohenstaufens, who had reigned over Swabia, accelerated this process. As the ❸ Savoyards in the southwest and the ❹ Habsburgs in the north began to dominate, cities and farm communities that sought to maintain independence allied against them.

The original cantons of Uri, Schwyz, and Unterwalden united in 1291 in an ❷ "eternal league" (*Ewiger Bund*), which became the nucleus of the Old Swiss Confed-

The Oath of Rütli for the foundation of the Swiss Confederation, 1291, painting by Henry Fusely, 18th c.

eration. Once the league had defeated the Habsburgs at Morgarten in 1315, the cities of Bern and Zurich, among others, joined the confederation by 1353. The confederation's Habsburg allies, the Burgundians under Duke Charles the Bold, were defeated in 1476 at Grandson and Morat; Charles himself fell in the Battle of Nancy in 1477. The Swiss intervened independently in the war between France and the Habsburgs in Italy. Though they were able to take Ticino, they adopted neutrality following their defeat by the French at ❺ Marignano in 1515. Clashes still occurred with the Savoyards—who relinquished Vaud and Geneva. Switzerland was also affected by the Thirty Years' War, as was Grisons, which was not then a member of the confederacy. Switzerland's independence was universally recognized at the Peace of Westphalia in 1648.

William Tell

William Tell is seen as the symbolic figure of Swiss independence. According to legend, he was forced by the Habsburgs' Bailiff Gessler to shoot an apple from his son's head. He later took revenge and in so doing ignited a rebellion against the Habsburgs. Friedrich von Schiller used the tale, which is probably fiction, as the basis for a drama, which in turn inspired Gioahino Rossini's opera of the same name.

Tell shooting the apple from his son's head, colored lithograph, early 20th century

King Francis I of France in the Battle of Marignano, painting by Fragonard, ca. 1836

Chillon Castle on Lake Geneva, rebuilt by the Earls of Savoyen

The Habsburg in Aargau, residence of the Habsburgs since the eleventh c.

1291	Formation of the "Ewiger Bund"	1476	Battles of Grandson and Morat	1515	Battle of Marignano
1315	Battle of Morgarten	1477	Battle of Nancy	from 1519	Reformation teachings by Zwingli

Internal Development from the Reformation to the Special Alliance

The present-day Swiss federal state developed during the 19th century out of an alliance of more or less sovereign cantons.

The Swiss Confederation, which used the name of one of the original cantons, Schwyz, as an overall designation, was built up from the 13 old cantons, additional new cantons, and subject and allied territories, all tied to one another through a complex system of agreements and governmental relationships. To the old cantons belong important cities such as Zurich and ❼ Bern. The new cantons were not full members of the confederation; they were tied to the confederation by alliances, but were internally autonomous.

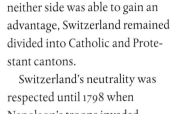

6 Ulrich Zwingli, painting, 16th c.

8 Fight in the *Sonderbundskrieg*, wood engraving, 19th century

Among these were the principality of Neuchâtel, the monastery of ❾ St. Gall, the bishopric of Basel, and the city-state of Geneva. There were also separate territories ruled by the old cantons. The

View of the city center of Bern with the tower of the minster and the cupolas of the *Bundshaus* or federal state building

only common institution of the confederation was the *Tagsatzung* (parliament), in which the emissaries of the cantons consulted.

Religious differences overlapped with structural differences between the cantons during the Reformation. In the 16th century, independent of each other, ❻ Ulrich Zwingli and ❿ John Calvin spread the ideas of the Reformation from Zurich and Geneva, respectively. Violent confrontations took place between Protestants and Catholics during the "Wars of Kappel" in 1529 and 1531, and battles at Villmergen from the 16th through early 18th centuries. As

neither side was able to gain an advantage, Switzerland remained divided into Catholic and Protestant cantons.

Switzerland's neutrality was respected until 1798 when Napoleon's troops invaded. Napoleon supported the liberal factions by forming a central state, the Helvetic Republic, although it was exposed from the onset to powerful internal resistance. A compromise between the new centralism and the old federalism was brought about through Napoleon's ⓫ Mediation Act of 1803. The cantons regained their sovereignty after the collapse at the Congress of Vienna in 1815, but disagreements over a common constitution continued. In 1847, the conservative Catholic cantons founded the *Sonderbund* ("Special Alliance") against the liberal Protestant cantons, who held a slight majority in the Tagsatzung (federal as-

sembly). A ❽ civil war, the *Sonderbundskrieg*, lasted one month, with fewer than 100 casualties, and ended with the defeat of the Sonderbund. This led to the founding of the Swiss federal state in 1848, centralizing lawmaking, defense, and trade.

9 Library in the monastery of St. Gall, 18th century

The Swiss Guards

Up until the 19th century, almost every European army employed Swiss mercenaries, as they were considered indomitable and warlike; for the Swiss, the poor mountain regions of their homeland offered few other forms of livelihood. Only the papal Swiss Guard at the Vatican, from 1505, has survived to this day.

Swiss Guard in the Vatican in the uniforms designed by Michelangelo in the 16th century

10 The reformer John Calvin, French painting, 16th century

11 Napoleon Bonaparte receives a Swiss delegation and hands over the Mediation Act, wood engraving, 19th century

from 1536	Calvin preaches in Geneva	**1798**	Invasion by Napoleon	**1847**	Founding of the Special Alliance
1648	Peace of Westphalia	**1803**	Mediation Act	**1848**	Founding of the Swiss State

FRANCE IN THE HIGH AND LATE MIDDLE AGES 843–1515

Charles II (the Bald), Charlemagne's grandson, was awarded the western portions of the Frankish Empire—future France—in the Treaty of Verdun in 843. The election of Hugh Capet over the last Carolingians in 987 established the rule of the Capetian dynasty over France, various branches of which ruled into the 19th century. The Capetians gradually built up a centrally governed state despite the resistance of the great princes in their kingdom, particularly in the Hundred Years' War through 1453 against the English kings, who possessed vast estates in France.

Reims Cathedral, where France's kings were crowned, 13th century

2 The Carolingian King Charles II—the Bald—book illustration, ninth c.

The Rise of the Capetians

Once the threat from the Carolingians had been eliminated, the Capetians consolidated and expanded their rule in France.

3 Coronation of Hugh Capet in Reims in 996, wood engraving, 19th century

The last **❷** Carolingians became enmeshed in struggles with the German Saxons over the possession of Lorraine. The Capetians, who as dukes of Paris had gained great prestige in repulsing the Normans, made use of this conflict; members of this family had already been elected in 888 and 922 over Carolingian candidates. When the Carolingian Louis V died without issue in 987, **❸** Hugh Capet took the throne with the help of the Saxons.

The kings at first possessed only a small realm in the Île-de-France around Paris out of which they could finance their reign. Many de facto autonomous dukes and counts ruled the rest of France. Un-

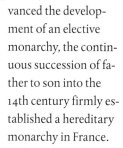

4 Louis VII with Eleanor of Aquitaine and Abbot Suger of St.-Denis, stained glass window, 19th c.

like the Holy Roman Empire, where the lack of adult heirs to the throne and consequent dying out of imperial dynasties advanced the development of an elective monarchy, the continuous succession of father to son into the 14th century firmly established a hereditary monarchy in France.

The kings sought support for their monarchy particularly from the rising cities and high-ranking clergy. Prominent among these was the **❹** Abbot Suger of **❺** Saint-Denis, who strengthened the kings' central authority, defended against insubordinate vassals, campaigned with **❻** Bernard of Clairvaux for the Second Crusade, and served as Louis VII's regent while the king took part in the Crusade. He also counseled Louis in his divorce from Eleanor of Aquitaine.

The Normans

A Viking tribe, the Normans not only plundered the coasts of Europe but also in the later half of the ninth century gradually settled the areas they terrorized—for example, Normandy, the region named after

Norman ships, *Bayeux Tapestry*, late eleventh century

them in northern France, which later became the Duchy of Normandy. It was from here that the Normans led by William the Conqueror occupied England in 1066. The English kings, William's descendants, also maintained their territorial interests in France.

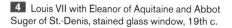

5 Tombs of the French kings in the Abbey of Saint-Denis

6 Bernard of Clairvaux preaches in 1146 on the Second Crusade

The Development of the Estates of the Crown

Philip II Augustus and his successors increased the possessions of the French crown.

The Capetians attempted to enlarge the territories they directly ruled through well-directed marriage diplomacy. In 1137 Louis VII married Eleanor of Aquitaine, the heiress of expansive estates in south-western France. However, the marriage was not a success and was dissolved in 1152. Eleanor then married Henry II Plantagenet, who was earl of Anjou, duke of Normandy, and from 1154

7   Battle of Philip II Augustus and John Lackland, book illustration, 14th century

king of England. Through this union, a dangerous enemy to the French king emerged in his own country. However, the struggle strengthened the French monarchy, which was supported by the popular will and by the Church, at a time when the English king was alleged to have encouraged the murder of the Archbishop of Canterbury, Thomas Becket.

In order to weaken the English, Philip II, the son of Louis VII from a second marriage, stirred up conflict between Henry and his son Richard the Lion-Hearted, and then between Richard and his brother John Lackland. John, as vassal of the French king, later refused to follow summons to the royal court in Paris. A trial in 1204 declared the majority of John's French lands forfeit. John then allied himself with his cousin, the Welf Otto IV, in a war against France, but ❼ Philip was victorious over John and Otto in the Battle

of Bouvines in 1214, which earned him the epithet "Augustus." At the same time, a war began against the ❽ Albigenses in southern France, who were supported by nobility, including the powerful ❾ counts of Toulouse and his ❿ vassals. After Philip's death in 1223, his son, and then his grandson (Saint) Louis IX, continued the Albigensian wars. Though they were waged as holy crusades, they also had the goal of gaining the prosperous, culturally and linguistically diverse southern France for the crown.

9   A Seal belonging to Count Raymond VII of Toulouse, 13th century

8
A heretic is burned at the stake while Philip II Augustus looks on, book illustration, 15th century

The Albigensian Wars

The community of Albigenses, or Cathari, the pure ones—whom the popes considered heretical—formed in the region around the town of Albi in southern France. The Cathars believed in a dualistic division of the world into good and evil, wherein the Roman Catholic Church belonged to the latter. Crusaders from northern France and the Inquisition, established solely for this purpose, eventually exterminated the Cathars over 20 years of brutal persecution.

top: The fortress cathedral Saint-Cecile of Albi, built 13th–15th c.

Eleanor of Aquitaine

The independent Eleanor of Aquitaine was a patron of artists, particularly troubadours. Her lifestyle did not suit her husband King Louis VII of France, who was under the strong influence of his counselor Abbot Suger. She also had a falling out with her unfaithful second husband, Henry Plantagenet, King of England. Eleanor was held under house arrest for years in England because she had supported a conspiracy of her son Richard the Lion-Hearted against his father.

Depiction of Eleanor of Aquitaine on her tomb in Fontevraud Abbey, sculpture, 13th century

10
Carcassonne castle, seat of one of the vassals of the counts of Toulouse, built in the twelfth century

---

1154 | Henry II Plantagenet becomes king of England   **1214** | Battle of Bouvines

1204 | Trial of John Lackland   **1208–29** | Albigensian wars

France under the Last Capetians

The later Capetians consolidated the power of the monarchy and were able to dominate the papacy.

Louis IX was successful in the war against the ❷ Albigenses and the counts of Toulouse and was able to incorporate southern France into the crown estates. He also kept the upper hand in the ongoing conflicts with the English kings, who, even after the setbacks under John Lackland, held considerable territories in southwestern France. Louis IX was canonized in 1297 for his ❶ crusades to the Holy Land—during the last of which he died in 1270.

Louis's grandson, ❹ Philip IV, was forced to withdraw from Flanders in 1302 following a revolt and the Battle of the Golden

Ludwig IX boards for the crusade, book illustration, 15th century

Spurs at Courtrai, in which his army of knights was destroyed by Flemish rebels. Pope Boniface VIII opposed Philip's ❸ taxation of the clergy and in 1302, in the papal bull *Unam Sanctam*, formulated a claim to absolute world supremacy. Philip had the pope kidnapped. Boniface was later able to free himself, but died a short time later.

In 1305, Philip succeeded in having his friend, the archbishop of Bordeaux, elected pope. As Pope Clement V, he designated ❺ Avignon in southern France as the new permanent papal residence. Philip bought the city, which belonged to the Holy See. The Popes, totally under the will

of the kings of France, would live there for nearly 70 years. Philip soon began an assault on the Order of the Knights Templar, which had vast holdings in France. All of its leaders were arrested and charged with heresy by 1307. After confessing under torture, the ❻ grand master and other knights were burned at the stake, and the king confiscated the order's assets. At the king's request, the pope in 1312 officially disbanded the order.

After Philip IV's death in 1314, his three sons followed him on the throne in succession, but all died without producing a male heir, bringing the primary Capetian line to an end in 1328. In accordance with the Lex Salica of Clovis I, which allowed succession only through male lineage, Charles IV's cousin Philip VI from the House of Valois became king. However, the English king, Edward III, also laid claim to the French crown as he was the son of Charles IV's sister Isabella. This led to the beginning of the Hundred Years' War.

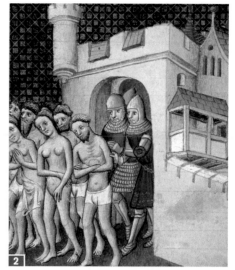

The expulsion of the Cathars from Carcassonne after their capitulation, book illustration, 14th c.

Philip IV and his councillors decide to tax the clergy, book illustration, 14th century

Philip IV watches the execution of Jacques de Molay, last grand master of the order of the Knights Templar, book illustration, early 15th century

Philip IV the Fair, king of France, steel engraving, 19th century

The papal palace in Avignon, photograph, ca. 1900

| 1270 | Death of Louis IX | 1302 | Battle of the Golden Spurs at Courtrai | 1305 | Election of Pope Clement V | 1314 | Death of Philip IV |
| 1297 | Canonization of Louis IX | 1302 | Boniface VIII issues the bull "Unam Sanctam" | 1312 | Dissolution of the Knights Templar | 1328 | Death of Charles IV |

The Hundred Years' War and the House of Valois through 1515

The war against England brought France to the verge of collapse. After a phase of reconstruction, the Habsburgs became the new opponents.

In 1346, in the Hundred Years' War, the English defeated the French in the ❼ Battle of Crécy. Edward "the Black Prince," son of Edward III, was again victorious

Charles VII of France, painting by Jean Fouquet, ca. 1444

in 1356 at the Battle of Maupertuis, where he took King John II of France captive. Through the Treaty of Bretigny in 1360, John regained freedom in exchange for a ransom and the secession of land. As he was unable to secure the ransom, he honorably returned to English captivity, where he died in 1364.

Charles V, who had taken over the regency for his captive father, followed him as king. First, he repressed peasant revolts in northeastern France. Then in 1369, he returned to war against England and was able to regain almost all of the English territories.

His son Charles VI acceded to the throne in 1380, but from 1392 was accused of mental insanity and therefore later called Charles the Mad. The struggle for regency among several of Charles's relatives resulted in a civil war. Henry V of England took advantage of this and in 1415 invaded France. After the Battle of Agincourt, Charles was forced to relinquish Normandy to Henry and recognize him as heir to the throne of France in the Treaty of Troyes in 1420. However, both died in 1422.

❽ Charles VII, claimant to the crown as the son of Charles VI, now had the south of France be-

❿ Joan of Arc, sculpture, 19th century

hind him, while Henry VI of England was supported by northern France. In 1428, with the siege of Orléans, the French seemed defeated, yet in the following year, led by ❿ Joan of Arc, the French drove out the English. Burgundy made peace with the French crown in the Treaty of Arras in 1435; Paris was liberated, and by 1453 the English had been expelled from France, with the exception of Calais. The outbreak of the War of the Roses in England deterred further attacks against France.

Charles VII and his successors set to work rebuilding the ❾ country. Louis XI fought Charles the Bold, duke of Burgundy, who strove for autonomy. After the latter's death in 1477, Louis lost a major part of the Burgundian realm through the marriage of Charles the Bold's daughter to Maximilian of Austria. This

Battle of Crécy in the northwest of France, book illustration, 14th century

Destitute mercenaries wander the country pillaging and murdering following the Hundred Years' War, book illustration, 15th century

strengthened the Habsburgs and they soon became France's new opponents.

The Valois had claims to the kingdom of Naples and the duchy of Milan which ⓫ Louis XII occupied in 1499. He was succeeded in 1515 by his son-in-law, Francis I, under whom conflict with the Habsburgs came to a head.

Joan of Arc, painting by Jean-Auguste-D. Ingres, 1894

Joan of Arc at the stake, wood engraving, 19th century

Joan of Arc

Joan of Arc was born into a family of peasants in 1412 and had religious visions as a child. She felt herself called to be the savior of France. Joan joined the army and was responsible for the victory at Orléans in 1429. Against the will of Charles VII, she continued the war in 1430, in the course of which she fell into the hands of the English. Pro-English clerics in occupied Rouen tried her for heresy and witchcraft. The French king made no attempt to save her, and she was burned at the stake in 1431.

Louis XII during a campaign in Italy, book illustration, early 16th century

| 1346 | Battle of Crécy | 1360 | Treaty of Bretigny | May 21, 1420 | Treaty of Troyes | 1429 | Relief of Orléans under Joan of Arc |
| 1356 | Battle of Maupertuis | 1415 | Battle of Agincourt | 1428 | Siege of Orléans | 1435 | Treaty of Arras |

1

Map of the divided Carolingian Empire after 870, Burgundy marked in yellow, 17th century

BURGUNDY AND THE NETHERLANDS 6TH–15TH C.

After the **➊** division of the Carolingian empire in the ninth century, France and Germany were unable to resolve the border region lying between them. Lorraine and the kingdoms of Lower and Upper Burgundy emerged from the Middle Kingdom. By the eleventh century these territories had become part of the Holy Roman Empire. In France, a side branch of the French royal family reigned in the duchy of Burgundy. In the 14th and 15th centuries, the dukes succeeded in building a powerful new Middle Kingdom, but it was divided between France and the Habsburgs after the last duke died in battle without a male heir in 1477. Arts in the Netherlands, especially painting and music, flourished under court patronage.

The Forerunners and Rise of the Duchy of Burgundy

During the Middle Ages various kingdoms emerged in the lands of historical Burgundy

In 534, the Franks conquered what, since the time of the Great Migration, had been the kingdom of the Burgundians. In the Treaty of Verdun of 843, the Carolingians divided Burgundy. The northwestern portion—the region of today's Burgundy— went to the West Frankish kingdom, the larger portion to the kingdom of **➋** Lothair I.

Lothair I's "Middle Kingdom" stretched from the North Sea coast to Italy. After his death in 855 it was once again divided among his sons. Louis II received Italy, Lothair II was given Lorraine— which is named after him—and Charles received Burgundy and Provence. Charles died in 863 without issue and his bro-

2

Lothair I on the throne, surrounded by guards, book illustration, ninth century

thers divided his territories among themselves. When Lothair II also died without heirs in 869, Louis II left Lorraine to his uncles Charles the Bald and Louis the German. However after prolonged disputes, it fell to the Holy Roman Empire. In 875 Louis II also died without producing a male heir.

In Lower Burgundy, Count Boso of Vienna, the son-in-law of Louis II, succeeded as king in 879. In Upper Burgundy, a member of the Welf dynasty, Rudolf I, was crowned king in 888. The Welfs supported the Saxons in Italy,

who in turn supported the Welfs in the annexation of Lower Burgundy in 933. Rudolf III signed an agreement in 1016 with his nephew, the German king Henry II, that led to the unification of Burgundy—called *Arelat* then after the capital **➌** Arles—with the Holy Roman Empire after Rudolf's death.

The duchy of Burgundy itself evolved from the ninth century out of the West Frankish part of Burgundy. This region was at first ruled by a side branch of the Capetians and in 1364 went to Philip the Bold and the Valois. Through **➍** marriage, Philip acquired Flanders, Brabant, and

3

The Carolingian Church St.Trophime, in Arles, the capital of the medieval kingdom of Burgundy

other territories of the Netherlands, where he first had to suppress the revolts of wealthy cities like **➎** Ghent and Bruges. In this way he created a significant power base for his dynasty.

4

Philip the Bold's wedding with Margaret, Countess and heiress of Flanders in 1369, book illustration

5

Medieval merchant houses on the river Lys in Ghent

Burgundy's Golden Age and End of Autonomy

Charles the Bold sought to substantially expand the collection of Burgundian territories, offending France and the Holy Roman Empire. After his death the kingdom rapidly disintegrated.

The murder of Louis of Orléans on the orders of John of Burgundy, book illustration, 15th century

Like his father, Philip the Bold, John the Fearless interfered in the regency of Charles VI of France. John ordered the ❻ murder of his adversary, Louis of Orléans, in 1407 and in the Hundred Years' War allied himself with Henry V of England against Louis's successor. In 1419, John himself was killed by a supporter of the future Charles VII, heir to the French throne. John's son, ❼ Philip the Good, continued the alliance with the English crown and handed Joan of Arc over to the English troops. But in 1435, he reconciled with Charles VII in the Treaty of Arras, after which Charles released Philip from his obligations as a vassal of the French crown. In the meantime, Philip had acquired further territories in the Netherlands and came to reign over a large complex of lands stretching between Germany and France. In 1464, he called the first ⓫ States-General, a delegation of all the estates over which he ruled. Although the regions always stressed their independence, the first step toward union had been taken.

❽ Charles the Bold, who succeeded his father, Philip, in 1467, wanted to unify his lands in a kingdom that would be independent of France and the Holy Roman Empire. He made a lot of enemies in his efforts to acquire the territories that separated his possessions in the Netherlands from the rest of Burgundy. He provoked Louis XI of France and the Habsburgs by occupying Lorraine, which belonged to the empire. He also put pressure on the free cities in Alsace, which were forced to seek support from the Swiss. Charles suffered a crushing defeat in 1476 at Grandson and Morat against an army fielded by the coalition between the Swiss and Lorraine. In 1477, the last duke of Burgundy was killed in the battle at Nancy.

Charles's only daughter ❾ Mary married the Habsburg

from left: Philip the Good, painting by Rogier van der Weyden; Charles the Bold, painting from the studio of Rogier van der Weyden, 15th century; Mary of Burgundy, painting by Niclas Reiser, ca. 1500

Battle between the Habsburgs and the French, by Tongern in 1482, wood engraving, 16th century

Maximilian of Austria, who later became emperor. When Mary died in Bruges in 1482, her husband inherited the estates, although he had to ❿ defend them against Louis XI of France. He succeeded in keeping most of the Burgundian territories, although the original West Frankish duchy of Burgundy passed to France.

"The Autumn of the Middle Ages"

Through textile production and international trade, the Netherlands had become the most advanced and wealthy region in Europe. Cities such as Bruges, Ghent, and Antwerp, and particularly the ducal courts in Dijon and Brussels, were centers of art and music. Fashion and court ceremony became the model for Europe. While paintings like those of the court artist Jan van Eyck announced the onset of the Renaissance, the exclusive Order of the Golden Fleece harked back to the age of chivalry.

above: Charles the Bold and the knights of the Order of the Golden Fleece, book illustration, ca. 1475
below: *The Sense of Taste*, tapestry from the southern Netherlands, late 15th century

Meeting of the States-General, chaired by the Duke of Burgundy, copper engraving, 18th century

ENGLAND IN THE MIDDLE AGES CA. 450–1485

Between the fifth and seventh centuries, the Anglo-Saxons founded a number of kingdoms on the territory of present-day ❶ England. In the ninth and tenth centuries, they united in defense against the Danish Vikings. Following a period of Danish rule, the French Normans conquered England in 1066. The holdings of the English kings on the Continent provoked France and, together with English claims to the French throne, led to the Hundred Years' War. In the 15th century, the disputes over the royal succession escalated into the War of the Roses. The nobility used the weaknesses of the monarchy to institutionalize their right to a share in decision making through the creation of a parliament.

First page of Bede's *Ecclesiastical History of the English People*, ca. 830

Settlement by the Anglo-Saxons and the Founding of Kingdoms

The Anglo-Saxons, and after them the Danish Vikings, conquered wide areas of the British Isles and drove out the native Britons as they settled in their territories. The native British tribes were pushed North and West into Scotland and Wales.

Germanic tribes from the North Sea coast landed in the British Isles around 450. They were initially summoned by the Celtic Britons as mercenaries against the Picts, who were invading from Scotland. However, under their legendary leaders, the brothers ❷ Hengist and Horsa, the Angles, Saxons, and Jutes settled permanently. The native Britons were pushed into the fringe regions of Cornwall and Wales, where Celtic princes were able to maintain their independence until the 13th century.

The occupation and settlement by the Germanic tribes, who merged to become the ❸ Anglo-Saxons, was complete by the seventh century. At that point, there were seven major Anglo-Saxon kingdoms: Mercia, Northumbria, East Anglia, Wessex, Essex, Sussex, and Kent. These were known as the Heptarchy. Northumbria's initial hegemony in the seventh century was overtaken by Mercia in the eighth century. However, it was out of Wessex, in defense against the Vikings, that the eventual unification of England came.

The first raid by Danish Vikings in 793 targeted the ❹ monastery of Lindisfarne off the coast of Northumbria. Further attacks and raids followed until the Danes, from around 866, set about the total conquest of the British islands. From the Thames estuary, they occupied the areas north of the river, the Danelaw. At the

3 Anglo-Saxon helmet, seventh c.

Hengist and Horsa land on the English coast, steel engraving, 19th century

same time, Norwegian Vikings conquered the coastal areas and islands of Ireland, Scotland, and England, where they founded kingdoms such as Dublin and the Isle of Man.

4 Ruins of the monastery on Lindisfarne or "Holy Island," northeast England

---

The Christianization of the Anglo-Saxons

St. Augustine, who was sent by Pope Gregory I to convert the Anglo-Saxons to Christianity, began his mission in Kent in 597. The reigning king, Ethelbert, had married a Christian Frank and, under her influence, converted to Christianity and was baptized. Augustine became the first archbishop of the city of Canterbury, which remains to this day the most important bishopric. Later, Anglo-Saxons themselves became missionaries, such as St. Boniface, who died in 754 and was known as the "Apostle of Germany."

King Ethelbert of Kent is baptized by St. Augustine of Canterbury, copper engraving, 17th century

---

ca. 450 | First landings of Germanic peoples on the British Isles   793 | Viking raid on the Lindisfarne Monastery   871 | Alfred the Great crowned in Wessex

from 597 | Christianization of the Anglo–Saxons   from ca. 866 | Conquest of England by the Danes

The Battle of the Anglo-Saxons against the Danes and Normans

The Danes were unable to conquer the kingdom of Wessex, which became the starting point of England's national unity.

King **❺** Alfred the Great of Wessex came to the throne in 871. At first he made a peace agreement with the Danes, but they did not abide by it. In 878, Alfred defeated the Danes in the **❻** Battle of Edington; in 886, he captured London, and by his death in 899 he had been able to extend his territories even further north. Alfred was also a notable legislator and a translator of historical and philosophical works from the Latin.

His successors continued the fight against the Danes. Alfred's grandson, Athelstan, completed the reconquest in 937 with a victory over the Danes and their Welsh and Scottish allies. Though the Danish kingdom on English soil was eliminated, further attacks ensued from Den-

mark itself. King Ethelred II tried in vain to buy off the Danes by paying large sums of **❽** "Danegeld" tribute. However, the Danish king Sweyn I Forkbeard forced him into exile with a military campaign of invasions that followed the massacre of England's Danish settlers. Sweyn's son, Canute the Great, eventually defeated Ethelred's son, Edmund

6 Battle between Anglo-Saxons and Danes, a still from the film *Alfred the Great,* 1969

II, in 1016 at the Battle of Assandun and was thereafter generally recognized as king of the English. Canute married Emma of Normandy, widow of Ethelred II, and converted to Christianity. After he also became king in Denmark and

Norway, he ruled over a vast kingdom situated on the coasts of the North Sea that also encompassed northern parts of Germany.

When Canute's son **❼** Hardecanute died in 1042 without an heir, Godwin, earl of Wessex, the leader of the Anglo-Saxon nobility, brought **❾** Edward the Confessor, the son of Ethelred II, out of exile in Normandy and made him the new king. Edward, however, became unpopular because he brought Norman counselors with him into the country and preferred them over the Anglo-Saxon nobility. When his marriage to Godwin's daughter remained childless, he designated his cousin, Duke William II of Normandy, as his successor. But the Anglo-Saxons chose Godwin's son **❿**, Harold II, as king after Edward's death in 1066. Harold was able to repulse an invasion by the Vikings, who wanted to

5 Alfred the Great, painting, 19th century

7 Hardecanute orders the body of his half-brother and usurper, Harold, exhumed, decapitated, and thrown into the Thames, copper engraving, 17th c.

reconstitute Canute's North Sea kingdom, but then was defeated in 1066 at the **⓫** Battle of Hastings by William of Normandy's invading troops. Harold fell in battle, and William the Conqueror had himself crowned king of England.

8 English coins used to pay the *Danegeld* tribute to the Viking invaders, tenth–eleventh century

9 Edward the Confessor, book illustration, late twelfth century

10 Coronation of Harold II, detail from the *Bayeux Tapestry,* late eleventh century

11 Armed with battle-axes, Anglo-Saxons fight against the Norman cavalry, detail from the *Bayeux Tapestry,* late eleventh century

Norman Rule in England

William the Conqueror and his successors introduced a well-organized central government to which the nobility and the Church were subordinate.

1
Caen Castle in Normandy, France, one of the largest medieval fortresses in Europe, built by William the Conqueror prior to his invasion of England

2
William the Conqueror lands on the English coast, engraving, 19th century

3
Archbishop Anselm of Canturbury, copper engraving, 18th century

4
Henry I, book illustration, 14th century

Danish Vikings who came to be known as Normans (or Norsemen) settled permanently around the estuary of the Seine in northern France toward the end of the ninth century. In 911, the West Frankish king Charles III was compelled to accept as vassal the Norman leader Rollo, who converted to Christianity and was elevated to count of ❶ Normandy. Through marriage, the counts and later dukes established connections with the French and English royal houses and became a significant power factor. Inheritance claims resulting from this led to the ❷ invasion of England by Duke William, a descendant of Rollo, and his ❺ coronation as King William I (the Conqueror) in 1066 ushering in Norman rule in England.

By 1071, William had conquered all of England. He quickly installed the European feudal system in England. The Salisbury Oath of Allegiance in 1086 swore vassals to loyalty to their sovereign lords. Rebel Anglo-Saxon nobles were dispossessed and their properties divided among the Norman invaders. William filled almost all the higher church, court, and state offices with his ❻ followers. As the Domesday Book of 1086 shows, at that point in time almost all private property was in the possession of the Normans. At the local level, however, the division of the country into shires, with a sheriff as royal officer, was carried over from the time of the Anglo-Saxons.

After William's death in 1087, a quarrel among his sons over the succession in England and Normandy developed. His youngest son, ❹ Henry I Beauclerc, emerged the winner. The Synod of Westminster of 1107 that settled the English investiture conflict over the appointing of clergy by laymen took place during his reign. ❸ Archbishop Anselm of Canterbury, a chief advocate of the philosophical movement of early scholasticism, was the King's opponent in the investiture question . In contrast to his son-in-law, the Holy Roman Emperor Henry V, however, Henry I asserted his right to the investiture of Church offices, despite opposition.

5
Coronation of William the Conqueror as King of England, in the background towns destroyed during his invasion

6
William the Conqueror feasts with his noble companions, detail from the *Bayeux Tapestry*, late eleventh century

The Domesday Book

In 1086, William the Conqueror ordered a complete survey of all land holdings and income in England. Together with a census of the population, this land register composed the Domesday Book and was the basis for calculating taxes. Nowhere else in Europe was there a similarly comprehensive administration at the time as that of the Normans.

The peasants harvest, supervised by the lord of the manor, book illustration, 14th century

The House of Plantagenet

The Plantagenet family attempted to consolidate the English monarchy while further enlarging its possessions in France.

Following the early death of his only son, Henry I forced the nobility to recognize his daughter Matilda as heiress to the throne. In her second marriage, she had wed the Frenchman Geoffrey, count of Anjou, who was named Plantagenet after a gorse-branch helmet decoration he wore in tournaments. When Henry died in 1135, his nephew Stephen, count of Blois, usurped the throne. After a long civil war between the two, Stephen was finally forced to recognize Matilda and Geoffrey's son, Henry Plantagenet, count of Anjou and duke of Normandy, as his successor in 1153. In 1154, after the death of Stephen of Blois, he became King Henry II of England.

In the turmoil, the central royal authority had deteriorated, and the nobility as well as the Church had gained in power. In order to strengthen his position, Henry tried to standardize the legal system. The reforms, however, diminished the power of the church courts; even the clergy was required to submit to the royal sec-

ular courts, which led to a ❼ dispute with Thomas Becket, the archbishop of Canterbury.

In 1169, Henry began the conquest of Ireland. However, his great success in power politics was his marriage to ⓫ Eleanor of Aquitaine, the divorced wife of the French king Louis VII. In uniting Anjou, Normandy, and Aquitaine with the crown of England,

❽ Richard I, wood etching, 19th century

the Plantagenets had founded the so-called Angevin kingdom, which challenged the power of the French king in his own country by rivaling his claims to French territories.

Henry's successor, his son ❽ Richard I (the Lion-Hearted), who took the throne in 1189, mar-

ched off to the Holy Land in the Third Crusade shortly after his coronation.

It was reports of the situation at home that persuaded him to return. However, on his return journey, he was taken ❿ prisoner near Vienna in 1192 by Duke Leopold V of Austria, with whom he had quarreled during the crusade. Leopold V demanded a huge ransom in return for Richard's release. The payments brought England to the edge of bankruptcy. Tax increases and the tyranny of John Lackland, who reigned as regent in the absence of his brother Richard, led to unrest in the population. These were the conditions that gave rise to the legend of ❾ Robin Hood, who stole from the rich to give to the poor.

After his return from captivity in 1194, Richard had to reconquer his lost French possessions, the major part of which had been occupied by Philip II Augustus of France in the meantime. However, he was killed in 1199 in battle against rebelling nobility in Aquitaine.

7 Dispute between Henry II and Thomas Becket, book illustration, 14th century

Thomas Becket

When Henry II decreed in 1164 that the clergy would be held accountable to the secular courts, Thomas Becket, the archbishop of Canterbury, objected. He was murdered in Canterbury Cathedral in 1170 by knights allegedly acting in response to Henry's rhetorical question "Will no one rid me of this troublesome priest?" Deeply distressed, Henry did penance at Becket's grave and repealed his decrees.

Henry II at the grave of Thomas Becket, engraving, 19th century

9 The mythical hero Robin Hood wakes up a sleeping Friar Tuck, wood engraving, 19th century

10 On his return from the crusades, a disguised Richard the Lion-Hearted is recognized and captured near Vienna, book illustration, late twelfth century

11 Tombs of Henry II (foreground) and Eleanor of Aquitaine, in the Church Notre Dame de Fontevraud, in France, painted stone, late 12th–early 13th century

1135 | Death of Henry I   **1169** | Beginning of Conquest of Ireland   **1189** | Coronation of Richard the Lion-Hearted

1154 | Crowning of Henry II   **1170** | Murder of the Archbishop of Canterbury   **1199** | Richard's death

The Struggle with the Nobility and the Development of Parliament

The kings were unable to subjugate the nobles and were forced to grant them a voice in political decision making.

In 1199, Richard's younger brother ➋ John, who as a result of disputes with Philip II Augustus of France had forfeited almost all of England's possessions in France, took the throne. King John was also known as John Lackland; as the fourth son he had inherited no land. Following King John's defeat by Philip at Bouvines in 1214, the English nobles rose up and coerced the king into signing the ➊ Magna Carta in 1215, by which the crown was compelled to recognize the rights and liberties of the nobility and Church. The Magna Carta became the foundation of English law.

John's son Henry III, who succeeded his father in 1216, had ambitious plans. He sought to secure the throne of the Holy Roman Empire for his brother, Richard of Cornwall, and win the crown of Sicily. Tax demands and the appointment of favorites from southern France to English state ministries led to a revolt of the

1

The Magna Carta, manuscript, 1215

English nobles, the Barons' War, led by Simon de Montfort in 1258. Although Simon de Montfort was initially one of the favorites promoted by Henry and thus an unlikely leader of the revolt, a feud between the two had developed when de Montfort had married Henry's sister Eleanor without his consent.

Henry was taken captive at the Battle of Lewes in 1264 and forced to agree to summoning a ➍ parliament, which was to include, along with the nobility, gentry from the shires and burgesses from the ➎ towns. Initially the representatives of the nobles, Church, and common people met together; only later did they separate into upper and lower houses. Although Henry's son, Edward I

3

Isabella of France presents her son Edward II of England to her brother Charles IV of France, book illustration, 15th century

defeated Simon de Montfort in the Battle of Evesham in 1265, he was forced to retain the parliament, as he was dependent upon the cooperation of the nobility and towns to finance his military campaigns. In 1297, he confirmed parliament's right to approve taxes. Despite this, Edward was able to restore the king's authority through a number of reforms. In addition, he succeeded in subjugating the last of the independent Celtic princes of Wales in 1284; the title "Prince of Wales" has

2

King John signing the Magna Carta, steel engraving, 19th century

been bestowed thereafter upon every English heir to the throne. On the other hand, Edward was only temporarily able to take possession of Scotland.

His son and successor in 1307, Edward II, was forced to give up his father's conquest of Scotland. He was confronted by a strong opposition of nobles, who opposed the influence of Edward's ➏ favorites, and his excessive financial demands. His own wife ➌ Isabella, a daughter of Philip IV of France, had the king deposed in 1327 with the help of her lover, the exiled baron Roger Mortimer and, it is assumed, had Edward killed.

4

English Parliament with clerical members (left of picture) and secular members, alcove painting, ca. 1400

5

London in the Middle Ages, old London Bridge over the River Thames, wood engraving, ca. 1600

6

Edward II and his favorite, Piers Gaveston, painting, 19th century

The Hundred Years' War and the War of the Roses

England spent its strength in the Hundred Years' War. The Houses of Lancaster and York, rival claimants, fought over the English crown and the inheritance of the Plantagenets.

When Edward III turned 18 in 1330, he exiled his mother and had her lover executed. As the grandson of Philip IV of France, he had laid ❼ claim to the French throne when the male line of the Capetians died out in 1328, triggering what became the ❾ Hundred Years' War. The king's eldest son, Edward— known as the Black Prince because of the color of his armor— was especially prominent as an army commander during the initial phase of the war. He died a year before his father in 1376, however, so in 1377 his young son became King ❽ Richard II at the age of ten. Although he successfully put down the Peasant's Revolt in 1381, Richard's reign became increasingly authoritarian and was directed at the claims of the nobility and Parliament, who openly supported a rebellion by Richard's cousin, the duke of Lancaster. Richard was deposed in 1399 and probably murdered. The duke of Lancaster then took the throne as Henry IV.

The war in France flared up again in 1415 during the reign of his son, Henry V. But the tide of

8
King Richard II worshiping the Madonna, painting, ca. 1395

the war turned against the English after the early death of the king in 1422. By 1453, under Henry VI, England had lost all of its continental possessions, with the exception of the harbor city of Calais. Worse still, the king became mentally ill. Various noble parties contested over the regency. One was led by a cousin of the king, Richard, duke of York, who himself had well-founded claims to the throne as both of his parents were direct descendants of King Edward III. Civil war broke out in 1455. As the House of Lancaster carried a red rose in its coat of arms and the House of York a white rose, the conflict became known as the War of the Roses.

Richard of York's son, ❿ Edward IV, usurped the throne in 1461 with the help of Richard Neville, earl of Warwick, known as "the Kingmaker." But Neville changed sides and Edward was forced to flee England in 1470. He returned with new troops and defeated Neville and Henry VI's son Edward, both of whom fell in battle. Henry VI was executed in the ⓬ Tower of London in 1471. Edward IV reigned undisputed as king until his death in 1483.

Edward was succeeded by his brother ⓫ Richard III, who had ⓭ Edward's underage sons excluded from the succession. Henry Tudor, a nephew of Henry VI, landed in England as the heir to the House of Lancaster and a descendant of an ancient Welsh royal house. Richard III fell in 1485 in the Battle of Bosworth. The new king, Henry VII, then united the claims of the houses of Lancaster and York by marrying Elisabeth of York, daughter and heiress of Edward IV, and became the first Tudor monarch.

7
Edward III dressed in the colors of England and France, leopards on a red background, and lilies on a blue background, book illustration, 15th century

9
English and French knights in battle during the Hundred Years' War, book illustration, 14th century

10
Edward IV unites the crowns of England, Ireland, and France after his victory over the House of Lancaster, book illustration, 15th century

11
Richard III, painting, 16th century

12
The Tower of London, built by William the Conqueror, begun in 1078

13
Murder of Edward's sons, painting, 19th century

| 1327 | Edward II deposed | 1376 | Death of "the Black Prince" | 1455 | War of the Roses begins | 1471 | Execution of Henry V |
| | | 1377 | Coronation of Richard III | 1461 | Throne seized by Edward IV | 1485 | Battle of Bosworth |

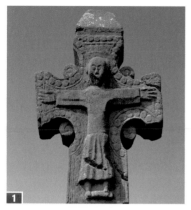

IRELAND AND SCOTLAND IN THE MIDDLE AGES CA. 450–1603

In ❶ Ireland and Scotland, neither of which had ever been part of the Roman Empire or conquered by Germans, many Celtic traditions that had disappeared in England were preserved. Both countries, however, were subjected to the English kings' expansionism. The English were able to take advantage of Ireland's internal divisions to subjugate clans and then the entire island, although English control remained weak. Scotland, on the other hand, maintained its independence until the dynastic unification with England.

Irish high cross, stone sculpture, twelfth century

Ireland

The rivalry among the clans prevented the development of a unified Irish state and made it possible for the English to extend their rule into Ireland.

The history of Ireland is dominated by the battles of a large number of hostile clans fighting among themselves, each attempting to build up a unified complex of dominions. Four large kingdoms emerged between the fourth and tenth centuries—Connacht, Leinster, ❷ Munster, and Ulster—in addition to numerous other smaller kingdoms. The title of an overall Irish ❸ "high king" remained hotly

St. Patrick's Cathedral in Cashel, the former capital of the kingdom of Munster

contested among the clans. In the fifth century, ❺ St. Patrick Christianized the whole of Ireland from the see he established in Armagh. A distinctive Irish type of Christianity, characterized by autonomous ❻ monasteries, developed. The monasteries ushered in a cultural golden age, particularly in literature, while also maintaining the old Celtic epics. Moreover, the monks traveled in active missionary work—for example, Gallus among the Germans on the Continent, and St. Columban of Iona in Scotland in the sixth century.

A plea for help to Henry II of England from a minor Irish king in battle against his rivals brought an ❹ English invasion in 1169. Initially only a portion of the east

coast was occupied, and the English kings were satisfied with nominal sovereignty. Not until the time of the Tudors was an attempt made to control the entire island, but then Henry VIII assumed the title of king of Ireland in the year 1541. The deliberate settlement of English people and later also Scots, particularly in Ulster, that began in the 16th century was meant to secure English rule. Religious conflicts developed, however, because the new settlers were Protestants while the Irish remained Catholics. After several rebellions, the revolt of Hugh O'Neill in 1595 became a serious threat to the English crown's rule over Ireland. Despite support from Spain, the Irish were overcome. The Irish supported the pro-Catholic Stuarts in the English civil war and during the Glorious Revolution, which they paid for through appalling retaliatory measures and a wide-reaching deprivation of rights by the English up to the 19th century.

The miracle of St. Patrick, painting by Tiepolo, 18th century

Broach from Tara, the seat of the Irish high kings, twelfth century

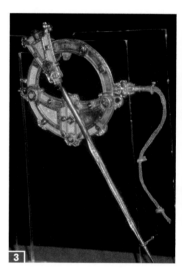

English fleet navigating a stormy Channel on the way to invade Ireland, book painting, ca. 1400

The round tower of Clonmacnoise Abbey, built in the twelfth century

Scotland

The Scottish kings had to establish national unity and independence in the face of the Scottish aristocracy and the claims of the English.

In Roman times Scotland was inhabited by tribes with a ❼ Celtic culture. The Romans called them Picts ("the painted"), because of their tattoos. In the third century, Celtic "Scottis"—after whom Scotland was named—began invading from out of Ireland; they settled and founded a kingdom. In the ninth century, their king, Kenneth MacAlpin, united the Picts and Scots in the Kingdom of Alba.

MacAlpin's descendants died out in 1018. A relative, Duncan I, took the throne, but was murdered by the usurper ❽ Macbeth in 1034. Macbeth then fell in battle against Duncan's son, who became king as Malcolm III of Scotland in 1057.

English influence in Scotland increased during the reign of Malcolm III and afterward. The Roman Catholic Church suppressed the Irish-Scottish form of Christianity. The feudal system in the English form became established in the Southeast and the ❾ Lowlands. The Highlands, however, remained ruled by the

7

Ossian on the bank of the Lora invoking the Gods to the strains of a Harp, painting by Gérard, 19th c.

8

Macbeth and the three witches, scene from Shakespeare's Scottish play *Macbeth*, painting, 19th century

clans as in Celtic times.

Once Malcolm's dynasty was extinguished at the end of the 13th century, the powerful Bruce and Balliol families fought over the succession. Edward I of England saw an opportunity and helped John de Balliol to the throne, in

return for which he was to recognize English suzerainty. However, after winning the crown, Balliol refused to submit to English interests, whereupon the English occupied the country. Sir William Wallace and Robert the Bruce organized the resistance against the English occupiers. In extended fighting, Robert, who was crowned king in 1306, was able to defend Scottish independence. The Scots were able to strengthen their position further as England became embroiled in the Hundred Years' War and the War of the Roses.

In 1371, the Stuarts replaced the House of Bruce. Despite the marriage of James IV Stuart to Margaret Tudor, the daughter of Henry VII of England in 1503, clashes with the English continued. Nevertheless, this marriage formed the basis for the claim of James's granddaughter ⓫ Mary Stuart to the English throne and led in 1603 to the unification of both kingdoms under Mary's son ❿ James VI of Scotland and I of England.

William Wallace

William Wallace—known as "Braveheart"—led the Scots to victory over a superior English army in the Battle of Stirling in 1297. However, the Scottish nobility refused to support Wallace, who rose out of modest circumstances, and so he was soon defeated by the English in 1298 at Falkirk. Wallace was later betrayed by a Scottish noble, taken captive, and executed in London in 1305.

above: Statue of William Wallace by the walls of Edinburgh Castle

9

Edinburgh Castle, built from the late seventh century on, in Edinburgh, capital of the Scottish Lowlands

10

James VI of Scotland and James I of England, painting, 1605

11

Mary Stuart with her second husband, Lord Darnley, engraving, 1565

ITALY IN THE MIDDLE AGES CA. 600–CA. 1500

Northern Italy was closely tied to France and later to the Holy Roman Empire. A Norman kingdom developed in southern Italy, then later went to the German Hohenstaufens and the French and Spanish royal houses. The papacy reached the pinnacle of its secular power in the 12th and 13th centuries. Its influence had decreased again by the Late Middle Ages as it was divided by the Great Schism. Simultaneously a self-confident middle class, whose early capitalist economy expanded over the Continent in the course of the following centuries, emerged in ❶ northern Italy. One northern Italian city-state, Venice, rose to become Europe's most significant economic power.

View over the city center of Siena in Tuscany, with the Palazzo Pub-blico and the Bell Tower built in the Middle Ages

The Kingdom of Italy After the Carolingians

Several dynasties fought for the monarchy following the end of the Carolingians. Eventually, the Saxon Ottonians added the Italian monarchy to the German royal crown.

❹, ❺ Charlemagne conquered the kingdom of the Lombards in northern Italy in 774. His sons and grandsons ruled over the Italian territories into the ninth century.

After the Carolingians died out, rulers of various families seized the Italian ❷ royal crown; most of these were descended from the female line of the Carolingians, although some were simply usurpers. None of the kings were able to establish a permanent dynasty,

however, and thus an unstable period followed in which local nobility and later cities were able to build up their independence.

In 951 the widow of Lothair II, ❻ Adelaide of Lombardy, sent a plea to the German king Otto the Great for help against the new king, Berengar II of the House of Ivrea. ❸ Otto defeated Berengar and became king of Italy. He united the

3 Berengar II of Ivrea before Otto I the Great, 1150

kingdom and then integrated it into the Holy Roman Empire. The German kings and emperors never had a power base of their own in Imperial Italy and were instead dependent upon the great nobles,

2 The "Iron Crown," the Lombard royal crown with an iron ring within, allegedly made from a nail of Christ's cross, sixth–ninth century

the powerful cities, the Church, and the papacy during their rule. They attempted to play the individual parties off against one other, for example, by granting increased royal prerogatives to win over individual parties, but this ultimately undermined their authority. Thus Italy ultimately disintegrated into numerous independent city-states.

4 Charlemagne marches into Pavia, capital of Lombardy, wood engraving, 19th c.

5 Charlemagne holds the Iron Crown, crown of the Lombard kings, drawing, 19th century

6 Figures of the Empress Adelaide and Emperor Otto I the Great at the dome of Meissen

Southern Italy from the 8th to the 15th centuries

Normans and Hohenstaufens made a model state of the kingdom of Sicily. French and Spanish dynasties fought over the wealthy Hohenstaufen crown.

Lombard principalities had survived in southern Italy. Furthermore, there were still Byzantine bases that had in part fallen into the hands of the Muslim ❽ Arabs who had occupied Sicily and Puglia in the ninth century. Since the eleventh century, Normans in the service of the southern Italian princes as mercenaries had also seized domains for themselves. The popes tried to bring the Normans under their control by legitimizing their rule through official investiture; in 1059 Robert Guiscard was made duke of Puglia and Calabria, and his brother Roger I count of Sicily. ❼, ⓫ Roger II combined the Norman possessions and was granted the title of king by the pope in 1130. Catholic and Orthodox Christians, Jews, and Muslims lived at his ⓭ court in Palermo, a leading European cultural center of the time.

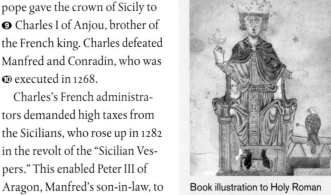

7 Coat for the crowning of Roger II, 12th century

In 1194, the Hohenstaufen emperor Henry VI, son-in-law of Roger II, gained the crown of Sicily. His son, Emperor ⓬ Frederick II, found Sicily more welcoming than the more northerly parts of the Holy Roman Empire and ruled from his home and power base there. Because of his education, Frederick was known by his contemporaries as "Stupor Mundi" ("Wonder of the World"). After Frederick's death in 1250 and that of his son Conrad IV in 1254, Conrad's illegitimate brother Manfred ruled Sicily in the name of Conrad's son, Conradin. In order to eliminate the Hohenstaufens for good, the pope gave the crown of Sicily to ❾ Charles I of Anjou, brother of the French king. Charles defeated Manfred and Conradin, who was ❿ executed in 1268.

Charles's French administrators demanded high taxes from the Sicilians, who rose up in 1282 in the revolt of the "Sicilian Vespers." This enabled Peter III of Aragon, Manfred's son-in-law, to occupy the island. Charles, who died shortly thereafter, retained only his mainland possessions, which became the kingdom of Naples. A number of battles over succession in Naples took place among Charles's descendants. The last monarch of the House of Anjou, Queen Joan II, first designated King Alfonso V of Aragon and Sicily as her heir, then a French cousin, Louis of the House of Valois. After her death in 1435, Alfonso secured the kingdom of Naples for his family. His nephew, Ferdinand the Catholic of Aragon, united Sicily and Naples in 1501. The possessions, along with the Spanish inheritance, went to his grandson, Charles V of the house of Habsburg after Ferdinand's death in 1516.

8 Arabs besiege and conquer Messina in 842–43, book illustration, 13th century

9 Charles I of Anjou travels to Italy by sea (left); his investiture by Pope Clemens IV with the kingdom of Sicily (right), wood painting, 14th century

11 Depiction of Roger II of Sicily crowned by Christ

12 Frederick II receives Arab deputies at his court, painting, 19th century

Salimbene di Adam, from his Cronica, about

Emperor Frederick II

"Frederick ... was crafty, wily, avaricious, lustful, malicious, wrathful; and yet a gallant man at times, when he would show his kindness or courtesy; full of solace, jocund, delightful, fertile in devices. He knew to read, write, and sing, to make songs and music."

Book illustration to Holy Roman Emperor Frederick II's book on falconry, 13th century

10 Execution of Conradin in Naples, copper engraving, 17th century

13 Palace of the Normans in Palermo, built from the ninth century onward

| 1220 | Manfred becomes regent of Sicily | Mar 30, 1282 | Sicilian Vespers revolt | 1501 | Unification of Sicily and Naples |
| 1268 | Execution of Manfred by Charles of Anjou | 1282 | Occupation of Sicily by Peter III |

■ The Papacy in the Middle Ages

The papacy reached the pinnacle of its power in the High Middle Ages, strengthened by the Cluniac and Gregorian reforms. Division in the Church over doctrinal and theological issues as well as secularization led to the gradual decline of the papacy.

2
Jesus gives Peter the keys to Rome, as a sign of his supremacy over the other apostles and the Church's right to territory in Rome, painting, 15th century

The popes—bishops of ❶ Rome and successors to the ❷ Apostle Peter—claimed a position of supremacy within the Catholic Church. Furthermore, once the Roman emperors no longer resided in Rome and the state structure in the Western Empire disintegrated, the popes increasingly assumed secular functions. The extent of their authority is demonstrated, for example, by Leo I, who was able to convince the leader of the Huns, Attila, to halt his march on Rome. The popes based their claims, among other things, on a falsified document known as the ❼ "Donation of Constantine" by

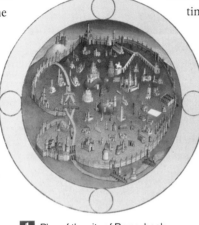

1 Plan of the city of Rome, book illustration, early 15th century

which Emperor Constantine the Great supposedly left most of the Western Roman Empire to the papacy. In the East, the patriarch of Constantinople and head of the Byzantine imperial church rejected the primacy of the Roman popes. The final break came in 1054 in the Eastern Schism, when Pope Leo IX and Patriarch Michael Cerularius excommunicated one other.

At the turn of the seventh century, ❸ Pope Gregory introduced the central administration of papal lands. From this developed what became known as the Papal States (*Patrimonium Petri*); of the former Papal States, only the Vatican remains under the pope's control today.

In 753 the new Frankish king, Pépin III, extended the Papal States by a bequest of lands known as the "Donation of Pépin." In return for this, he was recognized by Pope Stephen II as the successor to the Merovingians. The Franks became the protectors of the Church and defended the popes against Italian princes and Roman patricians. The alliance was cemented in 800 when Pope Leo III ❹ crowned Charlemagne as emperor. The Saxon Ottonians, who became kings of Italy in 951, continued the tradi-

tional close ties between the imperial crown and the papacy. Concurrently, the Cluniac reforms sought a spiritual renewal of the Church and the elimination of abuses such as the marriages of priests, simony, and lay investitures.

The Salians, who succeeded the Saxons, helped put a reform-minded pope in office. Now politically and spiritually renewed, the papacy turned against the instrumentalization of the Church by secular rulers by taking on the investiture controversy. Pope Gregory VII formulated the clergy's position of supremacy over the secular rulers in his *"Dictatus Papae."* The renewal movement gained further political weight through the Gregorian reforms. The symbolic submission of Emperor Henry IV to Gregory VII in his "journey to Canossa" in 1077 attested to the power of the papacy. The investiture controversy was officially settled in 1122, although the conflict between the pope and secular rulers continued.

3
Pope Gregory I (the Great) studying at his desk in his residence, ivory carving, tenth century

5
Pope Martin V is elected at the Council of Constance, book illustration, 15th century

6
Innocent III confirms the rules of the Franciscan order, fresco by Giotto di Bondone, ca. 1300

4
Pope Leo III crowns Charlemagne as emperor, copper engraving, 19th c.

440–61 | Pontificate of Leo I   **753** | Donation of Pépin   **ca. 1050** | Beginning of the investiture controversy   **1077** | Journey to Canossa

600 | Implementation of papal central administration   **8th–9th century** | Fabrication of the "Donation of Constantine"   **1054** | Eastern Schism

Between 1198 and 1216, the papacy under Pope Innocent III was able to take advantage of the power struggle between the Hohenstaufens and the Welfs in the Holy Roman Empire and reach the height of its political power. Innocent called for crusades against the Albigenses in France and the Muslims in the Holy Land and for the ❻ founding of the Franciscan and Dominican orders. In 1231 the latter was entrusted with the Inquisition, which served to combat heresy and monitor the implementation of Church doctrines.

The popes lacked temporal instruments of power such as armies, however, while their ultimate spiritual weapon—the threat of excommunication—had lost much of its impact through its frequent usage. In response to the overreaching claims of absolute world power that Pope ❸ Boniface VIII formulated in 1302 in the bull "Unam Sanctam," King Philip IV of France demonstrated the autonomy of

7 Constantine the Great gives Pope Silvester I the symbols of imperial power, fresco, 13th century

8 The Pope's palace in Avignon, France, built in the 14th century, papal residence 1309–1377

9 The Castel Sant'Angelo in Rome on the banks of the Tiber, tomb of Emperor Hadrian, refuge of the popes

10 The old St. Peter's Cathedral in Rome, in the background the new cupola, built in Renaissance style

11 Crowning of Pope Clement VII, book illustration, 14th century

the state by forcing the papacy to move to ❽ Avignon in France in 1309. Here it remained until 1377, constantly under the influence of the French kings. Similarly, excommunication by John XXII in 1324 no longer held the power to

intimidate the Bavarian emperor Louis IV. He continued to support the Franciscans against the papacy in the poverty controversy— the Franciscans saw the poverty of Christ as a model for the Church, a view the papacy did not share.

Because the papal properties in Italy were threatened, Gregory XI returned to ❾ Rome from Avignon in 1377. After Gregory's death, however, conflict erupted between the French and Italian cardinals; both parties wanted to elevate a fellow countryman to the papacy—and both did. In 1378, two popes were elected: Urban VI in Rome and ⓫ Clement VII, who continued to reside in Avignon. The Great Schism (or Western Schism)—after 1409, there were even three competing popes—was finally ended in 1417 at the Council of Constance with

the election of ❺ Martin V as the sole pope. During the schism, the spiritual authority of the papacy naturally suffered. Councils such as that of Basel, which met from 1431 to 1449, claimed to supersede the decisions of popes. The popes, however, succeeded in splitting the council movement, and in 1459 it was declared heretical by Pius II. Thus a possible instru-

12 Pope Pius II, fresco by Bernardino Pinturicchio, early 16th century

ment of Church reform was also eliminated.

In the 16th century, the inability to make spiritual reforms finally resulted in the rupture of the Catholic Church's authority on spiritual matters by the Reformation. The Reformation gained additional impetus from the secularization of the papacy, which was ushered in by ⓬ Pius II and his predecessor Nicholas V, under a series of ❿ Renaissance popes.

13 Pope Boniface VIII, gold-plated bronze structure, 1301

Northern Italy under the Salians and Hohenstaufens: Welfs and Ghibellines

Out of the power struggles between the emperor, the pope, the aristocracy, and cities came the feud between the Welfs and Ghibellines.

The new trading routes that the Crusades opened up brought enormous ❸ economic prosperity to the Italian cities in the 12th century. As a counterweight to the popes and the nobility, ❹ emperors had granted the cities increasingly more freedom. The cities, however, now insisted on pursuing their own goals. The investiture controversy had already reduced the emperor's authority. In addition, the conflict between the Welf (or Guelf) and Hohenstaufen houses spread into Italy as both families claimed the rich inheritance of Matilda of Tuscany. When the Hohenstaufen emperor ❻ Frederick I claimed ownership of Italian territories

1 The Piazza della Signoria in Florence with the Palazzo Vecchio, the government domicile of the city republic and the Loggia dei Lanzi (right)

3 A clothier at his loom, fresco by Lorenzetti, 14th century

4 Crowning of a German emperor with the Iron Crown of Lombardy, wood engraving, 19th century, after a relief from the late 14th century

6 Frederick I Barbarossa on horseback fights for a Lombard city, painting, 19th century

Mathilda of Tuscany

The countess of Tuscany held a key position due to her wealth and the strategic location of her estates in central Italy. An adherent of Church reform, Matilda mediated between Henry IV and Pope Gregory VII, who met at her family seat in Canossa in 1077. She rewrote her will several times before she died childless in 1115. At one point, she named the Church, and at another point the emperor, as heir to her fortune. Eventually the Welfs, the family of her last husband, also laid claim to the inheritance. The conflict was finally settled in 1213.

Henry IV asks the Countess Mathilde to mediate in his conflict with the pope, book illustration, early 12th century

and wanted to enforce his tax demands, the northern Italian cities formed the Lombard League against him. The Lombards defeated the emperor in the Battle of Legnano in 1176 and were thus able to secure their financial and political freedom.

Two factions emerged out of this conflict: The Welfs supported the papacy, while the Ghibellines, who got their name from the Hohenstaufen castle of Waiblingen, supported the emperor. The partisanship in the dispute between the Welfs and Hohenstaufens, however, gradually slipped out of focus. "Guelf" and "Ghibelline" evolved into designations for rival factions in many feuds between families or political groups, particularly in the communes, which were split by outright civil wars. For defense they retired to fortified towers, the ❺ "tower houses," which were also meant to demonstrate the families' wealth and power.

The Guelfs in 13th-century ❶ Florence saw themselves principally as good patriots who defended the liberties of the city. They had been exiled from the city but when the emperor died

2 Florentine merchant in his warehouse, wood engraving, late 15th century

5 The town of San Gimignano in Tuscany, from the Middle Ages, with numerous fortified towers

had come back to power. The declaration of the ideal of civic patriotism was meant to keep the hostile Ghibellines out of power. At the end of the 14th century, the Guelfs were mainly the representatives of the ❷ rich upper class in Florence, while the political representatives of the middle class belonged to the Ghibellines.

1096 | Beginning of the Crusades   1176 | Battle of Legnano   1312 | Coronation of Emperor Henry VII

1167 | Founding of the Lombard League   12th–13th c. | Fight between the Guelfs and Ghibellines   1312 | Giangaleazzo Visconti becomes duke of Milan

Northern Italy in the Late Middle Ages: Signori and Condottieri

New territorial states rose up among the many Italian cities and small dominions. These were characterized by unstable political conditions and conflict with neighboring states.

In the 13th century, after the end of the Hohenstaufen line, there was a power vacuum in northern and central Italy. The popes were then resident in French Avignon, and the papacy would later be split by the Great Schism. In southern Italy, the kings of Naples from the House of Anjou were fighting against the kings of Sicily from Aragon. France was distracted by the Hundred Years' War with England. The German kings and emperors from ever-changing royal houses concentrated primarily on Germany in their power politics and no longer had the resources to be active in Italian politics. The poet Dante expected Emperor ❼ Henry VII of Luxembourg to bring peace and unity to Italy, but the early death of the emperor in 1313 prevented the realization of these plans.

In this chaotic period, northern Italy dissolved into innumerable city-states and dominions. Civil war–like clashes between factions

❼ Henry VII of Luxembourg adjudicates a trial of the rebellious citizens of Milan, book painting, ca. 1350

and family feuds between Guelfs and Ghibellines plunged the cities into chaos. Communes were consequently forced to grant near-dictatorial powers to a single strong "city lord," the *signore* (or *signori*)—when he did not usurp these powers himself. The signori were descended either from old noble families such as the Estes in Ferrara, the Gonzagas in Mantua, or the ❾ Visconti in Milan or, like the Medici in Florence, from the wealthy middle class. Some of the signori were able to establish hereditary titles so that city-republics became principalities in the course of time. By ❿ subjugating neighboring signori, they were able to create expansive territorial states. The signori usually engaged mercenary leaders, the ❽ *condottieri*, and their forces for the countless wars against each other.

The condottieri were eventually also able to establish territories for themselves, as was the case with the Sforzas, for example, who succeeded the Visconti in Milan in 1450.

In the meantime, the Valois in France and the Habsburgs in the Holy Roman Empire consolidated their dominions. The Valois, as relatives of the Visconti and Anjou, laid claim to Milan and Naples. The Habsburgs inherited southern Italy along with Spain,

❾ Grave monument of Giangaleazzo Visconti, first duke of Milan from 1395, marble, 16th century

❽ Equestrian statue of the Condottiere Gattamelata in Padua, bronze statue by Donatello

Italy

"Ah! servile Italy, grief's hostelry! / A ship without a pilot in great tempest! / No Lady thou of Provinces, but brothel!...

And now within thee are not without war / Thy living ones, and one doth gnaw the other / Of those whom one wall and one fosse shut in!"

From Dante's The Divine Comedy (Purgatorio: Canto VI, translation by Henry Wadsworth Longfellow)

Dante Alighieri, painting by Justus van Gent, ca. 1476

and attempted to reestablish the traditional supremacy of the Holy Roman emperor over Italy. Consequently, Italy was caught between the ⓫ fronts of the great powers, and drawn into their conflicts.

❿ *The Battle of San Romano* in 1432 between the quarreling city republics of Florence and Siena, painting by Paolo Uccello, ca. 1456

⓫ 1525 battle between emperor Charles V and Francis I of France, near Pavia in Lombardy, 16th-century tapestry

---

1433 | Gianfrancesco Gonzaga becomes margrave of Mantua **1450** | Rule of the Sforzas in Milan begins **1525** | Battle near Pavia

1434–64 | Cosimo d'Medici the Elder leads the republic of Florence **1452–71** | Borso d'Este becomes duke of Modena and Ferrara

Genoa and Pisa

Though the sea powers Genoa and Pisa were able to accumulate great wealth, internal instability meant that politically they lost their freedom of action.

The Crusades and the Spanish Reconquista in the Middle Ages ended Muslim rule in the Mediterranean region, and this vacuum was filled by the Italian maritime cities—first and foremost ❶ Genoa, Pisa, and Venice. Initially they profited by using their own fleets to ❹ transport the crusading troops. Then they established trading posts in the

Genoa, wood engraving, late 15th c.

The Cathedral of Pisa, built from the 11th century on, with the Leaning Tower of Pisa, 12th century

Crusaders board ships heading for the Holy Land from a Mediterranean port, book illustration, 15th century

Crusader states—in the Byzantine Empire, around the Aegean Sea, and on the Black Sea coasts—and these became significant power bases. The Italians imported coveted goods such as silk, brocade, damask, pepper, incense, porcelain, pearls, and perfume to Europe via Arab middlemen. The Italians also borrowed an efficient accounting system from the Arabs, as well as Arabic

numerals. In addition to trade, banking and credit transactions gained in importance.

Through naval campaigns against the Arabs during the 11th century, Pisa and Genoa were able to build up supremacy in the Western Mediterranean. The Italian rivals, however, constantly waged war against each other. At first, Pisa dominated, and its great wealth was invested in costly ❸ building programs. In the middle of the 13th century, there was a shift to Genoa's advantage. Emperor Michael VIII Palaeologus granted extensive trade concessions as a reward for Genoa's support in returning him to the imperial Byzantine throne in 1261. In 1284, the Genoese military crushed the Pisan fleet in the naval battle of Meloria.

Domestically, however, Genoa and Pisa were caught up, like most of the Italian communes, in the spreading factional fighting. Ghibelline and Guelf noble families waged war against each other. In addition there were disputes with the *popolo*—literally "the people," but referring to the rising middle class of small

View into the Basilica of San Marco in Venice with mosaics in the Renaissance style, built in the eleventh century

merchants and craftsmen, who wanted a share in power. Consequently, popoli and signori from various noble families repeatedly replaced each other as magistrates. By supporting diverse factions, foreign powers were able to gain influence in the city-republics. Pisa was subjugated by ❺ Florence in 1406 and Florence became the new dominant power in Tuscany. Genoa maintained its independence but came under Milanese, ❻ French, and from 1528 Habsburg suzerainty.

Lombard and Giro

Many terms used in the financial world—for example, Lombard and giro—are reminders of the fact that the modern economy was first developed in northern Italy. From there, Italian bankers and traders spread early capitalism in Europe. In London, Lombard merchants settled in Lombard Street in London City, which even today is the address of many banks.

Early banking, depiction of a banking house in Genoa, book illustration, late 14th century

Victory of the Florentines over Pisa in 1505, fresco, ca. 1570

Louis XII of France and his troops attack a Genoese fortress, book illustration, ca. 1510

Venice

The Republic of Venice grew rich through control of much of the trade with the East and became a strong power for a time.

The settlements on the lagoon islands of Venice—to which the population had withdrawn during the age of the Great Migrations— were under Byzantine sovereignty and were never part of the Holy Roman Empire. Therefore, Venice was strongly influenced by Byzantine ❷ cul-

7

The doge's palace in Venice, left of the Campanile

ture as well. Byzantium appointed the first political leaders, the ❸ doges (from the Latin *dux*, "leader"), in the eighth century, but free election of the doge was established later. The authority of

the doges was greatly curtailed in the 12th and 13th centuries by the Great Council and the Senate, whose members were required to be from leading families of the city whose names had been entered in the "Golden Book" of 1297—by which means the ruling class excluded the broad mass of the population from taking part in the political process. The annually elected Council of Ten and a police state monitored all state institutions, made sure a ❾ political balance was maintained, prevented civil wars, and ensured that Venice was free of the influence of foreign powers that was present in other Italian communes.

Venice became extremely rich through its prominent location on the trade routes to the ❼ Eastern Mediterranean via the Adriatic and to Northern Europe via the Alpine passes. The Venetian doge ❿ Enrico Dandolo was able to conquer Constantinople in 1204 with the help of the Fourth Crusade. Venice seized the majority of the spoils and in addition gained

10

The doge Enrico Dandolo at the storming of Constantinople in 1204, painting by Tintoretto, 1580

11

Conquest of the town of Zara on the Adriatic by crusaders and Venetians in 1202, painting, 16th century

8

Venetian deputies at an Oriental court, painting, 15th century

9

Execution in 1355 of the doge Marino Falier in 1355, who wanted to abolish the republic and establish a hereditary monarchy, painting, 19th century

vast territories on the Adriatic and Aegean coasts.

When Venice won the power struggle with Genoa for mastery in the Mediterranean in ⓫ the War of Chioggia (1378–1381) it became the greatest and unrivaled trading power in Europe, famous for its naval fleets and skills.

In the 15th century, Venice began expanding its territories on the Italian mainland, the *terra firma*, to guarantee a food supply of the ever-growing city. This resulted in numerous wars over territory, which the Venetians won. A gradual decline began only with the eastward advance of the Ottomans in the 15th century and the shifting of the trade routes from the Mediterranean to the Atlantic in the 16th century.

The Jewish Ghetto

In 1516 the Venetian government resettled the Jewish communities of the city on the island of Ghetto. Despite this, relative tolerance prevailed and many exiled Jews from Spain and Portugal settled in Venice. This ghetto set the precedent for a form of persecution that was forced on the Jews throughout Europe until after World War II.

Synagogue of the Spanish Jews in the ghetto of Venice

Marco Polo

The Venetian Marco Polo set out on a trading journey to China in 1271, where he reportedly became a close friend of Kublai Khan, the Mongol emperor of China. He first returned to Europe in 1295. He had his memoirs recorded, but their authenticity was doubted even by his contemporaries, as his accounts and descriptions were so extravagant and fantastical.

From Marco Polo's travel memoirs: The dog-headed inhabitants of Ceylon trading spices, book painting, ca. 1412

1

SPAIN AND PORTUGAL IN THE MIDDLE AGES 8TH–15TH CENTURY

Since the eighth century, Christian kingdoms in the north of the Iberian Peninsula had been resisting Arab conquest, and starting in the eleventh century, the kingdoms began the ❶ Reconquista. The Muslim rulers were expelled by 1492. Modern Spain was created through a marriage between the kingdoms of Castile and Aragon at the end of the 15th century. In the 1400s, Portugal became a major sea power.

A Muslim and a monk play chess in a tent, book painting, 13th century

The Kingdoms of Navarre, Castile, Aragon, and Portugal

From the eleventh century on, the Christian kingdoms in the north of the Iberian Peninsula steadily pushed the Muslims farther south.

Between 711 and 714, Muslim Arabs conquered the Visigoth empire. Christian rule in Iberia survived only in the impassable Pyrenees in the north. There, in 718, the Visigoth ❷ Pelayo, leader in the struggle against the Muslims, was chosen to be king of ❸ Asturias— later part of the kingdom of León. At the same time, the Basques made a stand against Charlemagne's conquest attempts—he had set up a short-lived Spanish *marca* (border) in 812. In 824, they chose Inigo Arista as the first king of Navarre. In the ninth century, the county of Barcelona also took shape on the territory of the marca.

2 Pelayo, bronze

Around 1016, the Christian kingdoms benefited from ❹, ❻ Muslim civil wars, during the course of which the last Umayyad caliph was deposed in 1031. Numerous minor rulers took his place, but they were too disunited to oppose the *Reconquista* ("recon-

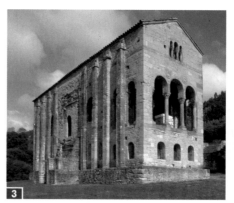

3 Reception hall of the Asturian kings in Oviedo, built ca. 850, later converted into a church

quest") begun by the Christian kings.

In the first half of the eleventh century, Sancho III Garcés "The Great" reigned as king over a significant kingdom in northern

Alcázar in Segovia, built 11th/12th c., since 14th c. residence of Castile kings

Spain. After his death in 1035, Sancho's kingdom was divided into three independent kingdoms: Castile, Aragon, and Navarre. In 1038, Ferdinand I "The Great," ruler of Castile, also became king of León through marriage. Aragon and Barcelona were also united through marriage in 1164. The French Count Henry of Burgundy married the granddaughter of Ferdinand of Castile and León and in 1097 received the country of Portugal as her dowry. Henry's son, ❺ Alfonso I, then established his independence from Castile and assumed the title of king in 1139. Thus in the twelfth century there were four kingdoms on the Iberian Peninsula: Navarre, Castile-León, Aragon, and Portugal.

5 Afonso I of Portugal "the Conqueror" takes Lisbon from the Moors in 1147, steel engraving, 19th century

6 Muslim rider in battle, fresco, ca. 1280

711–14 | Arab conquest of the Visigoth Empire   812 | Spanish march founded   1031 | Last Umayyad caliph deposed   1085 | Ferdinand I becomes king of Leon

718 | Pelayo becomes king of Asturias   824 | Inigo Arista first king of Navarre   1035 | Kingdom divided into Navarre, Aragon, and Castile

The Formation of Modern Spain and Portugal

In the course of the Reconquista, the Christian rulers recaptured all the Muslim territories on the Iberian Peninsula.

The Reconquista did not proceed without setbacks. The North African dynasties of the Almoravids and the Almohads, who ruled southern Spain from 1094 and 1147 respectively, were still able to win important victories over the Christian kings in the 12th century. There were isolated incidences of shifting coalitions among the Christians and Muslims, as illustrated by the example of El Cid. Spanish ❿ knightly orders—such as those of Calatrava,

7 Toledo, the Roman bridge "Puente de Alcantara" and the Alcázar in the background

8 The Cathedral of Córdoba, built into the former Great Mosque known as the Mezquita in the 16th century

9 Inquisition court under the chairmanship of Dominican friars, painting, end of 15th century

10 Castle of knights of an order in Ponferrada, founded in 1178

Alcantara, or Avis that kept alive the legacy of the Crusades—played an important role in the Reconquista.

The Portuguese kings meanwhile extended their territories along the Atlantic coasts. Lisbon, the future capital, was captured in 1147 and in 1250–51 the Algarve was conquered. ⓬ John I of Avis, crowned in 1385, conquered areas in North Africa in 1415. He and

his son, ⓭ Prince Henry the Navigator, who fitted out naval expeditions and founded a merchant navy college, initiated Portugal's ascendancy as a sea power.

In 1085 Alfonso VI of Castile had captured the former Visigoth capital of ❼ Toledo, which then became the Castilian and Spanish capital until the court was moved in 1561 to Madrid. Castile's expansion came to a temporary halt under ⓫ Ferdinand III after he conquered ❽ Córdoba in 1236. Only the Muslim kingdom of Granada in the extreme south of the peninsula remained.

Concurrently, Aragon was building up its power in the Mediterranean. In 1235 King James I captured the Balearic Islands and in 1238 the port of Valencia from the Moors (Spanish Muslims). His son Peter III occu-

El Cid

Rodrigo Díaz de Vivar, known as El Cid (from the Arabic al‑sid, "Lord"), fought as army commander for both the Christian and Muslim rulers in the Reconquista. He eventually captured the city of Valencia, which he defended against the Muslims until his death in 1099. El Cid thus came to embody the ideal of chivalry.

pied Sicily in 1282. Once it had brought Sardinia and Naples under its rule in 1326 and 1442, respectively, Aragon became a dominant power in the Mediterranean.

The 1469 marriage of ⓮ Ferdinand II of Aragon and Isabella I of Castile, jointly known as the "Catholic monarchs," set the stage for Spain's union and meant that both crowns went to the Habsburgs after Ferdinand's death in 1516. The two rulers completed the Reconquista with the subjugation of Granada in 1492. In Spain and Portugal, the persecution and eventual expulsion of the Muslims and Jews, as well as the so-called Moriscos (converted

Moors), were carried out with the aid of the ❾ Inquisition.

The kingdom of Navarre did not take part in the Reconquista. Several French royal families had succeeded each other since the 13th century. In 1572, Navarre fell to Henry of Bourbon, who also became king of France as Henry IV in 1589, combining both crowns. Ferdinand II of Aragon had already seized major parts of southern Navarre in 1512.

11 Ferdinand III "the Holy," book painting, 13th century

12 John I of Avis established as Portuguese king in the battle of Aljubarrota in 1385, book painting, 15th c.

14 Ferdinand II and Isabella I, wood engraving, beginning of 16th century

Henry the Navigator, painting, detail, 15th c.

1

NORTHERN EUROPE 8TH–16TH CENTURY

From Scandinavia, the Vikings started sailing along the European coasts during the eighth century. Initially they sailed as warriors and pirates, but later also as traders and settlers. In the ninth and tenth centuries, the kingdoms of Norway, Denmark, and Sweden emerged in Scandinavia. ❶ Christianity played a major role in the formation of these states. The kings were constantly opposed by a strong aristocracy. Even the Kalmar Union, which united the three northern kingdoms from the 14th to 16th centuries, could not obscure the structural weaknesses of the kingdoms.

Stave Church, Borgund, Norway, built in the 12th century

The Vikings and the Kingdom of Norway

Daring seafarers, the Vikings for a time ruled the seas around Europe. Norway experienced a golden age from the 13th century until it came under Danish rule in 1387.

The Scandinavians of the Early Middle Ages were also known as ❷ Vikings, Varangians, or Normans, though they formed no ethnic or political unity. Over

3

The Oseberg ship, found in a large burial mound in Norway, 9th century

time, various groups sailed from their northern homelands due to limited resources and political change, but also out of a thirst for adventure. Viking advances in ❸ shipbuilding technology en-

abled them to conduct warring and raiding expeditions along the European coasts and even up rivers far into the interior. Trade also played a significant role, as is testified to by the ❺ port cities, such as the North German trading settlement of Haithabu. Eventually, the Scandinavians also appeared as settlers and founders of empires in England, Ireland, Normandy, and Russia. The Vikings also reached Iceland and Greenland and, around the year 1000, led by ❻ Leif Eriksson, the North American coast.

In the homeland of the Vikings, the increasing power of the ❹ kings curbed the former

freedom and self-governance of the clans. Opponents of the new kingdoms usually joined the emigrants. ❼ Harold I Fairhair, about 870, was the first to unite the Norwegian monarchies.

Christianity was introduced, occasionally forcibly. In particular, Olaf I Tryggvason and Olaf II Haraldsson (St. Olaf) used the Church to support the centralization of the state in the eleventh century. As in other European countries, conflicts over the appointing of church offices arose in the twelfth century.

Sverre Sigurdsson was able to strengthen the power of the monarchy again by 1202. During the reign of his

2　Tyr, the Norse mythology god of warfare and battle, with a tied wolf of the underworld, bronze relief, 6th c.

grandson Haakon IV (the Old), Norwegian rule was extended over Greenland in 1261 and Iceland in 1262; for centuries before that, the institution of the Althing, an assembly of all free men in which political and legal affairs were discussed, had governed Iceland. In 1319 the Swedish Folkungs inherited Norway, and in 1380 it was inherited by the Danish queen Margaret I. Norway remained united with Denmark until 1814.

4　A king, Norwegian toy figure, 12th c.

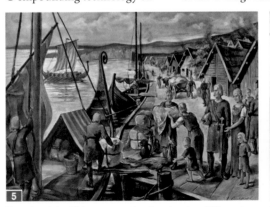

5

Port city of the Vikings, reconstruction drawing, 20th century

6

Leif Eriksson sees North America, painting, 19th century

7

Harold Fairhair and a giant, Iceland

Denmark and Sweden

In the Kalmar Union, Denmark attempted to dominate the Baltic Sea region. However, it came up against great opposition, particularly from Sweden.

The development of the Danish kingdom began with Gorm the Old, who about 940 subjugated the Vikings of Haithabu. His son ❿ Harold II Bluetooth followed him around 950, but was killed by

mar I (the Great) was able to conquer territories in northern Germany and along the Baltic coast, but his son Valdemar II was defeated in 1227 at the ❽ Battle of Bornhöved by the North German

a regent of the empire, completed the conquest of Finland, which had been the goal of Swedish ⓫ warriors, ⓭ missionaries, and settlers since the twelfth century.

Margaret I of Denmark, the

The Hanseatic League

Lübeck and other trading cities joined together between the 12th and 14th centuries as the Merchants' League of the Hanse. The Hanseatic League maintained common trading posts, secured the routes of their merchant ships—the so-called cogs—against pirate attacks, and intervened in the domestic politics of neighboring countries to gain more favorable concessions. The increasing strength of the Northern European states and the shift of the main trade routes to the Atlantic in the 16th century led to the decline of the Hanse.

Hanseatic League ship

8 Battle of Bornhöved, book illustration, ca. 1300

9 Kalmar Castle in southern Sweden, built 12th–16th c.

his son Sweyn I Forkbeard in 986. Sweyn and his son ⓬ Canute the Great occupied England and Norway, thus creating a great kingdom along the coasts of the North Sea. Only a few years after Canute's death in 1035, however, England and Norway regained their independence.

Denmark was weakened by struggles over succession in the further course of the eleventh and twelfth centuries. Beginning in 1157, Valde-

princes and the Hanseatic city of Lübeck. Following the Hanseatic War, Valdemar IV Atterdag was forced to recognize the demands of the Hanseatic League in the Treaty of Stralsund of 1370. His daughter Margaret I, widow of King Haakon VI Magnusson of Norway and Sweden, secured the Danish crown for her son Olaf and, after his death in 1387, took over the regency herself. In 1397, she united the three kingdoms as the ❾ Kalmar Union.

The history of the Swedish monarchy had begun in 980 with Erik VIII Bjornsson. His son Olaf Skotkonung III was baptized in 1008. Nevertheless, the entire period of the High Middle Ages was defined by clashes with non-Christian sections of the population and fighting over the throne by rival dynasties. In 1250, the House of Folkung came to the throne. The founder, Birger Jarl,

heiress of the last Folkungs, brought Sweden into the Kalmar Union. Sweden, in particular, chafed under the Danish domination of the Kalmar Union. The Swedish nobility rose up against Margaret's successors, particularly against the kings from the House of Oldenburg who reigned after 1448. This ended in 1523 when Gustav I Vasa, king of Sweden, broke away from Denmark.

10 Stone with runes of Harold Bluetooth, ca. 965

11 Mounted warriors on reindeers and soldiers on skis, wood engraving, 16th c.

12 King Canute the Great and his wife donate a cross, book illustration, 1031

13 Bishop Henry of Uppsala, a missionary in Finland, book illustration, ca. 1475

rwegian rule of Iceland   **1370** | Treaty of Stralsund   **1397** | Kalmar Union

1319 | Sweden inherits Norway   **1370** | Margaret I of Denmark regent over Norway and Sweden   **1523** | Sweden separates from Denmark

1

EASTERN EUROPE 10TH–15TH CENTURY

Following the Great Migration of Peoples, the Slavs spread into the areas of Eastern Europe abandoned by the German tribes. Around 900, the Magyars began to settle the central Danube region. In the tenth and eleventh centuries, the historical kingdoms of Poland, ❶ Bohemia, and Hungary emerged. The last to form a unified nation were the Lithuanians in the 14th century. The political development of all these countries was fundamentally characterized by the dominance of the nobility, while the kings continually sought to establish a dynastic rule of their realms.

Duke Boleslaw II of Bohemia gives an audience to St. Adalbert, Bishop of Prague, bronze relief, 12th century

▇ The Development of the Polish State in the Middle Ages

The long-ruling Piast dynasty was unable to establish a strong monarchy. Up until the 13th century, therefore, numerous territories were lost to Germany and other neighboring states.

Under the princely House of Piast, the West Slavic Polanie tribe, which settled between the Oder and the Vistula rivers, became the nucleus of the future Poland. Mieszko I came to power and converted to Christianity in the 960s. Although the Ottonians wanted to prevent too strong a concentration of power in the east, Mieszko I and his son

❻ Boleslaw I Chrobry (the Brave) initially maintained a cordial relationship with the German Saxon Ottonians. Only after the end of the Ottonian dynasty did Boleslaw assume the title of king in 1024 and thereby secure Poland's independence.

Boleslaw I's grandson Casimir I Odnowiciel had to contend with pagan revolts and repulse invasions from Bohemia and Kievan Rus. Boleslaw III Krzywousty in 1138 restructured the monarchy such that the eldest member of the dynasty would act as an overlord in the capital ❹ Krakow, while other family members would reign as autonomous princes over the provinces. Instead of the desired stability, however, this resulted in the fragmentation of Poland. The nobility and the Church benefited from the lack of a strong monarchy. After the catastrophic ❺ defeat in 1241 at Legnica (Liegnitz) against the Mon-

gols, Poland was saved only by the death of the khan and the subsequent withdrawal of the Mongol army.

In the meantime, the ❷ Germans were steadily encroaching from the west. By the twelfth century, the Slavic tribes between the Elbe and Oder rivers had lost their independence and, with few exceptions, also their cultural identity through the targeted policies of German conquest and ❸ colonization. In the 13th century the indigenous rulers in Pomerania and Silesia promoted the influx of German settlers, and in 1226 the Piast princes of Mazovia sought the help of the German Teutonic Order against the pagan Prussians. The "Germani-

2

Henry I, German king, conquers Brandenburg, colored lithograph, ca. 1900

3

The Polish town of Gdansk, which was founded as a German colony in 12th century near a Slavic castle

zed" territories leaned politically toward the German king. The Teutonic Knights became an adversary of Poland in the 14th and 15th centuries.

4

The king's castle Wawel in Krakow, residence of the dukes and kings of Poland until 1596

5

Battle of Legnica, copper engraving, 17th century

6

Boleslaw of Poland receives German missionaries, wood engraving, 19th century

Poland and Lithuania as Major Powers in Eastern Europe

The unified Poland-Lithuania under the Jagiellos became the largest state in Eastern Europe, although the domestic position of its rulers remained weak.

Following a period of Bohemian domination, Poland was reunited by Wladyslaw I Lokielek, who was crowned king in 1320 in Krakow. His son, Casimir III, became king in 1333. He took care of the extensive development of the country and invited ❿ Jews, who had escaped from pogroms in

8 | Quarrels between different factions of the nobility during a session of the Polish parliament

Western Europe, to settle down in Poland. He reached an agreement with the kings of Bohemia to abandon their claim to the Polish Crown in exchange for Silesia.

As the main line of the Piast dynasty ended with his death in 1370, he bequeathed the throne to his nephew, Louis I of Anjou, king of Hungary, known as the Great, in order to provide a counter-weight to the empire. But the Polish nobility used this transition to secure advantages for themselves. Louis was forced to make further concessions in the Pact of Koszyce of 1374 in order to secure the throne for his daughter, Jadwiga. The nobility immediately demonstrated its increased power by forcing Jadwiga to marry

❾ Jogaila, the grand duke of Lithuania, who was crowned king of Poland in 1386 as Wladyslaw II Jagiello.

Lithuania was at this time still a young, and for the most part pagan, country. The first grand duke of all Lithuania had been Jogaila's grandfather Gediminas, who

9 | Jogaila of Lithuania, crowned Wladyslaw II

fought against the Teutonic Order and benefited from the decline of Kievan Rus. In 1325, Gediminas captured Kiev and extended Lithuania's borders far inside today's Russia and Ukraine.

After their union under Jadwiga and Wladyslaw, Poland and Lithuania defeated the Teutonic Knights in the ⓬ Battle of Grunwald (Tannenberg). In the ⓫ Treaty of Torun in 1466, the order was forced to yield large territories to Wladyslaw's son Casimir IV and recognize him as sovereign. The Polish-Lithuanian kingdom now reached from the Baltic Sea to the Black Sea and was the largest territorial state of Europe.

Domestically, the Jagiellon dynasty was locked in contention

11 | Treaty of Torun, document with seals

with the great nobles, known as the magnates. Casimir IV therefore sought support from the lesser nobility, the *szlachta*, who were given tax privileges and admitted to the Polish ❽ *sejm*, or parliament. There, however, the magnates and the szlachta banded together, holding tight to the principle of the elective monarchy and demanding ever greater liberties from each new ruler. Casimir's successor in 1505 was forced to accept the *nihil novi* ("nothing new") law, according to which nothing was to be decided without the approval of the nobility. Possession of property became a privilege of the nobility, and the ❼ peasants were forced into serfdom. After 1652, any member of the sejm could alone thwart a decision through the "liberum veto." An aristocratic republic with a monarch evolved. However, the Polish kings of the 18th century were no match for the expansionist drives of the absolute rulers reigning in the neighboring countries of Prussia, Austria, and Russia.

7 | Peasant's wedding, engraving, 19th c.

10 | Old synagogue in Krakow, built in the 15th century

12 | Battle of Grunwald, painting, 20th century

Bohemia

The Czech Premysl dynasty founded the kingdom of Bohemia. Under subsequent dynasties, there were religious conflicts and disputes with the aristocracy.

In the ninth century, Premyslid princes unified the tribes of West Slavs that had settled in Bohemia. ❷ Prince St. Wenceslas sought ties to the Holy Roman Empire and promoted Christianity. In 929 he was murdered by his brother

Charles IV (left) and his son Wenceslas IV kneel before Mary, painting, 14th c.

Marchfeld, however, and control of Austria went to the Habsburgs. The Premyslids died out with Otakar's grandson Wenceslas III in 1306.

John of Luxembourg, the son of Emperor Henry VII, then

St. Wenceslas, altarpiece, 14th century

Battle of the Marchfeld, east of Vienna, Austria, painting, 19th century

Boleslav I, who was then forced to accept the suzerainty of the Holy Roman emperor. Bohemia became an autonomous part of the empire, and in 1198 the German emperor bestowed the hereditary title of king on the Premyslids.

King Otakar II of Bohemia occupied Austria in 1251 and also coveted the German crown. When Rudolf I of Habsburg was elected the German king in 1273, Otakar challenged him. Otakar fell in 1278 at the ❸ Battle of the

inherited the Bohemian crown by marrying Wenceslas's sister Elizabeth. He was followed in 1347 by his son ❶, ❼ Charles IV. The authoritarian regime of Charles's son ❹ Wenceslas IV caused a revolt of the nobility, in which even his relatives took part. The state structure collapsed completely when the conflict with the ❺ Hussites became a civil war. Wenceslas's brother Sigismund was refused recognition as king of Bohemia until shortly before his death in

1437, even though he had been Holy Roman Emperor since 1410.

When Sigismund's grandson ❻ László V (Posthumus) died in 1457, George of Podebrady, a local noble who had been regent for the underage László, was elected king. For the first time a king appealed to the moderate Hussites. In 1471 he was succeeded by

Murder of the clergyman John of Nepomuk, ordered by Wenceslas IV, wooden engraving, 19th century

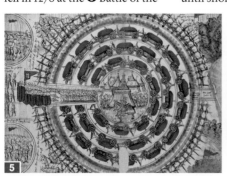

A corral used as a mobile fortress by the Hussites, book illustration, ca. 1450

László Posthumus, painting, 15th century

Karlstein Castle near Prague, built under Charles IV, 14th century

The Hussites

Jan Hus, a Bohemian reformer, attended the Council of Constance in 1415. He criticized the secularization of the Church and was therefore condemned as a heretic and burned at the stake. His followers in Bohemia rose up against Sigismund of Luxembourg, who had assured Hus safe conduct but was now seen as a betrayer. The Hussites terrorized wide stretches of the empire, and a number of crusades against them failed. Only a division within the Hussites in 1433 made possible a compromise with the more moderate faction and Sigismund's subsequent return to Bohemia.

Jan Hus is burned at the stake, copper engraving, 17th century

Wladyslaw (Ulászló) II, who also inherited Hungary in 1490. The Habsburgs once again gained control of Bohemia and Hungary through the double marriage of his children to the grandchildren of Holy Roman Emperor Maximilian I. The position of the Habsburg rulers in Bohemia, however, remained weak. The power of the Bohemian aristocracy was finally broken in the Thirty Years' War when they supported the adversaries of the Habsburgs.

929 | Wenceslas I murdered   **1001** | Stephen I becomes the first king of Hungary   **1251** | Otakar II occupies Austria

ca. 900 | Magyars advance under Árpád   **955** | Battle of Lechfeld   **1222** | "Golden Bull"   **1282** | Battle of the Marchfeld

Hungary

Hungary became a state under the Árpáds. Even in the face of the Ottoman threat, the self-confident nobility held onto their privileges.

From the time of the Huns in the fourth and fifth centuries, nomads continually pushed out of the Eurasian steppes into Europe. Around 900, the Magyars, or Hungarians, led by their prince  Árpád, moved into the power vacuum left by the Avars after their defeat by Charlemagne in 796. The Magyars traveled as far as Rome on their extended plundering raids, and only after their defeat by the German army in 955 at Lechfeld did they settle down in Transdanubia (Pannonia), present-day Hungary.

Prince Geza, a descendant of Árpád, became a Christian and secured a dominant position for his family. His son,  Stephen I

Sigismund escaping over the Danube after the Battle of Nicopolis

Baptism of Stephen I, painting, 19th c.

granted extensive autonomy. The Árpád dynasty ended with Andrew III in 1301.

Following much turmoil over the throne, a French Anjou came to power in 1307. Louis I (the Great) was enthroned in 1342 and

Louis II of Hungary and Bohemia, painting, 16th c.

Pressburg, present-day Bratislava, Slovakia, capital of the Hungarian Habsburgs after 1526

(St. Stephen), was crowned the first king of Hungary in 1001. With German help, he built up a government and an ecclesiastical structure. His successors conquered neighboring Croatia and Transylvania, where many Germans settled. In 1222 Andrew II was coerced by the nobles into issuing the "Golden Bull," which recognized the rights of the nobility and Church. The German regions in Transylvania were also

for a time was able to disempower the barons. In 1370, he also succeeded his uncle, Casimir III, as king of Poland. Upon Louis's death, his realm was again split, Poland being bequeathed to his daughter Jadwiga, while his daughter Mary and his son-in-law Sigismund of Luxembourg succeeded him in Hungary. In 1396, Sigismund suffered a crushing defeat against the Ottomans at  Nicopolis on the Danube. In

exchange for financial support, the barons were able to demand more and more privileges from the constantly cash-strapped monarch, who became German king in 1410, king of Bohemia in 1419, and emperor in 1433. After the death of Sigismund's son-in-law and heir, Albert of Austria, another struggle for the throne took place. In Hungary, the Hungarian nobleman János Hunyadi prevailed as regent for Albert's son, László Posthumus. After László's death in 1457, the Hungarians elected Hunyadi's own son,  Matthias Corvinus, as the new king.

During the reign of Matthias, who fostered a brilliant Renaissance court, Hungary reached its greatest territorial size. He occu-

pied wide stretches of Bohemia and Austria during his campaigns against George of Podebrady—who, as a Hussite, had been excommunicated by the pope—and Emperor Frederick III, who claimed László's inheritance. In the end, Matthias reconciled with Frederick and the successor of George Podebrady, Wladyslaw (Ulászló) II, who was elected king at Matthias's death as the latter had no legitimate children. Wladislaw's son  Louis II fell in the Battle of Mohács against the Ottomans, who occupied almost all of Hungary. Only in the  border region between Hungary and Austria was Louis's brother-in-law, the Habsburg Ferdinand I, accepted as king of Hungary.

The Hungarians appropriate land under the leadership of Árpád, painting, 19th century

Matthias Corvinus, marble relief, ca. 1490

1342 | Louis I becomes king of Hungary   **1415** | Murder of Jan Hus   **1457** | László V dies

1347 | Charles IV crowned king of Bohemia   **1437** | Sigismund recognized as king of Bohemia   **1490** | Wladyslaw II inherits Hungary

RUSSIA 9TH–16TH CENTURY

Under the influence of the Byzantine culture, Slavs and Scandinavian Varangians had been merging in the kingdom of Kiev since the ninth century. The ruling Rurik dynasty involved the country in ❶ struggles for the throne and the division of the dynastic inheritance. The divided principalities found themselves under Mongolian rule from the 13th century. At the same time, Moscow's rise began. Russia was united by Moscow in the 14th and 15th centuries and began its path to becoming a major European power. With the death of the last of the Ruriks, a period of chaos set in, ended only in 1613 by a new dynasty, the Romanovs.

Battling Russian principalities of Novgorod and Suzdal, icon, 15th century

Kievan Rus

The Scandinavian Varangians founded the first kingdom on Russian soil.

Scandinavian Vikings, known to Slavs and Byzantines as "Varangians" or "Rus," began moving into the territory of present-day Russia and Ukraine in the eighth century as warriors, traders, and

Varangian ship in the port of Novgorod, painting, 1900

settlers, using large rivers such as the Neva, Don, and Volga as transportation routes. The small defensive nuclei of the steppes became staging posts on a route

linking the Baltic to the Volga. Trading links, by way of the Black and Caspian seas, existed as far as the Byzantine Empire and the Abbasid caliphate. In Constantinople, Varangians formed the emperor's personal elite bodyguard.

According to the Primary Chronicle, the inhabitants of the old Slav trading metropolis of ❸ Novgorod in northern Russia elevated a Varangian named ❷ Rurik to the status of prince in 862 in order to settle their feuds; Varangians also came to power in other towns after being appointed by the Slavs or by taking them by force.

Rurik's successor Oleg the Wise advanced to the south and in 882 occupied Kiev, which became the capital of his realm,

known as Kievan Rus. A trade agreement with Byzantium in 911 also opened up the principality to Christianity; Rurik's daughter-in-law Olga was baptized in 957. Her grandson, Vladimir I (the Great), married the sister of the Byzantine emperor and converted to ❺, ❻ Christianity in 988 as part of a pact with Basil II of Constantinople. Kiev became the seat of an Orthodox bishop, who was

Slavic deputies kneel before Rurik, wood engraving, ca. 1890

The Russian Primary Chronicle

The Primary Chronicle recounts Kievan Rus history up to the twelfth century. It was compiled by an unknown author probably at the end of the eleventh century in Kiev's cave monastery. For a long time, it was known by the name of the monk Nestor, who was thought to have compiled it. However, he only revised it, shortly after 1110.

Manuscript illustration in a medieval Russian chronicle: looting of Kiev by an opposed Russian prince

Mosaic in the cupola of St. Sophie's cathedral in Kiev, 11th century

nominally subject to the patriarch of Constantinople until 1589.

When Vladimir died in 1015, his sons fought over the throne. Eventually, Yaroslav the Wise prevailed and by 1036 had subdued the whole of Kievan Rus. During Yaroslav's reign, Kiev experienced a golden era in ❹ architecture and culture influenced by Byzantine culture. Yaroslav was the first to codify Russian law—a combination of Byzantine laws and Slavic common law.

St. Sophie's cathedral in Novgorod, built under Vladimir I in the 11th c.

Baptism of Vladimir I, book illustration, 15th century

The Rule of the Mongols

The Mongols conquered the internally divided Kievan Rus in the early 13th century and obligated it to make tribute payments.

7 View over the city of Novgorod, copper engraving, 17th century

After the death of Yaroslav in 1054, Kievan Rus was divided among his sons. The eldest member of the Rurik dynasty was supposed to exercise titular sovereignty, yet after every change in ruler there were renewed struggles for the throne and further division of the inheritance. Even significant rulers such as ❽ Vladimir II (known as *Monomakh* or "sole ruler") and Mstislav the Great in the twelfth century were unable to reunite Kievan Rus. To make mat-

8 Crown of Vladimir II (*Monomakh*), ca. 300

sians at the Kalka River, northeast of the Crimea, in 1223 was without consequence at first as the Mongols under Genghis Khan considered it only a preparation for further conquests in the future. However, a decade after Genghis Khan's death, his grandson, Batu Khan of the Golden Horde, established the rule of the Mongols in Russia. The Russian princes were forced to pay tribute to the khans, pay taxes, and tolerate political control by Mongol envoys.

In 1240 the Rurik prince Alexander repelled a Swedish invasion at the Neva River, thus acquiring the sur-

name Nevsky. He also ❿ beat back the Teutonic Knights on the frozen Lake Peipus in 1242. In 1263, Alexander Nevsky entrusted the city of Moscow to his son Daniel as an independent principality. Daniel's son, ❾ Ivan I— known as *Kalita* ("moneybags")— bought the favor of the khans and began to subjugate neighboring principalities; in 1328 he assumed the title of grand prince. The head of the Russian Orthodox Church also moved his seat to Moscow.

Eventually, the Moscow grand princes turned against their

9 Ivan I Kalita with a silver pot, ca. 1900

Mongol overlords and successfully rebelled against them. Ivan's grandson, Dmitri Donskoi, won the first major victory over the Mongol army in 1380 at ⓬ Kulikovo on the Don, taking advantage of the fact that the Golden Horde had been disintegrating since 1357 and that the plague had hit them especially hard. Competing Turik khanates had emerged from the Crimea to Siberia, and these were later conquered by Russia. The last of these to come under Russian influence was the ⓫ khanate of the Crimean Tatars in the 18th century. At the time it had been under Ottoman suzerainty.

10 Battle between Russians and the Teutonic Order, movie scene

ters worse, economic decline set in. The profitable Black Sea trade, for example, was lost to the Venetians and Genoese in the 13th century. Only ❼ Novgorod continued to experience growth through trade with the Hanse.

Kievan Rus was politically splintered and shaken by wars and attacks on its borders. Thus the Mongols—known as "Tatars" to the Russians—were easily able to conquer the Russian principalities. The first defeat of the Rus-

11 Palace of the Crimean Tatar Khans in Bachtshissarai, painting, 19th century

12 Battle of Kulikovo, book illustration, 16th c.

| 1223 | Battle of the Kalka River | 1240 | Swedes repelled on the Neva | 1380 | Battle of Kulikovo |
| 1110 | Nestor revises the Primary Chronicle | 1227 | Genghis Khan dies | 1263 | Moscow made an independent principality |

■ Moscow's Rise

The Muscovite grand princes extended their territories and considered themselves the successors to the Byzantine emperors.

When Constantinople was conquered by the Ottomans in 1453, the grand princes of Moscow deemed themselves to be the legitimate heirs of the Byzantine emperor and defenders of the Orthodox Church. ❶ Moscow was to be the "third Rome." Grand Prince ❻ Ivan III married the niece of the last emperor in 1472

1 View over the city of Moscow with the Kremlin in the center, copper engraving, ca. 16th century

and from 1478 on assumed the title of "Sovereign of All Russia." From Byzantium, he adopted the heraldic double eagle on the Muscovy coat of arms, the court ceremonial, and the autocratic rule that characterized the Russian monarchy until its end in 1917.

Ivan had his royal residence in Moscow, the ❸ Kremlin, magnifi-

cently improved by Italian architects. In 1478 he annexed the merchant city of Novgorod, which had acquired vast territories in the north of Russia, and in 1480 ended his tribute payments to the Mongolian khans. Ivan and his son Vasily III steadily extended their Russian domain westward at the expense of the Polish-Lithuanian union.

When ❷ Ivan IV (the Terrible) inherited the throne from his father Vasily in 1533, he was just three years old, and a brutal battle for the regency flared up among the noble families, the *boyars*. When he reached adulthood in 1547 Ivan was crowned tsar, the first Russian ruler to use this title formally, and he began to break the power of boyars. With the help of the nobility (who earned their titles through service), the Church, and an elite military unit, the Strelitsi, he reformed the military, the legal system, and the government. To accomplish these ends, he used great ❹ brutality and the *oprichniki*, a bodyguard

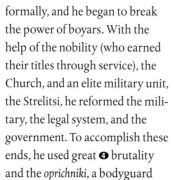

4 Ivan IV the Terrible has convicts roasted over an open fire, copper engraving, 17th c.

5 Ivan IV the Terrible with his dead son

Siberia

In 1558 Ivan IV charged the merchant Stroganov family with subjugating Siberia. They hired the Cossack leader Yermak, who in 1584 conquered the capital of the khanate of Sibir. The Cossacks were followed by merchants, fur traders, and settlers. A hundred years later, the Russians had reached the extreme east, where a treaty with China in 1689 established the Amur River as the boundary.

Yermak, the leader of the Cossacks, painting, 18th century

bound to him by an oath of loyalty. The opposing boyars were persecuted through deportations, expropriations, and liquidations, and their property was divided among the newly titled nobility loyal to the tsar. In 1570, Ivan had Novgorod razed and thousands of citizens murdered because the city had supposedly risen up against his authority. He even killed one of his own ❺ sons in a fit of frenzied rage. Peasants fled the state terror and sought refuge with the Cossacks in the steppe regions north of the Black Sea.

In international affairs, Ivan IV continued the expansionist policies of his predecessors. The khanates of ❼ Kasan and Astrakhan were conquered, which

2 Ivan the Terrible, painting by Victor M. Wasnezow, 1897

3 The Kremlin with the Cathedral of St. Michael the Archangel

6 Ivan III, wood engraving, 16th century

7

St. Basil's Cathedral, built by Ivan IV to celebrate his victory over Kasan

provoked a retaliatory strike by the Crimean Tatars, who devastated Moscow in 1571. The conquest of Siberia began in the east. In 1584, the northern port of Arkhangelsk was founded on the White Sea to facilitate trade with England.

When Ivan died in 1584, Russia had become significantly larger in territory, but internally was in ruins, the populace in poverty, and the leadership classes split by power struggles that broke out openly after the death of the czar.

The Cossacks

Ever since the 15th century, runaway serfs from Russia and the Ukraine and dispersed Tatars had been settling the steppes between the Black Sea and the Urals. Here they founded communities of free armed peasants and warriors, who chose their leaders by election. The Cossacks (from the Tatar qazaq, "adventurer") had a high reputation as skilled soldiers and were thus often hired as mercenaries by the Poles, Lithuanians, and Russians.

above: Assembly of Cossacks, painting by Ilya Repin, 19th century

▮ The Time of Troubles

After the death of Ivan the Terrible, the *Smuta*—Time of Troubles—began.

❾ Boris Godunov was the regent for his brother-in-law Fyodor I, the feebleminded son of Ivan IV and Anastasia Romanovna. Fyodor's only surviving brother, Dmitri, was murdered in 1591, probably on Godunov's command. When Fyodor died in 1598, ending the main line of the Ruriks, Godunov was elected to the throne. After a severe famine, social unrest and revolts plagued Godunov's reign as he made the serfdom of the peasants even harsher and more stringent.

Following Godunov's death in 1605 and the assassination of his son Fyodor II, Sigismund III Vasa of Poland-Lithuania sought to expand his influence in Russia and supported a pretender who claimed to be Dmitri, the son of Ivan IV. This Dmitri became tsar for a short time before he was assassinated by a boyar, Vasily Shuysky—who was then elected tsar by the boyars in 1606. Further revolts brought another false Dmitri, from Tushino, to prominence. Sigismund then claimed the tsar's throne for his son, the future Wladyslaw IV, and had Shuysky deposed in 1610. The Poles ruled in Moscow for two

8

Whipping in a Russian village, steel engraving, 19th century

years, until the folk hero ⓫ Kuzma Minin put together a Russian army and, with the support of the Cossacks, liberated Moscow in 1612. The following year, the boyars elected a new tsar, ⓪ Michael Romanov III, the 16-year-old son of an influential patriarch and—through his great-aunt Anastasia Romanovna—cousin of the last legitimate tsar of the House of Rurik. The Time of Troubles had finally ended, although the disputes over the autocracy of the tsars and the social problems of the starving and impoverished ❽ rural population that had erupted during the Time of Troubles would continue to plague Russia in the ensuing centuries.

Tsar Michael, who ruled until 1633 jointly with his father, the Patriarch Philarete, came to an understanding with Poland-

9

Boris Godunov, painting by Alexander Yakovlevith Golovin, 1912

Lithuania wherein the Polish territories under Ivan the Terrible's rule were returned.

The imperial dynasty of the Romanovs would rule as Russian tsars for 150 years and five generations from 1613 to 1762.

11

Prince Dimitrij Poscharsky and Kuzma, painting, 19th century

10

Michael Romanov ascends the throne, lithograph, 19th century

1571 | Crimean Tatars plunder Moscow   **1584** | Ivan IV dies, Time of Troubles begins   **1613** | Michael Romanov chosen as czar

1584 | Port of Arkhangelsk is founded   **1605** | Death of Boris Godunov   **1610–12** | Moscow under Polish occupation

THE BYZANTINE EMPIRE 867–1453

In the ninth through eleventh centuries, the Byzantine Empire once again rose to become a major power, but there were signs of internal discord. Attacks from outside weakened the state, and it did not fully recover from its conquest by the armies of the Fourth Crusade at the beginning of the 13th century. In 1453, Constantinople fell to the Ottomans, an event that sent shock waves through Christian Europe. ❶, ❷ Byzantine scholars who fled to the West brought with them the knowledge of the culture of classical antiquity preserved in the Byzantine Empire, which was central to the Renaissance and the rise of humanism in Italy.

John Bessarion, patriarch of Constantinople and scholar, painting, 16th c.

The Byzantine Resurrection under the Macedonian Dynasty

The Macedonian dynasty was able to reestablish the Byzantine Empire's old supremacy in the East.

Byzantine Emperor Basil I (the Macedonian 867–886) rose from modest circumstances. In 867, he ❸ murdered his patron, Emperor Michael III, and assumed the throne. Basil was soon able to ❻ reconquer territories in southern Italy and sought to win over the pope by temporarily relieving the anti-Roman patriarch, Photius I, of his office. Domestically, he had the Imperial Code retailored to allow a more centralized, strongly bureaucratic power for a government in which the emperor was considered the absolute ruler by divine right.

Basil's son, ❼ Leo VI, together with Romanus I Lecapenos, who led the government from 920 to 944, repulsed invasions by the Bulgars, the Russians, and the Arabs. In 922, the emperor sought to reform the system of land ownership, limiting the amount of land that large estate owners could acquire from small proprietors. Leo's son, ❹ Constantine VII Porphyrogenitus, wrote a number of works about the ceremonial customs and administration of the court.

In 963 Constantine's son and successor, Romanus II, was probably poisoned by his wife, Theophano, who then married his successor Nicephorus II Phocas, a successful general who had recaptured parts of Asia Minor and Syria, as well as the islands of Crete and Cyprus.

Theophano then turned to a younger relative of Nicephorus, ❺ John I Tzimisces, and together they plotted the assassination of the new emperor in 969. After this usurpation John married Theophano and quickly embarked on further military campaigns.

❷ Cross of John Bessarion, 14th–15th century

❸ Basil I murders Michael III in his bedchamber, copper engraving, 17th century

❹ Constantine VII Porphyrogenitus, gold coin, minted in 945

❺ Aided by Theophano, John I Tzimisces scales the palace walls in order to kill Nicephorus II Phocas, copper engraving, 17th century

❻ Basil I in battle against Arab invaders, book illustration, 13th century

Patriarch Photius I

Basil I initially attempted to cultivate a cordial relationship with the Roman papacy and removed Photius I, the patriarch of Constantinople, from office because of his emphasis on the independence of the Byzantine Church from Rome. Pope Nicholas I had also been angered by the success of the Slavic mission of St. Cyril and St. Methodius, initiated by Photius. After the death of his successor in 877, Photius was reinstated, which led to an open breach with Rome.

The "Slavic apostles" Cyril and Methodius, monument in front of the Bulgarian national library

❼ Leo VI at Christ's feet, mosaic, ca. 900

| 867 | Basil I seizes the throne. | | 963 | Romanus II murdered | | 976 | Reign of Basil II begins |

| 920–44 | Romanus I Lecapenos leads government | 971 | John I conquers eastern Bulgaria | 1014 | Boris II's victory over the Western Bulgars |

The Byzantine Empire and the Crusades

The attacks of the Normans, the Seljuks, and ultimately the crusaders brought the last golden age of the Byzantine Empire to an end.

The new emperor, John I Tzimisces, conquered eastern Bulgaria in 971 and advanced further into Syria and Palestine. He arranged the marriage of Theophano, the daughter of Romanus II, to Otto II, the future Holy Roman Emperor. John was succeeded in 976 by ⓫ Basil II, another member of the Macedonian dynasty. Basil conquered western Bulgaria after more than a decade of fighting. After the final victory in 1014, he had 14,000 enemy prisoners blinded, which earned him the title of the "Bulgaroctonus" ("Slayer of the Bulgars"). Basil's regency also marked the last great cultural flowering of the Byzantine Empire, which from then on was increasingly forced onto the defensive by the encroachments of its powerful enemies.

The advance of the Muslim Seljuks was particularly threatening. A crushing defeat of the Byzantines at Manzikert in Armenia in 1071 cleared the way for

8

Alexius I Comnenus, mosaic, 12th c.

the Seljuks to occupy Asia Minor, where they established the sultanate of Iconium.

At the same time, struggles over the throne grew in intensity. The female members of the court, notably ⓬ Zoe and ❾ Eudocia, played an important role in the dynastic intrigues of the period.

❽ Alexius I Comnenus, who became emperor in 1081, granted Venice, Genoa, and other leading Italian powers broad trading privileges to gain their support against the Normans, who had seized Byzantine possessions in southern Italy. In the long run, however, this undermined the Byzantine economy as the state lost control of its revenues. Despite the break with the Roman Catholic Church in the Great Schism in 1054, Alexius also sought help from

the pope in 1095 in his fight against the Seljuks. Although parts of Asia Minor were regained by Byzantium in the wake of the First Crusade in 1096, the new Crusader states in Syria and Palestine soon ceased to recognize the sovereignty of the Byzantine emperor.

Alexius' grandson, Manuel I, spent much of his reign fighting to regain lost provinces. Meanwhile, in 1175 the Venetians began to support the Normans, and the Byzantine Empire suffered a defeat in 1176 at the hands of the Seljuks at Myriocephalon. In 1185, the Bulgars also made themselves independent of the Byzantine Empire.

Under the influence of Venice, the Fourth Crusade used the ❿ struggle over the throne to sack Constantinople in 1203 and occupy it in 1204. The Byzantine Empire was reduced to a shell of small provinces.

9

Christ crowning Empress Eudocia and her second husband Romanus IV Diogenes, ivory carving, eleventh century

10

Murder of Alexios IV Angelos by Alexius V Dukas Murtzuphlos

11

Emperor Basil II stands over the defeated Bulgars, book illustration, early eleventh century

12

Empress Zoe, wife of three Byzantine emperors, golden diadem, eleventh c.

Feudalization

From the tenth century, the Byzantine emperors increasingly turned toward granting estates as payment for services rendered. It was also possible for large property owners to be granted immunity from taxes. When the estates and privileges became hereditary, the state also lost its control over the peasants, who had been pressed into serfdom. The authority of the central government in the provinces deteriorated in favor of the newly established domains of a developing nobility.

The Latin Empire and Other Successor States

Under the Emperor Michael Palaeologus of Nicaea, the Byzantines reconquered Constantinople.

After the ❸ fall of Constantinople, sacked by the Crusaders on 13 April in 1204, various crusader kingdoms and Byzantine successor states emerged on Byzantine soil. Among these was the empire of ❶ Trebizond founded in the northeast of Asia Minor, where a branch of the Comnenus family

The conquest of Constantinople in 1204, painting by Tintoretto, 16th century

reigned until 1461. In Byzantium itself the crusaders chose a Latin, Baldwin Count of Flanders, and crowned him as ❷ Emperor Baldwin I in Santa Sophia. The Patriarch was also a Latin: the Venetian Tomasso Morosini.

Venice also secured numerous strategically located islands and

"Tekfur Saray," the imperial palace, in Constantinople, built between the 12th and 13th century

ports, including Crete, most of the Aegean islands, Rhodes, and trading posts in the Peloponnese and Thrace. Crusader leaders built up feudal states after the European model in the kingdom of ❼ Thessaloniki, the duchies of Athens and Naxos, and the principality of Achaea. In theory, suzerainty was held by the Latin emperor of Constantinople, but he was dependent on the support of the feudal lords and Venice, keen to protect its trading privileges, in order to rule.

Greek Orthodox Christians were placed under Catholic clergy, which provoked violent resistance. They received support from the Bulgarian tsar, Kaloyan Asen, and at the Battle of Adrianople in 1205, Baldwin was seized and killed by the Bulgars. The Latin emperors in Constantinople thereafter followed one another in quick succession.

By the time Baldwin's nephew, ❹ Baldwin II, came to power in 1240, his empire consisted of little more than the city of Constantinople itself. His financial problems were so acute that he even married off his own son in return for a loan from Venice.

In Nicaea, the Byzantine state tradition was preserved by Emperor Theodore I Lascaris after the fall of Constantinople. From there, he and his successors sought to restore the empire. Although John III Ducas Vatatzes failed in the first attempt to retake Constantinople in 1235, he won territory in Thrace and Macedonia in victories over the Bulgars, and in 1246 he was able to reconquer Thessaloniki.

In 1259, Michael VIII Palaeologus usurped the throne from the young John IV Lascaris and founded the ❺, ❻ Palaeologan dynasty. He allied himself with Genoa, Venice's powerful rival in the Mediterranean, and the emerging Muslim power of Asia Minor, and succeeded in recapturing Constantinople in 1261.

The surprise attack was assisted by the absence of the Latin emperor, Baldwin II, who was on a mendicant visit to Western Europe. Michael Palaeologus thus restored the Byzantine empire, though in a much weakened form. The northern part of the Balkans remained under the control of the Bulgarians and the Serbs, while Thessaly and the Epirus were governed by the Greeks.

5 Manuel II Palaeologus, silver coin, minted ca. 1400

Hagia Sophia church in Trebizond, built in 1461 and later annexed by the Ottoman Empire

Venetian Doge Enrico Dandolo crowns Baldwin I of Flanders emperor of Byzantium, painting, 16–17th century

Venetian merchants meet Emperor Baldwin II, book illustration, ca. 1410

The "White Tower" in Thessaloniki, built during the 15th century

1204	Theodor I Laskaris becomes emperor of Nicaea	1240	Baldwin II becomes Latin emperor	1259	Michael VIII Palaeologus usurps the throne
	1205	Battle of Adrianople	1246	Reconquest of Thessaloniki	1261	Constantinople recaptured by the Byzantines

The Fall of the Byzantine Empire

After the restoration Byzantium was increasingly undermined by the powerful merchant empires of Venice and Genoa, while the mighty Ottomans finally captured Constantinople in 1453.

Although Michael VIII restored the Byzantine Empire, it was never again able to regain its former strength. The maritime republic of Venice maintained its stranglehold on commerce, while Genoa was rewarded for its help in restoring Michael to the throne

9 John VI, surrounded by the clergy at a synod, book illustration, 14th century

with trade privileges and the colony Pera, further undermining Byzantine power. The Latin feudal states held out in Greece, while the Serbs and Bulgars in the north and the successors of the Seljuks to the east all threatened Byzantine borders.

Despite this precarity, Byzantium enjoyed something of a **⓫** cultural resurgence in this period.

13 The Ottomans conquer Constantinople, 1453, copper engraving, 17th century

Michael's son, Andronicus II Palaeologus, came to power in 1282, but a period of dispute over the throne began in 1321 that brought the state close to complete collapse. After being coerced into recognizing his grandson, Andronicus III, as co-emperor, he

10 John VIII Palaeologus, painting by Benozzo Gozzoli, 15th century

was forced to abdicate in 1328. After Andronicus III's death in 1341, **9** John VI Cantacuzenus, supported by followers of *hesychasm*, usurped the throne in place of Andronicus's son John V. Although John VI was deposed, he regained the throne in 1347 with the help of the Ottomans. In 1354 he was deposed again and sent to a monastery. His son Matthaios, however, ruled until 1382 as despot of Morea, a center of late Byzantine culture.

The Palaeologans, restored in Constantinople, became increasingly dependent on the Ottomans. The fall of Adrianople in 1362 completed the encir-

8 "Greek fire," an incendiary liquid contained in a grenade, used by the Byzantines to set enemy ships ablaze, striking fear into enemy ranks

clement of the Byzantine Empire, which soon consisted of just Constantinople and its outlying districts. Calls for aid to the West went unanswered, and the fall of Byzantium was delayed only by the Ottomans' defeat by Tamerlane in 1402.

In 1439 Emperor **⓾** John VIII Palaeologus offered to recognize the supremacy of the pope in exchange for military aid against the Ottomans, but the deal failed

11 Chora monastery in Constantinople (Istanbul), built in the early 14th century, later transformed into a mosque

and provoked violent resistance from the Greek Orthodox population. He was succeeded in 1449 by his brother, Constantine XI, the last Byzantine emperor. When the Ottoman sultan Mehmed II began a siege of Constantinople in 1453, the **8** encircled populace offered determined resistance with assistance from Venetians and others in the city.

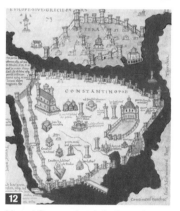
12 Map of Constantinople in the 16th century, with the Genoese trading colony of Pera in green

However, the Ottoman forces, using the heaviest artillery yet seen, were overwhelming. On the night of May 29, 1453, the **⓭** Ottomans broke through the **⓬** walls of the city. The last Byzantine emperor died in battle.

Ottoman bridge in Mostar, Herzegovina, built in the 16th century

SOUTHEAST EUROPE 7TH–15TH CENTURY

With the decline of the Eastern Roman Empire in the eighth and ninth centuries, numerous, often short-lived states developed in southeast Europe. Only the Bulgars and Serbs enjoyed periods of supremacy in the Balkans. The region was above all a zone of influence and a military thoroughfare for the neighboring major powers. The last of these was the ❶ Ottoman Empire, which by the 16th century controlled most the region.

◼ The Adriatic Coast

With only a few exceptions, the entire west and northwest of the Balkan Peninsula came under Ottoman or Habsburg control at the end of the Middle Ages.

The Southern Slavic Croats were ruled first by the Byzantine Empire and then by the Franks. In 925 an independent Croatian kingdom emerged, united with Hungary in a personal union from 1102 to 1918, which was ruled by a viceroy called ❸ Ban. After King Demetrius Zvonimir was crowned by the pope in 1076, Croatia aligned itself with the Roman Catholic Church. The ❻ Ottomans' endeavors to conquer Croatia were successfully repelled. By the 15th century, Venice had conquered Dalmatia, the Croatian coastal region, as it came to dominate the Adriatic.

Miklos Earl Zrinyi, Ban of Croatia, wood engraving, 16th century

The city-republic of ❺ Ragusa, today's Dubrovnik, was able to maintain its independence for centuries, until it was occupied by Napoleon's armies between 1806 and 1808. Bosnia was initially part of the Byzantine Empire but fell to Hungary in the twelfth century. Viceroy Stephen Kotromanic (Turtko) also conquered the region of Herzegovina. Following additional territorial gains, he named himself king of Serbia and Bosnia in 1377. The kingdom did not survive long after his death, however; the Ottomans occupied Bosnia in 1463 and Herzegovina in 1483.

Of the Slavic territories of the Balkans, only small Montenegro was able to maintain its autonomy against the Ottomans, because the inhabitants had inaccessible mountain fortresses from which they could hold out. From 1528, the Orthodox bishops of Cetinje headed a polity that

The Skanderbeg Château, where the Albanians defended themselves from the Ottomans in the 15th century

Prince George Kastrioti, known as Skanderbeg, wood engraving

consisted of loosely bound clans, who were at odds with each other. Toward the end of the 17th century, Peter I was able to make the office of bishop hereditary in his family. In 1852, Montenegro became a ❹ secular principality and in 1910 a kingdom that lasted for a mere eight years.

The Albanians, who are not of Slavic descent and are thought by some to be descended from the ancient Illyrians, were also able to resist the Ottomans for a long time. In 1443, ❷ George Kastrioti, also called Skanderbeg, was trained by the Ottomans and fought for them for many years. He later returned to unite the Albanian tribes. In alliance with Naples, Venice, and Hungary, he negotiated a ten-year cease-fire with the Ottomans in 1461. When Skanderbeg broke the agreement after only two years, his allies deserted him, although the Ottomans were not able to conquer the area until his death in 1468.

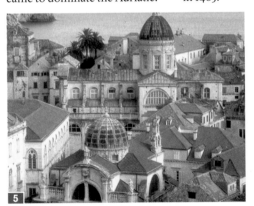

The old town of Ragusa, present-day Dubrovnik

The Ottomans besiege Agram (Zagreb), the Croatian capital

Greece and Romania

By the 17th century the Ottomans had conquered Greece. They appointed governors from the leading noble families in the Romanian principalities.

After the capture of Constantinople by the armies of the Fourth Crusade in 1204, a large number of independent ❶ dominions developed in present-day Greece alongside the ❼ Venetian strongholds.

8 | Marketplace in the German town of Schässburg in Transylvania, colored lithograph, 20th century

Often these consisted of only a small island or city and were ruled over by Greek, French, or Italian noble families. The most significant territory was the duchy of Athens, where the reigning French dukes were driven out in 1311 by Catalonian pirates, who were themselves ousted in 1388 by the Florentine Acciaioli family. In 1458, the Ottomans took Athens; the Ottoman conquest of the rest of

12 | Monastery of Voronet, built in 1488 on the orders of Stephen the Great, St. George, its patron saint

❿ Greece was not complete until into the 17th century.

The territory of present-day Romania was the home of the Vlachs, a people descended from the Romanized natives and the Gothic, Slavic, Hun, and Bulgarian invaders. Hungary's expansion in the eleventh century and the increasing number of ❽ German settlers pushed many of them out of Transylvania into the Carpathian Mountains and beyond, further

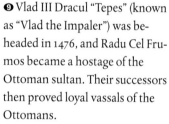

9 | Vlad III Dracul, "The Impaler," painting, 16th century

south and east into Walachia and Moldavia. Out of the Hungarian border provinces, independent

11 | Ruins of the Byzantine castle in Mistra in the Pelopennesus, 13th–15th c.

states under local princes—the voivods—developed in the 14th century.

Mircea the Old, the voivod of Walachia, made Bucharest his capital in 1385, and in order to avoid being deposed he accepted Ottoman suzerainty in 1396. His grandsons formed shifting alliances with Hungary and the Ottomans, which allowed them room to maneuver, but this was ultimately an unsustainable policy. The kings met grisly ends: Mircea was buried alive in 1442, ❾ Vlad III Dracul "Tepes" (known as "Vlad the Impaler") was beheaded in 1476, and Radu Cel Frumos became a hostage of the Ottoman sultan. Their successors then proved loyal vassals of the Ottomans.

⓬ Stephen the Great, voivod of Moldavia from 1457 to 1504, had more success in playing his neighbors off against each other, though in 1513, Moldavia was compelled to recognize Ottoman suzerainty. ⓭ Michael the Brave,

Count Dracula

Vlad III and Dracul Tepes were both 15th-century voivods of Walachia. Vlad III was notorious for his preference for executing the condemned by impalement. The Irish author Bram Stoker created the literary figure of Count Dracula at the end of the 19th century by combining these historical figures with popular vampire tales from Transylvania.

Vlad III Dracul Tepes dining during executions, wood engraving, 1500

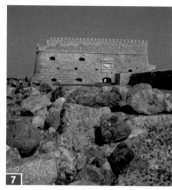

7 | Venetian fortress near Heraklion on the island of Crete

10 | Siege of Rhodes, Greece, by the Ottomans in 1480, book illustration, end of the 15th century

voivod of Walachia, together with the Moldavians, was the last to rise up against the Ottomans, but he was murdered in 1601. From the 17th century on, the Ottomans appointed nobles from different families as governors of the Romanian principalities.

13 | Michael the Brave is slain by a jealous comrade in arms, copper engraving, 17th century

Bulgarian Kingdoms

During the ninth and tenth centuries the Bulgars were the dominant power in the Balkans.

During the fifth century, elements of the Huns withdrew back into the steppes of southern Russia, where they mixed with related Turkic tribes and Slavic ethnic

Orthodox chapel overlooking Lake Ohrid, in present-day Macedonia, built in the late ninth c.

Fights between Bulgars and Byzantines outside Thessaloniki, book illustration, 13th century

groups to become the Bulgars. Their first major kingdom fell apart around 640 because of the advance of other steppe peoples, dividing the Bulgarian people into the Volga and Danube Bulgars.

Thereafter, the Volga Bulgars prospered on the trade route between Kievan Rus and the Islamic lands to the south until their kingdom was destroyed by Mongol invaders in 1236.

The Danube Bulgars established the first Bulgarian kingdom in the Balkans around 681 under their khan, Asparukh, who claimed to be descended from Attila. Boris I introduced ❷ Christianity in 865 to facilitate the unification of the kingdom. His younger son, Simeon, whom he had sent to Constantinople to be educated as a monk, usurped the throne in 893. Simeon I ("the Great"), the most significant Bulgarian ruler, waged several ❸ wars against Byzantium but was unable to capture Constantinople. In 925, he assumed the title "Tsar of All the Bulgars." Simeon presided over a cultural golden era in the Bulgarian Empire, promoting the use of the Cyrillic alphabet to en-

able Slavic translations of the Bible and to facilitate the population's conversion to Christianity.

Soon after Simeon's death in 927, during a time of conflicts with Kievan Rus, the decline of the empire set in. Bulgaria was so weakened in 1014 by its ❺ defeat at the hands of Byzantine emperor Basil II, the "Slayer of Bulgars," that four years later the Byzantines returned to annex all of Bulgaria, managing to hold it for almost two centuries.

The Bulgarian nobles Peter and Ivan Asen used the distraction caused by the attacks of the Seljuks on the Byzantine Empire to

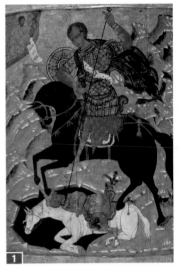

Ivan Shishman and his family, book illustration, 14th century

Kaloyan Asen in battle, mosaic, 16th c.

proclaim their independence in 1186. They founded the second Bulgarian kingdom, with its capital at ❻ Turnovo. Their brother, ❶ Kaloyan Asen, was recognized as king by Pope Innocent III in 1204. Shortly afterward, however, he turned away from Rome and supported the Greek Orthodox Christians in their struggle against the Latin Empire, defeating Emperor Baldwin I in 1205 at Adrianople. Kaloyan's nephew, Ivan Asen II, expanded the kingdom all the way to the Aegean and Adriatic Seas and in 1235 founded a Bulgarian patriarchate.

Following the invasion of the Mongols in 1242, the kingdom came under the rule of Mongolian khans. In 1330, Bulgaria was defeated by the Serbs at the Battle of Velbuzhd and was reduced to half of its previous size, thus becoming a relatively insignificant state. Bulgaria's last medieval tsar, ❹ Ivan Shishman, participated in the Christian defeat at the Battle of Kosovo in 1389 against the Ottomans, and by 1396 the Bulgarian territories were under the control of the Sultan.

Bulgar prisoners, blinded by Basil II, return from Byzantine captivity, wood engraving, ca. 1900

Fortifications and church of the old town Veliko Turnovo, above the Yantrain River, present-day Bulgaria

Serbian Kingdoms

From the 12th to the end of the 14th century, the Serbs were able to establish a large kingdom in the western Balkan region.

Like the Bulgars, the South Slavic Serbs, under Stephen Nemanja in 1167, used the decline of the Byzantine Empire in the twelfth century to establish an independent state. He reorganized the

7

Studenica Monastery, the largest in Serbia, founded by Stefan Nemanja after his abdication in 1196

10

Serbian Patriarchate Monastery in Pec, built in the 13th–14th centuries

Serbian kingdom and Church. New Serbian bishops were selected and Serbian became the liturgical language. In 1196 he abdicated and retired to a **7** monastery. His son and successor, **8** Stephan II Nemanja, initially turned toward the West and was granted the title of king by the pope in 1217. In 1219, as a counterweight to Stefan's pro-Roman policies, his brother **12** Sava founded the Serbian Orthodox Church, which later became a key part of Serbian national identity under foreign domination. The monasteries founded by St. Sava became cultural centers. Later in the 13th century, Serbia, which had previously been characterized by clan groupings, developed a feudal state after the Western European model, and the peasants effectively became serfs.

In 1330 at Velbuzhd, the Serbs won an important victory against

8

St. Stefan II Nemanja, king of Serbia, portrait surrounded by scenes from his life, Serbian icon painting, 16th c.

the Bulgars, which brought additional territories to the Serbian crown. **11** Stephen Dushan, crowned in 1331, continued these expansionist policies and conquered Greece as far as the outskirts of Athens. He had himself crowned "Emperor of the Serbs and Greeks" in 1346 in Skopje and established a Serbian **10** patriarchate. Domestically, he built up a hierarchical government organized along Byzantine lines and codified the legal system. His son, Stephan Urosh V, crowned in

9

János Hunyadi fighting against the Ottomans, wood engraving, 19th c.

11

Stephen Dushan, mosaic, 14th century

1355, was unable to hold the empire together and it splintered into a number of principalities in 1371. The North Serbian prince, Lazar Hrebeljanovic, tried in vain to halt the Ottoman advance. The Serbs suffered a massive defeat in the Battle of Kosovo on the "Field of the Blackbirds" in 1389, and Lazar's successors were forced to recognize Ottoman suzerainty.

In 1456, Belgrade was besieged by Mehmed II. On that occasion **9** János Hunyadi, the Hungarian regent, succeeded in relieving the city and forced the Ottomans to retreat before he himself died of plague in his army camp. Nonetheless, in 1459 the Ottomans deposed the last of the Serbian princes and integrated the region into their empire.

The Battle of Kosovo, "Field of the Blackbirds"

In June 1389, the armies of the Ottoman Sultan Murad I and the Serbian prince Lazar Hrebeljanovic faced each other at the town of Kosovo Polje, Serbian for "Field of the Blackbirds." With the defeat of the Serbs, the Ottomans became undisputed masters of the Balkans. Mythologized by nationalists in the 19th and 20th centuries, the battle still plays a role in Serbian national sentiment.

Battle at the "Field of the Blackbirds," copper engraving, 18th century

12

St. Sava, fresco in the monastery of Decani, Kosovo, 1572

1330	Serb victory over Bulgars at Velbuzhd	**Jun 28, 1389**	Battle of Kosovo	1456	Seige of Belgrade ended by János Hunyadi
1346	Stephen Dushan becomes "Emperor of the Serbs and Greeks"	1396	Ottoman conquest of Bulgaria	1459	Serbia annexed by the Ottomans

THE CRUSADES 11TH–15TH CENTURY

The Crusader movement, which began in the eleventh century, was in its causes and effects a multilayered phenomenon. The ❶ Crusades to the Orient led to the expansion of European trade with the Orient. They had a lasting effect on the development of Europe, particularly on its intellectual life. The Crusades in Europe itself, which were directed against the Muslims of the Iberian Peninsula and against heretics and pagans, were also of long-lasting political importance. The consequences of the Crusader idea were fatal for many European Jews, who also fell victim to the crusading armies and the fanaticized population.

Christ leads the crusaders, book illustration, 14th century

Background and Causes

Religious, material, and political reasons motivated aristocratic crusaders as well as poorer members of the population to set off for the Holy Land.

The religious life of the Christian West underwent revitalization in the tenth and eleventh centuries. Expressions of this included the reform movements within the Church, such as the Cluniac and Gregorian reforms, as well as the emergence of new religious orders such as the Cistercians. This sense of piousness also resulted in an increase in the number of ❷ pilgrimages to sites in Palestine, which had been under Muslim rule since the seventh century.

Into this situation came the ❺ Seljuks, whose advance into the Near East in the mid-eleventh century had been noticed in Europe. By 1074 Pope Gregory VII was already planning a Crusade to "liberate" the holy sites and

3   Knight on horseback, bronze sculpture, 13th century

overcome the Great Schism. When the Byzantine emperor Alexius I Comnenus turned to Pope Urban II with a request for aid against the Seljuks in 1095—the same year as the Synod of Clermont—the pope won over the

knights and princes of the West for a Crusade in support of the Byzantine emperor. Soon, however, the main aim of the war became to liberate ❹ Jerusalem from Muslim rule.

❸ Crusaders were promised a remission of their sins in the hereafter, which motivated many of the poorer participants. For most of the aristocratic crusaders involved, however, the possibility of material and political gains were also important motivating factors. Many of the younger sons of the aristocracy, who were excluded from hereditary succession in their homeland, saw the Crusades as an opportunity for an activity befitting their station that could lead to military glory,

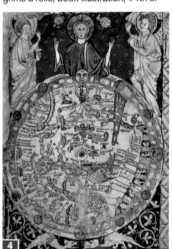

2   The patriarch of Jerusalem shows pilgrims a relic, book illustration, 14th c.

4   The world as a disc with Jerusalem at its center, illustration, ca. 1250

booty, and perhaps even a dominion of their own. At the same time, kings and princes used the Crusades to ideologically legitimize their reigns in their own countries by presenting themselves as truly Christian-minded rulers. Merchants, particularly in the Italian commercial cities, were lured by profits from outfitting and transporting troops, as well as the expansion of their trade interests.

5   Muslims hold a banquet after their victory over the Byzantines, Byzantine book illustration, 13th century

Pope Urban II's Sermon Promoting the Crusade, Clermont, 1095

"They [the Seljuks] have killed and captured many, and have destroyed the churches and devastated the empire. If you permit them to continue thus for awhile with impunity, the faithful of God will be much more widely attacked by them."

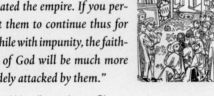

Pope Urban II preaches at Clermont

The First and Second Crusades

The First Crusade resulted in the establishment of crusader states in the Near East. These were soon on the defensive, however. A subsequent Crusade in their defense remained unsuccessful.

The pope's appeal was first answered in 1096 by relatively disordered bands of adventurers and social outsiders led by the monk ❻ Peter of Amiens. After being decimated by the Bulgars, the rest of the People's Crusade was wiped out by the Seljuks in Asia Minor. Around the same time, an army of German crusaders carried out pogroms against the Jews while still in Europe.

The first organized army of crusaders, the "Princes' Crusade," was led by Godfrey of Bouillon, his brother Baldwin of Boulogne, Raymond of Toulouse, and Bohemond of Taranto and was composed of French, Flemish, and southern Italian soldiers. When these crusaders reached Constantinople in 1097, Emperor Alexius I

7

Muslims are massacred by crusaders in a mosque, wood engraving, 19th c.

insisted that they swear an oath of allegiance to him, although this oath would not last long. Once the Christian army had beaten the Seljuks in 1097 at Dorylaeum, they were able to take Antioch in Syria in 1098. Meanwhile, Baldwin of Boulogne had been accepted as heir by Thoros, the king of Edessa on the other side of the Euphrates. When Thoros was assassinated, Baldwin erected the first of the crusader states there. Bohemond of Taranto then created the first principality in Antioch, and Raymond of Toulouse founded the county of Tripoli. In 1099, they conquered ❾ Jerusalem; Jews and Muslims alike were slaughtered in a ❼ massacre. Godfrey was elected "Protector of the ❽ Holy Sepulchre," refusing to be named king in the city where Christ had died. When he died in 1110, his brother Baldwin succeeded him and assumed the title of king.

By 1144, Edessa had been retaken by the Seljuks, whereupon the Cistercian abbot ❿ Bernhard of Clairvaux called for a second Crusade. Another army set off in 1147 under Louis VII of France and the German king, Conrad III. After a journey involving heavy losses and unsuccessful sieges of Damascus and other cities, the crusaders returned home in 1149.

6

Peter of Amiens calls for the Crusade, wood engraving, 19th century

8

The Holy Sepulchre in Jerusalem

Crusader States

The crusaders established several feudal states in Cyprus, Prussia, the Levant, Greece and Israel, along Western European lines. As few colonists from Europe were forthcoming, however, the small group of conquerors, after a wave of persecution and expulsions, adapted to the predominantly higher civilization of the Jews and Muslims and lived, if not with, then alongside them. In addition to warring with the Muslim states, the Christians also often fought among themselves, weakening each other's positions. After two centuries, in 1291, the last crusader state on the mainland fell.

above: Meeting of the Estates in Jerusalem under Godfrey of Bouillon, steel engraving, 19th c.

9

Jerusalem is captured by crusaders, 1099, book illustration, 14th century

10

Bernhard of Clairvaux calls for the Second Crusade, painting, 19th c.

1110 | Baldwin of Boulogne becomes King of Jerusalem   **1147** | Beginning of Second Crusade   **1291** | Fall of the last crusader state

1144 | Edessa retaken   **1149** | Crusaders return

The Third and Fourth Crusades

Led by Ayyubid Sultan Saladin, the Muslims retook large parts of the Near East, including Jerusalem, although it was then granted to Richard I of England.

Mount Hattin

The Second Crusade was unsuccessful in the Near East, but it had initiated the Reconquista on the Iberian Peninsula, where the Christians were advancing into the Muslim south.

In the Near East, the Ayyubids had supplanted the Seljuks as the dominant Muslim power. Sultan ❸ Saladin defeated the European crusaders in 1187 at ❷ Mount Hattin and ❶ recaptured Jerusalem, leading Pope Gregory VIII to call for a third Crusade. The rulers of the leading European countries—the Holy Roman Emperor, Frede-

Saladin conquers Jerusalem, illumination, ca. 1400

rick I (Barbarossa); the heir to the English throne, Richard I (the Lion-Hearted); and King Philip II Augustus of France—answered his call. Frederick won a victory in May 1189 at Iconium in Asia Minor but ❺ drowned in the Saleph River the next year. His son, Frederick VI of Hohenstaufen, led the German contingent to the Holy Land, from which a majority of them sailed home at once; the rest of the Germans, including Frederick VI, died of malaria.

❹ Richard and Philip were able to recapture the important port city of ❻ Acre in 1191. The French king then sailed home to France with his knights following a personal argument between the two monarchs. Alone, Richard was unable to recapture Jerusalem, but he did gain the secession of

the coastal regions of Palestine and Syria through negotiations. Saladin also guaranteed Christian pilgrims access to the holy sites.

The Fourth Crusade, initiated by Pope Innocent III in 1202, showed the corruption of the Crusade idea. The crusaders were redirected by the Venetian doge, Enrico Dandolo, to ❼ Constantinople, where they deposed the Byzantine emperor and established the Latin Empire that existed from 1204 to 1261.

The Children's Crusade of 1212 was a further low point. Thousands of boys and girls were led by religious fanatics to southern France where they were sold into slavery.

Monument to Saladin in front of the medieval citadel of Damascus, present–day Syria

Philip II Augustus of France and Richard the Lion-Hearted of England take the cross, book illustration, 14th century

From Annales Marbacenses, 1238:

The Children's Crusade

"Many of them [boys and girls] were kept back by the inhabitants of the land as farm hands and maidservants. Others were to go to the seaside, where boatmen and sailors would deceive them and ship them off to distant regions of the world."

above: Children's crusade, wood engraving, 19th century

Frederick I (Barbarossa) drowns in the Saleph River, wood engraving, ca. 1900

After the conquest of Acre, Richard I (the Lion-Hearted) orders the execution of Muslims, wood engraving, 19th c

Conquest of Constantinople, 1204, painting by Eugene Delacroix, 19th century

The Last Crusades and the End of the Crusader States

The Mamelukes drove the crusaders out of the Holy Land for good.

Emperor ❾ Frederick II had sworn a crusader's vow and set off in 1228 on the Sixth Crusade. He negotiated the return of Jerusalem, Nazareth, and Bethlehem from the Ayyubid Sultan al-Kamil in 1229. He achieved this through diplomatic negotiations with the Sultan, as a result of which he became popular in the Arab world. Jerusalem was handed over on the condition that Muslims would be allowed to go on pilgrimage to their holy sites.

After the Muslims retook Jerusalem in 1244, King Louis IX of France started out in 1248 on the Seventh Crusade to attack Egypt, the seat of Ayyubid power. Although he occupied Damietta in the Nile Delta in 1249, he suffered a defeat at Mansura and his army was ❿ captured. Louis was freed only after the payment of a ransom. Years later, Louis organized the last great Crusade, the Eighth. The king and many of his knights died of an epidemic outside the walls of Tunis in 1270. Louis was canonized in 1297.

In the meantime, the ⓬ Mamelukes, slaves recruited for the

8 Knight of St. John of Malta, a Maltese knight, painting by Caravaggio, beginning of 17th century

Ayyubids' military, had overthrown their former lords. By virtue of their centralist military regime, they were able to overcome the Mongols who invaded Syria in 1260. After that, they concentrated fully on subjugating the crusader states. In 1291, with the capture of ⓭ Acre, the last important bastion of the Christians, the

9 Emperor Frederick II crowns himself king of Jerusalem, wood engraving, 19th century

Mamelukes had reconquered Palestine and Syria.

The Christians were forced to withdraw from the Holy Land. Among them were the orders of Christian knights that had formed during the two centuries of the Crusades. The ⓫ Knights Templar concentrated on the administration of their territories in France, which constituted a threat to the crown, and they were disbanded in 1312. The Teutonic Knights had already sought a new field of activity in the Baltic with the mission of converting non-Christian peoples. Only the Knights Hospitaller continued to fight against the Muslims. In 1309, they moved their headquarters to ⓮ Rhodes, where they held off the Ottomans until 1522. Emperor Charles V allocated ❽ Malta to them, and it was not conquered until 1798 by Napoleon.

11 A Knight Templar, wood engraving

10 An imprisoned Louis IX, book illustration, 14th century

12 Mamelukes on horseback, Arabic book illustration, 15th century

13 Fortification in Acre dating from the times of the Crusades

14 Knights of the order of St. John in Rhodes, illustration, 15th century

Orders of the Knights

The knightly orders founded in the course of the twelfth century combined monkish and chivalrous ideals. Sworn to personal poverty, chastity, and obedience, the members initially dedicated themselves to the protection of pilgrims and caring for the sick. In addition, they increasingly took part in the fighting against the Muslims. The orders quickly developed into significant powers by virtue of their wealthy properties captured in the Holy Land and bequeathed to them in Western Europe.

above: Castle of the Knights of St. John in Syria, built ca. 1142

The Crusades in Europe and the Teutonic Knights

The crusaders also fought against heretics in Europe. Following the forced conversion of the Baltic Prussians, the Teutonic Knights erected a powerful military-monastic state in the Baltic region.

Crusades took place in Europe as well as the Near East. Examples of these include the Reconquista against the Muslims in the Iberian Peninsula and the campaigns against groups considered to be heretical, such as the Albigenses in southern France and the Hussites in Bohemia.

Military force was also employed in evangelical missions to non-Christian regions. Pope Eugenius III welcomed not only the Second Crusade to the Holy Land but also the one waged in 1147 against the Wends and Slavs in northern Germany by Henry the Lion, duke of Saxony—although undoubtedly an increase in their territory rather than the missionary work was uppermost in the minds of many of the German princes that took part.

As the Baltic Prussians, or ❷ Pruzzi, who lived on the coast between the Vistula and Neman Rivers offered especially strong resistance to Polish attempts to conquer and convert them, the ❻ Teutonic Knights were summoned to help in 1226. Emperor Frederick II, in the ❸ Golden Bull of Rimini, transferred their future conquests to them as possessions.

1 Albert of Brandenburg, the last grand master of the order of Teutonic Knights, painting, 16th century

The actual crusades against the Prussians first began in 1231 under Grand Master Hermann von Salza. In 1237, he merged his order with the Livonian Knights, founded in 1202 in Riga. By 1283 the Teutonic Knights had subjugated and officially Christianized the region, which was named Prussia after the Pruzzi. The whole of the eastern Baltic region except Lithuania then belonged to the Teutonic Knights, who erected

3 Golden Bull of Frederick II, 13th c.

their own state there. The head of the order was the grand master, who was elected by the general chapter and who resided in ❹ Marienburg after 1309. Province masters and commanders administered the order's districts. The half-brother commoners were placed beneath the brothers, who were knights and priests. The German patricians of the cities, as well as the Polish and German landed aristocracy, belonged to the upper class. The Prussian peasant farmers were underprivileged in contrast to the great number of new German colonists. Trade with the Hanseatic League brought great wealth.

The last people to convert to Christianity in the region were the Lithuanians, who did so after their union with Poland in 1386. This removed the need for proselytizing, which was the justification for the existence of the order. Furthermore, the order's state found itself in the grip of a powerful enemy, the

2
The Pruzzi kill the missionary Adalbert of Prague, 997, wood engraving, ca. 1900

united Polish-Lithuanian Commonwealth. After a decisive defeat in 1410 at the ❺ Battle of Grunwald and as a result of the two Treaties of Torun of 1411 and 1466, the order was forced to accept territorial losses. The last grand master, ❶ Albert of Brandenburg, secularized the remaining territories of the order in 1525 and declared it the Duchy of Prussia, a fief of the Polish king.

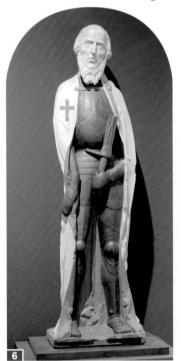

6 Teutonic Knight

4 Marienburg Castle in West Prussia, Poland, built ca. 1272   **5** Battle of Grunwald, painting, 19th century

Persecution of the Jews in Europe

Jews were not subjected to a direct campaign during the period of the Crusades but rather to persecution and discrimination.

Anti-Semitism was widespread in medieval Europe. The Jews were maligned as the "murderers of Christ." Accusations of ❽ ritual murder and desecration of the Eucharistic Host stubbornly persisted. A specific law governing the ❼ clothing of Jews was demanded at the fourth Lateran Council in 1215. A ban on ownership of real estate and membership in guilds forced the Jews into the textile trade. As the Christians were forbidden to loan money for interest, another source of income through financial transactions became open to the Jews—which in turn presented a source of new prejudices against Jewish usurers.

In the religiously inflamed atmosphere linked to the Crusades since the turn of the twelfth century, hate and jealousy repeatedly erupted against Jews in the form of frequent pogroms, during which Jews were tortured and murdered, along with the theft and destruction of Jewish property. A second wave of persecution occurred with the spread of the plague beginning in 1347, when Jews were accused of having poisoned the wells. More than 350 ❾ Jewish communities were destroyed during this period in the German territories alone.

Things were no better for Jews in other regions. In 1290, King Edward I had expelled all Jews from England, and they had been forced to leave ❿ France in 1394 due to alleged ritual murders of Christians. Jews who had lived in relative peace under Muslim rule on the Iberian Peninsula were either expelled or forced to convert during and particularly after the completion of the Reconquista in 1492; in the end, because even the forced converts were not to be trusted, they were completely driven out.

Primarily aimed at maintaining public order, laws were also repeatedly passed to protect the Jews. One example is Emperor Henry IV's Imperial Peace of Mainz from 1103, wherein the Jews were counted among those who were in need of protection— because they did not hold the status of free persons, they were not allowed to carry weapons and could not defend themselves. Rulers placed Jews under their protection in order to secure the high taxes that were extorted from them. They were particularly welcomed as settlers and tradesmen in ⓫ Eastern Europe.

8 Alleged ritual murder of a boy by the Jews in Trient, 1475, wood engraving, 15th century

9 Jewish ritual bath (*mikvah*) in Friedberg, Germany, built ca. 1260

from the chronicle of Salomo bar Simson:

A Crusader Discussing the Persecution of Jews

"*See we are on the long journey to the grave [of Christ] and to revenge ourselves on the followers of Islam, although in our midst are the Jews, whose forefathers killed and crucified him. …Let us take revenge on them and eradicate them among peoples … or let them take on our beliefs.*"

The burning of Jews as heretics, wood engraving, 15th century

10 Jews burned at the stake in France, painting, ca. 1410

11 Jewish cemetery in Prague, Czech Republic

7 Man wearing the typical headgear of the Jews, illustration, 14th century

1290	All Jews expelled from England	1410	Battle of Grunwald	1466	Second Treaty of Torun	1525	Prussia secularized
1394	All Jews expelled from France	1411	First Treaty of Torun	1492	Expulsion of all Jews from the Iberian Peninsula		

1

KEY IDEAS: ISLAM

Today, Islam is a subject more prevalent in the media of many Western countries than ever before, although comment is not always well informed. It has been depicted as an actual threat to the West due to the ❹ terrorism of radical Islamists, which reached a climax on September 11, 2001. In the prevailing political climate the distinction between radical and mainstream Islam has sometimes been blurred, and the common elements of Islam, Judaism, and Christianity, as well as the rich intellectual and cultural history of Islamic civilizations, are often overlooked.

Pilgrims in the Great Mosque of Mecca, colored engraving, ca. 1860

The theologization of politics, such as has occurred repeatedly in the history of man all over the world, has always tended toward radicalism and emotionalism and, above all, has often resulted in the suppression of, and intolerance toward, those of other faiths.

During its period of expansion and conquest, Islam, in contrast to Christianity, proved relatively tolerant, because respect toward other religions—particularly the other ❷ biblical religions Judaism and Christianity—is anchored in the Koran. The freedom to practice religion was very much the norm in the great Islamic empires—one need only consider Spain in the Middle Ages or the policies of the Ottoman Empire toward its many Christian subjects. The phrase "better the Turban than the Tiara" refers to the preference of some Orthodox Christians for the Sultan's rule rather than the persecution suffered under Catholics. It is ar-

4

The leader of the Al-Qaeda network, Osama bin Laden (right), speaking at an event

guably the humiliations suffered during the long years of colonization, and the support of the West for authoritarian regimes in the post-colonial Middle East, that have fed a hostile current of opinion in some Islamic countries vis-à-vis the West.

2

A Muslim reading the Holy Scripture in a mosque in Multan, Pakistan

The Beginnings of Islam

The prophet Muhammad and a small group of his followers, who declared their faith in the one true God, stand at the beginning of the history of Islam. Its development and diffusion were initiated by the Prophet's ❺ emigration, the *Hegira* (Arabic hijrah), from hostile Mecca to more receptive Medina in 622. The move was considered so important by the early Muslims that they used this

date as the start of the Islamic calendar. In Medina, Muhammad created the basis for a strong society of believers, with political as well as religious cohesion.

The Religious Teachings of Islam

"There is no god but Allah, and Muhammad is His Prophet." So states the Islamic declaration of faith, the *shahadah*. It contains Islam's two most important principles of faith: monotheism and the belief in the teachings and practices (*Sunnih*) of the Prophet, including the Koran as the instructions of God to mankind that were revealed directly to Muhammad. The Koran proclaims God as the creator of heaven and earth. It demands ❸ obedience to

5

The *Hegira* from Mecca to Medina in 622, copper engraving, 1844

the almighty, omniscient, and merciful God and describes a final judgment in which all mankind must answer to God for their deeds. Heaven awaits the believers, hell the nonbelievers. These aspects are also shared by Judaism and Christianity.

3

"Ma sha'a Allah"–"It is God's will"; Ottoman-era tile, 19th century

The standards of behavior demanded of Islam's followers are derived from the Koran and the examples of the Prophet. They are set down in Islamic law, known as the *sharia*, which constitutes a comprehensive guide to the righteous life. The most important regulations for the practice of the religion form the Five Pillars of Islam: the repetition of the *shahadah*, the five daily ❼ prayers offered to God, the distribution of alms, fasting during the holy month of Ramadan, and a pilgrimage to ❶ Mecca at least once in a lifetime.

Shia and Sunni

The most significant division of Islam was ignited by the issue of who the successor to Muhammad would be. After his death in 632, one group believed that only his son-in-law Ali and Ali's descendents were rightful heirs (*imams*) to the Prophet. This faction is known as Shia and its adherents Shiites—from Shiat Ali ("Party of Ali")—and comprises about 10–15

Worshipers perform Friday prayers on the street near the Bazaar in Istanbul, Turkey

percent of all Muslims today. Shiites in turn are divided into various groups, according to the number of rightful ❽ imams they recognize: There are the Fiver, Sevener, and Twelver Shiites. Shia also differs from Sunni, the largest group in Islam, in diverging teachings and traditions. The martyrdom of al-Husayn, a grandson of Muhammad, in 680 is very significant to the Shiites.

Spread and Expansion of Power

While Islam has been spreading in the world as a result of migration since the end of the 19th century, the expansion of Islam in its early stages took place by military conquest. Within the first 80 years, the caliphs and their army commanders had opened up to Islam an area that reached from the Indus River in the east to Spain in the west. A caliph ruled over the entire great Islamic em-

pire, while his governors ruled in the provinces. From the beginning, the system of rule was autocratic with divine authority invested in the ruler. However they were bound by Islamic law and were often restricted in their authority by influential legal scholars (*Ulema*) and religious clerics.

The first dynasty that reigned over a large Islamic empire was the Umayyads, followed by the Abbasids. Later phases of the expansion were carried out by the Turkic tribes and the Mongols of Central Asia. The last domain that combined major parts of the Islamic world, as well as other faiths, under its rule was the Ottoman Empire, which came to an end in 1923.

The political spread of Islam went with the Islamization of conquered countries, though seldom through forced conversions. Muslims and non-Muslims alike profited from political stability and a good infrastructure.

The Golden Mosque Al-Kazimain in Baghdad, a Shiite place of pilgrimage containing the graves of two imams

Pan-Arabism and Pan-Islamism

It was only in the 19th century that, under the influence of imperialism, nationalistic thought emerged in the Islamic world, out of which a secular pan-Arab consciousness developed. At first this new awareness was directed primarily against the Turkish Ottoman Empire and later against the European colonial powers. The Pan-Arab movement, whose most important figure in the 1950s and 1960s was Egyptian president Gamal Abdel Nasser, is based on historical, cultural, and linguistic characteristics, not on religion. It ultimately failed, due to differing ideologies and political goals. The goal of Pan-Islamism, on the other hand, was to foster a religiously motivated cooperation and solidarity. It had also been developing since the 19th century and strove to oppose nationalistic thinking through shared Islamic values.

Islamic States Today

By the end of the 19th century, the influence of Western politics as well as secular nationalism introduced by governments—such as that of Kemal Atatürk in Turkey—had already led to irreversible shifts in Islamic society, including changes in customs, Western clothing, and even the suppression of religion in daily life. A modern implementation of the Islamic principle of unity in religion and politics has succeeded in only a few nations.

One can only speak of "Islamic states" in a few cases. Although the Islamic Republic of Iran was created by a popular revolution of the faithful the civil society is complex. Secular lifestyles in

Street demonstrators brandishing a poster calling for Jihad ("Holy War")

large cities coexist with traditional Islam, although the highest state authority remains the religious committee of the guardian council. The country in which the legal system and public life are probably most determined by the sharia is Saudi Arabia. Most of the nations with Islamic populations have secular—but only in rare instances democratic—governments that profess a separation of religion and state. Islamic ❻ fundamentalism can be judged to be a counter-movement to this secularization of politics as well as to living conditions that often benefit only a privileged minority. A ❾ revival of Islam has been noticeable since the 1960s. Often, however, it is social conflicts and frustration with stifling and corrupt dictatorships that preside over closed economies and high unemployment that encourage the spread of radical and fundamentalist approaches to Islam.

Muslim woman wearing the chador, an outer garment that covers the body, worn by the devout in parts of Iran.

| 1453 | Ottomans capture Constantinople | 1923 | Collapse of Ottoman Empire | 1979 | Islamic Revolution in Iran |
| 11th–13th century | Crusades | 1492 | End of *Reconquista* in Spain | 1956–70 | Gamal Abdel Nasser president of Egypt |

THE SPREAD OF ISLAM 622–CA. 1500

Immediately after Muhammad's death, his successors, the caliphs, began to organize a rapidly spreading empire. By the early eighth century, Muslim armies had subjugated an area that stretched from Spain in the west to Pakistan in the east. However, driven by religious schisms resulting from debate concerning the legitimate successors of Muhammad, Islamic rule began splitting into regional autonomous dynasties after 800. Politically, early Islam had been dominated chiefly by Arabs and Persians, but after the 10th century, the Islamized Turkish peoples and, from the 12th and 13th centuries, the Berber tribes in the west and the Mongols in the east proved to be the principal forces.

The Grand Mosque of Mecca with the Kaaba, the main shrine of Muslims

Muhammad and the "Rightly Guided Caliphs"

Muhammad had already instituted the political organization of Islam, and under his first successors, the "rightly guided caliphs," its first triumphant campaign of expansion was initiated.

The Prophet Muhammad not only formulated the teachings of Islam but also acted as the political leader of a community. Following the Hegira, his migration to Medina in 622, Muhammad organized the ❷ battles and defense of the Muslim community (umma), drove out the Jewish tribes, and in 630 conquered ❶ Mecca almost without violence, where he declared the Kaaba to be Islam's main shrine.

Muhammad died on June 8, 632, in ❸ Medina without having designated a successor; therefore four "rightly guided caliphs" were chosen, one after the other, from among his most intimate circle. The first two were the Prophet's

fathers-in-law, the last two his sons-in-law. ❹ Abu Bakr, the first Muslim leader after the Prophet's death, held the community together based on the strength of his authority. Under him, parts of Yemen were brought under Islamic rule. It was his successor Umar I ibn al-Khattab, however, who would become the actual creator of the Islamic Empire. In 637 Umar consolidated the internal organization of the empire through military garrisons, land redistribution, pensions, and a poll tax levied on non-Muslims. His generals in 635–637 conquered all of Syria

Depiction of the main mosque of Medina showing the grave of Muhammad, ceramic tile

and Palestine, including Damascus and Jerusalem, as well as the Sassanian Persian Empire. They then subjugated Egypt in 639–641 and Iraq in 640–644. His successor, Uthman, dedicated himself primarily to domestic affairs, and in 653 had the ❺ Koran compiled in its present form. In 647, Muslim armies began pushing west out of Tripolitania (present-day Libya) and by 682 all of North Africa was under Islamic rule.

The fourth caliph, ❻ Ali, was the cousin and son-in-law of the Prophet and is considered by Shiite Muslims to be the true successor (imam) of the Prophet. He was a just and brave leader, but politically procrastinating and overly cautious. The first divisions of the Islamic community occurred under his rule, and he eventually lost the struggle against the Umayyads. The rule of these "rightly guided caliphs" is considered in the Sunni tradition to represent the "golden age" of a just and God-pleasing leadership of the Islamic community.

The battle of Badr in 624: Victory of the Muslims over the people of Mecca, miniature, ca. 1594–95

Muhammad and Abu Bakr hide from their persecutors in a cave, Turkish miniature, 17th century

Muhammad with his daughter Fatima, his cousin and son-in-law Ali ibn Abi Talib, and his grandchildren al-Hassan and Hussein, miniature, 18th c.

The Caliphate of the Umayyads

In 661, the Umayyads established a hereditary caliphate and from out of Damascus initiated the rapid spread of Islam to the east and west. In 750, they were deposed by the Abbasids.

The rule of the Umayyad dynasty began in 657, when Caliph Ali lost a battle at Siffin against the rebel Syrian governor Muawiya. After Ali's murder in 661, Muawiya, who already controlled a major part of the Muslim territory by 658, established the caliphate of his family. He made Damascus, where the magnificent ❼ Grand Mosque was built, his capital. ❽ Desert palaces in Syria and Jordan served as recuperative retreats as well as for agricultural purposes. In 674–678 Islamic troops advanced far into Byzantine territory and besieged Constantinople for the first time. Under Yazid I, the family of the Prophet's grandson al-Husayn was killed near Karbala in 680— an event that initiated the Shiite movement. Abd al-Malik began stabilizing the Umayyad Empire's political structures in 685. He wanted to make Jerusalem the new political and cultural focus of his reign, and had the flawless ❾ Dome of the Rock constructed in 691–692.

The second wave of Islamic expansion be-

7 The Grand Mosque of the Umayyads in Damascus, Syria, built in the eighth century

8 Qasr al-Hair ash-Sharki, desert palace in Syria, built starting in 729 under the Caliph Hisham

gan under al-Walid I. In 711, Islamic Arabs and Berbers under General Tariq crossed from Africa to Gibraltar and into Spain, destroyed the Visigoth Empire of Toledo, and within a short time conquered the whole Iberian Peninsula as far as Asturias. Soon they were advancing into southern France, but they were turned back

at Tours and Poitiers in 732 by the ⓫ Franks led by Charles Martel. Between 694 and 711, Arab troops also advanced out of southern Persia into present-day Pakistan and conquered Afghanistan, Bukhara, and Samarkand in 704, as well as the Indus Valley to Multan. In 724, Transoxiana and Tashkent also fell to the Islamic forces.

Troops of al-Walid's successors besieged Constantinople again in 717–718 and regularly plundered Byzantine Asia Minor. Caliph Hisham proved himself to be a capable administrative expert by regaining control of the unrest among the Berbers and new Muslims through the just distribution of ❿ monies and the financing of public buildings and municipal water supplies. He also promoted culture, the arts, and education. The bloody elimination of the Umayyad caliphate in 749–750 by the Abbasids, who were related to the Prophet's family, was facilitated by revolts under Hisham's successors and struggles for the throne in the ruling house.

The Tragedy of Karbala

After the abdication of his older brother al-Hassan, al-Husayn, the younger son of Ali, was recognized by the Shiites as the third imam and rightful ruler. In 680, the citizens of al-Kufa persuaded him to rise up against the Umayyads' rule. During a march through the desert, Husayn and 72 family members were surrounded by Caliph Yazid's troops, starved, and annihilated. The tragedy of Karbala on Muharram 10, 680, (October 10 according to the Western calendar) is commemorated by the Shiites in the Ashura festival with plays and flagellant processions.

above: Preperations for the battle of Karbala, Turkish miniature

9 Mosque of Omar, or Dome of the Rock, in Jerusalem, built 688–691

10 Silver coins minted by the Umayyads

11 Battle at Tours and Poitiers in 732

The Early Abbasids

After removing the Umayyads, the Abbasids took over the caliphate and built up Baghdad as the world center of Islam. However, a rapid decline in power was already evident by the ninth century.

Al-Mansur (ruled 754–775) became the founder of the Abbasid Empire after the Abbasid caliphate had been made secure through the extermination by his brother Abu l-Abbas ("the Bloody One") of all Umayyads, with the exception of Prince Abd al-Rahman. He led the Islamic world to a high point In 762, he established a new capital at Baghdad on the boundaries of the Arab and Persian worlds, which became a world center of Islamic culture, science, and art and a prosperous trading city in subsequent centuries. His son al-Mahdi established the dynastic and absolute rule of the ca-

liphs, with Sunni Islam as the state religion. He suppressed internal rebellions but lost Spain, where an

1 Harun ar-Rashid

independent caliphate had been established at Córdoba in 756.

Al-Mahdi's son was the luxury-loving **❶**, **❷** Harun ar-Rashid—known from the "Tales of the Arabian Nights"—during whose reign the empire reached its first high point. The gap between the caliph and the people, however, was growing ever wider. The Barmakid family of viziers, who administered the empire wisely, led the government until 803.

The power struggle among Harun's sons was won in 813 by al-Mamun. He elevated to state doctrine the rationalist teachings of the Mutazilites, who propagated the divine origin of the Koran. He also created an intellectual center with the founding of a comprehensive library in 830, the House of Science in Baghdad. He ordered the writings of the scholars and philosophers of ancient Greece to be translated, thus eventually making them available to the Western world. Al-Mamun began the practice, followed by his successors, of relying on Turk-

ish mercenary troops, converts to Sunni Islam.

In 836 al-Mutasim moved his capital and the Turkish guards from Baghdad, which had been repeatedly shaken by unrest caused by tension between the population and the Turkish troops, to the newly founded **❸**, **❹** Samarra. The strict believer al-Mutawakkil limited the influence of philosophers and the Mutazilites during his reign from 847 to 861. Disputes over succession and frequently changing caliphs weakened central power under his successors. The capital was returned to Baghdad in 883, but de facto autonomous local rule developed after 800, and the decline of the empire continued to accelerate. These weaker caliphs, who increasingly came under the control of the Turkish troop commanders, became a power elite under the caliphs in the tenth century.

2
The deputies of Harun ar-Rashids at an audience with Charlemagne

3
Stucco ornaments from Qasr al-Achiq ("the lovers' castle"), built in the late ninth century

4 Minaret of the Grand Mosque of Samarra, built in 859

Avicenna (Arabic: Ibn Sina)

Centers of Islamic Sciences

In Baghdad and other centers of Islamic sciences, the legacy of Greek antiquity was adopted and further developed, far outstripping progress in the West. It was principally in the areas of mathematics, astronomy, medicine, and optics that supreme achievements were made; philosophy also reached a new high point with the universal scholars al-Kindi and Ibn Sina (Avicenna), both of whom had a significant impact on Renaissance scholarship in Europe. For centuries, the textbooks of Islamic scholars comprised the scientific canon.

762 | Baghdad becomes royal capital   **830** | Founding of "House of Science"   **846** | The Aghlabids plunder Rome

786–809 | Caliph Harun ar-Rashid   **836** | Samarra becomes new capital   **932** | Renewal of caliphate under the Buwayhids

The End of the Abbasid Caliphate

The Abbasids' loss of power in the ninth century favored the autonomy of local kingdoms and the Shiite counter-caliphate of the Fatimids. The caliphate ended with the Mongol invasion.

The local kingdoms that developed under the Abbasids mostly proved to be politically strong and made their courts into independent cultural centers. The Aghlabids (800–909), who ruled in eastern Algeria, ❻ Tunisia, and Tripolitania, were able to settle southern Italy and Sicily after 827 and plundered Rome in 846, while the ❼ Tulunids (868–905) and Ikhshidids (935–969) ruled in Egypt, Syria, and Palestine. The Tahirids (821–873) in northeastern Persia (Khorasan) and the Saffarids (861/67–903) in Afghanistan and parts of Transoxiana made themselves independent

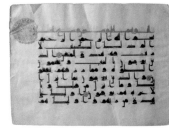

5 Handwriting from the Koran in script of the Kufi from the Grand Mosque in Kairouan, tenth century

and were then supplanted by the Samanids, who resided in Samarkand. The Maghreb and Spain withdrew from the control of Baghdad.

The Shiite Fatimids became Baghdad's greatest challenge when they advanced out of Tunisia, where they had made ❺, ❽ Kairouan their capital. The Fatimids conquered Egypt in 969, took control of Syria, and erected a Shiite counter-caliphate in the newly founded city of ❾ Cairo. Their founder Ubayd Allah al-Mahdi took advantage of Shiite expectations of salvation to hold his realm together. His successors al-Muizz and al-Aziz made Cairo into a center of science and culture and, with ❿ al-Azhar Mosque, founded a mission center for Shiism (today the leading Sunni school of Islamic theology).

The religious eccentricities of Caliph al-Hakim led to unrest

and, in 1017–1021, to the founding of the religious community of the Druze, who worshiped him as a god. In 1036–37 the Fatimid Empire, which was also undergoing an economic decline, lost Syria and Palestine to the Seljuks . The Ayyubid sultan Saladin was able to dispose of the Fatimid caliphate in 1171 because of a religious and political schism that had developed in 1094. Out of this schism the sect of Assassins, notorious for their murderous attacks, also emerged.

In the meantime, since 932 the caliphs in Baghdad had become mere puppets of the Shiite military dynasty of the Buwayhid emirs, who reestablished the power of the caliphate and revived Persian culture. The most notable of the Buwayhids, Adud ad-Dawlah, emir of Baghdad from 977 to 983, subordinated the whole of Iraq to his power. Between 1056 and 1062, the last of the Buwayhid line in Baghdad and Kerman was removed by the Seljuks. The caliphs then became

6 Ribat, fortress in Sousse, Tunisia, built in the late eighth century

7 The Mosque of Ibn Tulun in Cairo, inner courtyard with fountain, built 876

pawns of the Seljuks and the Khwarizm-shahs. They were able to once again restore their sovereignty to a great extent through an-Nasir and al-Mustansir, who built the Mustansiriya Madrassa in Baghdad. The last caliph, al-Mutasim, refused to submit to the advancing Mongols as demanded and died with thousands of his subjects when they stormed Baghdad in 1258.

8 The Grand Mosque of Kairouan, Tunisia, first built in 672, enlarged and rebuilt in the eighth century

9 Bab Zuweila, Fatimid city gate in Cairo, eleventh c.

10 The Al-Azhar Mosque in Cairo, Muslim university since 998, built 970–972

969 | The Fatimids conquer Egypt　　　　**1036–37** | The Seljuks conquer Syria and Palestine　　　　**1171** | End of Fatimid caliphate

1017–21 | Founding of the Druzes　　　　**1056–62** | The Buwayhids driven from Baghdad　　　　**1258** | End of Abbasid caliphate

The Emirate/Caliphate of Córdoba

After the Islamic conquest, the Spanish Umayyads guided their empire into a political and cultural golden era. In 929, Abd al-Rahman III assumed the title of caliph.

Since the conquest of the greater part of the Iberian Peninsula (from 711) by Arab and Berber troops, the province of al-Andalus had been ruled by governors of the Umayyad caliphs. Following their removal by the Abbasids, the only surviving Umayyad prince, Abd al-Rahman I, established an autonomous emirate in ❹ Córdoba in 756. Thereafter, al-Andalus experienced an economic heyday due to its excellent state administration,

3 Ivory box in the style of the Umayyads, from Medina az-Zahra, a palace city near Córdoba

cleverly devised irrigation and cultivation techniques, and extensive trade relations with Africa and the Orient. This was accompanied by an ❸ artistic and intellectual blossoming. Córdoba became an important religious site with its ❶, ❷ great mosque called La Mezquita; the enormous palace-city Medina az-Zahara was constructed just outside the city during Abd al-Rahman III's reign.

Abd al-Rahman I and his son

Hisham I consolidated power and several times advanced into southern France. An Orientalization of the cities and refinement of court manners occurred during the reign of Abd al-Rahman II (822–852). The ruler and the nobility emerged as poets and patrons of the arts, and Córdoba was soon able to compete with Baghdad and Samarra as an Islamic center. The central government began to lose its authority under his successors. Local rulers such as the Hafsun family in Bobastro, who controlled large parts of Spain, restricted the power of the emir, as did the Christian kings whose strength was growing and pushed southward from their bases in northern Spain—Asturias, León, and Castile.

Islamic Spain reached its political apogee under Abd al-Rahman III. He not only restored lost power, but after 920 also brought the whole of western Maghreb under his control and gave the empire a

well-organized civil and military administration. In 929, he proclaimed himself caliph and thus created a third caliphate alongside those in Baghdad and Cairo. His erudite son, al-Hakam II, had one of the largest libraries of his time built and furthered philosophy, science, and the arts. General al-Mansur assumed the regency for Hisham II, who was underage at the time of his father's death. Al-Mansur restored the military power of the empire in more than 50 campaigns against the Christians and, in 997 conquered Fez, as well as the Christian pilgrimage city of Santiago de Compostela. His son Abd al-Malik held onto power, but the caliphate sank into civil wars and the squabbles of

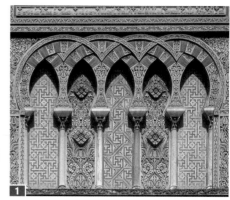

View of the east facade of the Grand Mosque, La Mezquita, in Córdoba, Spain, built 785–990, used as cathedral since 1236

Interior of La Mezquita in Córdoba, Spain

semiautonomous rulers after 1009. The last caliph, Hisham III, died in 1031 and the caliphate splintered into autonomous *taifas* (Islamic city-states) that were later conquered by powers from the north.

4 View of Córdoba with the bridge over the Guadalquivir and the Grand Mosque with the later cathedral

Islam in Spain and the Maghreb

The political weakness of the Arabs in Spain led to the rise of the Berber dynasties, which reached from Morocco into Spain. While Islam was being forced to retreat in Spain, the Berbers claimed the Maghreb.

Between 1013 and 1091, al-Andalus broke up into 26 tiny factional states, taifas, that were ruled over by Arab or Berber dynasties. In the meantime, the Almoravids, Berber border warriors, rose to power by about 1060, and in 1082 they advanced out of Marrakech into Algiers. Summoned to aid the local kings of Islamic Spain against the Christians of the north, the strictly religious Almoravids, who had started to build up an empire in Morocco, defeated the Christians but then took control of Spain themselves and eliminated the

5
The mosque of Tinmal, Morocco, from the Almohad period, built 1153–54

factional kingdoms between 1090 and 1094.

Beginning in 1124, opposition emerged in ❺ Tinmal, Morocco, in the form of a strict ascetic mass movement, the Almohads, led by

the preacher Ibn Tumart. In 1147, their leader Abd al-Mumin did away with Almoravid rule in Marrakech and ❻ Seville and by 1160 had absorbed into his empire almost the whole of Maghreb, including Algeria, Tunisia, and parts of Tripolitania. The Almohads put an end to the religious tolerance previously practiced by Muslim rulers in Spain and restricted free philosophy in favor of orthodox beliefs. After initial military successes in Spain, in 1212 they suffered a crushing defeat by the Christians at Las Navas de Tolosa, and after 1224–1232 they were subjugated by former vassal princes in Spain. Before long, the Christians reclaimed all of Spain except the ❾ Nasrid emirate of Granada, which had been founded in 1232 with the ❼ Alhambra palace as its center of power. This last Moorish stronghold lasted until 1492, when the Catholic kings drove out the last ruler, Muhammad XI, and eliminated Muslim rule in Western Europe.

The Berber dynasty of the Merinids ended Almohad rule in Morocco in 1269 and stayed in power for 200 years until 1465, building up its residence ❽ Fez with mosques and *madrassas* (Islamic schools) and extending its power over Algeria. The Hafsids, residing in Tunis, were in competition with the Merinids (1229/1236–1574) and ruled the former Al-

6
Torre del Oro, fortification tower in Seville, Spain, built in 1220

mohad lands in Tunisia, eastern Algeria, and Tripolitania. They took the title of caliph after 1258. Under the Hafsids, Tunis became the center of Mediterranean trade in the Magreb.

8
The Kairaouine Mosque in Fez, Morocco, founded in the ninth century

7
The Alhambra of Granada, residence of the Nasrids 1231–1492, left, the famous Courtyard of the Lions in the center of the palace grounds

Muhammad XI

Besieged by Christian forces, the Nasrids of Granada had been required to pay tribute to the kings of Castile since 1431. The last sultan, Abu Abdallah Muhammad, also known as Muhammad XI and in Spanish as Boabdil, "the little king," ruled from 1482 to 1492, except when temporarily expelled by his uncle in 1483–1487. He hardly resisted the advance of the Catholic kings and left Granada to them on January 2, 1492. This "farewell of the last Moor" was often artistically represented. He was exiled to Morocco and died in 1527.

right: Boabdil's dagger

9
The battle of Higueruela on July 1, 1431 between John II of Castile and the Nasrids of Granada, Spain, fresco 16th century

| 1031 | End of the caliphate of Córdoba | 1124 | Emergence of Almohads | 1232 | Founding of emirate of Granada |

| 997 | Conquest of Santiagos de Compostela | 1082 | Berber conquest of Algiers | 1212 | Battle of Las Navas de Tolos | 1492 | Expulsion of Boabdil, last sultan |

The Seljuk Empire

The Great Seljuks unified their domain under the "Sunni state," which was officially ruled by the caliph. After the disintegration of the Seljuks, only a small branch of the dynasty remained in Anatolia.

Islamized Turkish tribes took over power in the Middle East with the rise of the Great Seljuk sultanate. The Seljuks—named after the legendary tribal founder Seljuk—who at first settled in Transoxiana and followed a religion with shamanic practices, converted to Sunni Islam around 960 under the influence of the Persian Samanids. After their division into several tribal units, they pushed out of Nishapur and, following their victory over the Ghaznavids under the leadership of Tughril Beg, conquered western Iran (1042), advanced to Shiraz (1052), and then took control of Azerbaijan and Khuzestan in 1054. In 1055 Tughril Beg seized Baghdad, freed the caliph from the "protective rule" of the Shiite Buwayhids, and took his place as sultan. His nephew Alp Arslan, who assumed power in 1063, then created the Great Seljuk Empire, along with his exceptional vizier, the statesman and philosopher Nizam al-Mulk. In 1071, he achieved an important victory over the Fatimids, taking Aleppo, over ❶ Byzantium at Manzikert. Following Alp Arslan's murder in 1072, Nizam remained the dominant figure under his son Malik Shah. In 1092, Nizam became the first prominent murder victim of an attack by the Assassins.

As they themselves possessed no religious authority, the Seljuks, now rulers of all the Arab

❸ The mausoleum of Sultan Sandjar, probably the reception hall in the palace of the Great Seljuk in Merv, present-day Turkmenistan, 12th century

East save the far South of the Arabian Peninsula, acted as ❸ "rulers of the lands of East and West, renewers of Islam" (the title Tughril Beg took in 1062) on behalf of the caliph. They created a great and powerful empire with excellent administration, connected by secure roads, ❺ trade routes, and comfortable ❷ caravansaries from Central Asia across ❻ Persia to Iraq. A network of notable *madrassas*—schools for general education and the teaching of Islam—and the integrated "Sunni state" served to train the future administrative elite efficiently.

The Great Seljuk Empire disintegrated through struggles over the succession following Malik Shah, and in 1157 it was destroyed by the Khwarizm-shahs. However, a Seljuk branch had established its independence in Anatolia in 1078. Its sultan Qilich Arslan II maneuvered between the Crusaders and the Byzantines and created a well-organized and militarily stable state with its capital at ❹ Konya. Ala ad-Din Kay-Qubad I was its most significant sultan, ruling from 1219 to 1237. The westward-moving Mongols increased their pressure after 1242, and the Seljuks suffered a defeat in 1279 against the Ilkhans, the successors of the Mongols in Persia. Masud II, the last sultan of the Anatolian Seljuks, died in 1308.

❶ Battles between the Byzantines and the Seljuks in the eleventh century, Byzantine book illustration

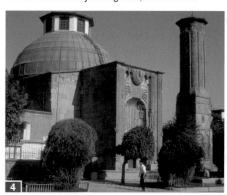

❷ Former caravansary in Baghdad, built in 1358

❹ The Ince Minare Medrese in Konya, Turkey

❻ Tiled mosaic in the Mosque of Isfahan, Iran

❺ Cobandede Bridge, part of the silk trade route built by the Seljuks, Anatolia, Turkey, 13th century

1042	The Seljuks conquer West Iran	**1063**	Sultanate of Alp Arslan	**1092**	Murder of Nizam al-Mulk	**1171**	Saladin eliminates the Fatimids
	1055 Tughril Beg captures Baghdad		**1071** Battle of Manzikert		**1157** Expulsion of Seljuks		

The Ayyubids and the Mamelukes

The time of the Crusades favored the rise of military dynasties in the Middle East. Sultan Saladin became the outstanding general on the side of Islam. He was followed by the Mameluke rulers

The Seljuks were not able to bring the local dynasties in the Palestine–Syria–northern Iraq area under their control. A Kurdish dynasty established the first political unity in the region under its founder, ❼ Saladin—one of Islam's most important statesmen and conquerors.

Saladin (Salah ad-Din) was initially a military leader for the Fatimids, but he removed them in 1171 and reinstituted Sunnism in their former area of dominion. In quick succession, he seized Tripoli (1172), Damascus (1174), ❽ Aleppo (1183), and Mosul (1185–1186) from the ⓫ Crusaders and local rulers. In 1187 he was able to take Jerusalem, which he proclaimed an open city for all religions. A mixture of brilliant tactics, negotia-

7
Sultan Saladin

ting, and chivalrous generosity characterized Saladin's political dealings, which won him respect even in the West. As the ruler of a reunited Egypt, Syria, and Iraq, Saladin negotiated with the army of the Third Crusade, led by ❿ Richard I (the Lion-Hearted) and persuaded the crusaders to end the

weak siege of the city of Jerusalem in 1192.

Saladin's brother al-Adil was able to reunite the empire that fractured upon Saladin's death in 1193, but al-Adil's successors had to use the help of Caucasian military slaves (Mamelukes) against the Crusaders. In 1250–1260, the ❾ Mamelukes removed the last of the Ayyubids and took power for themselves, ruling over Egypt and Syria until 1517 from their capital Cairo. The Mameluke leader Sultan Baybars I, an outstanding military strategist, halted the west-

8
The Grand Mosque of Aleppo in Syria, destroyed in 1169 and rebuilt under the Ayyubid Nur ad-Din

10
Richard the Lion-Hearted in the Battle of Arsuf against Saladin's troops

ward movement of the Mongols in 1260 and restricted the rule of the Crusaders, who were driven out of their last bastions in Tripoli and Acre in 1289–1291 by his successors. The Mamelukes developed Cairo into one of the most important hubs of Asian

The Conquest of Jerusalem

Saladin's victory over the Crusader army at Hattin on July 4, 1187, was a tactical masterpiece that paved the way for the retaking of Jerusalem on October 3. Saladin proved his chivalry when he allowed the inhabitants of Jerusalem to choose the knight Balian of Ibelin as their commander for the defense—although the knight was actually Saladin's prisoner—as he did not want to win a victory over women and children. After taking the city, he spared the Christians and allowed almost all of them to buy their freedom. He also granted freedom to hundreds without any ransom.

above: The 1187 battle of Hattin: The crusaders' defeat against Saladin's army

trade in the Mediterranean and under Sultan Barkuk resisted the Mongolian conqueror Tamerlane. They established their religious legitimacy through the Abbasid shadow caliphs, whom they controlled. Mameluke decline began after 1450, and in 1517 they were swept aside by the Ottomans under Selim I.

12 Lamp from Sultan Barkuk's mosque, 14th century

9
The tombs of Mameluke caliphs, in Cairo, laid out 1250–1517

11
Crusaders' castle Montreal, Shobak, in Jordan, built in 1115

The Islamic Regional Rulers of the East and Mahmud of Ghazna

Following the Samanids in the East, it was Mahmud of Ghazna and his successors who spread Islam through Central Asia and all the way to India.

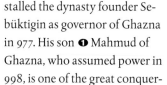

The Islamic East went through a development that was generally independent of that of the West. After the Arab armies had advanced as far as Bukhara, Samarkand, and Pakistan after 700, these dominions fell in 821 to the Tahirids, whose governors in Samarkand, Ferghana, and Herat were the Iranian ❹ Samanids (from 819). Nasr I used the decline of the Tahirids in 873 to make himself independent as the Abbasid caliph's governor in Transoxiana. He developed Bukhara into his royal

2 Khorasan ceramic plate, tenth c.

residence, and at the end of the tenth century it became a cultural center with Persian characteristics. His brother Ismail conquered Afghanistan and a major part of Persia including ❷ Khorasan by 903. The empire then reached its greatest extent under Nasr II (914–943) stretching from Baghdad, Kerman, and the Persian Gulf to Turkistan and India. His successors lost Khorasan to the Ghaznavids in 994 and Transoxiana to the Qarakhanids in 999. The last Samanid ruler was murdered in 1005 while fleeing.

With this, the Turkish tribes had taken over power in the East. The Ghaznavids, who were originally Turkish mercenaries and generals of the Samanids, in-

stalled the dynasty founder Sebüktigin as governor of Ghazna in 977. His son ❶ Mahmud of Ghazna, who assumed power in 998, is one of the great conquerors of Islam. By 999, he had conquered the Samanids in Khorasan and seized major areas of Persia and Punjab with his swift mounted armies. In 1027, he had the caliph in ❺ Baghdad award him the honorary title of "protector of the caliphate" and as a strict Sunni, fought the Shiite Buwayhids. He was driven by religious faith and the quest for wealth. Between 1001 and 1024, Mahmud subjugated the north of India in 17 campaigns and made possible Islam's penetration into India. He dealt harshly with the "idolatrous" Hindus and destroyed their temples. Mahmud's son Masud I focused on India and suffered a crushing defeat against the Seljuks in 1040 with the result that the sovereignty of the Ghaznavids became confined to ❸ eastern Afghanistan

1 Victory column of Ghazni, built under Mahmud of Ghazna

3 Kohi-Baba, mountain range in eastern Afghanistan

and northern India. In 1161, the Ghurids of central Afghanistan forced them out of Ghazna and in 1186 out of northern India as well.

4 The Samanid mausoleum in Bukhara, Uzbekistan, built from the ninth to the tenth century

5 Bab El Wastani, one of the city gates of Baghdad, late eleventh century

The Court of Mahmad of Ghazna

The court of Mahmud of Ghazna was a center of Islamic intellectual life. Poets and scientists were generously supported. He also took them with him on his campaigns so that they could conduct their studies there. Among the most notable scientists surrounding Mahmud was the universal scholar al-Biruni, who described the areas of life in his In the Garden of Science, and Firdawsi, who was commissioned by Mahmud to write his Persian book of kings Shah-nameh.

Firdawsi, when he was still an unknown poet, meets the court poets of Sultan Mahmud of Ghazna (980), cover picture of the *Shah-nameh* ("king's book") of Firdawsi

Central Asia and the Khwarizm-Shahs

Following the Seljuks and Qarakhanids, the northern Iranian Khwarizm-shahs erected the greatest empire of the old Islamic world. Due to their rapid expansion, they provoked the westward movement of the Mongols.

6

Uighur yurt at the Tian Chi in China

The Qarakhanids were a Turkic people belonging to the ❻ Uighurs who originated in the Asian steppes. They made themselves independent after 840 under a dual khanate in the west and east and converted to Islam in the tenth century. In 992, the Qarakhanids conquered Bukhara and by 999 had appropriated the Transoxianan dominions of the Samanids. They made ❼, ❾ Bukhara their royal residence, and after 1042 Samarkand, too. At first they were able to resist the Ghaznavids and Seljuks, but were finally forced to recognize the sovereignty of these and indeed later became their vassals. Under the rule of the Khwarizm-shahs after 1180, they were removed from the west khanate in 1210–1211 and from the east khanate in 1212.

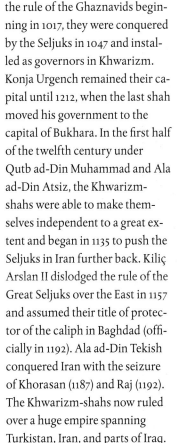

7

The Kalan Minaret in Bukhara, Uzbekistan, built in the early twelfth century by the Qarakhanids

The greatest Islamic empire before the western migration of the Mongols emerged under the Khwarizm-shahs (Khorezmi) who settled in Central Asia. Under the rule of the Ghaznavids beginning in 1017, they were conquered by the Seljuks in 1047 and installed as governors in Khwarizm. Konja Urgench remained their capital until 1212, when the last shah moved his government to the capital of Bukhara. In the first half of the twelfth century under Qutb ad-Din Muhammad and Ala ad-Din Atsiz, the Khwarizm-shahs were able to make themselves independent to a great extent and began in 1135 to push the Seljuks in Iran further back. Kiliç Arslan II dislodged the rule of the Great Seljuks over the East in 1157 and assumed their title of protector of the caliph in Baghdad (officially in 1192). Ala ad-Din Tekish conquered Iran with the seizure of Khorasan (1187) and Raj (1192). The Khwarizm-shahs now ruled over a huge empire spanning Turkistan, Iran, and parts of Iraq.

Ala ad-Din Muhammad expanded the empire once again by driving the Ghurids out of Afghanistan in 1206, and in 1210–1212 he overthrew the rival

8

Turkish tribes killing Mongolians, Indian miniature from the Mogul period

Qarakhanids in Transoxiana. Both territories were absorbed into the empire. Furthermore, he drove the ❽ Qara-Khitai Mongols back to the east. Ala ad-Din was now ruler over an Islamic empire of a size until then unknown. But in overestimating himself, he provoked the invasion of Mongolian army under ❿ Genghis Khan in 1218 by refusing to make amends for the arrest of Mongolian merchants by one of his governors. Ala ad-Din died trying to escape; his son Djalal ad-Din was murdered after an adventurous life as a fugitive in 1231. The empire then fell to the Mongols.

9

Cupola bazaar in Bukhara, with the Kalan minaret left in the background

10

Genghis Khan, wood engraving, 16th c.

| 1157 | Reign of Khwarizm-Shahs | 1187–92 | Conquest of Iran | 1206 | Ghurids driven out of Afghanistan | 1210–12 | Qarakhanids driven out of Transoxiania | 1218 | Invasion of Genghis Khan |

THE MONGOLIAN EMPIRE AND ITS SUCCESSORS 12TH–15TH CENTURY

The conquests of ❶ Genghis Khan and his successors fundamentally changed the structures of Asia and Eastern Europe. The "Mongolian storm" that hit Baghdad in 1258 brought about the end of the old Islamic world. The destructive force of the mounted nomads resulted in the downfall of many cities and kingdoms. The Mongols' religious tolerance enabled them to assimilate into the dominant cultures of the territories they conquered, such as China and Persia. The huge empire founded by Tamerlane in the 14th century saw itself as heir to both the Mongolian and Islamic traditions but rapidly disintegrated after his death.

1 Genghis Khan, founder of the Mongolian empire

The Campaigns of Conquest of Genghis Khan

Genghis Khan united most of the Mongolian tribes and undertook campaigns of conquest in every cardinal direction. With them came dreadful devastation.

Yurts–Mongolian tents–covered with felt, Persian miniature, 14th century

Even before the rise of Genghis Khan, Central Asia had been dominated by Turkish and Mongolian ❷ nomadic tribes since the migrations of late antiquity. Their strength lay in their ❸ swift and flexible fighting methods, which included attacks by mounted archers in small, mobile units. Between 1133 and 1211, Mongolians of the Qara-Khitai tribal group ruled vast stretches of central Asia, but they were driven back to the east by the Khwarizm -shahs after 1200.

At the end of the 12th century, Temujin, who was descended from the ruling family of a small tribe in the northeast of present-day Mongolia, was able to unite several tribes and assemble

3 Mounted Mongolian warlord, painted ceramic tile

a strong army. In 1206, he took the title Genghis Khan ("Universal Ruler") and began his carefully planned campaigns of conquest. First he subjugated southern Siberia in 1207 and in 1211–1216 conquered ❹ northern China. He made an unsuccessful attempt to advance into central China, but the Uigurs submitted to him in 1209. A careless act by the Khwa-

rizm-shahs presented the opportunity for a longplanned campaign in the west. Between 1219 and 1221 Genghis Khan overran Transoxiana and also wide stretches of the Khwarizm territories. In 1220, he founded his capital, Karakorum, in the north of Mongolia. He then captured northern Persia, Armenia, and Georgia and defeated the Russian princes in 1223.

Genghis Khan waged his campaigns with extreme cruelty and presided over widespread plundering and destruction. He did, however, lay the foundation for an empire supported by caravan trade, establishing a huge network of trading posts and communications points; he also kept the Silk Road free of banditry. The Mongolians also demonstrated a pragmatic tolerance of different religions. The subjugated empires were absorbed into a "friendship union" and required to pay tribute, from which considerable Mongolian state reserves were accumulated. Genghis Khan ❺ died in 1227, after which the empire was divided among his ❻ four sons.

4 Genghis Khan's Mongol army storms a fortress during the invasion of the northern Chinese province of Tangut, miniature painting, ca. 1590

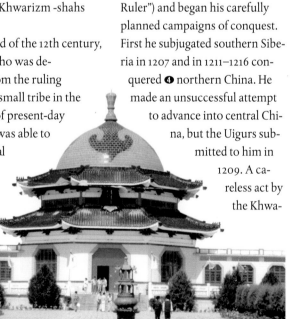

5 Genghis Khan's mausoleum, inner Mongolia

6 Meeting of Genghis Khan's sons, Persian book illustration, 14th c.

The Spread of Mongolian Rule

The empire may have been divided among the sons of Genghis Khan, but it was the third generation that proved its military power through the conquest of wide stretches of Asia and Eastern Europe.

Great khan Ögödei

Genghis Khan's son ❼ Ögödei, who succeeded him as the "great khan," decided in a war council in 1236 to conquer Russia, Poland, and Hungary and from there to move into the rest of Europe. His nephew Batu Khan subjugated most of Western Russia between 1236 and 1242. In 1240, he stormed Kiev and advanced almost to the Baltic Sea. In 1240–1241, his troops devastated Poland and Hungary and annihilated an army of German and Polish knights at ❽ Liegnitz, in Sile-

10

Great khan Kublai Khan

12

Occupation of fortresses strung along the Yangtse River in 1275 during Kublai Khan's invasion of China, from an Indian miniature, ca. 1590

sia, in early 1241. Europe appeared to lie open to the Mongolians when, in December 1241, Ögödei died and Batu Khan turned his army back east to settle the succession. In 1251, Mangu Khan, another grandson of Genghis Khan, became great khan in Karakorum and began the systematic construction of a great empire. In the meantime, his cousin ❾ Batu and his successors made themselves largely independent and founded the khanates of the Golden and Blue Hordes in Muscovy and Eastern Europe. However, they lost territory in battles against the Russian grand dukes in the 14th century, and in 1502 the states were destroyed. Mangu Khan, whose cultured court was characterized by religious tolerance, respectfully received a papal legation headed by Willem van Ruysbroeck in 1253. He charged his younger brother ❿ Kublai Khan, who in 1260 inherited the title of great khan, with new conquests to the East and South; Kublai Khan then invaded ⓬ China and founded the Yuan dynasty, which survived until 1368. Hülegü Khan conquered Persia

and led the Mongolian sacking of Baghdad that ended the caliphate and the old Islamic order in 1258. After disposing of the small principalities in the Middle East, he was finally halted by the Egyptian Mamelukes. Hülegü Khan founded the Il-khan dynasty, which ruled over Iran, Iraq, Syria, East Anatolia, and the Caucasus from the royal palace in Tabriz. The dynasty converted to ⓫ Islam

8

Battle of Liegnitz, April 9, 1241

9

Batu Khan on his throne, Persian book illustration, 14th century

11

Niche in the Friday mosque in Yazd, Iran, built in 1325–34

during the reign of Khan Ghazan in 1300.

In 1335, the Mongolian Empire disintegrated into a series of minor principalities. Though it only existed for 150 years, the Mongolian empire affected peoples and states across the known world, from China to Eastern Europe.

Baghdad before the Mongolian Attack on February 10, 1258:

"Together with them [two high officials and the army leader of Baghdad], the Baghdad army decided to withdraw, and much of the population hoped in this way to be saved. However, they were divided up between the thousand-, hundred-, and ten-man units of the Mongolian army and were killed. Those who remained in the city dispersed and hid themselves beneath the Earth and underneath the baths."

Rashid ad-Din's Book of The Tribes

The conquest of Baghdad by the Mongols led by Hülegü in 1258, Persian miniature

---

The Empire of Tamerlane

After 1370, the conqueror Tamerlane united Islamic and Mongolian traditions in his vast Asian empire. He brought scholars and artists to his capital, Samarkand, making it a center of culture.

In the 14th century, an aggressive expanding empire, combining Mongolian and Islamic characteristics once again emerged in Central Asia. The Jagatai khanate, the descendants of the second son of Genghis Khan, ruled in Central

3

In 1370 he occupied the Mongolian vassal Khwarizm, and in 1379 plundered the rebellious Konya Urgench. By 1381 he had conquered most of Afghanistan. He either integrated local rulers into his "union of friendship" or eliminated them. Tamerlane captured ❷ Isfahan in 1387 and seized Shiraz from the Muzaffarids in 1393. By 1391 he had made a fugitive of his most dangerous rival, Tokhtamysh, the khan of the Golden Horde, who had carved out an empire in western Russia and the Cau-

After defeating Ottoman armies in Anatolia, Tamerlane takes the Sultan Bayezid I prisoner, holding him in a golden cage, lithograph, 18th c.

casus. The conquest yielded enormous treasures that were hauled back to his royal residence in Samarkand. In 1393, Tamerlane occupied Iraq and Baghdad, crushing the local warlords ruling there. In 1394, he besieged Damascus, and then plundered it in 1401. In July 1402, Tamerlane annihilated the ❸ Ottomans in Anatolia and took Sultan Bayezid I, who had refused the offer of an alliance, prisoner.

The restless general, who ruled his world empire ❹ from his saddle, had already waged a military campaign against India in 1398–1399, in the course of which he occupied Lahore and Delhi and had 100,000 Indian prisoners executed. Tamerlane tended to treat cities and rulers relatively mildly if they surrendered to him, but showed no mercy to those who resisted. The fate of those who rebelled was even worse, as with the cities of Isfahan and Baghdad when they revolted in 1387 and 1401; Tamerlane had 10,000 inhabitants killed and their heads piled up in pyramids outside the city walls.

1

Tamerlane, artist's reconstruction based on contemporary descriptions

Aside from his conquests Tamerlane, who ruled over one of the largest empires in history, also gathered around him scholars, poets, and court painters. Many of these came from from the oc-

4

Tamerlane on horseback, atop a mound of skulls

2

Conquest of the city of Isfahan by Tamerlane, 1387

Asia, but its dominion had split into various tribal groupings during the 14th century. In the context of this political turmoil, a Turkic prince known as Tamerlane was able to emerge as a powerful leader. ❶ Tamerlane seized power in Samarkand in 1366, and in April 1370 united the majority of the khanates of ❺ Transoxiana under his leadership.

cupied territories, carried off to Samarkand where they made the capital the "center of the world" and the "threshold of Paradise," building magnificent mosques and madrassas. Tamerlane was a strict Sunni, but also sought to preserve the pre-Islamic Mongolian nomad traditions. In the autumn of 1404, he set off to the north with an enormous army to conquer China, but died in Utrar on February 19, 1405.

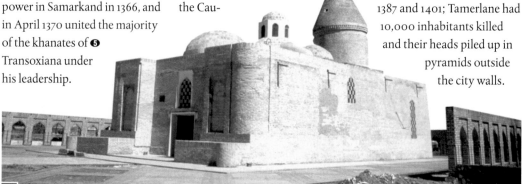

5

Hiob's well in Bukhara, one of the most important cities in Transoxiana (present-day Uzbekistan) built in the 14th century

The Rule of the Timurids

The empire that Tamerlane founded was divided up among his successors, but these new kingdoms continued to influence Central Asia well into the 16th century.

Tamerlane's heirs, the Timurids, divided the empire among themselves as dictated by Mongolian tradition after Tamerlane's chosen successor—his grandson Pir Muhammad, governor of Kandahar—was murdered in 1407. In the course of time, Tamerlane's youngest son, Shah Rokh, who had reigned in Herat since 1405, established himself as the most important of the heirs and head of the clan. He gained control of Transoxiana and Persia, and most of the rulers of the Uzbeks and the Golden Horde submitted. Iraq, however, was lost to local dynasties. Shah Rokh, a notable patron of the arts and sciences, was one of the more peaceful and cultivated Timurids.

His son, ❼ Ulugh Beg, who had been an autonomous khan in Samarkand since 1409, was one of the most significant scholars of his time. In 1428–1429, he had an observatory with telescopical instruments constructed, from which he made the most exact calculations of the stars possible in the period. The capital, Samarkand, which had been founded by his grandfather Tamerlane, continued to shine under his reign. The rulers were also buried ❽, ❾ here in a magnificent necropolis. In 1447, he waged war against his own son

6 Timuridian miniature painting from Herat, Afghanistan, ca. 1488

7 Ulugh Beg Madrasa in Samarkand, built between 1417–20, painting by W.W. Werestschagin, ca. 1870

9 The necropolis, Shah-i Zinda, outside Samarkand, painting by W.W. Werestschagin, ca. 1870

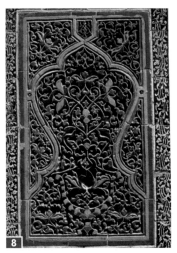

8 Ceramic tombstone from a mausoleum in Shah-i Zinda, Samarkand

Abd al-Latif over the succession to the empire of Shah Rokh. The conflict ended with the murder of Ulugh Beg in 1449 and Abd al-Latif a year later.

Abu Said, a great-grandson of Tamerlane, emerged victorious from the ensuing turmoil to rule over Transoxiana. In 1469, he was taken captive and executed by Turkic tribesmen of the Aq-Qoyunlu, the "White Sheep Turks," who advanced out of Persia. His son, Sultan Ahmad, held on to the Samarkand area, but was constantly under pressure from the Uzbek Shaibanids. Ahmad's nephew was Babur, the first great Mogul of India. The last Timurid still ruled from Herat over a part of ❿ Afghanistan, but died in 1506 during a campaign against the Shaibanids, after they attacked the city. The last rulers descended from Tamerlane are remembered more for their ❻ patronage of the arts than for their conquests.

The Gur-e Amir Mausoleum

Tamerlane and his successors were buried in the magnificent mausoleum Gur-e Ami, in Samarkand. In 1941, Russian scientists under the direction of anthropologist Mikhail Gerasimov investigated the remains, and Gerasimov reconstructed the facial characteristics of Tamerlane and his sons, Miranshah and Shah Rokh. An examination of Tamerlane's skeleton showed deformities on the right elbow and the right hip; the right kneecap had also grown together with the thigh. He was practically a hemiplegic.

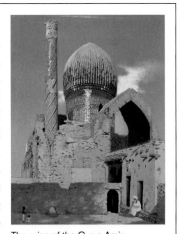

The ruins of the Gur-e Amir mausoleum, painting by W.W. Werestschagin, ca. 1870

10 The Blue Mosque in Mazar i-Sharif, Afghanistan, built ca. 1480

INDIA 500–1500

For centuries the north of India had experienced periodic Arab invasions and settlement. The arrival of Turkic Muslim invaders from central Asia after 1000 had a more lasting impact, not least through settlement. The Hindu kingdoms of north India were subjugated and by 1206 Delhi and the Ganges valley too. Only the South remained unaffected. Although the destruction of Hindu temples indicates persecution, a pattern of co-existence quickly emerged. Ultimately Indian culture proved adept at assimilating the new influences. The Muslim sultans were successful as military rulers but were displaced by the Moguls after 1500.

1 The Rajasimhesvara temple in Mahabalipuram, south India, built ca. 690–715 under the Pallava dynasty

The Hindu Empires in India

While northern India fell under the rule of the Muslim sultans, Hindu princes held onto power in most of central and southern India. The Vijayanagar Empire was the last significant Hindu state.

Distinctly Hindu or Dravidian dynasties reigned in central and southern India after 550. One of these was the ❷, ❸ Calukya dynasty that ruled in Bidjapur between 543 and 757 and subjugated a significant part of southern India between 609 and 642. A second ❺ Calukya dynasty ruled between 975 and 1189. They became involved in power struggles with the most important southern Indian dynasty, the ❶, ❻ Pallava of Kanchi, who had spread out in the seventh century into Deccan and the southern tip of India. They were supplanted by the dynasty of the Colas (888–1267), who enlarged their east coast kingdom northward. Under Rajaraja I (the Great), they rose to become the leading power in South India around 1000. They were also a naval power, their fleet sailing in 1001 to Ceylon and in 1014 occupying the Maldives.

The Hindu rulers of central India, including the Pala kings of Bengal (750–1199) or the Kanauj kings (840–1197), were eventually defeated by the advancing Muslim armies. The last great Hindu kingdom, ❼ Vijayanagar (City of Victory), was founded in 1336. Its capital, ❹, ❽ Hampi, was originally built on the site of a temple. It subsequently grew to become the preeminent kingdom in southern India. The flourishing city, with its magnificent temples and palaces, became a center of Indian literature and science. The kings of Vijayanagar regarded the Tungabadhra and Kistna rivers as the southern boundary of Islam and in 1380 compiled a collection of all the Brahman teachings, the *Sarvadarshana Sangraha*. While they successfully held off the invaders for some time, the last ruler, Ramaraja, fell in 1565 at Talikota in battle against the Muslim sultan Ahmadnagar.

Thereafter, only a small Hindu kingdom survived in Madurai. This was in turn annexed in 1684 by the Grand Mogul Aurangzeb.

5 Female dancer, sculpture, late western Calukya dynasty, twelfth c.

6 Buddha Maitreya, gold-plated bronze sculpture, seventh–ninth century

3 Vishnu, sculpture from the Calukyan period

2 Shiva, "king of the dance," with 18 arms, sculpture from the western Calukya dynasty, sixth century

4 Vithala Temple in Hampi, capital of the Vijayanagar kings, 16th century

7 Vijayanagar-style ceiling fresco, in the Virabhadra temple in Lepakshi, 16th c.

8 Narashima, the fourth incarnation of Vishnu, sculpture in Hampi

888–1267 | Cola Dynasty   **1001** | Conquests in India led by Mahmud of Ghazna   **1206** | Sultanate of Delhi founded

543–757 | First Western Calukya Dynasty   **975–1189** | Second Western Calukya Dynasty   **1193** | Construction of the Great Mosque in Delhi begins

The Sultans of Delhi

In the wake of the Ghaznavids and Ghurids, military dynasties of Turkish origin increased the spread of Islam in India. They came to an end with the Lodi rulers, who were defeated by the Moguls.

Ever since the first Muslim armies had advanced into Pakistan and India around 700, India had been coveted by Islamic rulers. Mahmud of Ghazna's campaigns of conquest after 1001 put great pressure on the Hindus, whose polytheism the strict Muslims vehemently rejected. The Ghaznavids dominated the north of India at the beginning of the 12th century, but in 1187 they were displaced by the powerful Afghan ❾ Ghurids in Lahore, who had already subjugated Multan in 1175. In 1193 Sultan Muizz ad-Din occupied Delhi and expanded his realm to Gujarat in the south and Bengal in the east. The driving force behind these conquests was the Turkish general Qutb-ud-Din ❿, ⓫ Aybak, who had ended the rule of the Buddhist princes in 1194 with the capture of Bihar, and pushed the Hindus to the south. He felt strong enough in 1206 to depose the Ghurid sultan and founded the "Slave King" sultanate of Delhi. His successor, Iltutmish (ruled 1211–1236) conquered Sind and made Delhi an independent Islamic kingdom.

In 1290, the House of Aybak was overthrown by the Khalji dynasty, which was also Turkish. They fended off the Mongols, conquered all of Deccan (central India), and advanced to Madurai in southern India. The sultanate divided the country into fiefs that were distributed to the Muslim nobility, each of whom was required to provide and maintain troop contingents in case of war. The Khaljis were later followed by the military dynasties of the Tughluqs (1320–1414) and Sayyids (1414–1451), under whom the state administration was Islamized. After 1388, many regions became increasingly independent from the government in Delhi and formed their own sultanates, including Bengal, Deccan, Gujarat, Jaunpur, and Malwa. In 1398–1399, Tamerlane invaded India and temporarily occupied Delhi.

After this shattering defeat, effective central authority re-emerged only under the Afghan Lodi dynasty which ruled from 1451 to 1526. Sikandar Lodi again extended the kingdom from the Indus to Bengal in the east. The last Lodi ruler, Ibrahim, fell in battle in 1526 at Panipat against the Mogul leader Babur, who had been summoned by Ibrahim's own emirs to depose him. Babur was then able to take possession of Agra.

❾ Adhaidinkajonpara mosque in Ajmer. The original Jaina school was converted into a mosque after its capture by the Ghurids in 1198

❿ The Qutb Minar, "tower of victory," built under Qutb ad-Din Aybak from 1199 on. In front and to the left is the mosque Quwwat al-Islam, the oldest Muslim building in Delhi.

⓫ Detail from outer wall of the Qutb Minar

Delhi

After Delhi became the capital of Islamic rule in India in 1193, various "slave kings" erected enormous buildings, often using the remains of destroyed Hindu temples. In the same year Delhi was captured, work began on the construction of the great Quwwat-ul-Islam ("Power of Islam") mosque. In 1236 the magnificent sepulchre of Sultan Iltutmish was integrated into it. Qutb-ud-Din Aybak began construction of the Qutb Minar ("Tower of Victory") in 1192.

above: Detail from the Qutb Minar, near Delhi

CHINA AFTER THE HAN DYNASTY 220–1279

For more than 300 years after the fall of the Han dynasty, China was divided into rival kingdoms. Then the ❶ Tang dynasty ushered in a cultural blossoming in the seventh century. Following half a century of turmoil and division, the Song dynasty began to unify the country once again in 960, although it remained militarily weak. The Songs eventually had to make way for the Chins and withdraw to the south. Here too, however, a cultural golden age began that lasted until the conquest of the Mongols in 1279.

1   Li Yuan, founder of the Tang dynasty, drawing 19th century

■ The Tang Dynasty 618–907

Several centuries of unrest were brought to an end by the Tang dynasty. Chinese culture and territorial expansion both reached high points.

2   Armor-plated and saddled horse from Wei dynasty, fifth-sixth cntury

3
The view of the citadel near Turfan, built to protect the Silk Road

4
Emperor Xuanzong flees in 755 from the revolt of An Lushan, painting, 8th c.

Following the fall of the Han dynasty in the third century, numerous wars took place between three rival kingdoms. Nomads from out of the steppes north of the Great Wall repeatedly attacked, until they were eventually able to bring the north under their control; China then remained divided into north and south until the sixth century. Numerous factions competed for control in the north until the ❷ Wei dynasty was able to bring them under its control in

439. During its brief reign, the Sui dynasty was able to restore the unity of China to a certain extent from 589 to 618, but was defeated in a war against the peoples of southern Manchuria and northern Korea. The uprising led by the later ruler Li Yuan, resulting primarily from domestic policies, prepared the way for the Tang dynasty from 618 to 907.

The Tangs stabilized China from their capital Ch'ang-an (present-day Xi'an) at the eastern end of the ❸ Silk Road. The ru-

lers were not afraid to allow broad tolerance in culture and religion, as the central government was solidly organized with well-trained ❺ civil servants and efficient regulations and laws. Chinese ❻ literature and the arts experienced a golden age. Trade relations by land and sea flourished, and conquests as well as international agreements secured the Tang dynasty's influence all the way into central and southern Asia. In the eighth century, however, China was forced to accept the expansion of the Tibetan Tu-fan kingdom, which conquered Tang territories.

Domestically, the Tang dynasty failed through its own success. The growth in population brought on by the booming economy destroyed the financial foundation of the state. Emperor ❹ Xuanzong, who tried to make reforms, was weakened by court intrigues that culminated in 755 in a revolt of the governor and general An Lushan. A civil war began, ending eight years later at a cost of millions of lives. The weaknesses of the state led to internal re-

pression. Persecution of the ❼ Buddhists, during which thousands of monasteries and temples were destroyed, began in 845. Regional govenors began to function more independently, until Zhu Wen deposed the emperor, ushering in the Five Dynasties and Ten Kingdoms Period.

7
Bodhisattva Avalokiteshvara, the personification of compassion, marble, 8th c.

5   Civil servant, statue, 7th-8th c.

6
House of the poet Du Fu near Chengdu in the province Sichuan

since 220 | Division of the empire in Shu, Wei, and Wu   **618–907** | Tang dynasty   **from 845** | Persecution of the Buddhists

589–618 | Unity of China under the Sui dynasty   **755** | Revolt of General An Lushan   **880** | Revolt under Huang Chao

The Song Dynasty 960–1279

The Song dynasty was able to stabilize the country until China was conquered by the Mongols.

A further revolt in 880 broke the power of the Tang dynasty over China. The country fell apart into minor regimes from 907 to 960, while the Mongolian ⓬ Liao dynasty built up a strong empire in the north between 907 and 1125.

❽ Chao K'uang, the first emperor of the Song dynasty, acceded to the Chinese throne in 960. Over the next 20 years, the Songs captured vast areas of China and ruled the empire from their ❿ capital Kaifeng. Like the Tangs, the Songs organized their power centrally: department ministries controlled corresponding

8 The first Song emperor, Chao K'uang, drawing, 19th century

areas of responsibility and the military was placed under civilian officials. In 1004 the Song dynasty, after several unsuccessful wars, was forced to secure peace with the Liao through tribute payments and the cession of territories they had previously annexed in the north.

The country prospered culturally and economically in this period until a crisis began around 1050. The population grew faster than the state could assimilate it, and the tax revenues soon could not cover the state's expenditures, particularly for protecting the northern borders. During the reign of Shen Tsung (Chao Hsü) in the eleventh century, comprehensive reforms were carried out, including a land reform in favor of the farmers, who then paid taxes according to their income.

The Songs, together with the Chin dynasty that ruled in Manchuria from 1115 to 1234, defeated the Liao, but they were then forced to the south by the Chins, and in 1126, also lost Kaifeng. This ended the empire of the Northern Song and began the era of the

Southern Song, who resided in Hangzhou from 1135. There the Songs once again flourished. Many technological innovations—including book printing with movable type, gunpowder, and ⓫ porcelain—were introduced. Academies trained landscape painters, Neo-Confucianism became the new state philosophy, and the philosopher Chu Hsi created the new Chinese language.

Like many other dynasties, the Songs were forced to give way to the ❾ Mongols coming out of the northern steppes. Genghis Khan had already conquered the Chin empire and its capital Beijing by 1215. In 1279, Kublai Khan also incorporated the Songs into the Mongolian world empire.

9 Mongols storming a Chinese fortress, Indian miniature, 16th century

10 Boat traffic in Kaifeng, painting on silk, ca. 1100

11 Three urns with figurative decoration, ceramics, 12th-13th century

12 Death mask from Liao dynasty times, bronze, tenth-twelfth century

Hangzhou

The Italian traveler Marco Polo visited the capital of the Southern Song dynasty in the 13th century. The 12,000 bridges of the city, which is situated on a lagoon, reminded him of his hometown of Venice. Hangzhou, he said, was "the most beautiful and magnificent city in the world."

View of the lagoon city, French book painting, ca. 1412

JAPAN CA. 400–1338

Influenced by China, a Japanese empire began developing in the fourth century and experienced its blossoming in the eighth century. During the ensuing period, great ❶ cultural achievements were accompanied by a decline in imperial power. With the emergence of the samurai class between the 8th and 12th centuries, the form of feudalism developed that would remain characteristic for Japan into the 19th century.

1 Pagoda in Nara in the family temple of the Fujiwara, built 710

Development of State and Culture

Following the phase of state building, the Nara Period was a cultural high point.

According to mythology, the state of Japan was founded in 600 B.C. when the god Ninigi descended on Mount Kirishimayana and was the forerunner of Jimmu, the first emperor. In reality, there probably existed only various subkingdoms that were first united into a large empire around 400 A.D. under the ❹ Yamato dynasty, which still reigns to this day. The Yamatos based their claim to rule on their descent from the sun goddess Amaterasu, the highest god in ❻ Shintoism. This combined in the Japanese emperor, the *tenno*, the functions of a high priest and political power.

Many cultural achievements were adopted from China, such as script and metallurgy. Buddhist missionaries began arriving on the islands in 552. Empress Suiko and her designated prince regent ❷ Shotoku later promoted Buddhism. In 604, a 17-article constitution was promulgated that contained, among other things, moral maxims and the principle of a hierarchical order of society.

2 Prince Regent Shotoku-Taishi's marriage to a princess, painting, 14th century

The Taika reforms introduced in 646 followed Chinese precedent and were meant to strengthen centralized imperial power over the aristocracy. The country would be ruled from the capital city Nara through imperial officials. All land was claimed by the emperor, who granted estates to loyal nobility as fiefs.

Japan experienced a cultural high point during the Nara Period, particularly during the reign of Emperor Shomu, who ruled until 756. He modified the Taika reforms in 743, giving the nobility the right to bequeath their properties. Consequently, they were in a position to build up a power base and thus to increasingly weaken central authority over the course of a few generations. The gradual rise of the Fujiwara family, of which Shomu's mother and wife were both members, began during his reign. Sho-

3 Bodhisattva, from the Nara period, varnished sculpture, eighth century

mu also promoted ❸ Buddhism. He had the famous ❺ Todaiji temple with the 48-foot- (14.6-meter) high *Daibutsu* ("Great Buddha") erected in Nara.

To avoid the growing power of the Buddhist priests and monasteries, Emperor Kammu moved the capital in 784 to Heian-kyo—modern Kyoto—and the Heian Period began.

4 Burial gift from a ruler of the Yamato Period, clay sculpture, seventh century

5 Archway of the Todaiji temple in Nara, built in the eighth century

6 Shinto ceremony in Kyoto: Drummer playing the big Taiko drum, which is used to call and entertain the gods

Shoguns, Samurai, and Daimyos

The imperial court lost political power with the development of feudal structures governed over by shoguns and based on military force and samurai warrior groups.

The arts, particularly literature, became highly refined during the Heian Period, from 794 to 1185; the ladies of the court especially were notable authors. While court culture blossomed, the political power of the emperor continued to wane. His functions became limited to ritual religious tasks, while the real power rested with the noble families who had built up their estates into autonomous dominions and then entangled the country in ❾ civil wars. Initially, the ❼ Fujiwara family was the leading dynasty.

During the war to expand the empire into the north in the eighth century, the fighting efficiency of the army of conscripts proved insufficient. The well-trained ❿ samurai mercenaries were much more effective in battle—and also in the civil wars.

Villa of the Fujiwara family in Kyoto, built in 1052, later converted into a temple

Certain families specialized in leading these samurai and became a warrior nobility. The system was multi-tiered in which individuals swore allegiance to particular leaders, who in turn were loyal to certain powerful families. Among these dynasties, the Taira and the Minamoto clans increasingly challenged the power of the Fujiwaras.

The Tairas displaced the Fujiwaras after a ⓫ civil war in the mid-twelfth century and were in turn defeated in 1185 by the ❽ Minamotos. In 1192, ⓬ Minamoto Yoritomo had the emperor give him the hereditary title of *shogun* ("imperial general") and created the Kamakura shogunate, named after his seat of government. Early in the Kamakura Period, which lasted from 1192 to 1333, however, a shift of power again

8

Minamoto no Yoshitsune, the "ideal knight" of the Japanese "middle ages," wood engraving, 19th century

took place, with the Hojo clan rising to become hereditary regents of the shogunate in 1203, while the shoguns were pushed into the background.

The *daimyo* class led the samurai warrior caste during the twelfth century. The Hojos were dependent upon them to drive off the invasion attempts of the Mongol Kublai Khan in 1274 and 1281. They succeeded—purportedly assisted by divine winds, the *kamikaze*—but because it was not a conquest and there were no spoils, the daimyos' loyalty to the central government diminished.

9

Burning of the palace in Kyoto during a rebellion in 1159, painting, 12th–14th century

10

Helmet and steel face mask of a samurai warrior in the style of the 14th c.

11

Battle scene during the civil war against the Fujiwaras, painting

**From *The Pillow Book*
of the Lady of the Court
Sei Shonagon**

*"A groom who is happy to see
the father-in-law / A bride,
that pleases the mother-in-law
A liegeman, who never de-
fames his master ...
Men, women, and priests who
maintain a lifelong friendship.
Many books capture that of
which does not know a single
one."*

Lady of the court, painting, 17th c.

Emperor Go-Daigo took advantage of this dissatisfaction in 1333 and overthrew the Kamakura shoguns and their Hojo regents with the help of samurai from the Ashikaga family. This Kemmu Restoration lasted only until 1338, when Ashikaga Takauji, who himself had hoped to be shogun, took over power in a coup.

12

Minamoto Yoritomo, painting, 19th c.

SOUTHEAST ASIA 5TH–15TH CENTURY

Once the Burmese Pagan Kingdom and the Khmer Empire of Angkor had divided ❶ Indochina between them, the Thais replaced the Khmer in their position of power and became the main rivals of the Burmese. A number of different kingdoms, both Hindu and Buddhist, followed one another in Indonesia until the Europeans built up their colonial rule in Southeast Asia.

The coasts of Southeast Asia, Portugese naval map, 16th century

■ Empires of the Southeast Asian Mainland

While the Khmer were greatly influenced by Indian culture, the proximity to China was evident in Vietnam. New conflicts were ignited by the advance of the Burmese and lastly by that of the Thais.

The area settled by the Khmer stretched from southern Thailand and southern Laos to the Mekong Delta. They were the trading power Chinese sources referred to as "Funan," which flourished from the first or second century A.D. to the sixth or seventh century. In the seventh and eighth century, small Khmer kingdoms emerged that were strongly influenced by Indian culture. Indravarman I was the first to establish a large kingdom; his son, Yashovarman I, founded Angkor ("the city") around 900.

The kingdom of Angkor expanded its power in the tenth century. Its rulers were followers of Shivaism and built monumen-

3 Jayavarman VII, sculpture, 12th–13th century

tal temples. The famous temple of ❺ Angkor Wat was built under Suryavarman II. Following an ❻ invasion by the Cham, ❸ Jayavarman VII expanded the Khmer kingdom over large parts of Asia. He was a follower of Mahayana Buddhism and built up the walled capital of Angkor with ❼ numerous Buddhist temples. Raids by the Thai led to the loss of Angkor in 1369 and in 1389. The capital was moved south in the 15th century to Longvek, Udong, and Phnom Penh, also for reasons of trade.

The state of Nam Viet (today's North Vietnam) was conquered in 111 B.C. by the Chinese Han dynasty. China's powerlessness following the Tang dynasty in 931

made possible the founding of a kingdom called Dai Viet in Tonkin, with its center in the Red River Delta. It was ruled by the Ly dynasty from 1009 to 1225. Chinese influence, as well as the great significance of Confucianism, remained evident. The Ly were followed by the Tran, who ruled

Buddhist monk praying in front of the hand of a 48-foot (14.6-m) Buddha statue in Sukhothai

Pagoda in Pagan, eleventh century

from 1225 to 1400 and in 1287 repulsed a Mongol invasion.

The Cham had settled in the southern regions in central and southern Vietnam. There they founded the kingdom of Champa by the fourth or fifth century. In 1177, the Cham conquered Angkor, but in 1181 were beaten back, and from 1192 to 1220 fell under the rule of the Khmer. Champa came under pressure from the Vietnamese and the kingdom was annexed ca. 1471.

The Burmese migrated in the ninth century down into present-day Burma and founded the ❷, ❽ Pagan Kingdom around 849. Until its destruction by the Mongols in 1287, the kingdom shared domination over southern Asia with the Khmer. Two separate state systems emerged after the fall of Pagan, and they were not reunited until the 18th century.

Tribes speaking the Thai language moved into Yunnan in the

5 The Hindu temple complex Angkor Wat, or Vishnuloka ("the world of Vishnu"), Cambodia, built in the twelfth century

6 War of the Khmer against the Cham, sandstone relief, ca. 1200

southwest of China from about the second century B.C. The kingdom of Nan Zhao developed there in the seventh century; the Mongols destroyed it in 1253. The ❹ kingdom of Sukhothai formed in the middle of present-day Thailand in 1238 is considered to be the political and cultural origin of Thailand. The kingdom experienced its high point in the second half of the 13th century under

7 Partial view of the Buddhist temple Angkor Thom, built ca. 1200

King Ramkhamhaeng, who expanded his dominion to the Gulf of Thailand at the expense of the Khmer and Burmese. Around 1283, he devised the traditional Thai script that is still in use today. His successors dedicated themselves only to religion and science, so that in 1350 the local Thai prince of Ayutthaya was able to take over the kingdom without a struggle.

8 Temple of Pagan in Burma, present-day Myanmar

The Island Kingdoms of Southeast Asia

Indonesia had always been influenced by Indian culture and religions. Various Buddhist and Hindu kingdoms existed there until Islam began its advance in the 14th century, after being introduced onto the island by Arabian merchants.

Until the 1300s, both Buddhist and Hindu kingdoms existed in the Indonesian archipelago. The most notable Buddhist realm was the maritime kingdom of Srivijaya, which emerged in the seventh century on the southeast coast of Sumatra. From its capital Palembang, Srivijaya spread its area of dominance throughout

the South China Sea and adjoining regions. Local rulers began making themselves independent again in the eleventh century. The Shailendra dynasty, which was also Buddhist, left the temple complex of ❾ Borobudur on Java.

The Hindu Majapahit empire, which replaced Srivijaya as the dominant power, was established

9 Temple of Borobudur on Java, Indonesia, built in the eighth century

in 1293 in eastern Java by King Vijaya. It existed until about 1520, experiencing its golden age in the 14th century when King Gajah Mada controlled Indonesia.

Around 1300, Arabian merchants introduced Islam into Indonesia, and it was rapidly accepted almost everywhere. Only the island kingdom of ❷ Bali remained ❶ Hindu. In the mid-15th century, the prince of Paramesvara on Sumatra founded the Malacca sultanate, with Palembang as its capital. It was the leading trading hub of the region until it was conquered by the ❿ Portuguese in 1511.

In the 17th century, Java was controlled for the most part by the ❸ kingdom of Mataram. The Dutch, who had replaced the Portuguese as the most important European trading power, established the trading base of ❹ Batavia on Java in 1619 and from there brought Indonesia under their control. In 1755, they

10 Portuguese shipwreck, Indian miniature, 16th century

brought about the division of the once-mighty Mataram into the two principalities of Surakarta and Yogyakarta, thus effectively curtailing its power.

11 Water temple on Bali

12 Pavilon and lotus pond in a palace on Bali, built in the 17th century

13 Nandi bull in a Hindu temple of the kings of Mataram, built in the tenth c

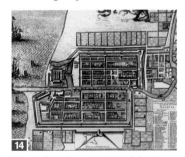

14 Map of Batavia, present-day Jakarta, copper engraving, 17th century

SUB-SAHARAN AFRICA 5TH–15TH CENTURY

It was not only in the north of Africa that impressive empires developed in the Middle Ages. Especially in western Africa, kingdoms that had become prosperous through ❶ trans-Saharan trade with the African north existed for centuries. Maritime trade also made the cities on the Swahili coasts in the east of the continent rich. Their connections reached into the interior of Africa to the kingdom of Zimbabwe, to which they were drawn by the treasures of its gold mines.

Caravan in the Sahara, film still

West Africa

From the fifth century, several large kingdoms existed south of the Sahara, controlling the caravan routes there.

Various kingdoms emerged along the caravan routes in West Africa in the Early Middle Ages. The kingdom of Ghana with its capital Koumbi Saleh developed south of Morocco in Mauritania in the fifth century. In the eighth century, Berbers reigned over black subjects until the latter expelled their overlords. The trade in gold and salt led to wealth, but the Arab traders, who had introduced Islam around 1000, we-

3 Portugese man with a musket, bronze relief from the Oba of Benin's palace, 16th c.

re soon followed by conquerors. Ghana was destroyed in the eleventh century by the North African Almoravids. A war ensued, ending in the Islamization of the country.

In 1203, the Soso people conquered Koumbi Saleh and ruled over Ghana for a brief period, but they were subjugated in the mid-13th century by the ❷ Manlinkas, who had founded a kingdom in Mali. The Manlinkas also converted to ❹ Islam. Under their ruler Mansa Musa, a period of great prosperity that spread from the capital of Niani began at the beginning of the 14th century. However, the kingdom disintegrated in the 1400s and was replaced by the Songhai.

The Songhai originated in the Nigerian northwest, and in the eighth century they spread their territory along the Niger River and built up an

2 Shrine of the legendary patriarch Malinkas, built in the 13th century and renewed every seven years

4 Mosque in Dienné in Mali, ca. 1400

economically flourishing kingdom around the capital of Gao. King Kossoi and his subjects converted to Islam around 1000. The city-state league of Kanem-Bornu that developed northeast of Lake Chad and existed into the 19th century converted to Islam in the eleventh century.

Only in the coastal areas on the Gulf of Guinea was Islam unable to gain a foothold. The Yoruba

Mansa Musa

Mansa Musa, the ruler of Mali, undertook a pilgrimage to Mecca in 1324 accompanied by a great caravan; he was reportedly accompanied by 60,000 bearers. The amount of gold that Musa spent in Cairo alone ruined the Egyptian currency for decades. Musa had a great mosque constructed in Timbuktu and developed an Islamic school that became a center of Islamic learning.

Caravan of pilgrims on their way to Mecca, painting, 19th century

founded several kingdoms there. Among these, ❻ Ife was the political and cultural center between the eighth and 13th centuries. It was then replaced by the Kingdom of Benin. The kings, called ❺ *obas*, made numerous military expeditions in the 15th century during which captives were taken; beginning in the 16th century, they began to be sold as slaves to the ❸ Europeans.

5 An oba of Benin on horseback with two servants, bronze relief, 16th c.

6 Head of a ruler of Ife, brass sculpture, 12th–15th c.

5th century | Founding of the Ghana Kingdom   **10th century** | Zagwe dynasty   **11th century** | Destruction of Ghana by the Almoravids

8th century | Development of the city-state league of Kanem-Bornu   **ca. 1000** | Introduction of Islam

South and East Africa

The East African coast was characterized by trade links reaching all the way to China, and Zimbabwe in southern Africa.

Christian Ethiopia shifted its center from Aksum to the highlands so that it could more easily defend against Muslim attacks. There, the Zagwe dynasty took over power in the tenth century. The Zagwe rebuilt Ethiopia from in Rome and Portugal, which actively supported the struggle against the Muslims in the 16th century.

On the East African coast, from the north of Somalia down to Mozambique, a relationship

Church cut from the rock, dedicated to the Virgin Mary, Lalibela, twelfth century

babwe in the twelfth century. Tens of thousands of people resided within the mighty walls that surrounded the capital ⓬ Great Zimbabwe. Finds of Chinese ceramic from the Ming period attest to its far-reaching trade connections. Zimbabwe's main exports were ores and gold.

The Shona empire was replaced in the 15th century by the Mozambican ⓽ Monomotapa, which for a time stretched far to

8

Fort in the harbor of Kilwa, Tanzania

9

King of Monomotapa

developed between African and Islamic Arab elements, the Swahili culture (from the Arabic *sahil*, "coast"), whose cities were made wealthy and powerful through their ⓾ trade on the continent as well as overseas with Arabia, India, and China. ⓼ Kilwa in Tanzania held the leading position among the coastal cities in the 14th century.

Their trading partners in the interior were the Bantu tribes, who primarily delivered copper and ivory. The Bantu people had spread out from the interior of the continent to the south and

Bantu

The word bantu means "person" and has come to signify a great linguistic family that today is spoken by around 100 million people in southern and central Africa. Half of this number speak the Swahili language. Bantu-speaking peoples migrated from Nigeria and Cameroon through East Africa down to South Africa.

Traditional housing of the Bantu-speaking Zulu in South Africa

10

Trade in African slaves, Arabic illumination, 13th century

their royal residence at ⓻ Lalibela. In 1268, they were supplanted by the Solomonic dynasty, which claimed descent from Menelik, the legendary founder of the nation. They were in permanent conflict with their ⓫ Muslim neighbors and rebellious provincial princes. To enforce the state church, which legitimized the rule of the emperor, heretics and Jews were persecuted. In the 15th century, contact was once again established with Europe, primarily with the pope

east shortly after the first century A.D., making their linguistic group one of the largest in Africa.

The Bantu-speaking Shona developed a state system in the region of Mozambique and Zim-

the west. Great bastions were also erected there, but the kingdom had already come under the control of the Portuguese and its decline and ultimate end in the late 1600s could no longer be avoided.

11

Battle between Ethiopians and Muslims, painting ca. 1412

12

Ruins of Great Zimbabwe, built from the 13th c. onward

| **12th century** | Rise of the Shona empire | **1325** | Pilgrimage of Mausa Musa to Mecca |

| **11th century** | Rise of the Mali empire | **1268** | Salomonid dynasty | **15th century** | Founding of the Monomotapa empire |

THE SETTLEMENT AND EARLY HIGH CULTURES OF AMERICA CA. 15TH CENTURY B.C.–15TH CENTURY A.D.

After the settling of the Americas, various cultures developed in North America, some of which were culturally very sophisticated. Predominantly hierarchically organized empires developed in Central and South America, each of which took over the political and cultural leadership of the region for a certain time. These included the empires of the ❶ Olmec and Toltec as well as the Maya and Aztec in Central America and of the Chimú, Chavín, Moche, Nazca, and finally the Inca in South America.

1 Colossal stone head depicting an Olmec god

North America

A large number of diverse American Indian cultures characterized the northern continent.

Nomadic Stone Age hunter-gatherers moved into North America toward the end of the last ice age, roughly 13,000 B.C., across a land bridge that existed at the time between Asia and America. They spread out over the entirety of the

2 Bison hunt, wood engraving, 19th c.

Americas in the course of the following millennia.

Around 300 B.C., members of the Hohokam cultures migrated northward from Mexico and settled in villages whose agricultural areas were irrigated by large-scale canal systems. The various American cultures flourished from the beginning of the Christian era until the eighth century. The ❻ cliff-dwelling ❸ Anasazi culture developed around 500 A.D. in the American Southwest. They were settled agriculturalists who dwelled in multistory stone houses and are the predecessors of the ❺ Pueblo Indians, who were then conquered by the Spanish in the 16th century.

The Mississippian culture unfolded about 750 around the city of Cahokia, near modern St. Louis, in which close to 50,000 inhabitants lived. The cultivation

3 Clay bowl of the Anasazi culture, 12th–13th c.

of corn served as their basis for life. Presumably the civilization was destroyed by epidemics introduced by Europeans—a fate that many Indian cultures met.

Tribes on the northwest coast existed by fishing, pursued trade with northern Asia, and held potlatches—complex gift-giving rituals that distinguished many of them. They are also known for their wood carvings, particularly their totem poles.

The ❹ tribes of the Great Plains were for the most part nomads, their culture dependent on the ❷ hunting of bison. As they more frequently came into con-

4 Totem poles of Indian tribes of the Great Plains of North America

tact with white settlers pushing westward, they were mistakenly thought to be typical of Indian cultures.

The lifestyles, social organizations, and political institutions of the Native Americans were very diverse. These were partly determined by the living conditions such as climate, terrain, and animal population, but even in similar environments there was a great diversity of social structures: settled and nomadic peoples with or without slaves, hunter and agrarian cultures, patriarchal and matriarchal societies, monarchical and democratic structures. The Wendat (Huron) confederations in the 15th century, and later the five-nation Iroquois League, had a parliament and constituted the first American democracy.

5 Settlement of the Pueblo Indians in New Mexico

6 Cliff dwellings of the Anasanzi culture, ca. 1200

| ca. 1500 B.C. | Advanced civilization of the Olmecs | ca. 300 B.C. | Northward migration of Hohokam cultures | 200 | Development of the Anasazi culture |
| ca. 1000 B.C. | Development of the Chavín culture | | | ca. 0 | Urban culture of Teotihuacán |

Central and South America

Sophisticated state-building civilizations developed in Mexico and Peru, some of which covered vast territories.

The nomadic hunter-gatherer communities of Central America became settled agrarian societies about 8000–9000 years ago. The Olmec formed the first advanced civilization; they left behind temple complexes and palaces from about 1200 B.C. The Olmec culture was dominant on the Mexican east coast until about 400 B.C. This culture was long considered to be the oldest in the Americas until 2001 when a city dating back to around 2700 B.C., and testifying to a sophisticated society that built pyramids as old as those of Egypt, was discovered in Caral, Peru.

Approximately 2000 years ago, a nation developed around the city of Teotihuacán not far from modern-day Mexico City, and it dominated Mexico from 450 to 700. The city at times had more than 100,000 inhabitants and a widespread trading network. It housed  ❶ sun and moon pyramids as well as numerous colorfully painted temples lining a wide thoroughfare.

Between 400 and 1200 A.D., the Toltec formed a militarily organized empire in the interior of Mexico, the first in Central America to use an army to subjugate its neighbors. In the twelfth century their empire fell, and the rise of the Aztec began in the ensuing decades.

The Maya peoples had been laying out settlements on the Yucatan Peninsula since 1200 B.C. Between 300 and 900 A.D., the Classic ⓭ Maya period, numerous ⓬ city-states ruled by ❽ priest-princes formed on the peninsula. For reasons unknown, these were given up in favor of the cities of the Postclassic Period, which were situated farther north.

In South America almost 3000 years ago, the Chavín culture emerged in Peru. It lasted into the third century B.C. and was replaced by the Mochica or Moche in the north and in the south by the Nazca. The latter, famous for their rock paintings, survived into the sixth or seventh century. Between 300 and 900, the civilization of the ❾ Tiahuanaco dominated the region around Lake Titicaca, which was possibly developed from the earlier Chavín culture and which influenced the Huari empire that ruled Peru from the seventh to eleventh centuries.

The ❼ Mochica built temples and pyramids that are among the largest in the Americas and created characteristic pottery that occasionally depicted human sacrifice. They gave up their cities at the beginning of the eighth century. The Chimú, who had an intricate irrigation system, succeeded them about 200 years later on the Peruvian coast. Their empire and its capital Chan Chan, which had around 50,000 inhabitants, was conquered by the Inca in 1470.

The ❿ Amazon region was first settled by humans in the third millennium B.C. The people occupying the southern tip of South America nearly 10,000 years ago were almost completely eradicated by colonization and epidemics.

7 Mochica culture vessel in the shape of a head, clay, first c. B.C.–sixth c. A.D.

9 Gateway of the Sun from the Tiahuanaco culture, Bolivia, model

10 Indians from the Amazon region wearing traditional garments

8 Head of a Maya prince, Tuff, ca. 700

11 The 213-foot-high (65 m) sun pyramid in Teotihuacán, ca. 0

12 Ruins of the city Tikal, Guatemala

13 Mayan vessel showing a palace scene, decorated clay

| ca. 750 | Development of the Mississippian culture | 1470 | Conquest of the Moche empire by the Incas |
| **300–900 A.D.** | Old Maya empire | **from the 12th century** | Rise of the Aztecs | **16th century** | Conquest of the Pueblo Indians by the Spaniards |

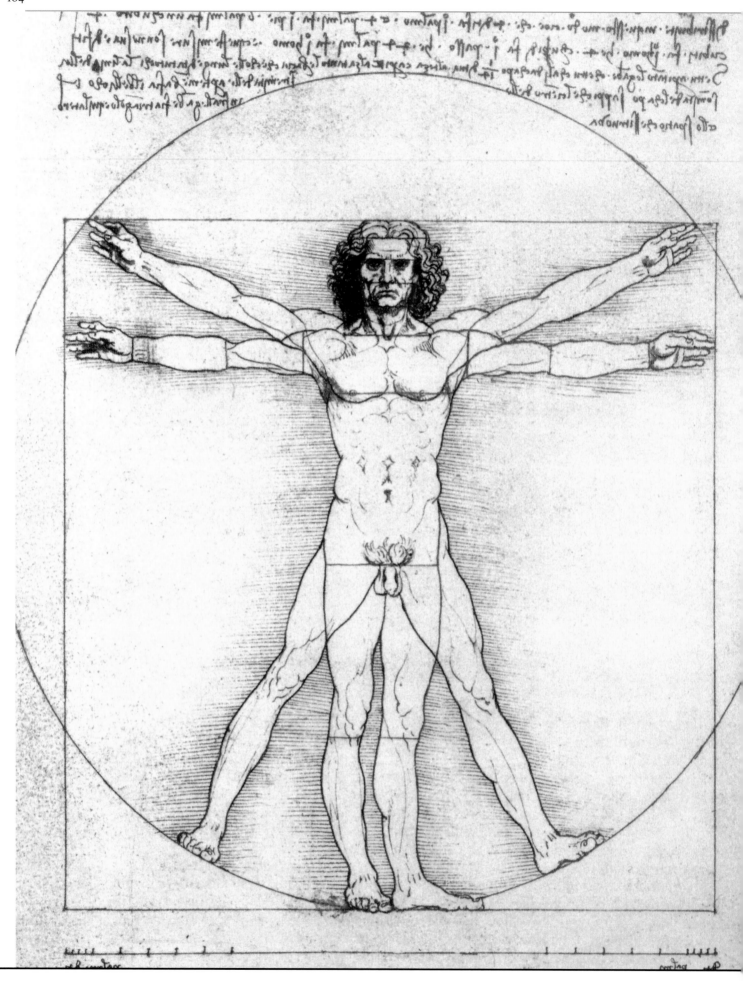

The Early Modern Period
16th–18th century

The smooth transition from the Middle Ages to the Modern Age is conventionally fixed on such events as the Reformation and the discovery of the "New World," which brought about the emergence of a new image of man and his world. Humanism, which spread out of Italy, also made an essential contribution to this with its promotion of a critical awareness of Christianity and the Church. The Reformation eventually broke the all-embracing power of the Church. After the Thirty Years' War, the concept of a universal empire was also nullified. The era of the nation-state began, bringing with it the desire to build up political and economic power far beyond Europe. The Americas, Africa, and Asia provided regions of expansion for the Europeans.

Proportions of the Human Figure by Leonardo da Vinci (drawing, ca. 1490) is a prime example of the new approach of Renaissance artists and scientists to the anatomy of the human body.

1

Breaking out of the worldview of the Middle Ages

2

Humanist scholars including Luther and Erasmus

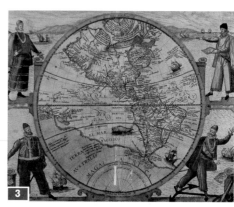

3

Map with Columbus, Vespucci, Magellan, and Pizarro

THE EARLY MODERN PERIOD

The beginnings of the Early Modern Period can be seen around 1500 in the reshaping and expansion of the ❶ worldview of the Middle Ages that was taking place. Despite symbolic dates such as the discovery of the New World by Christopher Columbus in 1492 and the beginning of the Reformation in 1517, this transformation did not take place abruptly but took the form of cumulative changes throughout the era.

Humanism and the Renaissance

As early as the 14th century, Italian authors such as ❺ Dante, Petrarch, and Boccaccio built on the ideals and erudition of the scholars of antiquity. In contrast to the universal world view that was prevalent during the Middle Ages, the Humanists (Latin: *humanitas*, "humanity") placed humankind at the center of their conceptualization of the world. The ideas of the *Renaissance* (French, "rebirth") emerged from a interaction with the teachings and philosophies of antiquity. This led to a new independence of the sciences and

5

Dante, Petrarch, and Boccaccio, painting by Giorgio Vasari, 16th century

a disentanglement of philosophy from Christian dogma and to a flourishing of the arts. Cosmopolitan scholars such as Erasmus of Rotterdam tried to unify humanism and Christian piety, while from the court of the Medici in Florence and the papal court of Rome, Renaissance art and its innovations spread throughout Europe.

Reformation, Counter-Reformation, and Nation-States

Even before ❷ Martin Luther initiated the Reformation, criticism of the increasingly worldly Church had been growing. Jan Hus of Bohemia, for example, was a significant reformer who, however, failed due to resistance from the aristocracy. In contrast Luther, during the peasant wars, for example, explicitly put himself on the side of the princes, who in turn

supported the Reformation because they hoped for an increase in power through the development of national churches. The Catholic world responded to the Reformation with an internal renewal of the Church. A significant agent of this renewal was the ❹ Jesuit order, which saw its duty in missionary work and also in combatting heretical movements. The Jesuit order also took over the development of the Catholic educational system. The Counter-Revolution was based on the redefinition of the Catholic faith and Church in the Council of Trent. The Council of Trent laid down the principles of Catholic faith in the same way that the "Augsburg Confession" definitively set down the tenets of the Protestant faith.

4

Ignatius of Loyola, founder of the Jesuit order, 17th century

Inventions and Discoveries

The rapid spread of the Reformation was facilitated by the invention of the ❻ printing press around 1445 by Johannes Gutenberg, as communication of new ideas was much facilitated and speeded up by this new medium, which made possible the mass production of texts that could be carried far from where they were written. Discoveries in the field of natural sciences,

6

Johannes Gutenberg at his printing press, etching, 18th century

such as that of the heliocentric universe by Copernicus in 1507, revolutionized the worldview of the time. A thirst for new discoveries and the search for new trading routes led to great ❸ sea voyages: The search for sea routes to India led the Portuguese to sail around Africa at the end of the 15th century; Christopher Columbus landed in America in 1492; Magellan sailed around the world for the first time from 1520 to 1521. In the wake of beginning world trade and colonialism,

| 1445 | Invention of printing press | 1507 | Theory of the heliocentric universe | 1530 | "Augsburg Confession" |
| 15th century | Beginning of the Era of Absolutism | 1492 | Landing of Columbus in America | 1517 | Beginning of Reformation |

Chinese Pavilion in Sanssouci, Potsdam, Germany

Newton discovers gravity by observing a falling apple

A middle-class cultural Salon in Paris, 18th century

European states established hegemony in many parts of the world. As a result of this they damaged and destroyed many cultures and forced millions of people into slavery. The discovery of new societies, however, also resulted in a fascination for the ❼ "exotic," particularly the cultures of Persia, China, and that of the Ottoman Empire. In the 17th and 18th century, elements of each of these were imported to Europe. In the Ottoman Empire, in Persia, and in India under the Great Moguls, and in China under the Manchu dynasty—states that were at the height of their power and prosperity between the 16th and 18th century—serious conflict with the Europeans did not take place and their excursions were given only marginal attention.

Absolutism and Enlightenment

In the Early Modern Era, absolutism—the concentration of undivided power in the hands of the princes—prevailed as the form of government in many countries. It was based on theories formulated by political philosophers such as Niccoló Macchiavelli, Jean Bodin, and Thomas Hobbes from the 16th and 17th century onward. In these tracts, concepts such as that of the raison d'état ("reason of state") and the absolute sovereignty of the ruler were developed. The primary instruments of power of the absolutist princes were the standing army and an administrative bureaucracy that was solely responsible to the ruler.

A particular form of absolutism emerged in conjunction with the Enlightenment of the 18th century that attempted to apply humanism, as well as the philosophical and scientific discoveries of the 17th century, throughout society. Since the 17th century scholars such as ⓫ René Descartes, John Locke, Baruch de Spinoza, and Gottfried Wilhelm Leibniz had found methods to free deduction from religious dogma. Scientists such as Galileo Galilei and ❽ Issac Newton shaped a new worldview based on knowledge gained through scientific discovery. The great Enlightenment philosophers of the 18th century such as Montesquieu and Voltaire championed freedom of the spirit, of religion, and the decoupling of knowledge from religious doctrine. They also demanded

a review of the methods of government on the basis of reason and an image of mankind that presumed the equality and community of all mankind. The philosophers Jean-Jacques Rousseau and ❿ Immanuel Kant, however, attacked absolutism through their critiques of the politics and institutions of the state, and above all of the church.

Enlightened Absolutist princes took advantage of the already present structures of church and state to achieve their goals: the good of the state and the welfare of their subjects. The centralization of the state was in this way pushed forward, while the influence of the church, particularly in the school and education systems, was decreased. However, even the reform-minded monarchs such as King Frederick the Great of Prussia or Emperor Joseph II were not prepared to give their subjects, particularly the upward striving bourgeoisie, a political voice. The division of powers, for example, demanded by the Enlightenment philosophers was never implemented.

Immanuel Kant, painting, 18th century

The Rise of the Bourgeoisie

Humanism and the Reformation particularly influenced the thinking of the European middle classes, which had become wealthy through early capitalism. This new wealth brought with it respect and a new and influential position in society. In order to maintain a counterweight to the power of the princes and the church, the absolutist princes leaned on the middle classes: with access to a university education, increasing numbers were able to hold state offices. In the state economies, trade and business, which lay in the hands of the middle classes, was promoted. Also in ❾ cultural life the middle classes took on increasing significance. Despite this, the bourgeoisie, as the middle classes became known, were prevented from taking part in political decision-making processes. The conflicts that arose out of this contradiction culminated in the French Revolution of 1789, which, together with the American Declaration of Independence, marked the beginning of the "Age of the Bourgeoisie" and the rise to power of the middle classes.

René Descartes, painting, ca.1640

THE GERMAN EMPIRE: THE REFORMATION AND ITS CONSEQUENCES 1517–1609

With the support of powerful protestant German princes, the Reformation initiated by Martin Luther was carried through rapidly in large parts of the empire. Following the first religious wars, the Peace of Augsburg created a balance of power between Catholics and Protestants, but the peace was unstable, as it made no concessions to the Calvinists. Thus conflicts as a result of confessional differences took place even after the Peace of Augsburg. Through a series of stages, the conflict progressively intensified through to the eve of the Thirty Years' War.

The German Emperor Charles V, painting by Jakob Seisenegger, 1532

■ Reformation and the Peasants' War

Martin Luther's Reformation of the church was radical, as it was associated with socially revolutionary demands.

Martin Luther, painting, 1528

Thomas Münzer, "Manifesto of the Mansfeldian Youths" from 1524:

"Go to it, go to it, while the fire is hot. Let not your sword become cold, do not let it become lame! Forge, clink clank, on the anvil of Nimrod, throw their tower to the ground! It is not possible, as long as they live that human fear should become empty. One can tell you nothing of God, while they govern over you. Go to it, go to it, while it is day. God precedes you, follow, follow!"

After the death of Maximilian I, his grandson ❶ Charles V was elected Holy Roman Emperor in 1519—his election was ensured by the payment of enormous bribes to the electors. The Habsburgs raised the money by going into debt with the merchant house of ❷ Fugger, whose trading network covered the whole of the known world. Meanwhile, the Reformation had begun.

Initially the Reformation was a reform movement within the Church that had been incited by the Church's practice of selling indulgences. In 1517 in Wittenberg, ❸ Martin Luther made public his 95 theses to reform the Church. He broke with the Church in 1520 when the pope threatened him with excommunication, and in 1521 Luther defended his theses at the ❻ Diet of Worms. The move-

ment developed momentum through the backing of powerful German princes. Elector ❼ Frederick of Saxony sheltered Luther in Wartburg Castle, where he worked on a translation of the Bible into German.

The Reformation soon became linked to the social upheaval of the time. In 1522–1523 there was an uprising of imperial knights under ❹ Ulrich von Hutten and Franz von Sickingen, who saw themselves as representatives of humanism and the Reformation, in opposition to the Catholic German princes. Peasants rebelled against the aristocratic landowners in 1524–1525, plundering manors and monasteries in Franconia and Swabia. Luther sided with the princes against the peasants, while the radical reformer ❺ Thomas Münzer led the peasa-

Anton Fugger burns the first debenture bonds of Charles V, in 1535

4 Humanist, writer, and imperial knight Ulrich von Hutten

nts in Thuringia. In 1525 the peasant army was defeated at Frankenhausen by the princes, and Münzer was executed. In 1533–1534 the radical Anabaptists seized control of Münster.

Thomas Münzer, engraving, 1608

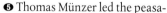

Martin Luther before Emperor Charles V at the Diet of Worms on April 17–18, 1521, painting by Anton von Werner, 1900

Frederick III, (the Wise) Elector of Saxony

The Organization of the Protestants and the Religious Peace of Augsburg in 1555

After 1530, a large portion of the empire became Protestant. The emperor won the religious wars against the Schmalkaldic League, but the Protestants, who were supported by France, the rivals of the Habsburgs, won the balance of power in the Peace of Augsburg of 1555.

8

The later German king and Emperor Ferdinand I, painting, 1521

9

Count Philip the Magnanimous of Hesse, painting, ca. 1534

10

The elector Duke Maurice of Saxony, painting by Lucas Cranach, 1548

Holy Roman Emperor Charles V ruled a vast empire on which "the sun never set"—it spanned Spain, the New World, Austria, northern Italy, and the Netherlands. He completely understood the necessity of Church reforms, yet his claim to a universal empire also required that all his subjects be of a unified religion. He therefore saw the Reformation as a politi-

cally destabilizing factor and fought energetically against it. As he was often absent from the empire, he had his brother ❽ Ferdinand I crowned Roman king of the Germans in 1531. Ferdinand was then responsible for negotiation between the Protestant and Catholic imperial princes and maintaining peace.

The elector of Saxony and

Count ❾ Philip the Magnanimous of Hesse placed themselves at the head of the Reformation movement and supported Luther in developing evangelical state churches. The new state churches did not answer to a higher church authority, which meant a huge increase in their power and influence. In 1530, the Protestant princes formulated their "Augsburg Confession" and presented it before the Diet, and in 1531 they organized as the Schmalkaldic League. When Brandenburg declared itself on the side of the Reformation in 1539, the whole of the southwest, east, and north of the empire—with the exception of Brunswick-Wolfenbüttel—was Protestant. The German princes secularized Catholic dioceses and installed their younger sons in them as hereditary rulers, hereby forcing the emperor's hand, by challenging his rule in numerous territories of the empire.

In the wars of the protestant ❶ Schmalkaldic League, Charles V

defeated the Protestants under the leadership of Saxony and Hesse, captured Count Philip, and transferred the Saxon electoral lands and titles to Duke ❿ Maurice of Saxony, who had fought on his side. However, Maurice then changed sides and marched to Austria as leader of the regrouped princes' opposition in 1551–1552, forcing the emperor to flee. In 1552 Maurice extracted from King Ferdinand the Peace of Passau, which guaranteed the Protestants freedom of religion. This treaty prepared the way for the Peace of Augsburg between the emperor and the Protestants, which was signed on September 25, 1555. It stipulated that each prince could determine the religion of his territories and that of his subjects ("*Cuius regio, eius religio*"). Maurice of Saxony was also able to acquire vast lands and power for his family.

Henry the Younger of Brunswick-Wolfenbüttel

Henry the Younger (1489-1568), who strongly opposed the Reformation, was an absolutist ruler of Brunswick-Wolfenbüttel since 1514, and remained a strict Catholic and loyal to the emperor while the other Welfs became Protestant. He fought against the Protestant cities of Brunswick and Lübeck. An intensive literary polemic was created around "Hank of Wolfenbüttel"; Martin Luther wrote "Against Hanswurst" about him in 1541. His ousting in 1542 eventually provoked the religious wars of the Schmalkaldic League. When Henry died in 1568, his son Julius converted to Protestantism.

11

Emperor Charles V triumphs over the Saxon army in the Battle at Muehlberg during the Schmalkaldic War of 1546–1547, copper engraving, 17th century

May 1525	Battle of Frankenhausen	1531	Founding of Schmalkaldic League	1546–47	Schmalkaldic War
	1530	Augsburg Confession	1533–34	Anabaptist rule in Münster	1555	Peace of Augsburg

■ The Division of the Empire and Calvinism

Despite being left out of the Peace of Augsburg, Calvinism was later able to gain a foothold in the empire while the emperor endeavored to reach religious compromises.

1 The German Emperor Charles V, archduke of Austria, and also Charles I of Spain, painting by Titian, 1548

2 The French-Swiss reformer John Calvin, painting in the style of the Flemish school, ca. 1530

3 The German Emperor Ferdinand I, archduke of Austria, king of Bohemia and Hungary, painting, ca. 1550

4 Huldrych Zwingli, former Catholic priest and German-Swiss reformer, painting by Hans Asper, 1549

5 The Emperor Maximilian II, painting by Anthonis Mor, ca. 1560

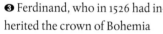

6 Elector August of Saxony, painting by Zacharias Wehme, 1586

Fatigued and sick with gout, **❶** Charles V gave up the throne in 1556, splitting his enormous empire between his brother Ferdinand (the Austrian line) and his son Philip (the Spanish line). **❸** Ferdinand, who in 1526 had inherited the crown of Bohemia and Hungary, received Austria and the title of emperor in 1558. The religious and political peace in the empire remained volatile. Ferdinand had been able to include a clause in the Peace of Augsburg stipulating that a prince was required to relinquish his power if he converted to Protestantism, but the Protestants were always able to work around this requirement. Furthermore, the Catholic majority of the seven electoral votes was minimal after Brandenburg, the Palatinate, and Saxony had become Protestant.

Meanwhile, the Reformation movement was also divided by doctrinal differences. In 1525 **❹** Huldrych Zwingli, a former Roman Catholic priest, had brought the Reformation to Zurich, but his version differed from the Lutheran, above all over the issue of Communion. Of even greater consequence was **❷** John Calvin's 1541 brand of Reformation in Geneva, which introduced a severe church discipline and established a form of theocracy in the city. Calvinism spread rapidly to France, the Netherlands, and the west of the empire. In 1560s the Palatinate electorate under Frederick III the Pious converted to Calvinism, and western German earldoms such as Nassau followed. Because the Calvinists had not been included in the Peace of Augsburg, the Palatinate leaned heavily toward France under Frederick III and even more so under his son John Casimir, bringing the emperor into great difficulties.

Charles V and Ferdinand I had repeatedly urged the pope to make the reforms to the Catholic Church that were finally made by the Council of Trent, which met intermittently between 1545 and 1563 and which redefined Catholic doctrine. Ferdinand remained a Catholic but was ready to make concessions, for example, over the issue of the marriage of priests, which he was prepared to allow in view of the many priests cohabiting. His son **❺** Maximilian II, emperor from 1564, was indifferent to religion, if anything leaning slightly toward Protestantism. The political lines were vague: Saxony under **❻** Elector August (elector since 1553) fought for the rights of the Protestants, but remained staunchly on the side of the emperor; on the other hand, the Catholic dukes of Bavaria were ready to weaken the Habsburgs to their own advantage. Protestantism was at the height of its power in the empire under Maximilian, when most of the important imperial cities had become Protestant.

The Counter-Reformation and Intensifying Religious Differences within the Empire

Spreading from southern Germany, the Catholic Counter-Reformation gained ground. The confessional differences sharpened, culminating in the outbreak of the Thirty Years' War.

7

John Sigismund von Brandenburg in a dispute with Wolfgang Wilhelm von Neuburg over the Jülich-Clevian succession, color print, 19th century

8

The German Jesuit Petrus Canisius preaches before Pope Gregory XIII and Emperor Rudolf II, painting, 1635

The beginning of the Catholic Counter-Reformation can be tied to the founding of the order of Jesuits by Ignatius of Loyola in 1540. The Bavarian dukes, among others, joined this order in 1564. The driving power behind it was the cardinal of Augsburg, Otto Truchsess of Waldburg, who unified Catholic forces. In 1563 he handed over the University of Dillingen, which he had founded in 1554, to the ❽ Jesuits, who were taking control of universities and establishing Catholic seminaries in all of the empire's territories. Also, in Austria where the Protestants had won significant freedoms, Archduke Ferdinand—later Emperor Ferdinand II—increased his efforts for a return to Catholicism from 1594.

Under the Emperor Rudolf II, whose reign began in 1576, the religious differences increased, especially after 1600 when the increasingly mentally ill emperor retired from public view. The occasion that sparked the war came during the crisis of Cologne in 1582–83, when Archbishop Gebhard Truchsess of Waldburg—a nephew of Cardinal Otto—attempted to transform Cologne into a hereditary Protestant principality with the aid of Protestant German princes and Dutch Calvinists. As this would have meant the loss of the majority in the Electoral College, Catholic forces, with the help of Spain, drove the archbishop out of Cologne and installed the young line of Bavarian Wittelsbachs, which ruled until 1777.

Since 1606 the fraternal feud in the House of Habsburg had been weakening the central power. ❿ Archduke Matthias won control over Hungary (1608) and Bohemia (1611) from Rudolf, who was by then almost incapable of governing. The emperor allied himself with the Protestant estates of Bohemia and granted them religious freedom in 1609. All signs pointed to a storm in the empire when in 1607 ⓫ Duke Maximilian I of Bavaria occupied the Protestant city of Donauworth, where a Catholic procession had been attacked, and re-established Catholic rule. As a result, the Protestant Union was formed in 1608 and, in response, the Catholic League in 1609. The ❾ battle lines of the Thirty Years' War had been drawn and the ❼ Jülich-Clevian dispute gave a foretaste of what was to come.

The Dispute over Succession in Jülich-Cleves

By 1609, the religious wars were already imminent when the last Catholic duke of Jülich and Cleves died and a dispute over the succession flared up. The princes of Brandenburg and Neuburg, both Protestant, each laid claim to the duchy. They agreed upon a division of the territory in 1614 only after the Brandenburgs had secured Dutch help by converting to Calvinism, and the Neuburgs had gotten aid from the Wittelsbachs and the Spaniards after converting to Catholicism.

9

A protestant flyer with a polemical depiction of the "real church of Christ" (Protestants) confronting the "antichrist" (Catholics) copper engraving, 1606

10

The German emperor Matthias, painting, ca. 1580

11

Maximilian I, Duke and since 1623 first Elector of Bavaria, painting, ca. 1620

THE THIRTY YEARS' WAR   1618–48

In the Thirty Years' War, the growing tensions between the Holy Roman Emperor and the Catholic powers on the one hand, and the Protestant regions and estates on the other, erupted into violence. The conflict began in Bohemia but soon spread throughout the empire and drew in almost all the European powers. Spain supported its Catholic relations, Denmark and Sweden supported the Protestants, and France was mainly interested in weakening the Habsburgs. In the Holy Roman Empire, and especially in Bohemia, whole districts were devastated by passing armies that would terrorize the local population and requisition their property.

The Battle of White Mountain in Bohemia, painting by Pieter Snayers, 17th century

■ The Palatine-Bohemian Phase   1618–1623

In Bohemia the country princes disposed of the Habsburg Ferdinand II and chose Elector Count Palatine as king. However, he was soon expelled by the Catholic League.

During his lifetime, the childless Emperor Matthias, who succeeded his brother Rudolf in 1612, assigned the crown of Bohemia (1617) and Hungary (1618) to his cousin, ❹ Ferdinand II. The Bohemian country princes, who were mainly Protestant, feared that the Jesuit-educated Ferdinand would suspend the Letter of Majesty of 1609. This had stipulated that all subjects should enjoy freedom of conscience in religious matters. Insisting on their right to freely elect their king, the princes deposed him and voted in the leader of the Protestant Union, ❺ Elector Frederick V of the Palatinate, as his replacement in 1618. The election caused bitter enmity between the religious parties of the Bohemian aristocracy.

❹ Ferdinand II

On May 23, 1618, Protestants threw the Catholic imperial governors, Slawata and Martinez, and a secretary out the window of the ❸ Prague Castle (the ❷ "Prague defenestration") and thus threw down a challenge to the Habsburgs. The violent conflict had begun.

Ferdinand sent his cousin, Duke Maximilian of Bavaria and head of the Catholic League, to Bohemia with troops under the command of the Bavarian ❻ General Tilly. On November 8, 1620, the league's forces ❶ defeated those of the Protestant princes at the Battle of White Mountain, near Prague.

Prague Castle

Frederick V, mocked as the "winter king" for his short-lived reign, was forced to flee to Holland. A tribunal then convened in Bohemia, and 21 leaders of the rebellion were executed, while a large amount of Protestant property was confiscated. The crown of Bohemia became the property of the Habsburgs until 1918.

In 1622 troops of the Catholic League and of Spain occupied the Palatinate, and in 1623 they made Maximilian elector palatine,

The "Prague defenestration," 1618

whereupon power relations in the Electoral College shifted significantly in favor of the Catholics. The Protestants in the empire felt challenged and threatened.

❺ Elector Frederick V of the Palatinate   ❻ Bavarian General Tilly

From
Mother Courage and Her Children
by Bertolt Brecht

I won't let you spoil the war for me. / It is said it kills off the weak, but they're done for in peace, too. / It's just that war feeds its own better, / and if it gets the best of you / then you're simply not there for the victory. / War is nothing more than business, / but with bullets instead of cheese.

Helene Weigel as "Mother Courage"

The Danish War 1625–1629

Denmark allied itself with the Protestants of Lower Saxony and fought against a northward attack by the imperial troops under Wallenstein.

7 Albrecht von Wallenstein, painting by Anthony van Dyck, 17th century

In his battle against Frederick V, Tilly advanced well into Westphalia. The Protestants of northern Germany feared Catholic domination and prepared their **8**, **10** troops under Ernst of Mansfeld and Christian of Brunswick-Wolfenbüttel. The war thus began to spread beyond Bohemia. Christian IV of Denmark led the Protestant forces, together with Duke von Holstein, the most senior Protestant prince in the region of Lower Saxony.

On the Catholic side, the rise of **7**, **12** Albrecht von Wallenstein commenced. The Bohemian aristocrat had converted to Catholicism, acquired an immense fortune through the purchase of confiscated Protestant goods, and offered his services to the emperor. An excellent strategist, he quickly made a name for himself as a military commander. Wallenstein marched his army to northern Germany and there defeated Ernst of Mansfeld at **13** Dessauer Bridge on April 25, 1626. Shortly afterward, Tilly also defeated Christian IV at the Battle of Lutter am Barenberg on August 27, 1626.

In 1626 Wallenstein, now commander in chief of the imperial army and duke of Friedland, and Tilly went on to conquer Holstein, Schleswig, and Jutland, expelling the dukes of Mecklenburg and appropriating their lands. The Danish king was forced to agree to the Peace of Lübeck in 1629. Ferdinand II now stood at the height of his powers, and on March 6, 1629, he decreed his Edict of Restitution, which demanded that the Protestants **11** return all the secularized Church lands and called on the Catholic imperial estates to actively re-Catholicize. However, Wallenstein's draconian demands alarmed many; at the Diet of

8 Band of soldiers attacking local peasants, wood engraving, 17th c.

Regensburg in 1630, his enemies and rivals, notably **9** Maximilian of Bavaria, conspired to secure his dismissal from the post of commander in chief of the imperial armies.

9 Maximilian I of Bavaria, painting, 17th century

Albrecht Eusebius von Wallenstein (1583–1634)

Wallenstein was convinced of the power of the stars over his fate. He had the famous astronomer John Kepler draw up his horoscope.

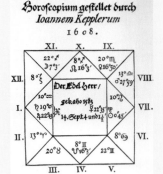

Horoscope made for Wallenstein by the astrologer John Kepler, showing the position of the planets on the day of his birth

10 Band of soldiers robbing and killing their victims, wood engraving, 17th c.

11 Castle Güstrow, Wallenstein's residence in Mecklenburg, north Germany

13 Wallenstein's victory in the Battle at the Dessauer Bridge, 1626

12 Wallenstein's palace in Prague, built in 1621

■ The Swedish War 1630–1635

The plight of the German Protestants caused the Swedish king to act. After a triumphant march through Germany, King Gustav fell in battle against Wallenstein.

Sweden was alarmed by the advance of imperial power in northern Germany and the Baltic region where, by the Peace of Lübeck of 1629, Christian IV of Denmark had agreed not to intervene in German affairs. Fearing for his hegemony in the North, the Swedish Lutheran ❶ King Gustav II Adolph championed the cause of the German Protestants. In 1630, encouraged and financially supported by Cardinal Richelieu of France who also wished to reduce imperial influence, Gustav moved south and began his march through Ger-

1

King Gustav II Adolph of Sweden

2

Battle of Breitenfeld, 1631

many. The Swedish army was a formidable and well-disciplined fighting unit. The imperial forces under Tilly were not strong enough and suffered a defeat against the ❸ allied Swedish and Saxon forces at ❷ Breitenfeld on September 17, 1631.

From Mainz, Gustav pushed southward in spring 1632 to occupy Augsburg, and in May of 1632 moved into the Munich residence of the Elector Maximilian, who had fled to Nuremberg. The city of Munich offered heavy bribes to prevent the Swedish and Saxon armies from looting, but many churches and monasteries in southern Germany were devastated by Swedish soldiers.

At this point the emperor had no choice but to reappoint Wallenstein as commander of the troops. Wallenstein cut off Swedish support in southern Germany and forced Gustav to confront him in Saxony. At the ❺ Battle of Lützen on November 16, 1632, Gustav was killed, but

3

Commemoration of the Protestant alliance between Gustav II Adolph of Sweden, the Elector John George I of Saxony, and George William of Brandenburg, 1631

6

Duke Bernhard von Weimar

4

Murder of Wallenstein by his officers in Eger, February 25, 1634

the Protestants still triumphed. However, the Swedish chancellor, Axel Oxenstierna, could not keep the Protestant alliance together, particularly as Wallenstein and the Saxon commander, Hans Georg von Arnim, were secretly

7

Battle of Nördlingen, 1634

5

Gustav II Adolph prays for victory before the Battle of Lützen, 1632

negotiating peace. The strange behavior of Wallenstein, who probably wanted to join the Protestant troops under ❻ Bernhard von Weimar at this stage, convinced Emperor Ferdinand of his commander's betrayal, and he gave his consent for ❹ Wallenstein's murder in Eger by a group of his officers.

The subsequent defeat of Weimar and the Swedes at ❼ Nördlingen led to the Peace of Prague between the emperor and most of the Protestant princes of the empire on May 30, 1635. Ferdinand abandoned the implementation of his Restitution Edict, and all sides agreed to expel foreign powers and mercenaries from the empire. A general war weariness saw all sides embrace the peace.

1630	Gustav II Adolph arrives in Pomerania		**Nov 16, 1632**	Battle of Lützen / Death of Gustav II Adolph		**Sep 1634**	Battle of Nördlingen
		Sep 17, 1631	Battle of Breitenfeld		**Feb 25, 1634**	Wallenstein murdered	

From the Franco-Swedish Phase to the Peace of Westphalia

1635–1648

France engineered the continuation of the war. The last phase was particularly devastating for the civilian population until the Peace of Westphalia ended the conflict in 1648.

Documents marked with the seals of the combatants establishing the Peace of Westphalia in 1648

The end of war in Germany was not in the interests of France, since it was clearly placing a major strain on the rival Habsburgs. Cardinal Richelieu of France continued to support the Protestant commanders with large sums of money and urged them to pursue the war. With this assistance, Swedish general Johan Banér defeated the imperial forces at ❽ Wittstock in 1636, and again at Chemnitz in 1639. Duke Bernhard of Saxe-Weimar also triumphed over imperial troops at Rheinfelden in 1638. In 1645, the Swedes marched as far as Vienna, while French troops were forced back in Bavaria.

After three decades of war the empire was devastated. Whole re-

General Banér in the Battle of Wittstock, 1636, wood engraving, 19th c.

gions in northern Germany, the Palatinate, and Brandenburg were depopulated and desolate and would remain so for decades; in some parts of the empire, as much as half of the population had ❿ died. Prosperous cities had been reduced to small towns or even large villages. The people, particularly the ⓫ peasants, had

suffered appalling hardships: torture, famine, and disease. Bands of desperate people wandered through Germany begging and stealing whatever they could.

From 1644 to 1648, representatives of all powers took part in peace negotiations at ⓬ Münster and Osnabrück, which after long and hard bargaining led to the ❾ Peace of Westphalia. Bavaria retained the title of elector palatine, and an eighth electorate was created for the reinstated son of the "winter king." Switzerland and the Netherlands officially resigned from the Imperial Alliance, and the power of the emperor was restricted to Hungary and Bohemia, his hereditary lands. The princes of the empire gained significantly in power and created their own alliance of sovereign states, of which the emperor was only the nominal head. The actual victors were France and Sweden, who gained territory and underlined their status as great European powers. The Netherlands, too, profited from the weakening of the empire. The Peace of Westphalia established the principle that states could not interfere in each other's affairs on grounds of religious differences.

Song of Praise for the Peace by Paul Gerhard

Praise God! A noble word of Peace and joy rings out,
Which will from now on still The spears and swords and their murdering.
Take courage and take once more to your string,
Playing O Germany and sing songs,
In a high full choir,
Lift your spirits to your God and say,
Lord, Your mercy and goodness Still remains eternal.

Peace of Münster is announced to a crowd in the town square

Mass public hanging, etching, 1632

Peasants flee from the advancing armies, ca. 1645

Peace negotiations in Münster, 1648

The Castle of Nymphenburg in Munich

THE HOLY ROMAN EMPIRE UNDER ENLIGHTENED ABSOLUTISM 1648–1806

The Peace of Westphalia brought the German states complete independence and some, most notably Prussia, would become European powers. Absolutist monarchies came to predominate as a form of rule. The Enlightenment and the belief in reform and progress are reflected in the "enlightened absolutism" of Prussia and Austria. Influenced by the French Revolution and under pressure from Napoleon's military victories, the Holy Roman Empire was finally dissolved in 1806.

■ The Absolutism of the German Princes

With the 18th century came new wars that taxed the empire. Of all the German princes, the electors of Saxony and Bavaria were the most significant.

By 1700, the empire had largely recovered from the damage done by the Thirty Years' War, but new wars—the Eight-Year War (1689–1697), the War of the Spanish Succession (1701–1714), and the Great Northern War (1700–1721)—brought fresh strife.

The German princes of the Baroque period sought to rule like kings. ❶ Prestigious buildings, after the French model, turned

left: Augustus the Strong middle: Maximilian II Emanuel, Elector of Bavaria
right: Klemens August, Elector of Cologne

The Battle of Hochstadt, August 13, 1704

The "Zwinger," a baroque castle in Dresden, painting by Canaletto

the greatest courts into cultural centers and drove the less wealthy into debt and ruin. The most magnificent German court was maintained by Elector Frederick Augustus II of Saxony, who in 1697 also took the throne of Poland. Known as ❷ "Augustus the Strong," he commissioned a number of ❻ architectural projects and was infamous for his nu-

merous love affairs. He made a disastrous attempt to annex territories from Sweden during the Great Northern War, and was temporarily driven out of Poland. ❸ Maximilian II Emanuel of Bavaria was governor of the Spanish Netherlands. In 1683 he was among those who fought the Turks outside Vienna and later fought on France's side in the War of Spanish Succession. After the French defeat at ❺ Hochstadt he was forced out of Bavaria—occupied by the Austrians—and not allowed to return until 1714. Maximilian's son Charles Albert (elector from 1726) occupied Bohemia in 1740 before being elected Holy Roman Emperor, as Charles VII, in Frankfurt in 1742. His brother ❹ Klemens August, "the sun

prince," was elector of Cologne from 1723. In 1714 George Louis, of the House of Hanover, became King George I of Great Britain and Ireland, and his descendants ruled until 1901.

The persecution of the "witches"

The last "witch-trial" in Germany took place in 1775 at the abbey of Kempten. Her story is similar to that of many other victims: The maid Maria Anna Schwegelin had lost her employment, after a suitor had broken their marriage engagement. The woman was put away into a workhouse, where she had to bear the continuous ill-treatment of an attendant. After several arguments the attendant accused her of being in league with the devil, and branded her a "witch."

A witch prays to a demon, wood engraving, 16th century

■ The End of the Empire

Napoleon abolished many of the smaller priestly principalities. Austria's defeats saw the larger German princes assert their independence from the Holy Roman Empire after 1801.

The priestly principalities of the empire were also under absolutist rule. The ruler was often a Prince-Bishop, who held both spiritual and temporal authority over his realm. Both Catholic and Protestant bishops usually originated from ruling royal houses or great noble families and often held several dioceses in their hands. The southwestern German Catholic area was shaped by the ❽ Schönborn family. After 1719, the imperial chancellor and

7 Karl Theodor, Baron of Dalberg

elector of Mainz since 1694, Lothar Franz, gave the most important bishoprics to his four nephews; Johann Philipp Franz in Würzburg, Friedrich Karl in Bamberg and Würzburg, Cardinal Damian Hugo in Speyer and Konstanz, and Franz Georg as elector of Trier. They built up the residences of ❿ Würzburg and Bamberg as well as the palaces of ❾ Bruchsal and ⓫ Pommersfelden and ruled in a manner that has come to be known as enlight-

ened absolutism.

While the princes of the Rhine were swept aside by the French Revolutionary armies after 1792, other German princes successfully allied with Napoleon to weaken Austrian influence. After the 1801 Treaty of Luneville between France and Austria, which headed the Holy Roman Empire, Mainz elector and imperial chancellor ❼ Karl Theodor Baron of Dalberg succeeded in bringing about the Diet's Recess on February 25, 1803. The west side of the Rhine was annexed by France and many of the smaller principalities were abolished, but the major German princes received compensation and their dominions were extended at the expense of city-states and through the requisitioning of Church land. After further defeats Austria's Francis II laid aside the crown of the Holy Roman Empire and declared it dissolved.

The Napoleonic wars had a lasting impact on the political map of Germany, consolidating what had been a patchwork of small states into fewer but larger and more powerful states.

8 Frederick Charles Schönborn

9 The Castle of Bruchsal, begun in 1722

11 Hall of Mirrors in the Castle of Weissenstein, Pommersfelden, built between 1711 and 1718

10 The bishop's residence in Würzburg; frescos painted by Giovanni Battista Tiepolo

◼ The Rise of Austria from Leopold I to Charles VI

Under Leopold I and his sons, Austria increased its power in Europe. Under the command of the talented general, Prince Eugène of Savoy, Austrian forces succeeded in halting, and then reversing, the advance of the Ottoman Turks. Meanwhile the emperors managed to keep France in check.

While Ferdinand III (emperor from 1637) presided over major disruption in the empire resulting from the Thirty Years' War, Austria's political and economic ascendance began under his son ❷ Leopold I, who became emperor in 1658. First, Leopold had to defeat the powerful Turkish army that had advanced out of the Balkans and in 1683 reached the gates of Vienna. An imperial army, under Charles V of Lorraine and the Polish king John III Sobieski, saved the city. They pushed back the Turkish army after a narrow victory at the ❶ Battle of Kahlenberg. Thereafter Leopold promoted himself as "vanquisher of the Turks." In 1696 work began on the building of his imperial residence, the ❸ Schonbrunn Palace.

Despite the victory at Vienna, Leopold was still forced to fight a war on two fronts. While he confronted France's claims to hegemony in the west and in the north of Italy, he continued to fight the Turks, who were allied with France, in the east. His bril-

The Battle of Kahlenberg on September 12, 1683, detail from the tapestry

liant general, ❹ Prince Eugène of Savoy, proved himself by comprehensively defeating the Turkish army at Senta, on the River Tisza, in 1697. In the Peace of Karlowitz (1699), dictated by the emperor, Austria took all of Hungary, Transylvania, and Croatia from the Ottomans. When war broke out again in 1717, Eugène captured Belgrade. The subsequent Peace of Passarowitz (1718) gave Serbia

to Austria and definitively ended the westward advance of the Ottoman Empire.

Leopold was succeeded by his oldest son, Joseph, in 1705. As ❻ Joseph I, he reorganized the government administration and forcibly repressed revolts in the kingdom of Hungary, whose Magyar nobility tended to jealously guard their autonomy and ancient privileges. After his death in 1711 the imperial crown fell to his brother, ❺ Charles VI, who had until then held the throne in Spain.

Under Charles VI Austria grew in economic and military power. As he had no male heirs, his major concern after 1713 was convincing the German princes to recognize his ❼ "Pragmatic Sanction," which changed the rules of succession to secure the crown for his daughter, Maria Theresa. The emperor made concessions to achieve this, but Prussia and Bavaria soon found reasons to disregard the agreement.

Leopold I in theater costume, painting

Interior of Schonbrunn Palace

Prince Eugène of Savoy

Charles VI (and Charles III of Hungary)

Joseph I

The "Pragmatic Sanction," 1713

Austria under Maria Theresa and Joseph II

Maria Theresa defended the Habsburg Empire against Prussia and introduced reforms. These were accelerated by her son, Joseph II, in the spirit of enlightened absolutism.

Francis Stephen of Lorraine, Holy Roman Emperor Francis I

Joseph II with his brother and successor, Leopold II, family portrait

Maria Theresa of Austria, portrait, 1750

In 1740 ❿ Maria Theresa inherited the thrones of Bohemia and Hungary. She immediately had to defend her birthright against King Frederick II of Prussia, who annexed Silesia, and Charles Albert of Bavaria, who occupied Bohemia. In the ⓫ War of Austrian Succession (1740–48), she succeeded in driving the Bavarians out of Bohemia, but Silesia remained Prussian. However, in 1745, Frederick II recognized the election of Maria Theresa's husband, ❽ Francis Stephen of Lorraine, as Holy Roman Emperor Francis I. The royal pair, together with their 16 children, founded the royal house of Habsburg-Lorraine.

Maria Theresa sought to bring greater uniformity and centralization to Austria through cautious reforms. Notably she reorganized the legal system, and improved education provision through a general school reform in 1774. With her chancellor of state, Prince Kaunitz, and in alliance with France and Russia, she attempted to win Silesia back from Prussia in the Seven Years' War (1756–1763). However, the war was not a success and the Treaty of Hubertusburg left the country financially ruined.

After Francis's death, his eldest son, ❾ Joseph II, became co-regent of Austria but did not attain real power until 1780. Strongly influenced by the ideas of the Enlightenment, he pushed through the enactment of many liberal reforms, such as the abolishment of torture and serfdom, complete freedom of the press, the emancipation of the Jews, and a reduction in the pomp of the court. In his Edict of Toleration (1781), Joseph granted complete freedom of religion, and later established new schools and orphanages. However his ambitious reform plans relied too much on central authority in a multi-ethnic state where special privileges for regions and groups were the rule. Thus Joseph's hasty attempts to impose enlightened ideas through despotic means swiftly ran into opposition and the results fell well short of his radical ambitions. His brother and successor Leopold II was more cautious but attempted to maintain the overall direction of the reforms. However, his son, Francis II, was forced to give up the imperial crown of the Holy Roman Empire in 1806.

Joseph II, portrait, 1785

Extract from Joseph II's *Edict of Toleration*, December 21, 1781

"*As we are convinced that every coercion that violates the conscience of humans is highly damaging; that in contrast extraordinary advantage for religion and the state come from true tolerance as prescribed by Christian love, so we have decided to implement these in all our hereditary lands.*"

Prussia defeats the army of Austria and Saxony at Hohenfriedberg

Joachim II from the House of Hohen-zollern, elector of Brandenburg from 1535 to 1571, copper engraving, 1570

The Rise of Prussia

After the Hohenzollern family had established themselves in Brandenburg, the Great Elector Frederick William made the region one of the leading forces in the empire. His son Frederick I secured the royal status of Prussia's rulers.

In 1411 King Sigismund made the Margraves of Nuremberg from the House of Hohenzollern governors of the province of Brandenburg. Four years later he granted them the title of elector. The first rulers quickly established their authority in the cities. ❶ Joachim II joined the Reformation movement in 1539 but, like his successor, stood by the emperor. The rise of Brandenburg began with ❷ John Sigismund, who converted to Calvinism in 1613. In 1614 he acquired Cleves, Mark, and Ravensberg on the Rhine during the dispute over the Jülich-Cleves succession. In 1618

he inherited ducal Prussia, which had been founded in 1525 on the lands once held by the Teutonic Order.

Brandenburg was ravaged by the Thirty Years' War, as troops of both sides marched through to battle. When ❸ Frederick William, the Great Elector, came to power in 1640, he resolutely set about reconstruction. After centralizing the tax system he acquired further territories (East Pomerania, Minden, and Halberstadt) through playing the emperor and France against one another. In 1675 he defeated the Swedish army at Fehrbellin and drove them out of Germany by seizing Swedish Pomerania and Rügen. His Pots-

John Sigismund, elector of Brandenburg

dam Edict of Tolerance (1685) was a landmark and paved the way for receiving the Huguenots, who were driven out of France. The absolutist ruler left his successors a centralized state with a strong standing army, which was well on the way to becoming a major European power.

His son ❹ Frederick III, together with his wife, the Welf princess Sophie Charlotte, turned the country into a glittering baroque state. They promoted the arts, built palaces (such as Berlin's Charlottenburg), and founded universities. In return for providing military aid to the emperor in the War of Spanish Succession, he was granted the royal status he had desired. On January 18, 1701, in Königsberg he had himself ❺ crowned Frederick I, marking the arrival of a powerful new dynasty in Europe.

3 Frederick William, "Great Elector" of Brandenburg, portrait painting, 1649

Frederick III, elector of Brandenburg, later Frederick I, king of Prussia

Coronation of Frederick I on January 18, 1701 in Königsberg, painting, 19th c.

Allegory of the reception of Protestants from Salzburg as they arrive in Frederick William I's Prussia

The Huguenots

When the Great Elector invited the Huguenots to settle in the cities and barren stretches of land in Brandenburg-Prussia, more than 20,000 accepted his invitation. By 1700 they made up about a third of the population of Berlin. Among them were craftsmen, who brought new skills with them from France, as well as prosperous merchants, who developed the city's connections to international trade, providing a major boost to the Prussian economy.

| Apr 18, 1525 | Teutonic Order's lands become Ducal Prussia | 1640 | Frederick William becomes Great Elector | 1675 | Battle of Fehrbellin |
| 1618 | John Sigismund inherits Prussia | 1660 | Prussia gains sovereignty | 1685 | Edict of Tolerance of Potsdam |

Prussia under the Soldier King and Frederick the Great

Through the creation of an effective centralized administration and a powerful army, the Soldier King, Frederick William I, and his son, the enlightened despot Frederick the Great, turned Prussia into one of the greatest powers in Europe.

Frederick William I inspecting the results of his education reforms in a Prussian school, painting

In 1713 Frederick William I, the "Soldier King," came to power. He was determined to cement his father's legacy with further reform to increase his dynasty's power and prestige. A straight-laced and thrifty Puritan, he sought to introduce a martial discipline into the bureaucracy and other aspects of the Prussian state. His was the largest standing army in Europe, accounting for three-quarters of the state's expenses. The mercantilist economy was forced to serve the needs of this military force. More progressively, he introduced ❻ compulsory primary education in 1717 and prohibited the physical punishment of serfs. Frederick William was pragmatic in foreign affairs, maintaining the alliance with Hanoverian England despite personal antipathy toward its rulers and occupying former Swedish West Pomerania without resistance in 1720. In 1732 he allowed the Salzburg Protestants, who had been expelled from Austria, to settle in the region, which boosted Prussia's economy. Prussia's "greatest domestic king" determined the character of the Prussian state until well into the 19th century.

His son ❼ Frederick II (the Great), despite severe conflicts with his unyielding father during his youth, retained Frederick William's system of government— contrary to expectations— yet was simultaneously a passionate adherent of the Enlightenment and French aesthetics. As the ❾ "philosopher of Sanssouci" and a ❽ talented flutist, he surrounded himself with eminent free-thinkers and artists, including ❿ Voltaire. He also used the army to expand Prussian territory, wresting Silesia from Austria in the War of Austrian Succession (1740–48). During the ⓫ Seven Years' War (1756–1763), Prussia was brought to the verge of destruction by the alliance of Austria, France, Russia, and Saxony, and was saved only by the death of the Russian empress in 1762. In 1772 Prussia participated, along with Russia and Austria, in the first partition of Poland. Domestically, Frederick bound the aristocracy into the leadership of the state and army and improved the educational system. The cost of his wars was borne by his subjects, but he made Prussia a dominant power and established the "Prussian myth."

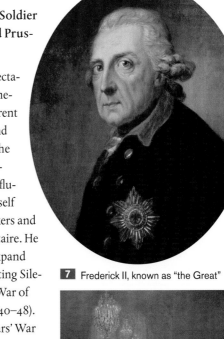

7   Frederick II, known as "the Great"

8   Frederick the Great gives a flute concert, painting by Adolph von Menzel, 1850/52

9   The Palace of Sanssouci in Potsdam

10   King Frederick II dining in Sanssouci, with guests including Voltaire and Friedrich von Stille, painting by Adolph von Menzel, 1850

Frederick the Great, 1743

"I hope posterity will know to differentiate in me the philosopher from the prince, the gentleman from the politician. I must admit: it is hard for he who is pulled into great European politics to maintain his honest and pure character."

11   Frederick the Great in the Battle of Zorndorf on the August 25, 1758 during the Seven Years' War

France: From the Wars of Religion to the Eve of the Revolution 1562–1789

The last kings of the House of Valois were bested by the Habsburgs in the struggle for supremacy in Italy. Domestically, they had to contend with religious schism and a powerful and fractious nobility. The kings of the House of Bourbon presided over conflict between Catholics and Protestants. After compromises failed, a policy of repression saw the forced expulsion of the Protestant Huguenots. A series of capable kings and ministers built up an absolutist monarchy and made France a great European power. French became the universal language of European diplomacy and aristocratic society while Paris became the center of European culture. Under weaker successors, costly wars drained the royal coffers, and political and economic crises paved the way for social upheaval and revolution.

The Castle of Chambord, built by Francis I

The Struggle Against the Habsburgs

Francis I and his successors tried to weaken the power of the Habsburgs. The spread of Calvinism led to the first conflicts. At the same time, Renaissance ideas and culture became predominant in France.

In 1515 ❶, ❷ Francis I, a member of a side branch of the House of Valois, ascended to the throne of France. During his reign, the

Double grave monument of Henry II and Catherine de Médicis in the Abbey of St. Denis near Paris

The Protestant church "Le Paradis" in Lyon, painting, 17th century

French court developed into a center of the European Renaissance, attracting important artists such as ❺ Leonardo da Vinci and Andrea del Sarto. Francis also spent money building up a considerable collection of Italian paintings including works by Titian and Raphael.

In foreign affairs, the king, like his predecessors, continued to compete with the Habsburgs for dominance in central Europe and Italy. Having lost out to Charles V for the emperor's crown in 1519, Francis was then defeated by him in the Italian Wars. Despite these reverses, Francis managed to cause his adversary considerable difficulty by allying himself with the Ottoman Empire and forcing the emperor into a war on two fronts. In the end, neither side managed to prevail.

Francis I was succeeded in 1547 by his son ❸ Henry II, who was married to Catherine de Médicis.

She was the niece of Pope Clement VII, an ally against the Habsburgs. Henry was under the political influence of his mistress, Diane de Poitiers, and on her advice, he took repressive measures against the ❹ French Protestants—even though he supported the Protestant princes of Germany with money and weapons—in their rebellion against the Habsburgs. Henry only accepted Habsburg dominance in Italy after a costly war that ended with the signing of the Treaty of Cateau-Cambrésis in 1559.

In the same year, the king was accidentally wounded in a joust and died from his injuries. His eldest son Francis II died one year after acceding to the throne. Charles IX and Henry III proved to be weak

2 Portrait of Francis I, bronze medallion by Benvenuto Cellini, 16th century

kings. The latter struggled to cope with the intrigues of his mother, Catherine, and the Duke of Guise, and with the religious turbulence that soon engulfed France.

Francis I at the death bed of Leonardo da Vinci, painting by Jean-Auguste-D. Ingres, 19th century

6

The Guise brothers, leaders of the Catholic faction; from left: Duke Charles of Mayenne, Duke Henry I of Guise, and Cardinal Louis of Lorraine, portrait from the 16th century

Excerpt from the Edict of Nantes, issued by Henry IV:

"We forbid all our subjects, of some state and quality that they are, to renew the memory, to attack, to feel, to scold, or to provoke each other by reproach of what took place, for some cause and excuse whether it is, to compete for it, to dispute, quarrel or offend itself or take offence actually or at word, but contain itself and live peacefully together as brothers, friends and fellow countrymen..."

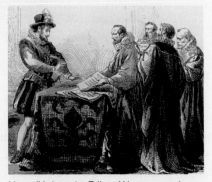

Henry IV signs the Edict of Nantes, wood engraving, 19th century

■ The French Wars of Religion and the Edict of Nantes

Bloody religious wars engulfed France during the reign of the last Valois king, Henry III. His successor, Henry IV of the House of Bourbon, was the first to be able to restore calm to the country with the Edict of Nantes.

Originating in the Swiss Cantons, Calvinism gradually spread to France and steadily gained followers from the middle of the 16th century on. They were called Huguenots, a French derivative from the German word *Eidgenossen* ("Swiss confederate"). A substantial proportion of the nobility became Huguenots— particularly the Bourbons, who not only had large holdings in France but also ruled as sovereign kings in neighboring Navarre. Being relatives of the Valois, they also had hereditary claims to the French throne. The mighty Catholic ❻ dukes of Guise were hostile to them.

Catherine de Médicis tried to play the factions off against one another to preserve the authority of the crown. To bind the Bourbons to her, she married off her daughter, Margaret, to Henry of Navarre in 1572. At the same time she planned to do away with the leader of the Huguenots, ❿ Gaspard de Coligny. When the assassination attempt failed, Catherine and the House of Guise, fearing revenge, initiated a massacre of thousands of Huguenots who had remained in Paris after the wedding on the ❾ night of St. Bartholomew's. Henry of Navarre fled to his kingdom, and his marriage to Margaret was later annulled.

A civil war broke out in France between the religious factions, including the nobility and the royal family. The "Holy League" of Catholics, founded in 1576 under the leadership of the dukes of Guise, allied with the Habsburgs, while the Huguenots were supported by England. In 1574, Catherine's third son, Henry III, then reigning as the king of Poland, ascended to the French throne. He had no children and when the last of his brothers died in 1584, Henry of Navarre became

7

Henry IV on horseback and wearing a suit of armor, statue, Paris

the successor. Five years later, a monk murdered ❽ Henry III, and the Bourbon Huguenot Henry of Navarre succeeded him as ❼, ⓫ Henry IV. In order to be recognized as king, he converted to Catholicism in 1593, famously saying, "Paris is worth a Mass." In 1598 he signed the Edict of Nantes that granted rights to France's Protestant minority. He was murdered in 1610.

8

Dominican monk murders Henry III, copper engraving, 17th century

9

The St. Bartholomew's Day Massacre, August 23–24, 1572

10

Gaspard de Coligny, portrait, 16th c.

11

Coronation of Henry IV in Chartres, 1594

Aug 23–24, 1572 | Saint Bartholomew's Day Massacre   **1589** | Assassination of Henry III   **1598** | Edict of Nantes

1576 | Founding of the "Holy League"   **1593** | Henry IV converts to Catholicism

The Rise of France under Henry IV and Cardinal Richelieu

Under the leadership of the cunning strategist Cardinal Richelieu, France was able to weaken the power of the Habsburgs in the Thirty Years' War and to centralize the French state.

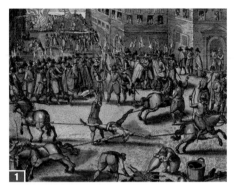

Ravaillac, the murderer of Henry IV, is quartered, colored copper engraving, early 17th century

After the turmoil of the Wars of Religion, Henry IV and his minister Sully set about reconstructing France. But in 1610 the king was murdered by the Catholic fanatic ❶ Ravaillac. ❹ Maria de Medici, the mother of Henry's son who was still a minor, ran the affairs of state for him. In 1616, she brought the future Cardinal Richelieu into the court. He won the confidences of the reserved ❸ Louis XIII and rose to become the leading minister in 1624. Such was his power that, following a conspiracy, he even forced the queen mother to flee the country.

Internationally, the gifted and unscrupulous power broker Richelieu sought to make France the leading power in Europe, while domestically he worked to strengthen the monarchy. He began by abolishing some of the special privileges of the nobility and oversaw a military campaign to crush the power of the French-protestant Huguenots. Provincial revolts against tax rises were also brutally suppressed. At the same time, he was a generous patron of the ❺ arts and founded the *Académie française.*

In foreign affairs, he seized the chance offered by the Thirty Years' War to weaken France's major rival, the Habsburgs. With cool calculation, he supported the Protestant princes against the Catholic emperor with both money and weapons. He also persuaded Gustav II Adolph of Sweden to fight the Habsburgs. Richelieu died in 1642, followed a year later by the king he had served, Louis XIII. France profited from the cardinal's aggressive policies in the Peace of Westphalia signed in 1648. The country gained territories in Alsace and the Pyrenees at the expense of the Habsburg Empire.

After his death, another Cardinal,

Cardinal Mazarin, copy of a painting by Champaigne, 17th century

Queen Anna of Austria, King Louis XIII, and Cardinal Richelieu, still from the film *The Three Musketeers*

the Italian ❷ Mazarin, became first minister of the French government. He initially ruled with Anna of Austria, Louis XIII's widow, who acted as regent for her son, Louis XIV.

The Three Musketeers

Today, Richelieu is less known for his political achievements and services to the arts and culture – he was elected principal of the Sorbonne in 1622 – than for the role he plays in Alexandre Dumas' novel The Three Musketeers. In it the young guardsman d'Artagnan fights together with the three inseparable musketeers, Athos, Porthos, and Aramis, against the sinister Richelieu. With the help of the mysterious Lady de Winter, the jealous cardinal is determined to uncover a love affair between Queen Anna of Austria and the English prime minister, Buckingham.

above: Duel between the king's musketeers and Cardinal Richelieu's guard, watercolor sketch

Triumph of the regent Maria de Medici, painting by Rubens, 1623

The chapel of the Sorbonne, sponsored by Richelieu

The reign of the the "Sun King" Louis XIV

Cardinal Mazarin continued Richelieu's policies and established the foundations of the absolutism of Louis XIV. During his reign France became the leading European power, both culturally and politically. The opulent royal court at Versailles became a model for rulers throughout the continent.

6 Inciting a crowd against Mazarin, the Louvre of Paris in the background, etching, 17th century

7 King Louis XIV of France, painting by Rigaud, 1701

Though the Peace of Westphalia in 1648 marked a major success for Mazarin, his domestic power base was weak. In a series of armed uprisings known as the *Fronde*, dissident French nobles **6** revolted against the authority of the king and his ministers between 1648 and 1653. It proved to be the last revolt of the French nobility, and henceforth they would be subordinate to the power of the ruling monarch and his royal court.

Upon the death of the cardinal in 1661, **7** Louis XIV took personal charge of the affairs of state. The **9** Palace of Versailles, the new royal residence located outside the capital Paris, became a symbol of the king's alleged claim *"L'état c'est moi"* ("I am the state"). Woods and **10** landscaped parks ran up to the palace, with the Hall of Mirrors and the **8** Royal Bedchamber as its center. The vast court of almost 20,000 people was the physical embodiment of Louis XIV's claim to rule by "divine right." His palace and his court were imitated by princes throughout Europe.

As in Versailles, everything in the state was supposed to be concentrated on the monarch known as the "Sun King." He did not tolerate overweening ministers like Richelieu or Mazarin. Several ministers together saw to the details of government for him. The finance minister, Jean-Baptiste Colbert, was also in charge of building up the fleet and an active colonial policy focussed on North America and India. Under his supervision the royal coffers swelled. His rival, the Minister of War, François Michel Louvois, built up one of the mightiest armies in Europe and pressured the king into an expansionist foreign policy. Despite fighting a series of wars both in Europe and the New World, France made few territorial gains.

The French Protestants suffered as Louis XIV sought to establish the supremacy of the French Catholic Church with himself at its head. He revoked the Edict of Nantes in 1685 and expelled the Huguenots from France. The flight of the Huguenots was a major loss to the French economy because the Protestants had played a significant role as merchants and skilled manufacturers. These refugees successfully established themselves in neighboring Protestant countries, building thriving communities in both Amsterdam and London.

8 The lavishly decorated royal bedchamber in the Palace of Versailles, near Paris

9 The Palace of Versailles, originally a hunting lodge but by 1682 Louis XIV's main residence

10 View from the Palace of Versailles, across the formal gardens, down toward the Grand Canal

	1648 Peace of Westphalia	**1661** Reign of Louis XIV begins	
1643 Cardinal Mazarin takes over affairs of state	**1648–1653** Civil wars of the Fronde	**1685** Revocation of the Edict of Nantes	

The Wars of Louis XIV

In his attempts to enlarge France's borders, Louis XIV drew other European states into a series of conflicts. The War of the Grand Alliance and the War of the Spanish Succession were inconclusive but nonetheless showed that France could not maintain its hegemony on the continent.

Louis XIV, with the help of his generals Condé, ❶ Turenne, ❷ Vauban, and Vendôme, waged numerous wars of aggression. Although territories were gained in the campaigns against Spain and the Netherlands—Spain, for example, was forced to relinquish Burgundy and parts of its Dutch territories in the Peace of Nijmegen in 1679—French expansionism led to a permanent alliance among the Habsburgs and most of the German princes, England, and the Netherlands.

Louis used the death of the Palatinate elector as an opportunity to make hereditary claims in the name of his sister-in-law,

2
Plan of the city of Freiburg showing the defenses established by Vauban, ink sketch, 1685

Elizabeth Charlotte, duchess of Orléans. In 1688 he occupied the Palatinate and other parts of the Holy Roman Empire, and in the process his armies pillaged a number of cities, including ❹ Heidelberg. This aggression ensured the unity of the Grand Alliance against France. A drawn-out war followed, in which the French navy was destroyed by a combined Anglo-Dutch fleet, but France held its

own on land. The 1697 Treaty of Ryswick did little other than restore the pre-war status quo.

The ❺ War of Spanish Succession began in 1701 after the line of the Spanish Habsburgs died out, and the throne was claimed by both the Austrian Habsburgs and the French Bourbons. Louis wished to place his grandson, Philippe Duke of Anjou, on the Spanish throne, while the Habsburgs backed a non-Bourbon candidate. Despite the defeat of the French armies in the war that followed, Philippe was confirmed king of Spain in 1713 at the Peace of Utrecht. However, he was removed from the French line to prevent a union of France and Spain. The Austrian Habsburgs also gained most of the former Spanish territories in the Low Countries and Italy.

Despite Louis XIV's attempts to expand his dominion through war and diplomacy, a policy that placed a ❸ heavy burden on the French population, French supremacy was replaced by a new

1
Henri de La Tour d'Auvergne, Count of Turenne, painting by Le Brun, 17th c.

balance of power in Europe, with the Habsburgs and English kings able to counterbalance France.

Liselotte of the Palatinate

Princess Elizabeth Charlotte, "Madame," was married to Philippe I, duke of Orléans and brother of Louis XIV, in 1671. The completely unpretentious duchess was known as "Madame." She had a difficult position at the French court alongside "Monsieur," her husband, who did not bother to conceal his numerous homosexual affairs. She vented her anger in innumerable often caustic letters to her German relatives: "Being a Madame is a wretched trade."

above: Elizabeth Charlotte of the Palatinate, Duchess of Orléans, portrait, ca. 1715

3
Collecting the taxes: "The nobleman is the spider, the peasant the fly," satirical cartoon, 17th c.

4
The Castle of Heidelberg, seized by the French army during the War of the Grand Alliance

5
Victory of the Austrians and British, led by Prince Eugène and the Duke of Marlborough, over the French army at Malplaquet, 1709

1667 | War of Devolution in the Spanish Netherlands   **1688** | War of the Grand Alliance begins   **1701** | War of the Spanish Succession begins

1679 | Peace of Nijmegen   **1697** | Treaty of Ryswick   **1713** | Peace of Utrecht

France under Louis XV and Louis XVI

Louis XIV's heirs possessed neither his political ambition nor his abilities, but they were confronted by endemic financial crises. At the same time the institution of absolutist monarchy came under increasing attack from radical writers inspired by the ideas of the Enlightenment.

Louis XIV outlived both his son and his grandson and was followed to the throne in 1715 by his five-year-old great-grandson ❻, ❽ Louis XV.

Even after coming of age, Louis XV left the running of the government to the acting regent Cardinal Fleury. The cardinal cleaned up the state finances and tried as far as possible to keep France out of international conflicts. Louis's marriage to Maria Leszczynska—daughter of the

❻ Louis XV's crown

Polish king Stanislaw I, who had been deposed and wanted to regain his throne—was the only entanglement. Instead of his throne, Stanislaw received the duchy of Lorraine in 1737, which reverted to France after his death in 1766.

After the death of Fleury in 1743, Louis increasingly came under the influence of his mistresses. Perhaps the most significant of them was the ❸ Marquise de Pompadour. She originated from the bourgeoisie and maintained an influence over French policies— even after her sexual relationship with the king ended— for almost 20 years, until her death in 1764. She was influential in France's alliance with Austria against Prussia and England in the ❿ Seven Years' War (1756–1763), which ended in defeat and humiliation for France. The huge expense of fighting against England in the New World, where France lost her last colonial possessions, took a massive toll on the royal finances.

The court was maintained in luxury at enormous expense, while the living standards of the ⓫ common people, on whom most tax burden fell, remained low. At the end of Louis' reign, France was virtually bankrupt. At the same time, the ideas of the Enlightenment were gaining currency. ❼ Voltaire, Montesquieu,

and Rousseau developed their ideas of a just and enlightened society and attacked the despotism of absolutist monarchy. Many minor writers popularized these ideas in satirical poems and pamphlets that stirred up resentment towards the king's lifestyle.

Louis XV's successor in 1774 was his grandson Louis XVI, who had been married since 1770 to ⓬ Marie Antoinette, a daughter of Maria Theresa. She was widely attacked in the radical press. As the financial situation worsened, Louis looked to reform but failed to win the cooperation of the nobility, who sought to protect their ❾ privileges. In an attempt to break the deadlock, the king summoned the States General in 1788, an assembly of the clergy, nobility, and commoners that had not met since 1614. Radical populist figures, backed by the hungry crowds of Paris, quickly came to dominate the assembly, firing the opening salvos of the French Revolution.

❽ Louis XV, painting by Maurice-Quentin de La Tour, 18th century

❿ French Québec in ruins after bombardment by the British fleet in 1759 during the Seven Years' War

❼ Voltaire, sculpture by Houdon, 1778

❾ A peasant carries the nobility and clergy on his back, cartoon satirizing the social order, 18th century

⓬ Queen Marie Antoinette, portrait by Élisabeth-Louise Vigée-Lebrun, 1783

⓭ Madame de Pompadour, portrait by François Boucher, 1756-58

⓫ *Old Peasant Couple Eating*, painting by Georges de la Tour, ca. 1620

THE RISE OF ENGLAND 1485–CA. 1800

The history of modern England began with the reign of the Tudors in 1485. They turned England once more into a player in European politics. The Stuarts, who reigned from 1603, united England and Scotland into an empire that has been named Great Britain since 1707, but did not succeed in establishing absolutism after the French model. Parliament was able to impose a constitutional monarchy during the civil war between 1642 and 1649 and finally in the "Glorious Revolution" of 1688–89. Furthermore, in the Act of Settlement parliament ensured that any future monarch of England would be Protestant. In 1714, the elector of Hanover inherited the British throne. In the 18th century, Great Britain finally became a world power through its ❶ sea trade and colonial policies.

Flagship of the British Royal Navy

■ England under Henry VII and Henry VIII

The first two Tudor rulers ruthlessly expanded the power of the monarchy. England was severed from the ecclesiastical sovereignty of the pope, and opposition in the country was suppressed.

In 1485, ❷ Henry Tudor, the Lancastrian heir, defeated Richard III from the rival House of York at Bosworth Field and seized the throne as Henry VII. He ended the War of the Roses by marrying Elizabeth of York, Richard III's niece. With strict economizing and high taxes, he brought the state finances into order. He also centralized jurisdiction in the royal supreme court.

The ascent to the throne of his son ❸ Henry VIII in 1509 was greeted at first with enthusiasm. Initially, his politics were determined by Cardinal ❺ Thomas

Henry VIII, painting by Hans Holbein the younger, 1540

Wolsey, who developed royal centralism and abroad followed a seesaw policy between the Habsburgs and France. In 1528, Henry

left: Henry VIII and his wives; Anne of Cleves, Kathryn Howard, Anna Boleyn, Catherine of Aragon, Catherine Parr, Jane Seymour, lithograph, 19th century
near right: Hampton Court Palace near London, residence of Cardinal Wolsey, later confiscated by Henry VIII during the church reforms
far right: Byland Abbey in Yorkshire, former Cistercian abbey, abolished by Henry VIII

decided to divorce his wife, Catherine of Aragon, the aunt of Charles V, partly because of the lack of a male heir but also because of his love for Anne Boleyn, a lady of the court. Under pressure from the Habsburgs, the pope wouldn't allow the divorce, and the process took years.

During this period, Henry's reign degenerated into tyranny. Cardinal Wolsey was dismissed in 1529 and charged with high treason. Thomas More, Wolsey's successor as lord chancellor, was executed. With the aid of the new, unscrupulous lord chancellor Thomas Cromwell, the king severed the English church from the papacy in 1534, creating an Angli-

Henry VII's coat of arms with the white rose and the red rose, the symbols of houses of Lancaster and York

can state church with the king as its head. Catholic ❻ church properties were confiscated or given to nobility, and monasteries were disbanded. After his first divorce, Henry VIII married five more times; two of his ❹ wives were executed. No English king had ever possessed so much personal power, which Henry used to dispose of opposing nobility and adversaries of his church policies.

| 1485 | Reign of Henry VII begins | 1516 | Thomas More's *Utopia* | 1534 | Anglican Church splits from Roman Church | 1547 | Edward VI crowned |

| 1509 | Cardinal Wolsey rules under Henry VIII | 1529 | Wolsey dismissed | 1535 | Thomas More murdered |

The Reign of the Tudors to Elizabeth I

Anglicanism strengthened its position during the reigns of Henry VIII's children, with but one interruption for a short phase of Catholic revanchism. Elizabeth I's naval policies simultaneously made England a great European power.

Henry VIII was followed in 1547 by his young son Edward VI, whose regency was contested by the dukes of Somerset and Northumberland. During his reign, the Anglican archbishop of Canterbury, Thomas Cranmer, formulated the creed and in 1553 the 42 articles of faith of the Anglicans as well as the renowned Book of Common Prayer. Edward was followed to the throne in 1553

The Catholic Queen Mary Tudor, painting, 16th century

Elizabeth I with the Armada in the background, painting, 1588

by his elder sister ❼ Mary, the Catholic daughter of Henry's first wife Catherine of Aragon. In 1554, she restored papal jurisdiction in England and married her cousin Philip II of Spain. Her brutal persecution of Protestants—among them Archbishop Cranmer, who was burned at the stake in 1556—

earned her the nickname "Bloody Mary."

In 1558, Mary's Protestant half-sister ❾ Elizabeth I, the daughter of Anne Boleyn, came to power. Though declared illegitimate, she had been magnificently educated in the "new learning" of the

❽ Sir Francis Drake, miniature, 16th c.

Renaissance. At first she acted cautiously in religious affairs, but then in 1564, with the "Thirty-Nine Articles" she finally secured the position of the Anglican state church. After the elimination of Mary Stuart's claims to the throne, Elizabeth supported the Protestant Netherlands in their struggle for liberation, which led to war with Spain. The English fleet annihilated the numerically far superior Spanish ❶ Armada in 1588, which dramatically marked the end of Spanish supremacy at sea and the rise of English sea power. Afterward, Elizabeth had

Spanish ships captured in an unofficial war by privateers like ❽ Francis Drake. It was increasingly clear that England was becoming a leading European power.

Domestically, the unmarried queen understood how to deftly play her ❿ favorites and aides against each other and assert the monarchy's authority. The Elizabethan Age produced a tremendous upswing in trade, as well as significant cultural achievements, of which the works of ❿ William Shakespeare are a shining example. In 1584, Elizabeth gave Sir Walter Raleigh permission to set up the first English colony in North America. It was named Virginia after the "virgin queen." In 1600, the East India Company— an important factor in trade and colonial policies—was chartered.

Confrontation of the English Navy (left) with the Spanish Armada (right), copper engraving, 18th century

Elizabeth I surrounded by her household, painting, ca. 1580

Thomas More

Thomas More, who in 1516 wrote about an ideal state in the novel Utopia, *became lord chancellor of England in 1529 after long experience as a member of Parliament. As he rejected the divorce of the king and the Reformation, he stepped down, but he was still accused by Henry VIII of high treason for refusing to recognize the Act of Supremacy that designated the king as head of the church and beheaded in July 1535. In 1935, the Catholic Church canonized him as a martyr.*

Arrest and execution of Thomas More, painting, 16th century

London Globe Theatre reconstructed to look as it did in Shakespeare's time

■ The Reign of the Stuarts

The personal union of the crowns of England and Scotland was brought about by James I, the son of Mary Stuart, in 1603. He and his son Charles I failed with their idea of an absolute monarchy, and Charles was executed.

When the House of Tudor died out with Elizabeth I in 1603, King James VI of the Scottish ❺ Stuarts succeeded in England as James I. James's mother, ❶ Mary

1 Mary Stuart, painting, 16th century

4 James I and VI, painting, 17th century

Stuart, known as Mary Queen of Scots, a granddaughter of Henry VII and a Scottish queen since birth, had raised a claim to the English throne in 1558. The Catholic queen saw in Elizabeth only the illegitimate child of Henry VIII and not a rightful claimant to the throne. During her reign in Scotland, a Calvinistic Reformation took place under ❸ John Knox that combined with civil wars and acts of violence even in the immediate surroundings of the queen. In 1578 Mary was deposed by a rebellion of Protestant nobles and imprisoned. She managed to escape to England, but was held captive there as well. When her intimate friends and England's Catholics tried to set her free, Queen Elizabeth had her charged with high treason and, in 1587, ❻ executed.

❹ James I tried to bring about a reconciliation between the faiths. He wanted to establish royal absolutism in England after the union of the two kingdoms, but failed due to the resistance of Parliament. The dispute over royal rights continued, but James adopted the Anglican state

church model, which disappointed the Catholics. He insisted on the principle of the Divine Right of Kings to rule.

James's second son ❷ Charles I, who took over the throne from his father in 1625, also tended toward absolutism and approached Spain against the will of Parliament. Up until 1640, he reacted to the resistance of the members of Parliament by repeatedly dissolving Parliament or not calling it into session, which inflamed the temper of the country. His unfortunate ecclesiastical policies led to revolts in Scotland and his permanent financial crisis forced him to summon the so-called Long Parliament, which ousted the king's favorites and leading ministers, and stayed in session until 1653. The parliamentary majority led by John Pym allied itself with the Scots, and in 1642 a civil war broke out, with the king and the

2 The Stuart king Charles II from three perspectives, painting by Paul van Dyck, ca. 1635

3 John Knox, copper engraving

royalist minority opposing the parliamentary majority, whose troops were commanded by Oliver Cromwell. After several defeats, in 1644–45 the king fled to Scotland but was handed over to the English Parliament in 1646. In 1647 he escaped and war broke out again, but in 1648 Charles I was recaptured and, after a trial before the Lower House, ❼ executed for high treason in London in 1649.

5 Holyrood Palace, the residence of the Scottish kings, construction begun in 1528, 19th century photograph

6 The execution of Mary Stuart, on February 8, 1587 in Fotheringhay

7 Execution of Charles I in front of the Banqueting House in London, copper engraving, 17th century

1587 | Beheading of Mary Stuart   **1625** | Charles I becomes king   **1642** | Civil war beaks out   **1646** | Charles I is handed over to the Parliamentarians

1603-25 | Reign of James I   **1640** | Calling of the "Long Parliament"   **1644–45** | Flight of Charles I   **Jan 30, 1649** | Beheading of Charles I

■ The "Glorious Revolution"

Oliver Cromwell abolished the monarch and ruled as lord protector over England, but in 1660 the Stuarts were restored to the throne. The Catholic James II was removed from power in the "Glorious Revolution" of 1688–89.

❽ Oliver Cromwell, leader of the English Puritans, abolished the monarchy in 1649 and proclaimed England a Protestant "free state," in the first stage of the English civil war. There was an immediate uprising by the Scots and Irish in 1649–1650, which Cromwell bloodily suppressed. Although he aspired to a republic, Cromwell dissolved Parliament in 1653 and, when it did not settle its internal strife, made himself "lord protector" with ❿ dictatorial powers, refusing the title of king. In foreign affairs, Cromwell strengthened England's supremacy at sea through well-directed colonial and trade policies and prevailed over the Netherlands in their trade rivalry. After his death in 1658, his son Richard could not

hold onto power and abdicated, clearing the way for the restoration of the Stuarts.

In 1660 ❾ Charles II, the son of Charles I, returned from exile. Though the new monarch punished the republicans, he worked for a political reconciliation of all parties. The Habeas Corpus Act, an important milestone in civil rights—under which no person may be held in custody without judicial review and being duly charged with an offense—was passed by Parliament in 1679.

8 Parliament in session, back of the state seal created by Oliver Cromwell in 1651

in 1686–87. The birth of his son in 1688 fed fears of a permanent Catholic and absolutist monarchy in England. Parliament, the army, and the middle class then offered the crown to the Protestant regent of the Netherlands, ⓫ William of Orange. In the "Glorious Revolution" of 1688–89, William landed in England and expelled James to France in December 1688. William III and his wife Mary II, James II's Protestant daughter from his first marriage, then ascended the throne as joint sover-

During Charles II's reign, the ❿ "Great Fire of London" broke out in 1666. It destroyed large parts of the city and made extensive reconstruction of the city necessary.

When Charles's Catholic brother, ⓬ James II, ascended to the throne in 1685, some of the nobles arose in protest but were subdued. Overturning a ban instituted by Charles II, James gave government posts to Catholics, and he proclaimed religious freedom for Catholics and those diverging from the state church

eigns after they had acquiesced to the "Declaration of Right" presented to them by Parliament and later incorporated into an Act of Parliament known as the Bill of Rights. The Bill of Rights established the rights of Parliament in relationship to the crown and a constitutional monarchy controlled by Parliament.

Charles II, painting, 17th century

Map of London after the fire of 1666, copper engraving, 18th century

11 William of Orange, the future king William III, sails to England, painting, 1689

13 Puritans under orders from Oliver Cromwell search and arrest noblemen, painting, 19th century

12 James II's cruelties to the Protestants in Ireland, copper engraving, 17th century

The Gunpowder Plot

Catholic nobility loyal to James I swore to blow up Parliament when it opened in 1605. They hid a great quantity of gunpowder in the cellar of Parliament, but the conspiracy was betrayed and the plotters caught and executed. The failure of the Gunpowder Plot is still celebrated in Great Britain on November 5 as Guy Fawkes Day.

Execution of the participants in the Gunpowder Plot, copper engraving, 17th century

■ The Reign of the House of Hanover

England fought against France's supremacy in Europe and developed its colonial territories. In 1714, Parliament established the succession of the Protestant Welfs (or Guelfs).

As regent of both countries, ❶ William III ended the conflict between England and the Netherlands. He defeated the Irish, who had supported James II, in the Battle of Boyne in 1690, and the Scots at the massacre of Glencoe. The king's engagement on the Continent, where he was fighting in alliance with the Habsburgs against Louis XIV's claims, was unpopular in England because he used English troops to defend his Dutch interests.

When the king died in 1702 at the start of the War of Spanish Succession, his sister-in-law ❷ Anne (1665–1714), the last of the Protestant Stuarts, followed

❶ William III depicted during the Battle of Boyne, painting, 18th century

him on the throne. During her reign, in 1707, England and Scotland were unified into Great Britain, with a single Parliament. However, Anne was a weak monarch who was under the controlling influence of the ❹ Duke

and Duchess of Marlborough.

In 1704, the English occupied Gibraltar and Menorca. After the victories of Marlborough and Prince Eugène of Savoy over the French in the ❺ battles of Hochstadt and Blenheim in 1704, Oudenaarde in 1708, and Malplaquet in 1709, Great Britain was the primary benefactor at the Peace of Utrecht in 1713 that put an end to the War of the Spanish Succession. It was allowed to keep its conquests and received part of the French colonies in North America.

In the Act of Settlement (1701), Parliament had excluded Catholics and anyone married to a Catholic from the succession to the throne as well as establishing

Memorial for Queen Anne Stuart in front of St. Paul's Cathedral, London

3   George I, colored copper engraving, ca. 1730

that Parliament determines who succeeds to the throne.

Thus the electoral widow Sophie of Hanover, a grandchild of James I, was the next Protestant heir apparent. After Anne's death, Sophie's son, Elector George Louis of Hanover, ascended the throne as ❸ George I. Great Britain and Hanover were ruled in personal union until 1837. The reign of the House of Hanover continued until Queen Victoria's death in 1901.

John Churchill, Duke of Marlborough

John Churchill had a very successful career as a military commander in the army under James II. He later shifted his allegiance to William of Orange, though he still maintained contact with James, which brought him under suspicion of treason. His wife, Sarah Jennings, was a close friend of Anne Stuart, who after ascending to the throne made Churchill commander-in-chief of the English troops in the War of Spanish Succession and in 1702 elevated him to duke of Marlborough. He was victorious over the French and was regarded as the savior of the motherland. In gratitude, Anne gave him land and money and had Blenheim Palace built for the duke and his wife. Sir Winston Churchill, a descendant of the first duke, was born there in 1874.

above: Blenheim Palace, Oxfordshire, built by John Vanbrugh and Nicholas Hawksmoore

John Churchill, first duke of Marlborough, painting, 1705

Battle of Hochstadt, copper engraving, 18th century

■ The Hanoverian Kings and the Growing Power of the Prime Minister

Parliament continued to gain power under the kings of the House of Hanover. Great Britain was able to expand its colonial territories at France's expense, but was forced to accept the American colonies' independence.

7   Sir Robert Walpole, Earl of Oxford, copper engraving

❼ Robert Walpole (1676-1745) was the first "modern" British prime minister in that he established collegiate Cabinet responsibility. He served the Hanoverian kings as Secretary for War, Chancellor of the Exchequer, and then Chief Minister. Completely trusted by King **❻** George I and then after 1727 by his son **❿** George II, as well as by a majority of the Whigs in Parliament, he determined Great Britain's policies be-

tween 1721 and 1742. He tried to ensure peace in foreign affairs, and when Great Britain became involved in the War of Austrian Succession, he resigned in 1742.

The Catholic pretender to the throne, Charles Edward Stuart— a grandson of James II and commonly known as Bonnie Prince Charlie—used a British defeat by the French as an excuse to land in Scotland. After initial successes, he and his Scottish supporters from the highland

clans were crushed at **⓫** Culloden in 1746.

The balance of European powers remained a foreign policy aim. Upon the urging of **❽** William Pitt the Elder, Great Britain intervened in the Seven Years' War and, under the Treaty of Paris in 1763, was able to take the French colonies in North America and India. George II was followed by his grandson, **❾** George III, in 1760. To become independent of the Whigs and gain more weight in the government, he turned to the Tories. His policies led to the war of independence of the American colonies. The focus of political decision making now clearly rested in Parliament. The king's mental illness also weakened the position of the crown. From 1811 until the death of George III in 1820, his son, the future George IV, reigned as regent. The most important prime minister under George III, **⓬** William Pitt the Younger, reduced state debt and brought the East India Company under government control. In 1793, war with France began.

An election party of the Whigs, copper engraving by Hogarth, 1755

Whigs and Tories

Two factions confronted each other in the British Parliament: the Whigs and the Tories. They were the only political parties in Britain until the mid-19th century. Both terms were originally derisive nicknames: "tory" came from an Irish word for outlaws, "whigs" were Scottish Presbyterian rebels. The Whigs stood for political and economic liberalism, a strong Parliament, and religious tolerance, the conservative Tories defended the rights of the Anglican Church and crown.

6

The Composer Handel and King George I at the Thames enjoying a performance of Handel's "Water Music," steel engraving, 19th century

8

William Pitt the Elder, Earl of Chatham, mezzotint, 18th century

9

George III, painting, 18th century

12   Caricature of William Pitt the Younger at a Parliament debate entitled "The Back-Less Pitt," etching, 1792

11   Charles Edward Stuart, called "The Young Pretender" or Bonnie Prince Charlie, in the battle of Culloden, steel engraving, 19th century

10   London at the time of George II, royal barque on the Thames and St. Paul's Cathedral in the background, painting

1763 Treaty of Paris	**1784** Government takes control of East India Company	
1721–42 Robert Walpole leads the government	**1775–83** American War of Independence	**1793** Declaration of war on France

THE NETHERLANDS: FROM THE STRUGGLE FOR INDEPENDENCE TO THE FRENCH OCCUPATION 1477–1795

1

The independence that the Habsburgs fought for after the Reformation led to the Netherlands' fight for liberation from the rule of the Catholic kings of Spain. It culminated in 1581 in the independence of the Protestant northern provinces under William I of Orange. The fight between the Calvinist-dominated north and the Habsburg-loyal, Catholic south was drawn out until 1621. The United Provinces of the Netherlands, under the regency of the House of Orange, experienced its golden age as a naval, trading, and ❶ cultural power in the 17th century but was eventually displaced by Great Britain.

The Nightwatch, a depiction of the Amsterdam citizens' brigade, painting by Rembrandt, 1642

The Beginnings of the Struggle for Liberation

The prosperous and self-confident Netherlands, under the influence of the Reformation and Calvinism, became involved in progressively more serious conflicts with their sovereign rulers, the Catholic Habsburgs.

In 1477, the Netherlands, which belonged to the dukes of Burgundy, was transferred to the Habsburgs through the marriage of Mary of Burgundy to the future Holy Roman Emperor Maximilian I of Austria. Maximilian combined most of the provinces into the "Burgundian Circle" in 1512. The privileges of the circle were greatly enhanced by his grandson Charles V, who ruled the Netherlands from 1506.

Calvinism gained a foothold in the Netherlands from 1540 on. An uprising occurred in Geneva, Charles's birthplace, in 1542, and radical Calvinists ❹ organized the destruction of Catholic chur-

3

Caricature depicting Duke of Alba and his violent regime in the Netherlands; the dead bodies of Egmont and Hoorn lie at his feet, copper engraving, 16th century

ches. The monarch Mary of Hungary, Charles's sister, pursued a policy of compromise, but when Charles ❺ abdicated in 1555 and the Netherlands fell to his son Philip II of Spain, Philip rejected any conciliation with the Protestants. He made his half-sister ❻ Margaret of Parma regent in 1559, and she reintroduced her aunt's policy of compromise, but by then the almost completely Calvinist nobility of the Netherlands demanded

the withdrawal of the Inquisition and the Spanish as well as religious freedom.

After fruitless negotiations, Philip II decided on harsh measures and in 1567 sent the ❸ Duke of Alba into the Netherlands leading Spanish troops, whereupon the regent stepped down. Alba restored monarchial rule by force, capturing the leaders of the opposition, the counts Egmont and Hoorn, in September and had

2

Mass executions in the Netherlands, copper engraving, 16th century

them beheaded in June 1568 in Brussels. Now the whole of the Netherlands was in open rebellion; the war of independence had begun. The Protestants, who were mockingly called Geusen ("beggars") by the Spanish, adopted the name for themselves and involved the Spanish in a guerrilla war. The Spanish answered with brutal ❷ retaliatory measures.

4

Looting and destruction of a Catholic church by the Calvinists, copper engraving, 16th century

5

Charles V assigns rule over the Netherlands to his son, Philip II, painting, 19th century

6

William of Orange protests at an audience with Margaret of Parma, painting, 19th century

1477	The Netherlands falls to the Habsburgs	**1542**	Calvinist uprising in Geneva	**1559**	Margaret of Parma becomes regent of the Netherlands
	1512 Founding of the "Burgundian Circle"		**1555** Philip II of Spain governs the Netherlands		

■ The Dutch War of Independence

The struggle for Dutch independence from Spain intensified under the repressive rule of the Duke of Alba. It culminated in independence in 1581. The leaders of the freedom fighters were William I of Orange and his family.

7
William of Orange, painting, 16th century

In 1556 Calvinist riots provoked Philip II of Spain to increasingly repress religious dissidents in the Netherlands. In 1568 **❼**, **❾** William I of Orange, of the House of Nassau-Dillenburg and originally a confidant of Charles V, took over the leadership of the Dutch Protestants. The Dutch republic owed its existence to William's devotion to the cause of independence from Spain.

William and his brothers John VI, the reigning duke of Nassau-Dillenburg, and Louis were leading exponents of a combative Calvinism in the empire. Louis traveled throughout Bohemia and Hungary to forge alliances with radical Protestants. Since 1567, about 60,000 of the empire's persecuted Calvinists had poured into the Netherlands and had fortified the resolve for freedom there. In 1572, William pushed into the Netherlands with Protestant troops and seized several cities from the Spanish. In the face of these successes, Philip II recalled the Duke of Alba as governor-general in 1573.

Following negotiations over a cease-fire, the final phase of the revolt began in 1576. William enacted laws for the northern provinces, but a union with the southern provinces failed due to **❽** Geusen unwillingness to compromise in matters of religion. In 1579, the seven northern provinces of Holland, Friesland, Gelderland, Zeeland, Overijssel, Utrecht, and Groningen—the United Provinces—formed the Utrecht Union, with William as its *stadhouder* or governor, and officially broke with Spain in 1581 to form the Republic of the United Netherlands. In 1579, the southern provinces had joined together in the Union of Arras and recognized the Spanish governor-general, **⓫** Alexander Farnese, duke of Parma; they later formed the **⓬** Spanish Netherlands, which was ruled by the Habsburgs. The war, however,

9 Equestrian statue of William of Orange

8
Catholic Geusen loot a farm in the southern provinces, painting, ca. 1600

10
William of Orange's tomb in the "Nieuwe Kerk" (New Church) in Delft, painting, ca. 1651

continued because Farnese wavered between peace negotiations and waging war. Philip II put a price on **❿** William's head in 1580, and he was shot by a Catholic fanatic in Delft in 1584.

Declaration of Independence of the United Provinces to Philip II, 1581 Dutch Act of Abjuration

"A prince is constituted by God to be ruler of a people, to defend them from oppression and violence as the shepherd his sheep; and whereas God did not create the people slaves to their prince ... but rather the prince for the sake of the subjects ... to govern them ... and support them as a father his children. ... And when he does not behave thus, but ... exacting from them slavish compliance, then he is no longer a prince, but a tyrant."

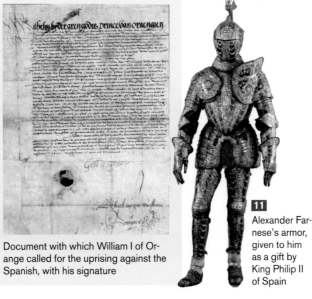

Document with which William I of Orange called for the uprising against the Spanish, with his signature

11
Alexander Farnese's armor, given to him as a gift by King Philip II of Spain

12
Grande Place in Brussels, capital of the Spanish Netherlands

The Independent Netherlands to the Middle of the 17th Century

The war of the United Provinces against the southern Netherlands ended in 1609. A power struggle then developed between the *stadhouder* (governor) from the house of Nassau-Orange and the powerful merchants over who would rule the United Provinces.

The fleet of the Dutch East India Company, painting, 1675

Isabella Clara Eugenia of Spain, painting by Rubens, ca. 1613/15

The "Mauritshuis" in The Hague, home of Maurice of Orange

After declaring independence, the United Provinces had to continue to fight against an invasion of Spanish forces under the command of Alessandro Farnese; internally it took action against the Catholics. In 1584 the Stadhouder William of Orange was murdered by a Catholic fanatic. In 1585, Antwerp was taken by Farnese, and the United Provinces accepted an offer of aid from Elizabeth I of England, who sent 8000 English soldiers under the command of the Earl of Leicester to their aid. The war dragged on with varying intensity until Maurice of Nassau, son of William of Orange, after two years of campaigning finally succeeded in expelling Spanish forces from the Protestant Netherlands in 1607. Finally, in 1609, the governor-general of the Spanish Netherlands, Archduke Albrecht of Austria and his wife ❶ Isabella Clara Eugenia, a daughter of Philip II, concluded a truce. In 1621, Philip III of Spain finally recognized the independence of the United Provinces.

The northern Netherlands recovered rapidly from the wars and, due to the powerful ❹ middle class in its cities, soon rose to become perhaps the wealthiest nation of Europe in the 17th century. For a time it was the leading ❷ naval and colonial power, with territories reaching from North America (New Amsterdam, later New York) and the Caribbean to Indonesia and Japan. It also dominated culturally, particularly in the field of painting. Political relations within the United Provinces were difficult, however, as they decided in 1590 against having a single head of state.

In 1585, the eldest son of William I of Orange, ❸ Maurice, replaced him as stadhouder of the provinces. Holland, financially the strongest of the United Provinces, was dominated by a rich ❺ merchant and legal elite, whose leader, Johan van Oldenbarnevelt, was the second political head alongside Maurice begining in 1586. Although Maurice wanted to continue fighting, van Oldenbarnevelt accepted the truce with the Spanish Netherlands in 1609 in the interests of continuing trade. A power struggle developed, and Maurice ousted van Oldenbarnevelt and had him executed in 1619. The conflict was symptomatic of the unsettled power struggle between the Orange governors and the municipal representatives, which would dominate Dutch history until 1786. Maurice's half-brother, ❻ Frederick Henry, succeeded him as stadhouder in 1625, conquered fortresses in the south from the Spanish during the Thirty Years' War, and turned his court in The Hague into a center for arts and culture.

Wedding portrait of a Haarlem merchant, painting by Frans Hals, c. 1622

Representatives of the cloth merchants' guild, painting by Rembrandt, 1662

Frederick Henry depicted as messenger of peace and independence, painting by Jordaens, 1652

| 1609 | Cease-fire | 1652–54 | First Anglo-Dutch naval war | 1667 | Navigation Act | 1668 | Alliance with England against France |
| 1621 | Recognition of independence | 1665–67 | Second Anglo-Dutch naval war | 1667–68 | France attacks | 1672 | Murder of de Witt |

The Netherlands up to the French Occupation

In 1672, the House of Orange was finally able to prevail with William III. His heirs were driven out in 1795 by French revolutionary troops, and later controlled by Napoleon.

William III of Orange, king of England, painting, c. 1700

Frederick Henry's son, William II, attempted to occupy ❼ Amsterdam in 1650 and make himself king but died before he could. The ruling grand pensionary of Hol-

The mayor's house on the "Damplatz" in Amsterdam, painting, ca. 1668

land, Johan de Witt, who represented the liberal bourgeoisie of the cities hostile to the centralizing monarchy, was forced into two naval wars with England over the Navigation Acts. These effectively broke Dutch naval supremacy. In 1667–1668, France seized parts of the Spanish Netherlands, whereupon de Witt made an alliance with England in 1668 and

forced Louis XIV to withdraw. But then England changed sides, joining France in an attack on the United Provinces, particularly Holland, by land and by sea. Consequently, de Witt was literally torn to pieces in a rebellion in August 1672 and William III of Orange, the son of William II, was installed as supreme commander and stadhouder. He ended the war with England in 1674 and with France in 1678. In 1689 he was ❽ granted the English throne as James II's son-in-law. The prosperity of the country was maintained by the Dutch East India Company, founded in 1602, and ❾ colonial territories in Africa (Cape Colony), the Americas (Guyana, Netherlands An-tilles), and Asia (Indonesia).

After William III died in 1702, there was no unified leadership until 1747 when William IV Friso, a member of the House of Orange, became stadhouder of the United Netherlands. From 1780 to 1784, his son and successor William V waged war against Great

Britain over colonies, which weakened the Netherlands as a colonial power; to prevail against the French, he supported the ❿ "Patriots" in 1785 and 1787, who had ousted him from office as stadhouder in some provinces.

The Spanish Netherlands went to the Habsburgs in 1713 in the Peace of Utrecht, which ended the War of Spanish Succession, and were thereafter called the ⓫ Austrian Netherlands. Occupied by French revolutionary troops in

Whipping of a black slave in Dutch Guyana, copper engraving, 18th century

1792, the southern provinces were incorporated into France in 1794. The following year, the French also occupied the United Provinces, drove out William V, and proclaimed it the Batavian Republic. In 1806, Napoleon Bonaparte made this French satellite state into a kingdom and handed it over to his brother Louis.

Caricature of the suppression of the uprising against William V of Orange, etching, 1787

Laeken Castle near Brussels, built for the governor of the Austrian Netherlands, Maria Christina of Austria, between 1782 and 1784

Intellectual Freedom in the United Provinces

During the 17th century the United Provinces were a stronghold of intellectual freedom in Europe. Hugo Grotius, the famous scholar of international law, was the pensionary (chief magistrate) of Rotterdam from 1613 to 1618. The founder of modern Rationalism, René Descartes, found refuge in the Netherlands in 1628–1648. The Jewish philosopher Baruch de Spinoza also lived in The Hague.

Grotius' *De iure belli ac pacis* ("on the law of war and peace"), 1626

THE ITALY OF POPES AND PRINCES

CA. 1450–CA. 1800

Between the 15th and the 18th centuries, Italy was contested by the rulers of France, Spain, and the Holy Roman Empire. It disintegrated into interdependent political structures that quarreled with each other and maneuvered between the great powers. The popes and the northern Italian princes were united by ruthless power and family politics in their battle against municipal freedoms and fashioned their courts into shining centers of the ❼ arts and literature.

View of Pont Sant' Angelo and St. Peter's Basilica, Rome

■ The Renaissance Papacy

The popes of the Renaissance were politically unscrupulous and had a love of splendor and worldly pleasures. They made their families exceedingly rich and were also patrons of the arts.

In the Papal States, the "Renaissance papacy" began in the middle of the 15th century. While its first representatives in the mid- to late 1400s, notably Nicholas V and ❷ Pius II (formerly the celebrated poet Enea Silvio Piccolomini), were significant and respected humanists, moral decay set in with the pontificate of Sixtus IV in 1471. The popes sold Church offices and favored their families. ❶ Rome became a city of frivolous celebrations, rather than of religious piety. Popes and cardinals, who were mostly members of leading noble families and related to one another, enriched themselves with church properties and monies. However, the court of the Renaissance popes was also a center of culture and the arts where significant artists such as Raphael and ❼ Michelangelo were commissioned by the ecclesiastical princes to create artworks.

The integrity of the papacy reached a low point with the self-aggrandizing Alexander VI between 1492 and 1503. His successor, Julius II, personally fought at the head of his troops in defense of the Papal States and against the rivalling Italian cities, while the popes from the Medici family, ❹ Leo X and Clement VII, were patrons of the arts. Clement VII allied himself with France against the Holy Roman emperor and consequently provoked the plundering of Rome by imperial mercenaries in the ❸ sacco di Roma in 1527. ❻ Paul III (Alessandro Farnese) and Julius III were transitional popes who, although they continued to live like Renaissance princes, were coaxed by Emperor Charles V into making reforms. ❺ The Council of Trent, which was convened in 1545 and lasted until 1563, eventually introduced a far-reaching program of internal ecclesiastical reorganization after years of debate.

Enea Silvio Piccolomini, the future Pope Pius II, being crowned as poet laureate by Emperor Frederick III, fresco by Pinturicchio, ca.1502

Charles' mercenary army ridicule the pope during the sacco di Roma, copper engraving

Pope Leo X, copy after the painting by his protégé Raphael

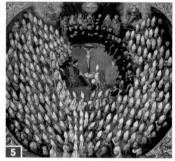

Congregation of the Council of Trent, painting, 18th century

The creation of Adam, from ceiling fresco of the Sistine Chapel painted by Michelangelo, 1511

Paul III's Palazzo Farnese in Rome, built 1534–89

■ The Papacy during the Counter-Reformation

A moral renewal of the papacy occurred under the influence of the Counter-Reformation, but it also brought about a curbing of intellectual and scientific freedoms, and the papacy ignored the Enlightenment for a long time.

Cesare Borgia, Son of Pope Alexander VI, painting, ca. 1520

After the reform plans of popes such as Hadrian VI, Pius III, and Marcellus II failed because their pontificates were too short, Paul IV in 1555 and Pius V in 1566 were able to establish an uncompromising papacy of the Counter-Reformation. The moral renewal under these popes, however, was accompanied by the Inquisition's reign of terror. Among the Italian clergy active at this time was the later canonized Carlo Borromeo, who as cardinal-archbishop of Milan after 1560 worked toward comprehensive Church reform.

Popes who held fast to the concept of the Counter-Reformation included Gregory XIII, who introduced the modern Gregorian calendar in 1582, and Sixtus V, who rid the Papal States of its bands of robbers and developed papal centralism through a complete reorganization of Church administration that remained in force into the 20th century. In

Tomb of Pope Alexander VII in San Pietro di Vaticano, designed by Bernini, 1676–78

the 17th century under Paul V and Urban VIII, Rome once again became a world center of ❾ art and culture, but it was also under them that the dispute with ⓫ Galileo Galilei about the Copernican conception of the world took place. Gregory XV founded the Congregation for Propagating the Faith (*Propaganda Fide*) in 1622, which was responsible in the following centuries for coordinating the spread of Catholic missio-

nary work all over the world. Innocent XI stood out among the successors of Urban VIII, bringing about a grand coalition of European powers against the Ottomans' 1683 siege of Vienna.

The papacy closed its mind to the enlightening currents of the 18th century through censorship and the banning of books. The liberal and enlightened ❿ Benedict XIV, who was described by Montesquieu as the pope of the scholars, demanded internal ecclesiastical enlightenment, but his successors rescinded his reforms—provoking the opposition of enlightened absolutism, which had by that time established itself in the Catholic countries. Austria, Spain, and Portugal forced the reactionary Clement XIV to

8 Pope Pius VI and the Emperor Joseph II, copper engraving, 18th c.

dissolve the powerful order of the Jesuits in 1773. His successor, ❽ Pius VI, was a victim of these developments; in 1782 he traveled to Vienna in a fruitless attempt to persuade Emperor Joseph II to tone down measures against the Church. In 1797 Pius lost the papal enclave at Avignon in southern France, and in 1798 he was captured by French troops who had occupied Italy on Napoleon's orders and was deported, along with a major part of the Church's treasures, to France.

10 Pope Benedict XIV, painting, 18th c.

11 Galileo defends himself before the inquisition court, painting, 17th century

1582	Gregorian calendar reform		1633	Galileo's trial		1798	Capture of Pius VI
1545–63	Council of Trent	1622	*Propaganda Fide*	1773	Jesuits disbanded		

The Nobility and the Papal States in Northern and Central Italy

The numerous Italian princes' palaces became, despite their comparatively minor political importance, significant centers of the Renaissance and the baroque. They were matched in their displays of splendor by the confident noble families in the city-republics.

The Battle of Pavia, wood engraving, ca. 1530

Lorenzo de Medici, painting by Vasari, 16th century

While the Kingdom of Naples and Sicily was ruled over by Spain or by Spanish collateral family branches into the 18th century, local ruling dynasties of varying origins reigned in the north and center of the Italian peninsula. The Milanese Sforza family, descended from a mercenary soldier (*condottiere*), was ousted in 1515 when Francis I of France occupied Lombardy after his victory at Marignano. Following success over the French at ❶ Pavia in 1525, the Habsburg emperor Charles V then seized Milan as an imperial fief.

The history of the Medici family in ❸ Florence was eventful. They rose to become the unofficial rulers of the city and particularly distinguished themselves as patrons of the arts. Cosimo the Elder summoned the sculptor Donatello to his court in the 15th century. Michelangelo and Botticelli worked for his grandson ❷ Lorenzo the Magnificent in Florence. After Lorenzo's death, however, the family was driven out by the monk ❹ Savonarola, who established a form of theocratic republic in 1494. The Medici returned in 1513. After the murder of Alessandro de' Medici—who, as son-in-law of Charles V gained the title of duke of Florence for his family in 1532—Cosimo I, a distant cousin, took over the dukedom in 1537 and became a leading power in northern Italy. Cosimo established himself as absolute ruler, founded the famous collection of paintings in the Pitti Palace, and conquered Siena, which he absorbed into Tuscany in 1555. In 1569 he was elevated to grand duke of Tuscany. When the Medici line died out in 1737, the grand duchy was given to Francis Stephen (later Emperor Francis I) in exchange for Lorraine. His son Peter Leopold, the later Emperor Leopold II, transformed Tuscany into a model state of enlightened absolutism and a center of independent sciences through extensive social reforms.

The ancient royal house of Este was granted the imperial fiefs of Modena and Reggio by the emperor in 1452 and in 1471 was awarded ❺ Ferrara as a dukedom by the pope. Ercole I laid out Ferrara as a modern city with wide, straight streets. His son Alfonso I was married to the pope's daughter Lucrezia Borgia. When the direct line died out with Alfonso II in 1597, the pope took back Ferrara as a papal fief in 1598, but Este relatives still ruled in Modena until the French occupation in 1796.

The main branch of the Gonzaga family reigned in Mantua. Margrave Giovanni Francesco III was married to ❻ Isabella d'Este, who made Mantua into an important cultural center. Their son Federigo II gained the title of duke in 1530. The extinction of the direct line in 1627 led to the War of Mantuan Succession (1628–1631).

The Cathedral of Florence with the bell tower by Giotto di Bondone and the dome by Brunelleschi

The emperor seized Mantua as an imperial fief in 1708.

Pope ❼ Paul III of the House of Farnese made his illegitimate son Pier Luigi the duke of Parma and Piacenza in 1545. However, the duke was murdered and the land

Castello Estense in Ferrara

Savonarola's execution in Florence, painting, ca. 1500

| 1452 | Este rule in Modena and Reggio | 1515 | French occupation of Lombardy | 1528 | End of French rule in Genoa |
| **ca. 1500** | Medici rule in Florence | 1525 | Charles V seizes Milan as an imperial fief | 1545 | Farnese rule in Parma and Piacenza |

Isabella d' Este, Duchess of Mantua, painting by Rubens, ca. 1605/08

Pope Paul III and his nephews, painting by Titian, 1546

was then occupied by imperial troops. His son Ottavio was able to regain the estates in 1538 through his marriage to Margaret, the illegitimate daughter of

Andrea Doria depicted as sea god Neptune, by Bronzino, ca. 1530

Emperor Charles V. Their son Alexander became governor of the Netherlands in 1578. The Farnese line died out in 1731, and Parma was initially seized by the emperor as an imperial fief, but eventually in 1748 through marriage came into the hands of the Spanish Bourbons, who also ruled Naples and Sicily.

Another papal family, the della Rovere, gained possession of Urbino. Here, the governor and condottiere Federigo da Montefeltro received the ducal title in 1474 and founded a dynasty, into which the nephew of Pope Julius II and great-nephew of Pope Sixtus IV, Francesco Maria della Rovere, married in 1508. Urbino was independent until 1631 when it re-

verted to the Papal States.

❽ Andrea Doria, who fought against the Ottomans as an admiral for Emperor Charles V, put an end to the French rule of Genoa in 1528 and reintroduced the old constitution of the aristocratic republic with the election of a doge as head of state every two years. In compensation for having lost the Mediterranean trade to the Venetians and the Turks, the Genoese rose to become the most important bankers of the Spanish crown. In contrast to ❿ Venice, Genoa was able to maintain a leading position in commerce. The Venetian republic had lost almost all of its territories in the Eastern Mediterranean to the Ottomans by the 18th century. The shifting of world trade to the Atlantic led to the gradual decline of the city. In 1797, the French occupied both Venice and Genoa, abolished the rule of the doges, and made both cities satellite states of the French Republic.

The most significant dynasty in Northern Italy was the house of Savoy. From ❾ Turin it ruled the Duchy of Savoy and Piedmont. It alternatively allied with the French and the Habsburgs in order to maintain its independence and expand its territories. After the Spanish wars of succession it gained the island of Sardinia and ⓫ its crown.

As in the other Italian states, branches of the Bourbons or respectively the Habsburgs ruled, it was able to lead the Italian independence movement in the 19th century as it was the only authentically "Italian" royal dynasty.

Niccolò Machiavelli

A diplomat and member of the government of the republic of Florence, Niccolò Machiavelli—in his work, Il Principe (The Prince), in 1513—*developed the principle of pragmatic politics as a fundamental law for modern European states: "The end justifies the means."*

above: Niccolò Machiavelli, painting, 16th century

The Basilica of Supergra containing the House of Savoy mausoleum, Turin

The doge of Venice's gondola, painting by Canaletto, ca. 1750

Coronation of Victor Amadeus II, Duke of Savoy, marble relief, 1713

1555	Conquest of Sienna	1598	Ferrara becomes papal fief	1737	Medici government ends	1797	French occupation of Genoa and Venice
1578	Alexander Farnese governor of the Netherlands	1628–31	War of Mantuan Succession	1796	French occupation of Modena		

SPAIN AND PORTUGAL 1500–1800

Voyages of discovery and merchant shipping made Portugal and Spain the leading sea powers of Europe during the fifteenth and sixteenth century. Under ❷ Philip II, Spain also became the major force behind the Counter-Reformation. A rapid economic and political decline took place in Portugal after 1580 and in Spain after 1600, accelerated by the often weak and conservative governments. This decline lasted until around 1750, when reforms associated with enlightened absolutism elsewhere were carried out in ❶ both countries. In the wake of the French Revolution, both countries fell under Napoleon's control.

1 Map of the Iberian peninsula, 1577   **right:** Philip II of Spain 2

Spain from the Catholic Kings to Philip II

The union of the kingdoms of Castile and Aragon paved the way for the final defeat and expulsion of the Arab Muslim and the rise of the Spanish kingdom. Under Charles V and Philip II, Spain became the leading Catholic power in Europe.

Spain was unified by the marriage of the "Catholic monarchs" ❺ Ferdinand of Aragon and ❹ Isabella of Castile in 1469. In 1492, they ❸ drove out the last of the Iberian Muslim rulers from Granada and then completed the *Reconquista* through the expulsion or forced baptism of Jews and Moors. In the same year, ❼ Christopher Columbus landed in America and claimed it for Spain. The royal heir to the Spanish throne, Joanna the Mad, married the Habsburg Philip the Handsome, the son of Emperor Maximilian I, in 1496. When Isabella died in 1505, Joanna was already mentally ill and was unable

3 The handing over of the key to Granada by the last of the Muslim rulers after the city's surrender, stone carving, ca. 1500

to govern in Castile. After Philip's death in 1506, Ferdinand of Aragon established his rule over all of Spain.

Only after Ferdinand's death in 1516 was his grandson Charles I, who became the Holy Roman Emperor Charles V in 1519, able to take up his inheritance. The Spanish cities rebelled against his Dutch advisors in 1520. Spanish conquest in the New World brought vast quantities of gold into the country but did not lead to any long-term improvements in the state finances. During his

frequent absences, Charles left the regency to his wife Isabella of Portugal or his son Philip II.

When Charles I abdicated in 1556, Spain along with its overseas possessions, the Netherlands, and Italy, were inherited by his son, Philip II. He became the leading figure of the Catholic Counter-Reformation in Europe. The extremely duty-conscious and hard working monarch took personal charge of the adminis-

4 Isabella I, portrait, ca. 1500

5 Ferdinand II, portrait, ca. 1500

tration of the kingdom from his ❻ Escorial Palace in Madrid. He was determined to combat the spread of Protestantism in Europe by any means. This led to the secession of the Netherlands, where Calvinism was strong, after a protracted war that began in 1568.

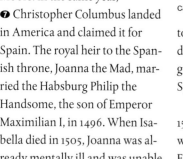

6 The Escorial Palace, residence and place of burial for the Spanish kings since 1563, built by Juan Bautista de Toledo and Juan de Herrera

7 Columbus returns with gifts from the New World, painting by Delacroix, 1839

High Point and Decline of Spanish Power

Spain's dominant position in Europe and the New World, attained under Philip II, declined under his successors. Under the last Spanish Habsburg the country was practically bankrupt, and its political influence greatly diminished.

8 Philip III on horseback, portrait by Velasquez, ca. 1634

From a position of strength, Philip II projected Spanish power across Europe. He supported the Austrian Habsburgs against the Protestants, ended the war with France in 1559, and married Eliza-

11 The windmills of La Mancha, setting for the famous 17th century novel *Don Quixote* by Miguel de Cervantes, who also fought in the Battle of Lepanto

beth of Valois, the daughter of Catherine de Médicis, in his third marriage. In the context of the Counter-Reformation he financed the Catholic League in the French Wars of Religion, but was unable to prevent Henry of Navarre from becoming king of France in 1589. In 1571 a Spanish-papal fleet under Juan de Austria won a major **9** naval victory over the Ottomans at Lepanto. However, Spanish naval supremacy was broken in 1588 when a large invasion fleet, the Spanish Armada, was defeated off the British coast in 1588.

In 1598 Philip II was succeeded by his son, **8** Philip III, who fell under the influence of royal favorites. He further stretched the state finances by underwriting the Catholic powers in the Thirty Years' War. In the same period, Spanish art and **11** literature was in full bloom at his **10** courts. **12** Philip IV was forced to declare the state bankrupt in 1627 and accept the loss of territory in the Treaty of the Pyrenees in 1659 after heavy defeats by the French. The repeated intermarrying of Austrian and Spanish Habsburgs

began to show clear signs of degeneration. **13** Philip's son Charles II, the last of the Spanish Habsburgs, was both impotent and mentally ill. Even before his death, the dispute over his succession flared up at the royal court. When he died in November 1700, the War of the Spanish Succession began.

9 Celebration of the victory over the Ottomans at the Battle of Lepanto, including PiusV, Philip II, Doge Alvise Mocenigo of Venice, and Don Juan de Austria, painting by El Greco, ca. 1577

10 Palace Buen Retiro and gardens in Madrid, painting, 17th century

Philip II, on the Defeat of the Spanish Armada Sent to Invade England:

"We must praise God for all that He does. And I thank Him for the mercy shown. In the storms which the Armada had to sail through, they could have suffered a worse fate, [and] that their misfortune was not greater is thanks to the pious and ceaseless prayers sent to heaven for their successful return(...)"

—*Extract from a letter to the Spanish bishops, 1588*

above: English naval victory over the Spanish Armada, engraving, 17th c.

12 Philip IV, portrait by Velasquez

13 Charles II, portrait by Velasquez

Portugal at Its Zenith as a Naval Power

Voyages of discovery, merchant shipping, and a well-run fleet made Portugal the leading sea power at the end of the 15th century. When the reign of the House of Aviz came to an end to be replaced by the Spanish Habsburgs, the country lost its dominant position.

1 Vasco da Gama before an Indian sovereign, wood engraving, 19th century

Since the time of Henry the Navigator in the first half of the 15th century, Portuguese explorers had dedicated themselves to finding a sea route around Africa to India and establishing bases on the African coast. John II (ruled 1481–1495) launched a major fleet-building program, had ❼ sea charts drawn up, and outfitted explorers and soldiers. In 1487-1488

2 King Manuel I the Fortunate with St. Hieronymus in Belem in the Hieronymus monastery, donated by the king, sculpture, 16th c.

Bartolomeu Dias sailed to the Cape of Good Hope. Ten years later, ❷ King Manuel I the Fortunate sponsored the expedition of ❶ Vasco da Gama, which sailed around Africa and reached the coast of ❸ India in May 1498. Pedro Alvars Cabral claimed part of today's Brazil for Portugal in 1500, thus securing Portugal's position in South America—confirmed by the papal "division" of the New World between Spain and Portugal in the Treaty of Tordesillas signed in 1494.

Manuel centralized the government as an absolute ruler and expelled the Moors and Jews—refugees from Spain—to North Africa in 1496. During his reign, and that of his son John III, Portugal reached its zenith as a

maritime power. The Portuguese constructed forts and trading stations along the African and Indian coasts and controlled the spice trade to Europe. Working with certain African tribal chiefs, they transported a great number of slaves for the European markets. Portuguese ❻ caravels ruled the world's seas. Francisco de Almeida, the first Portuguese viceroy in East India in 1505, and ❹ Alfonso de Albuquerque, secured Portuguese dominance in the Indian Ocean and took trading cities such as Goa and Malacca. Their successors conquered the Moluccas (Spice Islands) and Ceylon. John's grandson, ❺ Sebastian, succeeded him in 1557 and dreamed of a revival of the Crusades. He invaded North Africa with a large army in 1578 but was defeated by the sultan of Morocco at Ksar el-Kebir. As his body was never found, the Portuguese believed for

4 Afonso de Albuquerque

5 Sebastian, King of Portugal painting, 1571

3 Baroque church dating from the time of the Portuguese in Goa

a long time that he would return victorious, a rumor which several adventurers used to their advantage. His great-uncle, Cardinal Henry, who had already reigned as regent for the young Sebastian, succeeded him as king and had to pay an enormous ransom for the survivors in North Africa. The royal line of Aviz came to an end with the death of Henry in 1580.

6 Portuguese sailing boat, book illustration, 16th century

7 Portuguese map of the world, 1573

Portugal up to the Occupation by Napoleon

Neither under the Spanish nor under the House of Bragança did Portugal regain its former importance. Following reforms under Pombal, the country was occupied by Napoleon in 1807.

9 Philip II, King of Spain and Portugal, bronze sculpture, ca. 1570

10 A typical country estate of the nobility, in Villa Real in the north of Portugal, built in the 18th century

11 Heretics being burned at the stake by Jesuits, copper engraving, 1723

Since time immemorial, Portugal's rulers had made marriage alliances with the Spanish ruling houses. **9** Philip II of Spain, an uncle of King Sebastian, rejected claims by related dynasties in 1580 and occupied Portugal, which he absorbed into his empire. Portugal was further undermined through the weaknesses of the Spanish Habsburgs after 1598. The Dutch replaced their hegemony in the Indian Ocean and seized the Moluccas in 1663 and Ceylon in 1668.

A Portuguese **8** revolt against Spain, supported by England, brought John IV (of the Bragança dynasty, a side branch of the old royal house) to the throne in 1640. In 1654, he drove the Dutch out of the coast of Brazil and permanently secured it as a possession of Portugal. During the reign of John's successor, Portugal sought support from Great Britain against Spain. The country's economy suffered as a result of mass emigration to Brazil by those seeking to escape the rigidly hierarchical society, in which most of the land **10** was in the hands of the nobility. Change came in 1750, when Joseph I, an adherent of enlightened absolutism, came to the throne. His chief minister, the Marquês de Pombal, used an earthquake that struck **12** Lisbon in 1755 as an excuse to institute radical changes. He had the city rebuilt, improved its infrastructure, and worked to revive the economy. Between 1761 and 1763, he banned slavery in Portugal. He expelled the Jesuits,

who had led **11** the Inquisition, from the country in 1759–1760 and, Portugal contributed to the order's dissolution in 1773 through pressure on the pope. Pombal cemented a form of enlightened absolutism, reformed the universities, and brought Portugal into line with the more progressive of Europe's regimes.

Joseph's death in 1777 meant the fall of Pombal, because successive rulers again came under the influence of the Church. Since Portugal remained aligned with Great Britain, Napoleon occupied the country in 1807 and expelled the regent John VI, who set up a secondary royal court in Brazil.

8 Uprising in Lisbon against the Spanish king, etching, 18th century

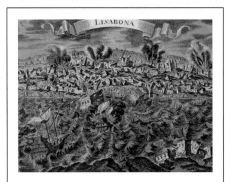

The Lisbon Earthquake

On November 1, 1755, a massive earthquake and subsequent tidal wave destroyed the city of Lisbon and took the lives of about 60,000 people. The event became a much-discussed subject in Enlightenment Europe. The optimism of the proponents of the Enlightenment was greatly shaken, and Voltaire wrote a mocking poem in 1756 that he entitled "Poem on the Lisbon Disaster; or, An Examination of the Axiom 'All Is Well.'"

above: The Lisbon earthquake, sketch, 18th c.

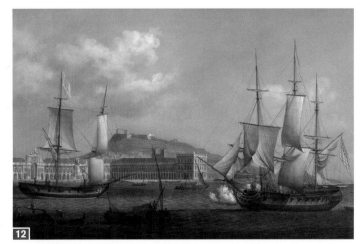

12 Ships entering the port of Lisbon with the central Praça do Comércio in the background, painting, ca. 1800

| 1580 | Philip II occupies Portugal | 1654 | Portuguese establish colony in Brazil | 1759–60 | Jesuits expelled | 1807 | Napoleon invades Portugal |
| Dec 1640 | Portuguese revolt | Nov 1, 1755 | Lisbon earthquake | 1761–63 | Slavery abolished |

Spain under the First Bourbons

As the Habsburg dynasty died out, the new Bourbon line temporarily brought Spain under the influence of France. Under mentally ill monarchs Spain lost territories and influence.

In 1700 Charles II, the last Habsburg, who had no heir, bequeathed the Spanish throne to his great-nephew ❷ Duke Philip of Anjou, the grandson of Louis XIV of France. The Austrian Habsburgs countered this with their own claims to the throne. They were supported by the British, who feared French hegemony. In the War of Spanish Succession,

the two sides fought for their claims. However, when the Habsburg pretender Charles III succeeded his brother Joseph I as Holy Roman Emperor, his erstwhile allies began to fear an increase in Habsburg power. In the end, the inheritance was divided: The grandson of Louis XIV was recognized as King Philip V of Spain in 1713–1714 by the treaties of Utrecht and Rastatt but was forced to renounce his and his descendants' claims to the French throne. The Habsburgs also received the Spanish possessions in the Netherlands and Italy, while Great Britain gained Minorca and Gibraltar. The psychologically unstable ❶ Philip V (ruled 1700–1746) was heavily influenced by his second wife ❹ Isabella Farnese,

1
Philip V, portrait by Rigaud, 18th c.

princess of Parma and Piacenza, who wished to secure crowns for her own sons. Through military and diplomatic pressure following the War of Polish Succession in 1734–1735, the Habsburgs were forced to relinquish Naples and Sicily. After the War of Austrian Succession in 1748, they lost Parma and Piacenza as well. Philip's attacks of depression soon escalated into phases of mental breakdown and paranoia, and he spent much of the time in retreat at his ❸ residences outside Madrid. Meanwhile, the aristocracy, who under the last Habsburgs had already made themselves largely independent on their country estates, blocked all social reform to alleviate the situation of the majority of the population who suffered from poverty and illiteracy.

In Philip's son Ferdinand VI, who succeeded him in 1746, the hereditary depression intensified into chronic mental illness. As he was incapable of governing, Chief Minister Marquis de la Ensenada ruled in his place. While in office he reformed the Spanish finances, making Spain independent of France, and began to introduce a range of Enlightenment-inspired political reforms in the country.

3
The gardens of La Granja de San Ildefonso, Philip V's summer residence

2
King Louis XIV proclaims the Duke of Anjou to be king of Spain, color lithograph

Farinelli

The Italian castrato singer, Farinelli, performed at the Spanish court from 1737. Born Carlo Broschi in 1705 in Italy, he first performed publicly in 1721 and was soon a celebrated star around the opera houses of Europe. Under Philip V and Ferdinand VI, he initially sang for a small circle of the illustrious—it is said that he was the only one who could please the depressive Philip—but then rose to become the "maître de plaisir" and an esteemed political advisor in the Spanish court.

Carlo Broschi, known as Farinelli, painting, 18th century

4
Philip V and Isabella Farnese and family, painting by Van Loo, 1743

Spain during the Reigns of Charles III and Charles IV

Charles III enacted reforms in the spirit of enlightened absolutism. Under his son Charles IV, the chief minister, Godoy, presided over a political reconciliation with the French Republic.

A reversal of conditions in Spain took place when Ferdinand VI was succeeded by his half-brother ❺ Charles III in 1759. As king of Naples and Sicily since 1735, Charles had already initiated social and economic reforms in southern Italy with the aid of his chief minister Tanucci. The single-minded and industrious king now brought enlightened absolutism to Spain. He began an extensive settlement program to recultivate the rural regions that had been barren for centuries, ordering modern techniques and new strains of plants for the peasants. Along with a number of ❻ palaces and hunting lodges, he built orphanages and workhouses for vagrants. He improved roads, established banks and carefully controlled colonial revenues. Charles III even took on the Catholic Church. He ended the Church's monopoly over education and abolished the ❾ courts of Inquisition. In foreign affairs, Charles formed an alliance with France in 1761 and participated in the Seven Years' War against Great Britain, which was allied with Prussia against France. In 1767, he expelled the Jesuits from Spain, confiscated much Church property, and distributed it to the ❼ peasants.

Charles III was succeeded in 1788 by his son ❽ Charles IV, who left much of the affairs of government to his energetic wife, Maria Luisa of Parma, and her protégé, ❿ Manuel de Godoy, who as chief minister from 1792 continued the policies of Charles III. Initially Godoy had been an opponent of revolutionary France, but in 1796 he entered into the alliance of San Ildefonso with the French Republic, which obliged Spain to take part in the war against Great Britain. In 1805, the British fleet under Admiral Nelson destroyed the French and Spanish fleets at Trafalgar. As a result Spanish trade routes were decimated.

In 1807, Godoy even attempted to negotiate with Napoleon over the division of French-occupied territories in the hope of gaining southern Portugal as part of the Spanish kingdom. In 1808, however, Godoy was ousted from Aranjuez in a popular uprising. To prevent Spain from defecting to the growing enemy camp, Napoleon forced Charles III and his son Ferdinand to renounce the throne and installed his own brother, Joseph, as king.

5 Charles III on horseback, 18th c.

Charles III, on the Clergy:

"The Bishops have nothing to give away; everything they own belongs to the poor; therefore they should sell it and distribute it as alms."

above: The Cathedral of Santiago de Compostela, built in the 18th century

Royal palace of Madrid, designed by Juvara, construction begun under Philip V and completed under Charles III, photograph, ca. 1890

A Village Bullfight, traditional pastime of the peasants, painting by Goya, ca. 1819

Charles IV and Maria Luisa with their children, family portrait by Francisco Goya, 1800

Public humiliation of man condemned by the Inquisition, painting, 19th c.

Manuel de Godoy during a military campaign against Portugal, painting by Francisco Goya, 1801

1759	Charles III comes to power	1767	Jesuits expelled	1805	Battle of Trafalgar
1761	Alliance with France	1796	Alliance with San Ildefonso	1808	Joseph Bonaparte becomes king of Spain

EASTERN EUROPE AND SCANDINAVIA 1500–1800

Poland experienced a turbulent period due to its elective and weak monarchy that struggled to maintain its authority in the face of an aristocracy that strove for independence. It was then divided up between the Great Powers in the partitions of Poland. In Hungary and Transylvania the Ottomans and Habsburgs fought for power. Protestant ❷ kings in Denmark and Sweden attempted to strengthen central authority and expand their sphere of influence. Sweden rose to become a European power under Gustav II Adolph after 1648, but Russia was able to break Sweden's dominance in the north after the death of Charles XII.

The Wawel Cathedral in Kraków used for the coronation ceremonies of Polish kings and built in the Italian Renaissance style

The Danish "Crown of the Absolute Monarchs," made in 1670–71

◾ Poland and Hungary in the 16th and 17th Centuries

The aristocracy's right of election and the disputes with its neighbors weakened the Polish kingdom. Hungary came under the rule of the Ottomans and the Habsburgs.

The position of the Polish kings was traditionally weak because it was an ❸ elective monarchy. The nobility held the peasants in servitude and expanded its privileges at every election in the Sejm or Diet. Sigismund I of the Jagiellon dynasty, king from 1506, was

Unification of Poland and Lithuania in the Lublin, wood engraving

Portrait of Sigismund III Vasa, king of Poland and briefly king of Sweden, ca. 1600

a promoter of the ❶ Renaissance and humanism. He ended the disputes with the Habsburgs in 1515 and with the Teutonic Order over East Prussia in 1525. His son Sigismund II Augustus unified the Lithuanian provinces with Poland in the ❺ Union of Lublin in 1569.

After the end of the Jagiellon line, the aristocracy forced through religious freedom and the right of resistance with the election of Henry of Valois in 1572, later Henry III king of France. In 1587 ❻ Sigismund III brought the Catholic line of the House of Vasa to power. His son Wladyslaw IV pushed far into Russian territory, but Wlady-slaw's brother ❹ John II Casimir later had to contend with the revolts of the Cossack leader Bogdan Chmelnizkij, who was supported by Russia and the Polish peasants, founded his own state in the Ukraine, and placed himself un-

der the czar in 1654. When Ukraine was lost to Russia, the king abdicated.

A branch of the house of Jagiellon had ruled in Bohemia and Hungary since the 15th century. A pact was made with the Habsburgs for the ❼ double wedding of the children of King Wladyslaw II, Louis and Anna, with the grandchildren of Holy Roman Emperor Maximilian I, Ferdinand and

John II Casimir, 18th c.

Polish general assembly for the election of a king in a field near Warsaw, copper engraving, 17th century

Mary, in 1515. When the young King Louis II fell in the Battle of Mohacs against the Turks in 1526, his brother-in-law, Ferdinand I claimed Bohemia and Hungary. But Ferdinand was only able to hold Bohemia; the Ottomans, who supported their own kings, occupied most of Hungary for a century and a half.

Double wedding between the Habsburg and the Jagiellon dynasty in 1515

| since 1386 | Jagiello rule in Bohemia and Hungary | 1525 | Secularization of Prussia | 1541 | Turkish Hungary becomes Ottoman province |
| 1515 | Poland gains Prussia as fief | 1526 | Battle of Mohacs | 1569 | Lublin Union |

Hungary and Poland to the 18th Century

The power struggle between the Ottomans and the Habsburgs also raged in Hungary and neighboring Transylvania. At first, Poland fought against Sweden in the Great Northern War but then came under the influence of Russia and finally ceased to exist as a state due to the Three Partitions.

8   Ferenc II Rákóczi, portrait, ca. 1700

10   Stanislaw I Leszczynski, steel engraving, 18th century

The battle for Hungary and Transylvania sapped the strength of the Habsburgs in the East. The Ottomans had supported local nobility against the Habsburgs over the centuries, beginning with John Zápolya, who was *woiwode* (governor) of Transylvania from 1511 and king of eastern Hungary from 1526. The Protestant Bethlen Gábor, for example, prince of Transylvania in 1613 and king of Hungary in 1620, pushed into Bohemia and Austria. The Habsburgs were first able to extend their rule over all of Hungary only after the victory of Prince Eugène of Savoy in 1697. For the last time, in 1704, **8** Ferenc II Rákóczi, prince of Transylvania and Hungary, once again led a revolt against the Habsburgs but in 1711 was forced to relinquish all his titles. Nevertheless, Hungary, which persisted in striving for independence, remained a hotbed of conflict until the end of the Habsburg monarchy.

9 John III Sobieski, who was elected king of Poland in 1674, helped defend Vienna against the

9   John III Sobieski with captured Ottomans, etching, 18th century

Turks. His attempt to establish a hereditary monarchy failed, however, due to the resistance of the nobility. Instead, the Saxon elector **11** Frederick Augustus I (the Strong) was elected as King Augustus II in 1697. He was driven out of Poland in the Great Northern War in 1701 by Charles XII of Sweden but was able to regain the crown after Charles's defeat at Poltava in 1709.

Upon Augustus's death in 1733, the Polish nobility chose the Polish noble **10** Stanislaw I Leszczynski, the father-in-law of Louis XV of France, who had once already been installed as king between 1704 and 1709 by Charles XII. However, Russia and Austria, fearful of losing their influence, forced the election of Augustus III, the son of Augustus the Strong, in 1733–1734. The consequent War of Polish Succession ended with a Europe-wide exchange of lands. Stanislaw Leszczynski received Lorraine as compensation and Francis Stephen of Lorraine got Tuscany. Augustus III continued to reign in Saxony and Poland. After his death, Empress Catherine II of Russia put her former lover **12** Stanislaw II Poniatowski on the throne in 1764. The king tried to make reforms, but Russia obstructed them. In opposition, the National Polish "Confederation of Bar" rebelled, while in support, the Ottomans started a war with Russia. After her victory, the empress undertook the **13** First Partition of Poland in 1772, in which Russia, Austria, and Prussia annexed large tracts of land for themselves. In two further partitions in 1793 and 1795, Poland was completely divided up. King Stanislaw II abdicated and the old Polish Empire ceased to exist.

11   Charles XII of Sweden encounters his opponent in war, Frederick I Augustus (the Strong) of Saxony and Poland, wood engraving, ca. 1860

12   Stanislaw II August Poniatowski, copper engraving, 19th century

13   Artistic representation of the first partition of Poland, with Catherine II of Russia, Stanislaw II of Poland, Joseph II of Austria, and Frederick II of Prussia, copper engraving, 18th century

Denmark and Sweden to the 17th Century

The kings in Denmark and Sweden carried out the Reformation, attempted to prevail against the nobility, and became involved in the Thirty Years' War. Sweden was one of the main benefactors of the war's peace treaty in 1648.

1616 poem by Gustav II Adolph:

Some day virtue will reward you, / When you have become Dust, / With high glory eternal / As you were promised.

Gustav II Adolph, 17th century

Christian IV, ca. 1640

Traditionally in Denmark and Sweden, the nobility tried to maintain their independence, while the kings sought increased central authority and supported their countries' sea power. ❷ Christian II, king of Denmark and Norway from 1513, brutally established his dominance over Sweden with the "Bloodbath of Stockholm"—the mass execution of his opponents in 1520.

❸ Queen Christina of Sweden on horseback, ca. 1652–54

Just three years later, however, he was driven out by the Swedish noble Gustav Erickson, who was elected the new king. As ❹ Gustav I Vasa, he established the modern nation-state of Sweden and introduced the Reformation in 1527.

His successors built upon this foundation in wars of shifting alliances against Denmark, Poland, and the Hanseatic city of Lübeck, which controlled the Baltic Sea trade. King Gustav II Adolph was thus able to gain territories in the Baltic from Russia in 1617 and from Poland in 1629, making Sweden the leading power in the north. In 1630, he intervened in the Thirty Years' War as leader of the Protestant powers. Sweden also ac-

Christian II, painting by Lucas Cranach the Elder, ca. 1523

quired land from Denmark in 1645 and was among the winners of the Peace of Westphalia in 1648, gaining the archdiocese of Bremen, the diocese of Verden, and parts of Pomerania. Gustav II's daughter and successor ❸ Christina, for whom Chancellor Axel Oxenstierna was regent until 1644, turned her court into a center of scholars but then abdicated in 1654, converted to Catholicism in 1655, and died in ❻ Rome in 1689. The kings of the House of Palatinate-Zweibrucken, who inherited Sweden from the Vasas in 1654, continued to develop Sweden's power and influence.

In Denmark the strengthening of the monarch's authority was served by the introduction of the Reformation in Denmark and Norway in 1536, because it placed the church under the control of the head of state. ❶

Christian IV centralized government and in 1625 entered the Thirty Years' War. In 1645, he was forced to recognize Sweden's hegemony in the Baltic region in the Peace of Brömsebro. His son, ❺ Frederick III, broke the power of the nobility in an alliance with the clergy and middle class in 1660, introduced the hereditary monarchy, and established absolutism by the Royal Law of 1665.

Gustav I Vasa, 19th-century painting

Frederick III, ca. 1648

Festivities for the reception of Christina of Sweden in Rome

| 1520 | Bloodbath of Stockholm | 1527 | Introduction of the Reformation in Sweden | 1645 | Treaty of Brömsebro |
| 1523 | Gustav I Vasa elected king | 1536 | Introduction of the Reformation in Denmark | 1654 | Sweden invades Poland |

■ Northern Europe in the 18th Century

Charles XII once again made Sweden the predominant power in northeast Europe, but with his death, all that was gained was lost again. Enlightened absolutism could only be hesitantly implemented in Denmark and Sweden.

❼ Charles X Gustav of the house Palatinate-Zweibrucken, who inherited the Swedish throne from his cousin Christina of Vasa in 1654, extended Swedish possessions in wars against Poland and Denmark—which was forced to relinquish all of southern Sweden, including Skåne and Halland, by the Treaty of Roskilde in 1658. Although his son ❽ Charles XI lost Pomerania to Brandenburg, he did finally break the power of the Swedish aristocracy by seizing the crown estates and establishing absolutist rule. Denmark, Russia, and Poland allied against his son Charles XII, who succeeded him in 1699, to regain lost territories from Sweden, but the king invaded Denmark and forced it to accept peace, and then in 1700, leading his troops, destroyed the Russian army at ⓫ Narva. In 1702 Charles XII expelled Augustus the Strong of Saxony and Poland out of Livonia, then in 1702 out of Poland as well, and in 1706 he invaded Saxony. In 1709, however, he suffered a crushing defeat against Czar Peter the Great on the plains of Poltava and was forced to flee to Turkey; he finally fell in Norway in November 1718. The Great Northern War, begun in 1700, was finally concluded at the Treaty of Nystad in 1721. Sweden was forced to turn over its possessions in the Baltic and southwest Finland to Russia.

Domestically, marriages and the inheritance of succeeding reigns by the German houses of Hessen-Kassel and Holstein-Gottorp weakened royal power in Sweden. ⓬ Gustav III Vasa restored the absolute power of the king in 1772 through a coup d'état and abolished aristocratic privileges in 1789. His was a splendid court, and he founded the Swedish Academy in 1786, but he was murdered in March 1792 by a conspiracy of nobles during a masked ball. His son Gustav IV Adolph waged unsuccessful wars against Napoleon and was deposed by his officers in 1809.

Denmark's inflexible absolutism prevented necessary reforms. Two chief ministers, Johann Hartwig Graf Bernstorff and his nephew Andreas Peter Graf Bernstorff, tried to govern in the spirit of enlightened absolutism. In 1771–1772, the physician of the mentally ill King ❿ Christian VII and lover of the Queen Caroline Mathilde, ❾ John Frederick of Struensee, intervened in politics with radical reforms, including the abolition of torture and censorship, but he was overthrown early in 1772 and executed.

Charles X Gustav, painting, ca. 1652

8 Statue of Charles XI in Karlskrona, 19th century

Struensee is led away to his execution, quill lithography, 19th century

10
Christian VII, copper engraving

11
Charles XII of Sweden conquers the Russian fortress of Narva in a crushing defeat of the Russians, copper engraving, ca. 1700

12
Murder of Gustav III in the Stockholm opera house, wood engraving, 19th c.

RUSSIA'S RISE AS A GREAT POWER 1613–1801

The rule of the Romanov dynasty which began with the election of Michael Romanov in 1613 stabilized the turbulent political conditions in Russia following the "Time of Troubles." Supported by an absolute authority, Czar Peter the Great could push through an authoritative and broad ❶ modernization of the Empire in all fields. His successors continued this modernization and, particularly under Catherine the Great, carried out aggressive Russian expansion policies, particularly against Poland and the Ottoman Empire. Catherine ruled as one of the most powerful "Enlightened monarchs" of the eighteenth century.

Caricature referring to the modernizing reforms of Peter the Great: A "reactionary's" beard is cut off, wood engraving, ca. 1700

Russia under the First Romanovs

The ruling Romanov dynasty reintroduced the autocracy of the czars and began to reconquer the lands lost to Poland and Sweden under previous rulers.

The election of ❷ Michael Romanov as Russian czar in 1613, ended the "Time of Troubles" (*Smuta*). His father Fyodor, the Orthodox patriarch of Moscow, stood behind his election. Another relative, the patriarch Philaret, governed Russia jointly with the czar until 1633.

Czar Michael I made peace with Sweden and Poland in 1617–1618, whereby Novgorod was brought back into the empire. The Church reforms led to the Great Schism. Michael's son ❸ Alexis curtailed the rights of the aristocracy and the Church further. The serfdom of the peasants was definitively laid down in law at this time. As a result of the sup-

The Election of Michael Romanov to Czar, watercolor painting, 19th century

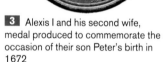

❸ Alexis I and his second wife, medal produced to commemorate the occasion of their son Peter's birth in 1672

port of the Cossack leader Bogdan Chmelnizkij, Russia won back parts of Ukraine with the old Russian capital of Kiev in 1654–1667, leading to conflicts with the Ottomans and the khans of the Crimea in the Ukrainian south.

After Alexis' death in 1676, his children from two marriages fought for succession. His son Fyodor III became czar but died six years later. Fyodor's sister Sophia then served as regent for her mentally deficient brother Ivan V and underage half-brother ❺ Peter I; in 1686 she allied with Poland and joined the Holy League against the

Ottomans. When Peter reached maturity, Sophia tried to retain power and get rid of Peter. However, he preempted her and took power in a coup in 1689, exiling ❹ Sophia to the Novodevichy convent. That year, Peter, who was sole ruler after the death of Ivan, brutally put down the ❻ streltzi uprising by a military unit of Sophia's supporters.

Sophia in exile in the convent, painting by Ilja Repin, 1879

Peter I the Great, painting by Jean Marc Nattier, 1717

After his return from Western Europe, Peter I has participants in the *streltzi* uprising executed

1613	Czar Michael I Romanov		May 16, 1703	Founding of St. Petersburg		1721	Dissolution of the Patriarchy
	since 1696	Reform phase under Peter the Great		1714	Introduction of a line of succession		1725	Catherine I crowned

■ From Peter the Great to Catherine the Great

Peter the Great's reforms made Russia a modern European great power. His successors, particularly Catherine the Great, carried out the expansion of the empire.

Fascinated by Western European culture,  Peter I (the Great) undertook a journey to Prussia, England, and Holland in 1697-98, where he was trained as an ordnance soldier and ❽ shipbuilding engineer. He completed his expansion of the army and fleet and then, in the Great Northern War, conquered Swedish territory in the southwest of Finland and in the Baltic region, giving Russia access to the Baltic Sea. Here, on the estuary of the Neva River, he founded his new capital, ❾ St. Petersburg, which was designed after the European example. Internally Peter initiated comprehensi-

8 Peter I learns shipbuilding in the Netherlands, wood engraving, 19th c.

10 Peter I founding St. Petersburg, painting, 19th century

11 Elizabeth, daughter of Peter I, painting, ca. 1744–51

9 Peter and Paul Fortress in St. Petersburg, with the Cathedral where the Romanovs are interred

ve modernization. He broke the power of the Church by disbanding the patriarchy and appointing a holy synod along the Lutheran model. The economy and social order were reformed by the establishment of early manufacturing organizations, expansion of the infrastructure, recruitment of foreign workers, founding of education institutions, and regulation of the aristocracy and administration.

As he had had his own son killed, Peter's widow Catherine I succeeded him in 1725. In 1741 his youngest daughter ⓫ Elizabeth came to the throne. She joined in alliance with Maria Theresa of Austria against Prussia in the Seven Years' War in 1756, and their forces had brought Prussia to the brink of total collapse when Eliz-

abeth died in 1762. This alone saved Frederick the Great, as Elizabeth's successor Peter III was an admirer of the Prussian king and ended the war immediately. In order to control Peter, Frederick had negotiated his marriage to Sophie von Anhalt-Zerbst, the daughter of a Prussian general, in 1745. Peter's reign was brief, however, as his wife, aided by a military putsch, disposed of him and took the throne as ❼ Catherine II within the year.

Influenced by Enlightenment ideas, Catherine II (the Great) communicated with many of the most significant thinkers of Europe, yet also gave away thousands of serfs as presents to her numerous lovers and favorites.

Catherine adopted strongly imperialist policies and conclusively turned Russia into a great power. In the Russo-Turkish War, Russia destroyed the Turkish Fleet in 1770 and conquered the northern Caucasus, ensuring Russian access to the Black Sea. Crimea, which had less than a decade earlier become independent, was annexed. In the three partitions of

7 Catherine the Great, painting, 18th c.

Poland in 1772, 1793, and 1795, Russia pushed its boundaries gradually west.

Catherine's son, ⓬ Paul I, took part in the Second Coalition in the Revolutionary Wars against France. In 1801, his plans for the conquest of India led to his murder by military officers.

Prince Potemkin

Prince Potemkin was a favorite and political advisor of Catherine the Great. He was a capable administrator and initiated ambitious constructions of city and settlement projects in the south of Russia. Those jealous of him defamed him by suggesting that he set up false facades—"Potemkin villages"—faked civic improvement with which to impress the Czar during her tour of the country.

above: Prince Potemkin

12 Paul I, painting, late 18th century

THE OTTOMAN EMPIRE, THE GREAT POWER OF THE EAST CA. 1300–1792

The Turkmen tribal group of the Ottomans, based in northwestern Anatolia, pushed steadily westward. After the capture of Constantinople in 1453, Sultan Selim I made the Ottoman Empire a major power by 1516-1517 with the conquest of the Near East and large parts of Africa. Under his successors, particularly ❶ Suleiman the Magnificent, the Turkish presence became a determining factor in European politics. After several successful advances against the Habsburg Empire, the Ottomans were forced onto the defensive by the Austrians and Russians after 1697. Internal political reforms were slow.

Sultan Suleiman the Magnficent's "tughra," the official seal or signature of a sultan

The Rise of the Ottomans

The early Ottoman sultans consolidated their power in Anatolia and began the conquest of the Balkans. In 1453, Mehmed II took Constantinople and ended the Byzantine Empire.

Osman I with his army commanders, colored lithograph

❷ Osman I, the dynasty founder from whom the name "Ottoman" is derived, led an independent tribal group in northwestern Anatolia around 1300. The tribe's warriors had dedicated themselves to a jihad against Byzan-

Interior of the Hagia Sophia, finished in the sixth century, mosque since 1453

tium. Osman's son Orhan took the title of sultan, made Bursa his capital, and conquered East Anatolia. In 1354, he gained control of Gallipoli, a foothold in the Crimea, which he then used as a base to begin his conquest of the Balkans. Murad I conquered Bulgaria in 1385-86 and triumphed over the Serbs in 1389 in the Battle of Kosovo, at the Field of the Blackbirds.

During the 14th century, the Ottoman tribal federation became a solid state structure. The sultans armed their military well and created an elite corps made up of Islamized Balkan Christians— the much-feared ❸ Janissaries. Bayezid I permanently subjugated Bulgaria in 1393, but suffered a crushing defeat near Ankara in 1402 against the Central Asian conqueror Tamerlane. A reorganization of the state interrupted further expansion until Mehmed I brought Asia Minor and a large

part of the Balkans under his control again. The siege of Constantinople began in 1422 under Murad II, who had subjugated all of Anatolia. In 1439 Murad annexed Serbia—which he crushed in 1448 in the second Battle of Kosovo—into his empire, and repelled the last Christian Crusade in 1444 at

Sultan Mehmed II

Janissary soldier

Varna. ❹ Mehmed II was able to conquer Constantinople on May 29, 1453, bringing an end to the Byzantine Empire. He had many churches converted into mosques, including the ❺ Hagia Sophia, and built the Topkapi Palace, where the sultans would reside from then on.

Critobulus of Imbros, History of Mehmed the Conqueror, 15th century, on

The Conquest of Constantinople:

"…but when Sultan Mehmed saw that the Palisade and the rest of the part of the walls (of Constantinople) had been pulled down and was naked of men and without defenders…he immediately called in a loud voice, 'We have the city, my friends, we have her already. With a small effort and the city is conquered. Do not get weak, but go with courage to the work and prove yourselves brave men and I will be with you.'"

The Ottoman army base outside Constantinople

The Zenith of the Ottoman Empire

Mehmed II's successor, Selim I, was responsible for making the Ottoman Empire a world power. During the reign of Suleiman the Magnificent, the empire was at its political and cultural peak.

Mehmed II considered himself the next world conqueror. While he avoided internal unrest by granting Christians and Jews cultural freedom through payment of a poll tax, his forces overran Serbia, Bosnia, and Albania and occupied the last Christian territories in the Peloponnesus in 1458-1462. He annexed Serbia in 1459. The Ottomans soon controlled the Eastern Mediterranean and the Black Sea through the conquest of Trebizond in Asia Minor and the subjugation of the khans of the Crimea in 1475, and then obligated to tribute payments. In 1480 Mehmed landed in southern Italy and was preparing to advance on Rome, the "heart of Christianity," when he died in the spring of 1481.

A time of military inactivity under the pious sultan ❻ Bayezid II ended in April 1512 with a coup d'état by his son, Selim I (the Grim). At his accession to the throne, Selim proclaimed that he was going to be lord of all civilization and successor to Alexander the Great. He was the creator of the Ottoman world empire. In 1514 he defeated the Safavid rulers of Persia at ❾ Chaldiran, occupied Azerbaijan and East Anatolia, and subjugated Kurdistan, which gave him control of the trade routes to Persia. The sultan used the Egyptian Mamelukes' call for aid against the Portuguese to occupy Syria in 1516 and seize Egypt in 1517. With that, Selim had doubled the area of the Ottoman Empire. He deposed the last caliph in Cairo, assuming the title himself, and took over the protectorate of the Islamic holy sites of Mecca and Medina. In order to secure the power of the sultan domestically from rivals and to avoid struggles of succession, he introduced the practice of a sultan murdering all of his brothers upon assuming the throne.

Selim's son ❼ Suleiman I (the Magnificent) led the Ottoman Empire to cultural grandeur. He dedicated himself to the modernization of the government, especially the legal and tax systems. He had magnificent ❿ mosques constructed by his brilliant master builder ❽ Sinan. Suleiman's armies pushed west. In 1521, they took Belgrade, which became their main base in the Balkans in the ensuing period, and they crushed the Hungarians in 1526 at Mohács.

7 Sultan Suleiman the Magnificent

In 1529, the Ottomans approached ⓫ Vienna for the first time and besieged the city, but this was unsuccessful and they were forced to withdraw. The 16th century was marked by the Ottomans' eventful battles against the Habsburgs and Spanish in the Balkans, their control of North Africa, and their domination of the Mediterranean.

6 Sultan Bayezid II

8 The architect Sinan

10 The Suleiman Mosque in Istanbul, 16th century

9 Battle against the Persians on the plain of Chaldiran on the August 23, 1514

11 The Ottomans besiege Vienna under Suleiman II from September 8 to October 15, 1529

1514	Battle of Chaldiran	1517	Conquest of Egypt	1521	Taking of Belgrade	1529	First Siege of Vienna
1453	Conquest of Constantinople	1516	Conquest of Syria	1520–66	Reign of Suleiman II	1526	Battle of Mohács

The Time of the Grand Viziers

Suleiman I's successors were generally weak rulers whose grand viziers ruled in their stead. Nevertheless, in 1683 the Ottomans once again stood at the gates of Vienna.

The naval battle of Lepanto on the Oct. 7, 1571

In the middle of the 16th century, Selim II and Murad III ushered in the period of the rule of insignificant sultans with no interest in state affairs. They abandoned themselves to immense luxury and became wrapped up in household intrigues, and the reign of the grand viziers began. Thanks to Grand Vizier Mehmed Sokollu, the empire remained politically stable even after its defeat at the hands of an allied Christian fleet in the naval Battle of ❷ Lepanto in 1571. The Turks opened diplomatic and trade relations with England in 1580 and with the Netherlands in 1603. Caucasia, with ❶ Tbilisi and Tabriz, came under Ottoman control in the 1579-1590 war against Persia, but after 1603 they were lost again to Shah Abbas the Great.

Revolts in Anatolia and Kurdistan provided signs of the internal disintegration of the empire. The Janissaries had become a powerful state within a state. But in 1622 when they murdered Sultan Osman II, who had attempted to curb their power, his brother Murad IV broke the Janissaries' dominion with barbaric ritual punishment. He was able to subdue the revolts of the Kurds and Druze in Syria, and in 1638 managed to ❸ retake Baghdad from the Safavids. During this period, many Albanians and Bosnians and a portion of the Bulgarians in the Balkans converted to Islam.

From the middle of the 17th century, the governance of the empire was in the hands of the Albanian Koprulu family of grand viziers, who proclaimed a war on corruption and strengthened the central authority. They were also able to snatch Crete from the Venetians in 1669 and Podolia from the Poles in 1672.

The ambitious ❹ Kara Mustafa became grand vizier in 1676 and marched his troops through Hungary. In 1683, he besieged Vienna, but the combined armies and their Polish allies defeated the Turks at the ❺ Kahlenberg heights and drove them back; Charles V of Lorraine and Louis William of Baden-Baden then pushed the Ottomans out of ❻ Hungary. In 1687, the Venetians occupied parts of the Peloponnesus, including Athens. A return to rule of the Koprulu grand viziers did not end Turkish losses in the Balkans.

Triumphant parade of the Ottoman army outside the walls of Tbilisi in Georgia after the Persians had abandoned the city in Aug. 1578, book illustration

The taking of Baghdad by the Ottomans

The Grand Vizier Kara Mustafa

The Battle of Kahlenberg Heights, Sept. 12, 1683

Austrian imperial troops attack an Ottoman army base

The Harem

The wives of the sultan, his concubines, and the countless servant girls who served them lived in the harem, closed off from the outside world and guarded over by eunuchs. At the head of the harem was the powerful mother of the sultan, with whom the women who had borne the sultan sons vied for power. The sultans' sons were also raised here in this "gilded cage." It was no wonder that many of them were blind to reality or even psychologically disturbed when they finally came to power.

above: Members of the sultan's harem play a game, painting, Francesco Guardi, 18th c.

1571	Battle of Lepanto	1656–76	Grand Viziers Mehmed and Fasil Ahmed Koprulu	1676–83	Grand Vizier Kara Mustafa
1565–79	Grand Vizier Mehmed Sokollu	1579–90	War against Persia	1669	Conquest of Crete	1683	Siege of Vienna

▪ The Empire between Decline and Reform

The Ottoman Empire was forced onto the defensive in the Balkans through the victories of Prince Eugène of Savoy and pressure from Russia. Necessary internal reforms were late in coming and strongly opposed.

Sultan Ahmed III in one of the courts of the Topkapi Palace, painting, 18th c.

Defeated by the Austrian general Eugène of Savoy in 1697 at Zenta, the Ottoman empire lost Hungary, Transylvania, and Slavonia to Austria, Podolia to Poland, and the Peloponnesus and parts of Dalmatia to Venice under provisions of the Treaty of Carlowitz; in 1700 Azov went to Russia. When Sultan ❽ Ahmed III gran-

ted asylum to Charles XII of Sweden in 1709, he provoked a war with Russia in 1710-1711, which the Ottomans won. In 1717, however, ❼, ❾ Belgrade was lost to the Austrian Empire, which by the Treaty of Passarowitz in 1718 also took the Banat, northern Serbia, and Little Walachia.

These military failures led to the overthrow of Ahmed III in 1730 and a renewed reign of the Janissary corps, which retook northern Serbia and Little Walachia in 1736-1739. While a military pact was made with Austria, Russia with its expansionist ambitions had become the major enemy of the Ottoman Empire by 1741. An alliance between the Ottomans and Prussia in 1761 ushered in cordial relations that continued up to World War I. The Russians advanced into Moldavia and Transcaucasia during the First Russo-Turkish War (1768-1774) and in 1770 destroyed the Turkish fleet. In 1774-1783, the Ottomans

lost ❿ Crimea to Russia and Bukovina to Austria. Catherine the Great of Russia then usurped the protectorate over the Christian princes Georgia in 1784. The Turks once again went to war in 1787-1792 against Russia and Austria. Russia made further territorial gains and replaced the Ottoman Empire as the dominant power in the Black Sea region.

The Ottomans hand over Belgrade to the Austrians in 1717, painting

The Tulip Era

The short period between 1718 and 1730 during the reign of Sultan Ahmed III is referred to as the Tulip Era. Following the Treaty of Passarowitz, Ottoman interest in the European baroque culture grew, as did Western interest in the Orient. During the Tulip era in Turkey there was a cultural blossoming of the arts. The tulip, an extremely popular and—as tulip bulbs could be sold for their weight in gold—valuable export from Turkey, became a symbol for the era.

Example of the famous ceramic tiles produced in Iznik, Turkey, with tulip, carnation, and rosette motif

The Battle for Belgrade, center Prince Eugene of Savoy, Aug. 18, 1717

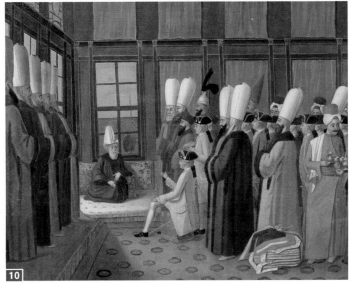

The Russian deputy sovereign visits the Grand Vizier in 1775 for negotiations

1689–91	Grand Vizier Fasil Mustafa Koprulu	1699	Peace of Karlowitz	1768–74	First Russo-Turkish War	1787–92	Second Russo-Turkish War
1697	Battle of Zenta		1718	Peace of Passarowitz	1770	Destruction of Ottoman fleet

NORTH AFRICA 16TH–18TH CENTURY

Algeria, Tunisia, and Libya were fiercely contested during the 16th century. The Ottomans eventually prevailed, yet the local elite was able to win increasing political and cultural freedom and became effectively independent by the 17th century. Morocco had particular difficulties defending itself against Portuguese conquest attempts. Under local dynasties, the land grew in prosperity and stability, but, like the whole of the Maghreb, it drew Europe's colonial interest around 1800.

1 Naval map of the Mediterranean and the Black Sea, 1551

Algeria and Tunisia in the 16th–18th centuries

The eastern area of the Maghreb was at first fought over by Spain and the Ottomans. The Ottomans were able to uphold their rule for a long time, but the regions won a large degree of autonomy despite their formal suzerainty.

3 Liberated Christians in Tunis express their gratitude to Emperor Charles V

While Syria-Palestine and Egypt had been firmly under the control of the Ottomans since 1517, the coasts of Algeria, Libya, and Tunisia were actively fought over in the 16th century. In the **1** Mediterranean, the Spanish and the Ottomans competed for both military and commercial supremacy. The Barbary pirates, or corsairs, were a constant source of uncertainty as they often changed allegiance and plundered coastal towns. The most successful of them during this period were the two brothers **2** Khayr ad-Din.

5 View of the important coastal city of Algiers from the sea

Attacks on Spanish galleons by Khayr ad-Din (Barbarossa) provoked Emperor Charles V into occupying **3**, **6** Tunis in 1535 and besieging **5** Algiers, the most important centers on the North African coast.

In the long run, it was the Ottomans who—at least nominally—won supremacy over the eastern Maghreb: Cyrenaica in 1521, Tripolitania (Libya) in 1551, Algeria in 1556, and Tunisia in 1574. From 1587 until 1671, Algeria was administered by a Turkish governor (*pasha*) until the local Janissaries took over rule as *deys* who were only officially dependent on the sultan; this system lasted until the French occupation of 1830. The Ottoman pasha was also deposed in Tunisia in 1591 in favor of a largely autonomous dey. In 1640 Hammuda ibn Murad seized power and founded the dynasty of the Muradid beys that stayed in power until 1702; they were followed in 1705 by Husain ibn Ali, whose dynasty of **4** Husainid beys ruled until the

declaration of the republic in 1957. In Tripolitania, the Qaramanli dynasty ruled from 1711 until 1832 as autonomous beys. Their ships' troops were feared as pirates. Even before 1800, this region was being eyed by France as potential colonial territory.

2 The Corsair Khayr ad-Din Barbarossa

4 Muhammad III, Bey of Tunis (1859–82)

6 Market place in Tunis, painting, 19th century

The Siege of Malta

After the Turks captured the headquarters of the Order of St. John of Jerusalem on Rhodes in 1522, Emperor Charles V gave the Order the island of Malta in 1530 as a fiefdom. From here they continued to defy the Muslim world. A Turkish-corsair fleet tried to conquer Malta in 1565, but the Knights of St. John, supported by the Spanish, held the island, despite a four-month siege. The hero of the defensive battle was the order's grand master, Jean Parisot de La Valette.

above: Turkish forces besiege Malta, May 1565

Morocco under the Wattasids and the Early 'Alawites

The Wattasids and the later dynasties of the Sa'did and 'Alawites defended Morocco's independence. Morocco experienced stability and prosperity under Mawlay Ismail and his successors as a result of its strategic position for trade.

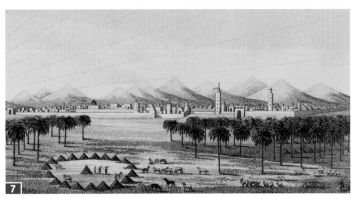

The capital Marrakech, which lies in an oasis where date palms grow

Detail from the Sadier tombs at Marrakech, built under Sultan Ahmad al-Mansur

❿ Morocco did not come under the rule of the Ottomans, but was forced to defend its independence against Portugal. The Wattasids, who had ruled Morocco since 1472, lost Melilla to the Spanish in 1497 and then Agadir and large expanses of their coastal regions in 1504 to the Portuguese, who then besieged ❼ Marrakech in 1515. In 1524 the Sa'did dynasty rebelled in southern Morocco, and in 1554 they deposed the last of the Wattasid rulers. Muhammad al-Mahdi, the founder of the Sa'did dynasty, assumed the title of sultan, made an alliance with the Ottomans, and declared himself a descendant of the Prophet Muhammad (sharif), and even a caliph of Islam. His descendant, ❽ Ahmad al-Mansur, crushingly defeated the invading Portuguese under King Sebastian in 1578 at Ksar el-Kebir, and through tight administration led the country to considerable prosperity. Through the policy of *makhzan*, a system of awarding land, he was able to make the elite of the country beholden to him. His sons divided the land in two ruling lines that governed Fez (until 1626) and Marrakech (until 1659).

The Sa'did sharifs were followed in 1666 by the 'Alawite dynasty of sharifs, who still rule Morocco today. Mawlay ar-Rashid, the first ruler, established himself in Fez and, in alliance with the Otto-mans, conquered Marrakech in 1669 and finally all of Morocco. His son, ❾ Mawlay Ismail, succeeded him in 1672 and was the most important ruling public figure of Maghreb in the 18th century. Politically shrewd, ostentatious, and violent, he broke the resistance of the local sheiks and religious brotherhoods, created a personal elite corps of 150,000 black slaves, and built the magnificent "imperial city" of Meknes. He maintained trading relations with many European powers.

Everything Mawlay Ismail had gained was at stake in the fratricidal war of his seven sons. However, his grandson, Mawlay Mohammed, was able to restore stability through the reorganization of the administration system and finances and by fostering the economy through the granting of trade licenses, primarily to France and the United States. His son Mawlay Suleiman continued these policies by easing tariffs for the European powers. After 1810, he changed his originally liberal policy concerning religion and persecuted religious brother-

The stables in Mawlay Ismail's Meknes

hoods and banned local customs, which led to general unrest. Around 1800 Morocco's prosperity caught the interest of France and Spain.

Moroccan landscape, small settlement with the Atlas Mountain range that stretches across northern Morocco in the background

| May–Sep 1565 | Siege of Malta | 1578 | Battle of Ksar el-Kebir | from 1666 | 'Alawite dynasty rule in Morocco | 1711 | Qaramanli Dynasty rule in Libya |
| 1574 | Ottomans occupy Tunisia | 1640 | Muradid Bey rule in Tunisia begins | 1705 | Husainid Bey Dynasty rule in Tunisia | | |

1 Map of Persia, 1681

PERSIA UNDER THE SAFAVIDS AND QAJARS CA. 1450–1921

The rule of the Shiite Safavids introduced a period of independent religious and cultural development in ❶ Persia after 1500. In particular Shah Abbas the Great, through his military and economic policies, made the country a major power in the Near East. For this reason, it was constantly in competition with the Ottoman Empire. Following the Safavids, Nadir Shah erected a short-lived empire that fell apart again under his successor. The Qajars, who came to power in 1796, were the first dynasty able to restore Persia's unity. At the same time, the Central Asian Uzbek empire was flowering under the Shaybanids.

■ The Beginnings of the Safavids and the First Safavid Shahs

Shah Ismail established Safavid rule in Persia in 1501. He laid the groundwork for the Shi'ite identity of the country, which was used as a foundation by his successors.

In the power vacuum left by the local dynasties, the heirs of the Timurid Empire established the Sufi Order of the Safavids, which converted to Twelver Shiism in the 15th century. The hereditary sheikhs of the order also fostered a military basis among their followers and were able to extend their power. The founder of the dynasty, and the first shah was Ismail I (ruled 1499–1524), ruler of the town of Ardevil, who descended from the Sassanid dynasty. A Shi'ite, he conquered all of Iran and Iraq and drove the Uzbeks east by 1507. In 1514, at Chaldiran, he suffered defeat against the Ottomans under Sultan Selim I.

Shah Ismail focused on domestic development. He concentrated religious and secular authority and made Twelver Shiism the state religion, dramatically influencing Iran's development as a nation-state. Ismail's rule, based on his own charisma, showed itself to be unsturdy under his son Tahmasp I, who succeeded him in 1524. The new shah, who was himself artistically talented, promoted painting and calligraphy. During his reign, magnificent editions of the Persian national epic, ❷, ❸ *Shah Namah*, and the

"Khamsa" by Nizami were created. During the course of his entire reign, Tahmasp was forced to wage war against the Uzbeks over Khorasan in the east and with the Ottoman Turks over Azerbaijan in the west. In 1548 he moved his capital from Tabriz to Qazvin. In 1554 he occupied Georgia, where he increased military recruitment of Caucasians, and in 1555 exchanged Iraq for Azerbaijan in a peace settlement with the Ottomans. The reigns of Tahmasp's sons, Ismail II (ruled 1576–77) and

2 From the *Shah Namah* or "Book of Kings" by Firdausi, 1567

Mohammad Khudabanda (ruled 1578–1587), almost led to the collapse of the state structure. Mohammed's son Abbas, who was declared shah in Herat in 1581, entered Qazvin in 1587 and forced his father to abdicate. In 1592 he moved the capital again from Qazvin to Isfahan.

3 From the *Shah Namah* or "Book of Kings" by Firdausi: Ardashir's fight against Arduwan, book illustration, 16th century

The Safavids

The Safavids came out of a Sufi order of Shi'a Islam. It was founded about 1300 by Sheikh Safi od-Din (1252–1334) in Ardabil in present-day Azerbaijan. Because of his socially revolutionary orientation and active proselytizing in neighboring countries, he soon became very popular. He supported himself militarily with his own troops, who were named Kizilbash ("redheaded ones") after their red turbans. The order founded the Safavid Dynasty in 1501.

Dance of the Dervishes, book miniature from the "Khamsa" by Dschami, early 16th century

1501 | Rule of the Safavid Shahs in Persia   **1514** | Battle of Chaldiran   **1581** | Shah Abbas I the Great

1507 | Conquest of Iran and Iraq by Ismail I   **1554** | Occupation of Georgia   **1590** | Ottomans gain Azerbaijan and Kurdistan

■ The Safavid Empire under Abbas the Great

Shah Abbas the Great led the Safavid Empire to its political, and economic zenith. The first of his successors were able to govern using the structures he had created. Encouragement of immigration and trade enriched his country. He rebuilt the capital, Ispahan.

Shah Abbas I (the Great; 1571-1629) was the most eminent of the Safavid rulers. He energetically oversaw the reorganization of the state. In 1590, he made peace with the Ottomans, at first conceding Georgia, Armenia, Azerbaijan, and Kurdistan to them, territories that he would later recover. He created a standing army of Christian Caucasians, Armenians, and Circassians under British officers that he organized after the model of the Turkish Janissaries. In 1598 Abbas retook Khorasan from the

Persian Carpets

The renown of Persian carpets, which persists to this day, was established during the reign of Abbas the Great. Carpets were already being manufactured in Persia, but only then did the export to Europe begin. Here they served, not as floor coverings as in the East where people prayed sitting, but as luxury coverings for tables and beds. The designs changed in this period from representations of figures to arabesques, blossoms, and leaves. The material—silk—was provided by the Armenians settled in nearby Isfahan, who monopolized the silk trade.

top: Carpet with trees, birds and a deer; in the center a pond with ducks, 16th century

5 Wall hanging from the Lutfallah-Mosque, Isfahan, early 17th century

Uzbeks, and he then annexed Bahrain in 1601, captured Azerbaijan, Armenia, and Georgia between 1603–08, and in 1623–24 retook Kurdistan as well as Iraq from the Ottomans, making Persia the supreme power of the Near East.

Abbas's greatest accomplishments were in the area of domestic politics. He settled Caucasian craftsmen in Iran and invited Christian and Jewish traders and

7 Caravan on the Shahrestan Bridge in Isfahan

merchants into the country, which brought the people prosperity and the state coffers enormous wealth. **❹** Isfahan, his new capital, was **❺** magnificently rebuilt. Under Abbas, the leasing and tax systems were simplified, and he maintained close **❻**, **❼** trade relations with the Moguls in India. Abbas seized the trading center of Hormuz from the Portuguese in 1622, from which he controlled the trade of the Persian Gulf. At this point, Europeans also discovered Safavid Persia; trade delegations, artists, and adventurers came into the country in swarms, some of them personally received by the **❽** shah. When Abbas the Great died in 1629, Persia stood at its political and economic peak, a modern empire with diplomatic contacts throughout the world.

It was during the reign of Abbas's grandson Safi I, who killed his family during a fit of paranoia, that Iraq was lost to the Ottoman Turks in 1638. It was thanks to Grand Vizier Mirza Taqi that Armenia wasn't lost as well. Safi's son Abbas II was the last of the

4 Isfahan, copper engraving, 1681

strong Safavid leaders, securing the streets and trade routes, and maintaining intensive economic exchange with European colonies. In his fight against corruption and the arbitrary use of power, he reformed the legal system.

6 The Caravan of the Persian Shah, painting by Alberto Pasini, 1867

8 Reception by a Persian Prince, miniature, end of the 16th century

1598 Conquest of Khorasan	**1603–08** Conquest of Azerbaijan, Armenia, and Georgia	**1629** Death of Abbas I the Great
1601 Annexation of Bahrain	**1623–24** Conquest of Kurdistan and Iraq	**1638** Ottoman conquest of Iraq

From the Last of the Safavids to the Qajars

During the reigns of the last Safavid rulers, the empire experienced its decline and fall. Only the conqueror Nadir Shah was able, in 1736, to once again create a great empire. After a short reign by the Zand, the Qajars came to power.

Afghan

Qajar

The "Peacock Throne"

When Nadir Shah defeated the Indian grand mogul, he took the Moguls' treasures for himself, bringing them back to Persia. In addition to the Peacock Throne and the famous Koh-i-noor diamond, which is today part of the British Crown Jewels in the Tower of London, they became a symbol of the shahs.

top: The Grand Moghul Shajahan on the Peacock Throne, Persian miniature

Following the reign of Abbas II (ruled 1642–1667), signs of a Safavid decline could be seen. He sought French aid against Constantinople, in return for commercial preferences. His son Safi II left the running of the government largely to palace eunuchs. In 1668 he assumed the throne for a second time under the name of Shah Suleiman, while his hostile neighbors pushed into Iranian territory unimpeded. Safi's son Sultan Husein (ruled 1694–1722) submitted himself completely to the rule of Shiite clerics. When he began forced conversions of the Afghan Sunnis, who had been subjugated in 1648, he provoked a revolt of the Afghans. In 1709 they murdered the Persian officials and soldiers and declared Afghanistan independent. In 1719 the Afghans marched into Persia under their leader Mir Mahmud and conquered the country. Sultan Husein was executed in 1726. Although Mahmud declared

himself shah in 1722, two shadow rulers of the House of Safavid continued to claim control until 1736. During the reign of the last Safavid, Abbas III, General Nadir of the Afshar, a Turkmen tribe, rose to power. Nadir drove the ❶ Afghans out of Isfahan in 1726 and by 1730 out of all of Persia, seized Azerbaijan and the Caucasus from the Ottomans, and then ascended the throne in 1736 as Nadir Shah. He moved his capital from Ispahan to Mashhad, on the route to India reoccupied Afghanistan in 1738, pushed into India taking Peshawar and, reaching Delhi in 1739. Afterward, he turned to Central Asia and conquered Chiva and Bukhara. In June 1747, Nadir Shah was murdered by his own emirs.

The Afshar dynasty didn't outlive Nadir Shah for long. His grandson lost the empire in 1749. Afghanistan,

Azerbaijan, and a large part of Persia proclaimed themselves independent. The Kurdish military leader Karim Khan Zand (ruled 1750–1779) established the Zand dynasty in central and southern Iran, with its capital at Shiraz. After his death in 1779, his sons fought each other until being replaced in 1794 by the ❷ Qajars.

The Qajars were Turkmen nomads from the northwest of Iran and followers of the Safavids. Their leader, Agha Muhammad Khan, made Tehran his capital in 1786, deposed the last Zand ruler in 1794, and then took the title of shah of Persia in 1796. The Qajar dynasty that he founded ruled until 1925. When he was murdered in June 1797, the dynasty was so well established that his nephew Fath Ali Shah (ruled 1797–1834) was able to assume power without opposition. Under his rule, Iran began a close ❸ association with the great powers of Europe, primarily the British who were concerned about the expansionism of Russia.

Asker-Khan, the Persian legate in France, painting by Joseph Franque

1648 | Subjugation of Afghanistan   **1719** | Afghan conquest of Persia   **1736** | Nadir Shah comes to power   **1739** | Persia expands to Delhi

1709 | Afghan revolt and declaration of independence   **1730** | Afghans driven out of Persia   **1736-1738** | Nadir Shah's conquests in Central Asia

■ Central Asia

Under the Uzbek successor dynasties following the Timurids, Central Asia—especially the capitals Bukhara and Samarkand—remained a cultural center of eastern Islam. During the 18th century, however, they fell under Persian and later Russian suzerainty.

4

Chanaka Nadir Diwan-Begi, an inn for pilgrims in Buchara, built in 1620

The cultural blossoming under the Timurids continued under their successors, the Uzbek tribal confederation. Beginning in 1500, the ❻ Uzbek leader Muhammad Shaybani Khan seized the territories of the Timurids, occupying Herat in 1507 and establishing the rule of the Shaybanids, a dynasty with Mongolian roots. He fell in 1510 at Merv against the Safavids attempting to conquer Khorasan, but his rule over Bukhara and the capital Samarkand was established. Ubaydallah and his successors further built up both cities with numerous mosques, ❽ madrassas, and inns for ❹ pilgrims. The former tribal warriors soon assumed the courtly culture of the cities and supported the ❼ Naqshbandi order, so that the region became a center for Islamic mysticism. Since 1540 one line had ruled in Bukhara, and Abdallah II, the last of the Shaybanids, was able to reunify the empire out of Bukhara in 1583 and successfully expanded his domination to the west, east, and north.

In 1599, Baqi Muhammad, leader of another Uzbek tribal confederation, the Djanids (or Astrakhanids), took control over Central Asia. They made Bukhara their capital and once more developed it splendidly, reigning there until 1785. In the 18th century, various conquerors cast an eye on Bukhara. Nadir Shah of Persia occupied large parts of the empire after 1737, including Balkh, Chiva, and Bukhara. Chiva remained under Persian and Turkmen domination until 1770. Czarist Russia, which was expanding eastward, sought to influence the politics of the khanate, until finally bringing the area under its control in the 19th century.

After Kokand and other regions had detached themselves

5　Alim Khan, the last Emir of Buchara

6

Uzbek commander Muhammad Shaybani Khan, painting, 1873

7

Members of an Islamic Order in Tashkent, painting

8

The madrassa Mir-i Arab in Buchara, built 1535–1536

9

The conquest of Samarkand by the Emir of Buchara, painting, 1868.

Setareje Mahe Chase, the summer residence of the last reigning Emir of Buchara, Said Alim Khan

10

from the central regime beginning in 1732, a rapid loss of power and a civil war among the Djanids occurred in 1747. The rulers fell under the regency of the related Mangits from around 1753 until Amir-i-Masum Shah, who acted as regent in Bukhara beginning in 1770, assumed the title of "prince of the believers" and established the khanate of the Mangits in 1785. He was able to assert himself in the Bukhara region in the early 19th century, but following ❾ internal unrest, the area fell under Russian rule between 1868 and 1873. The last ❺, ❿ Mangit khan was deposed in 1921.

A Mogul ruler in the region of Agra, Indian miniature, ca. 1650

MOGUL INDIA AND THE EUROPEAN TRADING COMPANIES 1526–CA. 1800

The Indian Mogul Empire had existed since 1526, blossoming under Akbar's rule beginning in 1556. The splendor and luxury for which the Moguls are famed developed under his successors. After the death of Aurangzeb, the last important ❶ Mogul ruler, the empire declined both politically and culturally, while the European trading companies that had established themselves on the coasts of India since 1500 increasingly influenced political affairs. The Portuguese, initially the most powerful European state in India, were later pushed aside by the Dutch and British. Eventually, the British politically and economically dominated the subcontinent.

■ The First Moguls to Akbar the Great

Babur, founder of the Mogul Empire, established his authority over wide areas of India, which were, however, lost again under Humayun. It was not until Akbar the Great that the empire was finally consolidated.

By 1526 ❸ Babur had conquered the north and middle of India, founding the Mogul Empire, which in the 16th and 17th centuries would reach almost unbelievable standards of splendor together with immeasurable wealth. The name of Babur's dynasty, the Moguls (Mongols), reflects his Central Asian heritage: He was directly related to Tamerlane on his father's side and Genghis Khan on his mother's. In 1497 Babur became the ruler of Samarkand. He went on to conquer Kabul in 1504 and then pushed steadily southward into India from Afghani-

stan through the Khyber Pass, taking Lahore in 1524. After his victory over the last Lodi ruler at Panipat in 1526, Babur controlled the majority of India and made Agra his capital.

Just how unstable his empire was became evident under his son, Humayun, who was driven out of India and into Persia by the brilliant commander Shir Shah Khan, who took Agra, Delhi, and Lahore, in 1540. Shir Shah established his own dynasty, consolidating and giving firm institutions to the Mogul Empire, but his kingdom collapsed after his mur-

der in 1545 and had disappeared by 1555. Humayun returned from Persian exile but had a fatal accident shortly afterward.

His son ❷ Akbar the Great ascended the throne at the age of 13 in 1556. He shaped the Mogul Empire and guided the Indian-Islamic culture to a new golden age. A capable general as well as politician, he extended the empire in all directions and controlled the area from Kabul and Kashmir in the west to Bengal in the east. Northern Deccan to the south, including the Rajput states of Rajasthan and Gujarat, were also parts of his empire. Akbar erected the royal city of ❹, ❺ Fatehpur Sikri as his new capital. He created a new class of nobility loyal to him from the military aristocracy of various tribes, implemented a modern government, and supported the economy. At the same time, he intensified trade with the European trading companies. Akbar allowed free expression and discussion of all religions—even Christianity and Judaism—at his court and organized colloquia and debates.

Akbar crosses the Ganges, Indian miniature, ca. 1600

The residence Fatehpur Sikri, illustration from the *Akbar-name*, ca. 1590

Babur, the founder of the Mogul dynasty in India, miniature, 17th century

The private audience hall of the emperor in Fatehpur Sikri

▪ The Empire at the Height of Its Splendor

Akbar's successors Jahangir and Shah Jahan were politically weak but are notable as great patrons of the arts and architecture. Their love of extravagance brought the state into difficulties.

6
The mausoleum of Akbar in Sikandra

A tolerant and far-sighted ruler, Akbar attempted to resolve the smoldering differences between Muslims and Hindus in his empire by establishing a new religion with strong characteristics of a ruler cult. *Din-i-Ilahi* ("Divine Faith") was a mixture of Islam, Hinduism, and other religions, but it failed due to the massive resistance of the Islamic court orthodoxy. Akbar's grand buildings —court

10
Court of the great Mogul, engraving by Jan Caspar Philips, 18th century

11
Jahangir with a picture of the Virgin Mary

studios in which magnificently illustrated books, ❽ carpets, and jewelry were created— served both political and symbolic functions.

❻ Akbar left his successors an internally stable empire, but before long the first signs of political weakness emerged. Akbar's son ⓫ Jahangir, who succeeded him in 1605, was addicted to opium, neglected affairs of state, and came under the influence of rival court cliques. The grandeur of the arts and ❿ immense court administration that developed under his reign fascinated foreign envoys. Great Britain in particular had been trying to establish diplomatic and economic relations since 1609 and was granted numerous trade privileges. Jahangir's reign was weake-

8
Indian carpet from Madras

ned by rebellions in his own family and in Deccan beginning in 1620. During the reign of his son ❼, ❾ Shah Jahan, the splendor and luxury of the court reached its zenith. He collected tens of thousands of jewels, exported the products of the Indian painting schools to the world, and commissioned the construction of the ⓬ Taj Mahal near Agra.

Shah Jahan was not only an enthusiastic builder but also a distrustful personality who took ruthless measures against his adversaries, suspected as well

above: Shah Jahan
right: Shah Jahan's favorite wife Mumtaz-i-Mahal

9

as real. As a strict Muslim, he attacked the Portuguese colony in India and left Christian captives who refused conversion to Islam to die in prison. The "grand mogul" retreated to his harem palaces, isolated from the outside world, and left the government of his empire increasingly to his ministers and eunuchs. The maintenance of the court began to cost more than taxes brought in. In June 1658 Shah Jahan was deposed by his sons.

Taj Mahal

Between 1632 and 1648, Shah Jahan had the Taj Mahal constructed out of white marble by 20,000 workers as a mausoleum for his favorite wife Mumtaz-i-Mahal ("Pearl of the palace"), who died in childbirth in 1631. A planned parallel mausoleum for Shah Jahan himself, to be built out of black marble, was never constructed. The Taj Mahal, whose interior is equally magnificently constructed and in which Shah Jahan was also laid to rest, is often called the "Eighth Wonder of the World."

above: The Taj Mahal in Agra. The central building with its 22 cupolas and minarets (ca. 131 ft high), made of marble and red sandstone that must be continually renovated due to its porosity.

12
Ornaments with blossom motifs in the Taj Mahal

1556 | Akbar the Great takes power   **1609** | Diplomatic relations established with Great Britain   **1658** | Shah Jahan deposed

        1605 | Rule of Jahangir   **1631** | Attack on the Portuguese Indian colonies

Aurangzeb and the Decline of the Moguls in India

During Aurangzeb's reign, the empire gained political strength once more, but his religious conservatism and intolerance undermined the stability of society. His successors became mere decadent shadow rulers.

1
The great Mogul Aurangzeb

3
The conquest of Kandahar by Aurangzeb

The conflict that had been building among the four sons of Shah Jahan and Mumtaz-i-Mahal since 1644 flared up immediately after their father was deposed. At first it seemed that the eldest, Prince ❷ Dara Shukoh, a supporter of the arts and of dialogue between religions, would prevail. However, the third son ❶ Aurangzeb, allied with Islamic orthodoxy against his brother and ascended the Mogul throne in June 1658 under the name of Alamgir ("world conqueror"). In 1659 he defeated Dara Shukoh and had him executed. Aurangzeb was a strictly orthodox Muslim, popular for his application of Sharia law. A talented military commander, he doubled the empire's territory, and the Mogul Empire reached its greatest expanse when he seized Deccan, ❸ Kandahar, and Kabul. In 1687, he conquered the Kingdom of Golkonda, the most significant state on the Indian subcontinent.

Domestically, Aurangzeb brutally suppressed all "unorthodox"

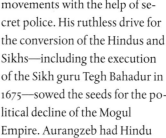

2
Dara Shukoh with his army

movements with the help of secret police. His ruthless drive for the conversion of the Hindus and Sikhs—including the execution of the Sikh guru Tegh Bahadur in 1675—sowed the seeds for the political decline of the Mogul Empire. Aurangzeb had Hindu temples systematicaly razed to the ground and erected ❹,❺ mosques in their place. In 1679 he reintroduced the poll tax for non-Muslims, which had been abolished under Akbar. When Aurangzeb, the last powerful Mogul, died in March 1707, many parts of the empire were in open revolt.

Aurangzeb's son, Bahadur Shah I, was able to make favorable contracts again with the princes of Bengal and the English trading companies, reform the tax system, and repeal the harsh religious policies of his father. However, after his death in 1712, the Mogul dynasty sank into chaos and violent family feuds. In the year 1719 alone, four Moguls successively ascended the throne. In 1739 Nadir Shah of Persia invaded

British Ambassador Sir William Norris, 1701, Describing his Encounter with Emperor Aurangzeb

"He was completely white, the clothing, the turban, and the beard and was carried by a crowd of humans in open gentleness. But he himself saw no one, as his eyes were directed towards a book in his hands, which he read during the entire way, not letting himself be distracted by any other object."

India and plundered the treasures of the palaces. The succeeding Moguls ruled only nominally and never left their palaces, where the British eventually found them vegetating under indescribable conditions. After a crushed rebellion which he led in 1857–58, the last "Mogul," Bahadur Shah II, was deposed by the British, who then took control of the country.

6
The Portuguese seafarer Vasco da Gama, who discovered the sea route to India, Portuguese book illustration, 1683

4
Mosque of Gyanvapi, built by Aurangzeb, in Benares on the Ganges, watercolor by R. Smith, 1833

5
The mosque of Gyanvapi with neighboring ghats in Benares, steel engraving, ca. 1850

| **1497–98** | Sea route to India discovered | **1612** | Naval battle of Suali | **1675** | Tegh Bahadur's execution |
| **1531–58** | British conquest of Indian west coast | **1658** | Aurangzeb comes to power | **1679** | Reintroduction of poll tax for non-Muslims |

From European Trading Companies to British Domination

The Portuguese controlled European trade with India in the 16th century, but after 1600 they were pushed aside by the Dutch, British, and French. The British eventually gained political control throughout the region as well.

During the rise and fall of the Mogul Empire, the ⓬ European trading companies were establishing themselves on the Indian coasts. Following ⓺ Vasco da Gama's discovery of a sea route to India in 1497–1498, the Portuguese—having defeated the combined fleets of Egypt and Gujarat at Diu in 1509—reached ⓻ Goa in 1510.

8 A frigate of the kind used by the East India Company off of the Indian Coast, from two perspectives, painting by Thomas Whitcombe

From there they proceeded to conquer the west coast of India in 1531–1558 and establish a ⓾ trade monopoly of goods from India and Indonesia in Europe.

In the 17th century, the Dutch and English entered into competition with the Portuguese, after Queen Elizabeth granted the British ⓼ East India Company a monopoly over British trade with

India in 1600. The British, who had already established a trading post in Agra in 1608, defeated the Portuguese in a naval engagement near Surat in 1612 and went on to set up outposts on both the east and west coasts of India. In 1658, Chennai (Madras) became the headquarters of the ⓫ East India Company, which had been diplomatically represented at the court of the Moguls since 1603. In 1668, the British also took Mumbai (Bombay) from the Portuguese. Meanwhile, the Dutch East India Company was able to establish itself in Surat in 1618 and Bengal in 1627 and drove the Portuguese out of Ceylon in 1638. That led to the bitter and bloody ⓭ struggle between the British and the Dutch, which the British eventually won.

In 1664, the French under Finance Minister Jean-Baptiste Colbert also entered the competition for Indian trade. The French *Compagnie des Indes Orientales* seized bases on the west and east coasts in 1668 and won, in 1739, the sou-

thern portion of the Kingdom of Hyderabad. Joseph François Dupleix, governor-general of the company from 1742 to 1754, was able to spread French influence across all of the southern Indian principalities. There were several clashes between the French and British in southern India between 1746 and 1763, which the British eventually won under the leadership of Robert Clive. In 1765 Lord Clive became governor of East India, and the East India Company was given Bengal, Bihar, and Orissa (Kalinga), making British dominance of the subcontinent a fact.

9 Warren Hastings

⓽ Warren Hastings, the first governor-general of Bengal from 1772 to 1785, put a complete end to French influence there and paved the way for British political domination of India. In 1784, the East India Company was placed under the control of the British government, which instituted British universities in India and anglicized Indian society to a far-reaching extent.

7 The St. Alex Church in Calangute, Goa, built in 1515

10 European merchant ships, presumably Portuguese, at the Indian coast, Indian miniature, late 16th century

After the last Mogul had been deposed, India was governed by a British viceroy, or *Raj*, from 1858 until Indian independence in 1947.

11 Two British officers of the East India Company are entertained with music and dance

12 Europeans smoking a water pipe, Indian miniature, ca. 1760

13 British warships at an island in Dutch East India, painting by Dominic Serres the Elder

1687	Conquest of Golkonda	1707	Aurangzeb dies	1746–63	Anglo-French war over southern India	1858	East India Company dissolved
	1690	Calcutta founded	1739	Persian invasion		1784	East India Company under British government

CHINA UNDER THE MING AND MANCHU EMPERORS 1368–CA. 1800

The native Ming dynasty established itself in China in 1368, but the central power of the ❶ emperor was already in decline by the 15th century. The country was under constant pressure from Mongolian tribes and also had to defend itself against the advance of the Europeans. Economic prosperity led to an enormous increase in the population. The country expanded into Central Asia under the Manchu emperors, but was showing internal stagnation in its bureaucratic and intellectual traditionalism.

The Forbidden City, residence of the emperor since the Ming era

■ The Beginnings of the Ming Dynasty

In 1368, the Mings drove the Mongolians out of China, but they were constantly forced to defend their rule against internal and external enemies. However, the court eunuchs eventually came to exercise real power.

2

Zhu Yuanzhang, Emperor Taizu

❷ Zhu Yuanzhang, a former Buddhist monk, drove the Mongolian Yuan dynasty out of China from the south and founded the Ming dynasty as Emperor Hung-Wu. A cruel despot, ❸, ❹ officials and ministers were limited to counseling functions, and the administration of the 13 provinces was carried out directly by the ruler—in this case a ruler who penalized the slightest infraction with cruel punishment. As the peasants had supported his rise to power, the emperor instituted a redistribution of land, made taxes more equitable, and established a work colony for the destitute. Defense against the Mongols and Japanese invasions on the coasts remained a pressing military problem during the whole of the Ming period. As early as 1387, China began building fortifications on the east and southeastern coasts and continued construction of the ❺ Great Wall.

Emperor Chengzu, who ascended the throne in 1402, built a fleet of ships and intensified overseas trade. The eunuchs were now increasingly replacing the officials in the internal administration until they became, under Chengzu's successor, the actual instrument of rule. The leading eunuch Zheng undertook sea voyages to Africa and developed a market for African products in China, an endeavor which he did not persue. After Chengzu, there followed a series of weak or very young emperors, who were effectively controlled by court cliques and the eunuchs, while Mongolian leaders were able to advance several times as far as Nanjing and Beijing. By 1550 all of the court offices and control of the bureaucracy were in the hands of the cliques and court favorites. Through the reinforcement of the teachings of Confucius in the academies and civil service schools, the internal structure of the state was able to remain relatively stable despite occasional rebellions in the rural provinces.

3 A civil servant (right) and a military servant (left) from the Ming era

4

Portrait of an educated dignitary from the Ming era

Wang Yangming

The greatest Ming philosopher, Wang Yangming (1472–1529), worked to counter the intellectual torpor in China. He combined Neo-Confucianism with Chinese Buddhism and reinforced the intellectual fusion of both systems. Furthermore, he developed the idea of "intuitive" as opposed to rational knowledge of what is good and bad, with which many political decisions were justified.

5
The Great Wall

1368 Ming Dynasty founded	**1421** Extension of the Great Wall	**1563** Elimination of Japanese pirates
1402 Emperor Chengzu	**1516** First Portuguese base in Canton	

The End of the Mings and Beginning of Christian Influence

The power of the Mings decreased during the 16th century until the Manchus deposed them in 1644. At the same time Europeans, the Jesuits in particular, were able to gain a foothold in China.

As the Ming emperors had to station large armies on the coasts and the northern and southern borders of the empire to defend against external enemies, colonies were established in the borderlands, leading to the settlement of previously uninhabited regions. Due to the Mongolian threat, the capital was also moved from Nanjing to Beijing.

The economy of the Ming period was based primarily on expanded trade and agriculture; experiencing an upswing in the 1600s with the cultivation of new, economically useful plants such as potatoes, ❻ tobacco, corn, and peanuts. As a result of the general prosperity, the population surged. A merchant and banking class emerged in the rapidly growing cities, making its way into the state administration, while the emperors remained weak through an extravagant lifestyle and the power of the eunuchs.

During the reign of Emperor Wan Li, the country was shaken by innumerable revolts. In addition, a Japanese attempt to occupy the Chinese vassal state of Korea in 1592 was answered with a costly defensive battle in 1593–98. Between 1594 and 1604, China also unsuccessfully attempted to decrease the influence of the East India Company through wars in Annam, Burma, and Siam.

❻ Ivory tobacco tin

After the Portuguese had established a trading colony in ❶ Canton in 1516—particularly for the ❼ tea trade—and Macao as a trading base in 1567, Christians began missionary work in China. The Jesuit ❿ Matteo Ricci lived in Beijing from 1601 and as a scholar had access to the highest court circles. In 1613, the emperor entrusted the Jesuits with reforming the calendar, and ❾ Johann Adam Schall von Bell,

7 A tea manufactory in China: Tea is pressed, packed, and sold to European merchants, 18th century

who worked on it, soon became director of the ⓬ imperial observatory, was conferred the rank of first-class mandarin, and functioned as the regent of the young emperor from 1651. The Jesuits assumed Chinese clothing and manner and considered Confucianism to be compatible with Christianity.

During the reign of the last Ming emperor, despite the political weaknesses of the empire, China experienced a blossoming of literature, science, the arts, and above all, ❽ porcelain production. The political weakness was exploited from the end of the 16th century on by Jurchen tribes in Manchuria, who, under the leadership of Nurhachi, rose up against the Chinese administrators and allied themselves with the Mongolians. By 1621 they had conquered Manchuria and under their leader Abahai marched toward Beijing. In 1636, the Manchus (Jurchen) proclaimed themselves an imperial dynasty under

9 Johann Adam Schall von Bell

the name of Da Qing ("Great Purity"). When the last Ming emperor, Chongzhen, committed suicide in 1644, the Manchus entered Beijing.

10 The Italian Jesuit Matteo Ricci

11 European trade branches in Canton

12 The royal observatory in Beijing

8 Vase with a dragon motif, beginning of 15th century

	from 1581 | Jesuit mission in China	1593–98 | War against Japan	1644 | Manchu capture Beijing
1567 | Portuguese trading colony in Macao		1592 | Japanese attack Korea	1636 | Qing Dynasty founded

■ The Reign of the Manchus

The foreign Manchu rulers soon assumed Chinese customs, promoted science and the arts, and expanded Chinese influence into Central Asia. This last imperial dynasty lasted over 250 years.

The ❶ Manchus, or Qings ruled over the last Chinese imperial dynasty (1644–1911). To consolidate power they had to first crush the revolts of rival tribes and do away with the remaining Mings in the south. They secured their influence in politics and the administration and then demanded the adoption of their customs, including the wearing of pigtails and traditional Manchu dress. Thousands of the ❷ native Chinese officials committed suicide, but the majority of the Chinese population soon accustomed themselves to the political and cultural dominance of foreigners.

The long reigns of the three Manchu emperors between 1661 and 1796 were political, economic, and cultural high points. The emperors promoted the publication of encyclopedias and literary works, and the educated officials and upper class occupied themselves with literature and painting. Christianity was initially tolerated if the representatives were open-minded scholars.

❹ Emperor K'ang-hsi brought about an extensive reconciliation of the various peoples of the empire, moved against official corruption, and integrated Taiwan into the empire after expelling the Dutch in 1662. By 1681, he was able to establish the central government's authority over all parts of the land. K'ang-hsi entered into a treaty with Russia in 1689—the first Chinese treaty with a European power—ending Russian encroachment in the Amur River region. In 1696, he drove off the Jungars, who had been advancing into East Turkistan and Outer Mongolia since 1678. When the Jungars occupied Tibet in 1717–1718, K'ang-hsi began an ❸ intensified Chinese engagement in Central Asia. Tibet was taken back in 1720 by the Chinese and integrated into the empire as a protectorate with authority administered by resident commissioners or *ambans*.

Although relative economic prosperity continued, the population explosion created a food crisis. The population of China rose (according to a popular census) from 60 million in 1578 to more than 100 million in 1662, 143 million in 1741, 275 million in 1796, and 374 million by 1814. Agricultural land-use, however, was not able to keep pace with territorial expansion and population growth. Farming methods also remained underdeveloped.

Emperor Schi-tsu, the founder of the Manchu (Qing) Dynasty

Infantrymen escorting two dignitaries by horse

The Panchen Lama lodged in this temple near Beijing when he visited the Qing court in 1780.

Emperor K'ang-hsi's second journey to the south, rolled picture by Wang Hui, silk painting, ca.1700

| 1662 | Annexation of Taiwan | 1689 | Treaty with Russia | 1705 | Ban on Christianity |
| 1681 | Rule established over entire empire | 1696 | Jungars repulsed | 1717–18 | Junggars occupy Tibet |

China under Yung-cheng and Hung-li

The preferential treatment of Christians ended abruptly under Yung-cheng. Hung-li then led the empire to international splendor and high esteem once again, but internally the seeds of intellectual inflexibility and corruption were being sown.

5

Emperor Yung-cheng

K'ang-hsi's son **❺** Yung-cheng instituted a complete change in politics and culture in China. He institutionalized imperial power in 1729 by replacing the ponderous "inner cabinet" with a modern state council as advisory body. He also prevented the influence of imperial relatives, excluded eunuchs from higher offices, and installed an information service and a secret police. He increased the wages of the civil servants to discourage second incomes and integrated the finance and tax systems. The open influence of Christians in China also ended during the reign of Yung-cheng. In 1705, the pope had declared Confucianism and Christianity to be incompatible, and Catholic missionaries had begun preaching against **❽** Confucius. The emperor thereupon banned Christianity, expelled the missionaries, and persecuted native Christians.

China reached the greatest extent of its expansion during the long reign of **❻** Hung-li (1735-1796). It was simultaneously forced to wage colonial wars for many years, bringing Uighurs, Kazakhs, Kirghiz, and Mongols under Chinese rule. Beijing was magnificently built up with **❼** residences and **❾** temples, yet the empire was showing signs of intellectual ossification: the Chinese civil service exams were filled with more questions about orthodox Neo-Confucianism than practical knowledge, necessary political and economic reforms did not occur, and the state administration became extremely conservative. The arbitrary use of power by officials provoked revolts of the populace, and mafialike secret societies frequently controlled whole regions. The government was forced to undertake a campaign against the strongest of them, the White Lotus society, between 1793 and 1803. The British sent **❿** diplomatic missions to the imperial court in 1793 and 1816 to gain trade concessions, but the court firmly held to its policy of isolationism and turned the British away. Despite this, from 1816 on, the British East India Company increasingly brought opium into the country and the smoking of opium became widespread among the Chinese.

6

Emperor Hung-li

7

A palace for the summer in Beijing, built under emperor Qianlong 1711–96, Chinese silk painting

8

Worshippers at a statue of Confucius

10

Lord Macartney's diplomatic mission to facilitate the trade with China, caricature from 1792/93

9

The sky temple in Beijing

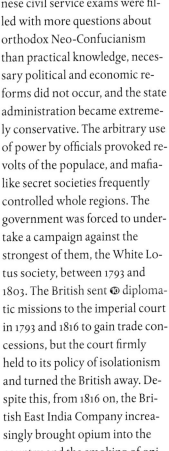

Official proclamation against the secret society of the Big Knives

Secret Societies

Secret societies and secret sects run throughout China's history. Mostly they originated out of local cult societies, founded by charasimatic leaders. They attracted charismatic members with religious and socially utopian promises of salvation, and trained fanatic fighters. The bloody Taiping Rebellion, which cost 20 million Chinese lives in 1850–1864, and the Boxer Rebellion of 1900 against Western influence have their roots in these secret societies.

1

Theater performance, detail from a colored tapestry, Muromachi Period

JAPAN FROM THE MUROMACHI PERIOD TO THE TOKUGAWA SHOGUNATE 1338–1868

During the Muromachi period of the Ashikaga shogunate, which began in 1338, political power in Japan was transferred to the military aristocracy and regional warlords. Their rivalry favored the rise of local centers, European trade, and Christianity. Starting in 1560, the three great "unifiers" of the country centralized political and military power. The Tokugawa shogunate of the Edo period pursued a policy of isolationism that brought inner stability but also persecution of Christians, and sealed off the country from European influences into the 19th century.

■ The Muromachi Period (1338–1573)

The shogunate of the Ashikaga brought the military aristocracy to power in Japan permanently. As the central power became weaker and weaker, the rise of the local military warlords began.

In the Muromachi period, governmental power went from the imperial government to the military aristocracy—the *samurai*, or *bushi*. The ❸, ❹ *bushi* were swordfighters who despised court life and lived in the provinces on their estates. They gave their personal allegiance to a local prince and had their own personal followers. The samurai code of ethics required them to fight for honor and family and, when necessary, to commit ritual suicide (*hara-kiri*). Their heroic deeds were immortalized in the cultic plays of the ❶, ❷ Noh theater.

The Muromachi period began with a power struggle. In 1334

Emperor Go-Daigo, based in Kyoto, tried to reestablish the power of the emperor that had been lost to the shoguns in 1185—whereupon the military leader, Ashikaga Takauji, installed a new imperial line loyal to him. In 1338 Ashikaga conquered the shogunate for himself and his family. The shogun became the sole ruler, with the emperor as a mere figurehead. Military leaders in the provinces, the *shugo*, gradually established civil administration and tax sovereignty for themselves. In 1379,

❷ Noh theater mask, ca. 1500

under the third shogun Yoshimitsu, the center of power was moved from ❺ Kyoto back to Kamakura. The sixth shogun, Yoshinori (1428-1441), was the last to intervene strongly in the political fate of the country; his successors dedicating themselves primarily to the arts. The Onin War of 1467–1477 erupted over the succession of the shogunate and devastated many provinces.

The power of the shugo brought the country considerable economic growth and great cul-

❸

An actor playing a Samurai, colored wood engraving, early 19th century

tural achievements, with many provincial courts able to compete with the major courtly centers. The development of fleets by the princes of coastal provinces led to vigorous trade with China but also attacks on China's coasts.

4

Japanese Samurai sword with an ivory sheath, 18th century

5

The Kinkakuji Temple, or "Golden Pavilion" in Kyoto, built in 1397

The Samurai

The Japanese knights, the samurai, lived according to the code of bushido, which fused three traditions. From Zen Buddhism came the ideal of inner peace and fearless composure, and from Shintoism, the honoring of the family and ancestors as well as unconditional loyalty to the prince. Finally, Confucianism imposed on the bushi the requirement of service for the good of society and country, and the protection of the weak. Samurai were also expected to be literate and take interest in the arts.

Armament of a samurai, 16th–17th century

The Reign of the Daimyo

The rule of rival local princes, the *daimyo*, favored the rise of Christianity in Japan. From 1560, the three great unifiers of the country formed a new, strong centralized power.

The political weaknesses of the last Ashikaga shoguns after the Onin War led to the effective takeover of power by provincial princes, who were known as *sen-goku-daimyo*, or feudal lords. The most powerful daimyo—there were between 200 and 300 in Japan—were able to raise armies of more than 10,000 men and replaced the individual combat of the ❻ samurai with the besieging of cities and the storming of strongholds by organized infantry troops. They pursued their own, shifting alliance policies. The rivalry among the daimyos also favored the spread of European influence and ❼ Christianity in Japan.

In 1543 ❾ ❿, ⓫ Portuguese merchants from Macao landed in Japan for the first time, south of Kyushu. Because the daimyo of Kyushu—and soon other daimyos as well—hoped to gain power through European trade,

they granted the merchants favorable concessions. In 1571, the port of Nagasaki became the Portuguese base in Japan, and in 1579 municipal authority was even transferred to them. There were always Christian missionaries in the retinue of merchants. The cofounder of the Jesuit order, ❽ the Spaniard Francis Xavier, had already landed in Kyushu in 1549 and was honorably received by the local daimyo. The work of Gaspar Vilela in Kyoto made it a center of Christian missionary work in 1560. By 1582 there were

already 200 churches and 150,000 Christians in Japan.

A new period of political strength began in 1560 under the three great unifiers—the shoguns Oda Nobunaga, Toyotomi Hideyoshi, and Tokugawa Ieyasu. They, too, were at first local daimyo, but were able to consolidate their power and influence through clever alliance and war policies. They recognized the need for a consolidation of the central authority and worked for policies that resulted in the expansion of trade and the importation of Western firearms.

Nobunaga began to eliminate his daimyo foes in 1560, seized Kyoto in 1568, broke the resistance of the Buddhist monasteries, and in 1573 ended the reign of the Ashikaga shoguns, whose authority, by this time, existed only in name. His rule also saw the development of the tea ceremony and kabuki theater.

6 Japanese helmet, decorated with a war fan, 16th century

8 The missionary Francis Xavier

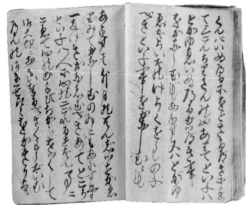
7 Book of Catholic faith in Japanese handwriting, 17th century

9 Portuguese trading ship in the port of Nagasaki, detail from a Japanese folding screen, 17th century

10 A Jesuit and a Portuguese merchant in Japan, detail from a Japanese folding screen, 17th century

11 Portuguese merchants, detail from a Japanese folding screen, 17th century

1549 Jesuit mission under Francisco Xavier	**1568** Conquest of Kyoto
1543 Portuguese merchants land in Kyushu	**1560** New political strength of Oda Nobunaga begins **1573** Last Ashikaga shogun

The Reign of the Unifiers

The political reorganization by Oda Nobunaga, Toyotomi Hideyoshi, and Tokugawa Ieyasu fundamentally changed the structure of Japan. Ieyasu was the first to be able to institute a dynasty of his family.

1 Osaka Castle, built 1583–1587 by Toyotomi Hideyoshi

Nobunaga established his power over the land by making vassals of the local daimyo or by fighting against them with his massive armies and siege techniques. At the Battle of Nagashino in 1575, his troops were the first to use firearms on a large scale. By 1582 Nobunaga had brought the greater part of Japan under his control. He then decreed a standardization of weights and measurements, taxes, and commerce laws, did away with the power of the local guilds, and supported the merchants.

2 Box depicting the preparation of tea, lacquer-work

After Nobunaga's death in 1582, his general ❸ Toyotomi Hideyoshi was able to gain control, occupying Kyoto in 1584 and allying himself with the powerful Tokugawa Ieyasu. In 1585, Hideyoshi eliminated the last of the daimyo with brutal force, while trying to win over the traditional elite for a constructive policy of peace, rewarding even former rivals with estates once they had proved their loyalty. He brought the daimyo together in a union and made himself the supreme feudal lord. In order to control them, he often held their families as "hostages of honor" at his court. From 1583 on, Hideyoshi built ❶ Osaka Castle as his capital and in 1591 he appointed himself regent for the emperor. He occupied Korea in 1592, but was forced to withdraw from the continent two years later.

In domestic policies, Hideyoshi undertook sweeping reforms. He had the whole country surveyed in order to reorganize the villages and family seats. He then put the villages together into production units and calculated the tax rate according to the whole village.

This measure was accompanied by a separation of ❷ farmers from the warrior class, ❺ tradesmen, and merchants that would prove decisive in the future. The farmers were forced to give up their weapons, while the bushi were kept out of the villages and were allocated to their princes in personal allegiance. In 1590, after a last victory over the Hojo, Hideyoshi was the undisputed master of Japan, but his attempt to establish a shogunate for his family failed.

When Hideyoshi died in 1598, his powerful ally ❹ Ieyasu, after a decisive victory in the Battle of Sekigahara, assumed power and was able to establish the Tokugawa shogunate in 1603 that his family would hold until 1867. Ieyasu built upon the achievements of his predecessor and laid the foundation for a rather conservative, isolationist

3 Audience hall of Hideyoshi in Kyoto, partial view of the interior, 16th century

form of politics, which, however, contributed to lasting peace and internal stability. He also centralized all of Japan's economic and trade policies, preventing local daimyo from trading with Europe.

4 The Japanese national coat of arms, the chrysanthemum, at the Higashi-Honganji Temple, founded in 1602 by Ieyasu

5 Merchants at the market and bathing people at the Shijo Gawa River in Kyoto, detail from a colored folding screen, ca. 1550

■ The Tokugawa Shogunate 1603–1867/68

After forcefully bringing peace to the country, the Tokugawa shoguns suppressed Christianity and resolved to seal the country off from European influences. This continued until the 19th century.

Taking over for Hideyoshi, Ieyasu first had to contend with a renewed rebellion of the daimyo families. He defeated his greatest rival, Ishida, and his "western alliance" in 1600. By the time he finally gained full control in 1603, 87 daimyo families had been eradicated. The centers of Tokugawa power were ❽ Kyoto and especially Edo (present-day Tokyo). In 1605 Ieyasu officially transferred the shogunate to his son Hideta-da, who played only a background role until Ieyasu's death in 1616. In the meantime, Ieyasu wiped out the last of the rebelling daimyos while ❾ seizing Osaka in 1614–15.

The third Tokugawa shogun, Iemitsu, completed the development of Ieyasu's system of rule and finally brought peace to the empire through strict military controls. Iemitsu, who enacted strict nationalistic marriage and dress regulations, forced the daimyo to recognize him as the sole lawgiver and in 1635 put all religious institutions under the supervision of the shoguns. The system of personal loyalty and allegiance was anchored at all levels. In 1639, the policy of "locking up the country," which isolated Japan from the outside world for 200 years, was proclaimed. As early as 1622, ❼ Christians had begun to be persecuted, and they were now perceived as foreigners. Religious and cultural policies gained extreme nationalistic characteristics after the ❻ foreigners had been expelled and the native Christians executed.

After Iemitsu, the Tokugawas increasingly refrained from active politics and left the government to the military leaders. The eighth shogun, Yoshimune, whose reign began in 1716, was able to reestablish the power of the shogunate through governmental and economic reforms. He encouraged new land reclamation and the cultivation of crops such as sweet potatoes and mulberry trees for the breeding of silk-worms. He also standardized the legal system and cancelled the debts held by farmers. Yoshimune also loosened the ban on the import of European publications in order to become acquainted with new administrative and agricultural breeding methods. His policies were actively resumed by the eleventh shogun, Ien-ari, from 1787. Japan experienced a new upswing, but the policy of isolationism remained in place until the country was forcibly ❿ opened by the United States in 1853–54.

❻ A native boy shows a great bird to a European, colored woodcarving, 18th century

❼ Martyrdom of the Jesuits in Japan, painting, 1622

❽ Nijo-jo Castle in Kyoto, residence of the Tokugawa Dynasty in the imperial city, built 1603–1626

Revolt of the Christians

The religio-political measures of the first Tokugawa shogun provoked the revolt of the Christians of Shimabara in 1637–38. The shogun brutally crushed the uprising, and initiated the extermination of Christianity in Japan. Even when restrictions on the import of Western writings were moderated in 1720, no publications with Christian content were allowed to enter the country.

Depiction of the Virgin Mary in a plaster form. Persecutors of Christians recognized Catholics by their refusal to desecrate the form by stepping on it.

❾ The conquest of Osaka 1615, detail from a folding screen, 17th century

❿ Delivery of a letter from US president Fillmore to the Japanese emperor by a delegation on June 14, 1853, lithography, 19th century

1622–23	Christians persecuted		1639	"Policy of locking up the country"		1853–54	The opening of Japan
	1637–39	Christians of Schimabara revolt		from 1720	European books allowed		1868	Last Shogun abdicated

SOUTHEAST ASIA 1500–1800

Burma and Siam were particularly significant kingdoms between the 16th and 18th centuries. The Portuguese and other Europeans established relations with trade agreements, particularly in Siam. While the French asserted themselves in Annam in the 18th century, the Portuguese were able to control the Malay Archipelago at first—and with it a monopoly on the spice trade—only to gradually lose it to the Dutch in the 17th century. Many South Asian kingdoms experienced a renaissance through trade with the Europeans.

Burmese rowing boat

Burma and Siam

The kingdom of Burma was able to temporarily extend its influence to Siam. The Portuguese, and later other European powers, made advantageous trade agreements with Siam (Ayutthaya).

After the fall of the Kingdom of Pagan in 1287, the Shan tribes established a kingdom in Upper Burma. The Mon, who founded principalities in the ninth and tenth centuries before the arrival of the ❶, ❷ Burmans, ruled in the south. In 1531, the Toungoo dynasty from Lower Burma unified the country. King Tabinshwehti subjugated the Mon and, with the aid of Portuguese firearms, conquered central Burma, establishing its capital at Pegu in 1559 and Ava in 1635. By 1559, his successor gained the principalities of the north and the Shan states. The empire was at its zenith and magnificent buildings were erected. In the 17th century, British and Dutch trading companies began establishing bases in the empire. After attacks by the Chinese and Siamese, the Toungoo dynasty fell in 1752.

The Burmese chief Alaungpaya unified ❺ Burma (present-day Myanmar) in 1753. His son Hsinbyushin, bringing many scholars to his court, rebuilt Ava as his capital in 1765 and between 1764 and 1767 pushed far into Siam. Burma occupied a large part of Siam by 1785, until the British, attacking from India, brought Siam under its control after the first Anglo-Burmese War (1824–26).

The Ayutthaya Kingdom in Siam (present-day Thailand), which had existed since the 14th century and stretched over the Malay Peninsula to Malacca, destroyed the Khmer Empire in 1431. King Ramathibodi II in 1516 allowed the Portuguese to set up trading posts. His successor fended off the Burmans, and in 1549 besieged Ayutthaya. The kings had been using European weapons against the Burmese since the 16th century, in exchange for which the Europeans were granted favorable trade agreements with Siam—a trading center for products from China and Japan. Religious tolerance in Siam also allowed for the influence of European culture.

France sent Jesuit missionaries to ❸ Buddhist Siam in 1662 and the French East Indian Trading Company came to Ayutthaya in 1680. However, ❹ French political intervention proved excessive and in 1688 King Phetracha had them expelled. Two years later, the Dutch forced the king to grant them a monopoly on the trade in animal skins by blockading the Menam River. After 1700, this trade brought considerable prosperity to Siam. Thai literature and art reached a high point during the reign of King Boromokot.

Starting in 1770, the general Phraya Taksin reconstituted the Kingdom of Siam, and made vassal states of ❻ Laos and Cambodia; at his death, the kingdom was as powerful as ever. In 1782, General Phraya Chakri ascended to the throne as Rama I and founded the Chakri dynasty, which still reigns in Thailand today.

Elegant man and woman from Annan, colored wood engraving

❸ Head of a Buddha, Siamese sculpture in the Ayutthaya style

The French ambassador arrives at the palace of the Siamese king

That Luang, Buddhist temple near Vientiane, Laos, 1566, reconstructed 1930

❺ The Shwe Dagon Pagoda in Rangun, Burma, altered in 1768–73

1431 | Ayutthaya destroy Khmer Empire   1521 | European discovery of the Philippines   1544 | Conquest of Central Burma   1662 | Jesuits in Siam

1516 | Portuguese trading posts in Southeast Asia   1531 | Toungoo Dynasty in Burma   1549 | Ayutthaya conquered by Burma

■ Indochina and Indonesia

The French gained influence in Indochina, while the Portuguese and Dutch waged war over the foreign trading posts in the Indonesian Archipelago.

In 1428, Annam in Indochina, under Emperor Le Loi (Le Thai-to), the founder of the Le dynasty, broke away from China. Through efficient administration, Annam under Le Thanh-tong in 1471 occupied the remainder of the Champa Empire. Central power declined during the 16th century,

8 Map of the Malay Archipelago, detail from a map of the world by Pierre Desceliers, 1550

and the country was ruled up to the 17th century by two great families, the Trinh and the Nguyen, who for a long time fended off landing attempts by the Europeans. France negotiated the first foreign basing rights in the region, with ❼ Nguyen Anh in Indochina in 1787, who declared himself Emperor Gia Long in Vietnam in 1802.

Muslim merchants and the Portuguese fought over influence in Indonesia and the ❽ Malay Archipelago. In 1511, the Portuguese conquered ❾ Malacca and made it their main base; from there, they set up trading posts in ❿ Java, Ambon, Banda, Ternate, and elsewhere and monopolized the spice trade. During the 16th century, a major part of formerly Buddhist Indonesian territory converted to Islam.

The chartering of the Dutch East India Company in 1602 led to bitter fighting. The Dutch established themselves in Jakarta in 1610 and then in 1619 set up Batavia as their administrative center.

They seized Malacca from the Portuguese in 1641, Sulawesi (Celebes) in 1666, and finally Ambon and Ternate in 1683 and so controlled the region, but were forced to allow British trade in their regions in 1784. The Dutch East India Company declared bankruptcy in 1798 and was dissolved by the Dutch government, which took over administration of the company's territories.

7 Nguyen Anh at the age of eight during his visit to Versailles, 1787

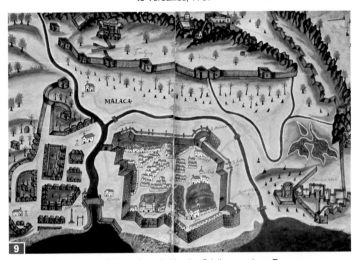

9 Harbor and capital of Malacca founded by the Srivijayan prince Parameswara, map of the city as a Portuguese trade base

The Philippines

By the end of the 15th century, Islam had spread from Borneo and Sulawesi to the Philippines. Magellan reached the island group in 1521 on his voyage around the world and clashed with the inhabitants. The islands were claimed by Spain and named after King Philip II in 1543. The structures of the local tribal governments were considered "primitive" and the northern islands were soon Christianized and economically developed by Catholic padres following the South American model, while the southern islands remain Islamic to this day.

Magellan fighting against the natives on the Phillipine island of Cebu

10 Dutch trading center at the coast of Bantam, Java

1688 | French expelled from Siam   **1753** | Founding of the new Burmese empire   **1782** | Chakri Dynasty founded in Siam

1680 | French East Indian Trading Company in Siam   **1752** | Fall of the Toungoo Dynasty   **1770** | Paya Tak reconstitutes Siam   **1785** | Occupation of parts of Siam

AFRICA 1500–1800

The diversity of African social development can be accounted for only to a certain extent. From the 16th to the 19th century, Africa became a focus of European trading interests. The coastal regions primarily drew the interest of the Portuguese and other European powers, who organized a complex slave and commodities trade with the African kings and chiefs, playing rival tribes against each other. In the North African kingdoms, there were constant struggles between Islam and Christianity in the upper classes, while the common people held fast to their traditional religions. Ethiopia had a special position in North Africa.

1 Map of the Indian Ocean showing East Africa, 16th century

■ East Africa, the Kongo Kingdom, and the Songhai Empire

While the Portuguese controlled trade on the African east coast, a Christian kingdom was established in the Kongo Kingdom. The Muslim Songhai Empire resisted Christianization.

The arrival of the Portuguese on the African continent in 1498, a year after Vasco da Gama had discovered India, changed the dynamics of Africa, especially on the ❶ east coast. Portuguese commercial enterprise would know no limits. The Portuguese used the rivalry between the coastal ❻ chiefs and city-states to destroy the trade there, eliminate Muslim traders, and gradually bring the entire coast under their control. In the meantime, the kingdoms of central Africa were able to survive, while Zanzibar became a new center for Arab traders under the rule of Oman.

In the the ❺ Kongo Kingdom, King Nzinga Nkuwu asked the Portuguese king to send missionaries to his Kingdom in 1482 and

3 Bronze head of an Oba, a king of Benin

converted to Christianity in 1491 as John I. He and his son Afonso I (Nzinga Mbemba I) constructed Christian churches and monasteries. The Kongo Kingdom experienced considerable prosperity as a result of the influx of Christian merchants and artisans, but the Kingdom's Christian upper class also participated in the ❹ slave trade of the poorer subjects. The Christian Kongo Kingdom declined in the 17th century and in 1668 the capital São Salvador do Kongo was devastated and plundered during

attacks by neighboring non-Christian tribes.

The most important Yoruba state, the Kingdom of ❸ Benin, traded with the ❷ Portuguese from 1486 and allowed them a trading post in the country. British expeditions to Benin beginning in 1530 led to regular clashes with the Portuguese, but the kingdom profited from the slave trade. The ban on slavery in 1691 led to the disintegration of the Kingdom of Benin.

Portugal also opened diplomatic relations and trade in 1484 with the Mali Empire, which went under in the 16th century with the expansion of the Muslim Songhai Empire. Songhai had already risen to become a properous kingdom in the 11th century through intensive trade contacts with the Arab world. Sonni Ali the Great turned the empire into the leading power in the Sudan by 1464 through expansion and in 1476 conquered Djenné. ❼ Muham-

2 Portuguese with helmet and trident, sculpture from Benin, 17th c.

4 Handcuffs of slave traders in sub-Saharan Africa

mad Ture founded the Askia dynasty in the Songhai Empire in 1493, which became a leading power in Upper Africa with a standing army, but was defeated by Morocco in 1590–1591.

7 The Tomb of Muhammed Ture of the Asaki dynasty in Gao, Mali

5 The king of Kongo receives a delegation, copper engraving, 1686

6 Monomotapa of the Bantu Empire, copper engraving, 17th c.

1476	Conquest of Djenné	1493	Askia Dynasty in Upper Africa	1543	Ethiopian victory under Negus Claudius
from 1482	Christianizing of the Kongo	1527	Somali Empire attacks Ethiopia		

Bornu, the West Coasts, and Ethiopia

Bornu became a strong Islamic empire, while the African west coast fell under the trade control of European powers. Ethiopia was largely able to maintain its own independent form of Christianity.

Castle at the Gold Coast, present-day Ghana, copper engraving, ca. 1750

The rising Bornu Empire under Ali Dunamani, who had reigned since 1472, replaced the declining Kanem Empire on Lake Chad. Ali expanded his empire in all directions with his armored cavalry and carried on trade with North and West Africa. Idris II continued this expansion and trade, which reached their height during the reign of Idris Alooma in 1580–1617. Northern Cameroon, northern Nigeria, and even the Yoruba nations were then under the influence of Bornu, but its supremacy declined in the 17th century. Islam had been advancing since the 1500s in the Hausa and Fulbe states, which had been largely able to retain their independence.

Competition developed among the European great powers for West African trade products, and the British and French eventually triumphed. In the 18th century, the British controlled the trade in the Gambia, Sierra Leone, and the Gold Coast (present-day Ghana), while the French dominated Senegal, French Guinea, and the Ivory Coast. ❾ Ghana, Togo, Nigeria, the Kongo, and Angola were centers of the ebony trade.

The Christian emperors in ❽ Ethiopia had been fighting the advance of Islam in Africa since the 14th century. Although they were determined to maintain political and ❿ cultural independ-ence, they were supported in the battle against Islam by the Portuguese from the 16th century on. Plagued since 1527 by the raids of Adel's Muslim Somali Empire, Negus Claudius was able to crushingly defeat it with Portuguese aid in 1543. Although Claudius and his successors emphasized the independence of Ethiopian Christianity, Jesuits were allowed to do missionary work in the country from 1557. The conversion to Catholicism of Negus Za Dengel in 1605 and Negus Susneus in 1622 led to bloody uprisings until Negus Fasilidas expelled all Catholics under penalty of death. During the reign of Jasus I (the Great),

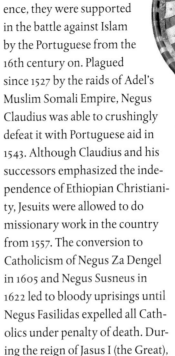

8 Leather buckle from Ethiopia

Ethiopia once again attained a political and cultural zenith at the turn of the 18th century but then sank into anarchy due to palace intrigues and the invasions of hostile neighboring tribes, finally crumbling into small local kingdoms. This condition persisted until Theodor II's reign in 1855. Theodore, a native of Amhara, married the daughter of the previous ruler.

10 Banquet, where wine is served in round clay jugs, Ethiopian book illustration, 17th century

---

The Ancient American Empires and the Conquest by Spain and Portugal

As in Southeast Asia, the Portuguese were forced out of Africa after 1600 by the Dutch. In 1637 the Dutch West India Company drove the Portuguese out of Elmina on the Gold Coast, took over the slave trade there, and made its own contracts with the Fanti chiefs of the Coast. In 1641, the Dutch occupied Luanda Island in Angola; they finally succeeded in expelling the Portuguese from Angola by force of arms in 1648. A largely peaceful reconciliation in trade eventually developed between the Portuguese and the Dutch.

Dirck Wilre, General Director of the West India Company on the south coast of Africa, painting by Peter de Wit, ca. 1669

1590–91 | Moroccan victory over the Songhai   **1641** | Dutch occupy Luanda Island

1557 | Jesuit mission in Ethiopia   **1637** | Dutch oust Portuguese from Elmina   **1648** | Dutch driven out of Angola by Portugal

THE ANCIENT AMERICAN EMPIRES AND THE CONQUEST BY SPAIN AND PORTUGAL CA. 1500–1800

The regionally splintered late ❶ Mayan cultures, as well as the Aztec and Inca peoples, built up—even as late as the 15th century—large and effectively administered empires in Central and South America. Their rapid collapse in the face of the Spanish conquest in the 16th century may be connected to the conquistadors' ability to exploit the enormous concentration of religious power in the hands of the native rulers. Under Spanish and Portuguese rule, it was primarily the missionaries who converted the Indians, though some of these clergymen also fought for the Indians' rights. Africans were also brought as slaves to the New World and exploited. Under the direction of the Jesuits, semi-autonomous Indian reservations were set up.

1 Maya incense holder in the form of the rain god Chac, painted clay

The Late Maya Empire

The late Maya culture was divided into a number of separate states. These were weakened by political strife in the 15th century and were conquered by the Spanish in the 16th century.

The Old Maya Empire and its temple cities were established by 300 A.D. In the fifth and sixth centuries, the Maya culture spread widely. An efficient agricultural system permitted a substantial increase in the population. In 987, the New Empire of the Maya emerged in the Yucatan under the leadership of the Toltec, who had emigrated from Campeche and mixed with the

ancient Maya. Other city-states joined the new entity. By 1204, the Cocom of Mayapán, who may have originated in Mexico, had assumed leadership of the empire. Some Maya tribes, led by Xiu of ❷ Uxmál, rebelled against their harsh rule in 1441. Political unification eluded the Yucatan, as 18 tiny city-states fought among themselves. Epidemics and natural catastrophes also served to weaken the states prior to the arrival of the Spanish.

In the highlands of present-day Guatemala were the Toltec-influenced states of the ❸ Quiché, the Cachiquel, and the Tzutuhil, with their capitals at Utatlán, Iximché, and Atitlán, respectively. Toltec tribes also settled areas of present-day Nicaragua, northwest Honduras, and El Salvador.

Despite its political decline, ❹ Maya culture was highly developed in the pre-Columbian period. The Maya used a ❺ hieroglyphic script, a numerical system, and a calendar that was more precise than the Gregorian calendar used in 16th century Europe. The people lived in large cities with stone houses and surfaced roads. Surpluses in the cultivation of maize supported artistic activities and skilled trades. The society was hierarchically structured, with the nobility and priests forming the ruling caste. Slaves were acquired through taking prisoners in war or debt servitude. The Maya traded over long distances, but metals and wagons were unknown to them.

2 Farmers in Uxmál

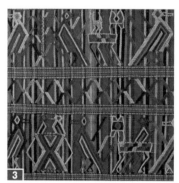

3 Traditional Quiché cloth decorated with animal motifs

Favored by this political fragmentation, the Spanish were able to conquer the highlands of ❻ Guatemala by 1525 and Yucatan by 1541, but the Guatemalan lowlands eluded Spanish control until 1697.

6 Necklace with jaguar-shaped beads, Guatemala, ca. 1200–1500

4 Mayan temple in Yucatan, built ca. 12th century

5 Maya fortune-telling calendar, known as the Tro-Cortes codex, which was probably made in Yucatán using the hieroglyphic script, 14th century

987 | New Maya Empire founded   **1204** | Rule of the Cocom of Mayapán begins   **1441** | Maya tribes under Xiu revolt

1100 | Aztecs migrate into Mexico   **1375** | Aztec capital Tenochtitlán founded

The Aztec Empire

In alliance with other cities, the Aztec ruled a mighty empire from their capital, Tenochtitlán, but in the 16th century they were rapidly subjugated by the Spanish conquerors.

The Aztec first migrated into Mexico around 1100. At first they were vassals of the Tepanec but steadily gained in strength. In 1375 the Aztec founded their capital, ⓫ Tenochtitlán, and then in 1428 they rebelled against the domination of the Tepanec, whose empire they destroyed in 1430 in

7 Aztec warriors, Indian drawing taken from the *Historia de las cosas de Nueva*

10
Moctezuma II

alliance with the city-states of Tetzoco and Tlatelolco. The Aztec rulers Moctezuma I, Axayacatl, and Ahuitzotl expanded the ❼ empire to the northeast in the second half of the 15th century, and peoples as far south as Guatemala paid tribute to them. They declared themselves the heirs of the Toltec and identified their ❾ war god Huitzilopochtli with the sun god, thus ❽ religiously legitimizing their policy of conquest. The Aztec Empire maintained alliances with its partner city-states, and all three profited from the enormous tributes and slaves that the subjugated peoples were forced to provide. At the time of the Spanish conquest, the empire was composed of 38 city-provinces.

In 1502, ❿ Moctezuma II Xocoyotzin, who would lead the empire to its zenith and then its rapid demise, came to the throne. He subdued the Mixtec in the highlands of Oaxaca and annexed the allies of Tetzoco in 1516. Moctezuma built up Tenochtitlán into the largest and most magnificent city in the Americas, with a population of about 300,000 people. The society was strictly hierarchical, and religiously charged court

customs allowed the ruler to stand far above his people. The nobility was hereditary, but warriors with outstanding service could also aspire to enter the noble caste.

In 1519 Moctezuma cordially welcomed the ⓬ Spanish under

8 Headdress of an Aztec priest, early 16th century

9 The Aztec god of war, Huitzilopochtli, lithograph

Hernán Cortés, because a prophecy had announced the return of the god Quetzalcóatl. Cortés, however, treacherously took the ruler captive and used him to

Human Sacrifices

The war and sun god of the Aztec, Huitzilopochtli—meaning "blue hummingbird of the south"—was regularly offered bloody human sacrifices on the temple platform's stone sun altar. The victims were usually anesthetized with intoxicating beverages before the chief priest sliced the hearts out of their living bodies. According to contemporary reports, in the final years of the Aztec Empire about 20,000 people were sacrificed annually, and human remains have subsequently been found that seem to confirm this.

above: Human sacrifices on the sun altar in Tenochtitlán

subdue the people. The Spanish put down a rebellion against the ⓭ destruction of Inca religious sites in 1520, and in the course of this Moctezuma was killed by a thrown stone. The Spanish went on to occupy the whole Aztec Empire by 1521.

11 The Aztec capital city Tenochtitlán (left) and the Incan capital city Cuzco (right)

12 Hernán Cortés leading his soldiers to the Aztec leader Moctezuma

13 Hernán Cortés destroys the religious sites of the Aztecs, 1520

1520 Death of Moctezuma		**1525** Spanish conquer highlands of Guatemala
1519 Hernán Cortés arrives in Tenochtitlán	**1521** Spanish occupy Aztec Empire	**1541** Spanish conquer Yucatán

■ The Rise of the Inca Empire

From their capital Cuzco, in present-day Peru, the Inca built the greatest empire in South America in the 15th century and ran a centralized government that organized almost all areas of life.

Following the collapse of the Tia-huanaco culture in the central Andes (part of present-day Peru and Bolivia) around 1100, local coastal cultures arose and formed numerous small states. The Inca, who inhabited the Cuzco Valley, gradually gained dominance under the ruler Manco Capac, who according to Inca tradition had migrated from Lake Titicaca around 1200. "Inca" appears to have originally been the name of the ruling family, then of the ruler, and finally the name of the whole people. The ninth Inca ruler, Pachacutec Yupanqui, who came to power around 1438, embarked on a series of military conquests that provided the foundations for the government of the Inca Empire. The capital

Headdress made of plaited lama hair decorated with feathers, 15th–16th c.

Cuzco grew rapidly, and other cities such as ❷ Machu Picchu were founded with ❹ monumental cult edifices. Pachacutec's son, ❸ Topa Yupanqui, conquered the Bolivian highlands and pushed into present-day northwest Argentina, subduing the coastal areas of the Chimú Empire and expanding Inca territory southwards. He sent raft expeditions out into the Pacific Ocean, which probably got

as far as the Galapagos Islands. At the beginning of the 16th century, under Huayna Capac, the empire was further enlarged to include much of present-day Colombia and reached its political and ❶ cultural zenith. The "Empire of Four Parts" was the mightiest realm in ancient America, ruling the surrounding peoples.

The Inca state had a tightly centralized administration and a carefully planned economic structure. At its head was the ❻ ruler, the Sapay Inca ("highest Inca"), revered as the son of the ❺ sun. In the empire's strict hierarchy, the Inca people constituted the nobility, while the subjugated peoples were used as laborers. All subjects were combined into administrative units and were required to accomplish specific labor and military services for the good of the state. Everything was recorded by means of knotted strings called ❼ *quipu*. An excellent network of paths through the mountains permitted the rapid transport of troops, news, and some produce between cities. Like the Maya, the Inca did not

The ruins of Machu Picchu, Peru

Topa Yupanqui on his throne with his wife at his side, artist's reconstruction from written descriptions, 1870

have knowledge of metallurgy or the wheel. A common language of the empire, Quechua, was used to simplify administration. For every 10,000 inhabitants of the Inca Empire, there were 1330 state officials, selected according to their abilities and trained for specific responsibilities and positions.

Carved rock sundial for cult ceremonies, Machu Picchu, Peru

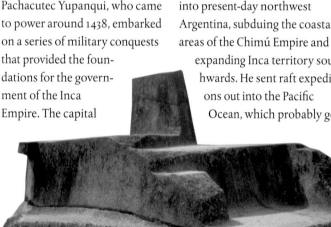
Inca sacrifice to the sun god, colored copper engraving, 17th century

Inca ruler, wood engraving, 16th c.

Inca quipu, 1430–1532

The Structure of the Inca Empire and the Spanish Conquest

Agrarian collectivism was overseen by the Inca Empire's administration, but the passivity of the masses and a fratricidal war facilitated the civilization's rapid conquest by the Spanish.

In Inca society the land belonged to the village community, which allocated certain areas of arable land to individual families, according to their size. Each family could live from the yield, but the community was also required to pay taxes for the support of the ruler, the priests, and communal buildings. Individuals also had to cultivate the community's fields to support the elderly, the ill, and those otherwise unfit for work. Woods and pastures were common land for the use of every member of the community, but the home and farm were family property. Harvest surpluses were delivered to central silos where they were stored for times of famine. Agricultural productivity was raised through ❽ terracing and irrigation systems and the use of fertilizer, primarily guano. The breeding of animals, notably the llama, and fishing along the coast, also played a significant part in the Inca economy. The manner in which the absolute

authority of the ruler and his state rested on divine ritual and went unquestioned may have made the structure more fragile, assisting the Spanish conquest.

In 1527, Huayna Capac died

Atahualpa, son of Huayna Capac

without designating a successor. Both his eldest son Huáscar, in Cuzco, and his favorite son Atahualpa, in Quito, laid claim to the throne. resulting in a fraticidal war that seriously weakened the empire. The Spanish under Fran-

cisco Pizarro used this division to their advantage to conquer the Inca Empire. At first they sided with ❾ Atahualpa, who was victorious when Huáscar was captured and murdered by his troops in 1532. But then Pizarro had Atahualpa ❿ imprisoned in 1533 and strangled, leaving the state without a Sapay Inca and thus paralyzed. The Inca Empire was largely conquered by 1539.

Resistance to the Spanish continued after 1535 in the border provinces of Vilcabamba under the leadership of a member of the former ruling family, Manco Capac II, whom the Spanish themselves had installed in 1533. He was murdered in 1544, but the Vilcabamba region was still able to resist the Spanish until 1572. A last revolt of the Inca, which attempted to restore the old religion, failed in 1565. Despite repression and conversion, ⓫ Inca culture survived and influenced the European colonists who came and settled in the former empire.

8 Irrigation of the Inca terraced fields, wood engraving, ca. 1560

The revolt against the Spanish in 1780–81

Attempts by Spanish government officials (corregidores) to force the indigenous peoples to adopt 18th-century Spanish lifestyles resulted in a revolt in Peru in 1780–1781 that was led by a descendant of a noble Inca family, Tupac Amaru. The revolt was violently crushed, but the corregidores concerned were replaced by new officials who then allowed the indigenous people greater independence.

10 Atahualpa is seized by Pizarro's soldiers, 1532

11 Drinking vessel in a mixed Incan-Spanish style, ca. 1650

1544 Manco Capac II murdered	**1780–81** Tupac Amaru leads failed revolt
1535 Inca revolt in Vilcabamba led by Manco Capac II	**1572** End of revolt in Vilcabamba

Spanish and Portuguese Domination of the Americas

The Spanish and the Portuguese colonized the "New World" after 1500. Black slaves were brought from Africa to work on the plantations and farms of the colonizers.

1

Columbus lands in the Americas, 1498

4

Cortés conquers Mexico, colored lithograph

Soon after their arrival in the Americas, the Spanish and Portuguese began to lay claim to the land. In 1498 ❶ Christopher Columbus reached the mainland for the first time (in present-day Venuezuela) and the following year, Amerigo Vespucci landed on the coast of Colombia. The Europeans proceeded to explore and conquer much of the continent: the area of Mexico by ❸,❹ Hernán Cortés in 1519–1521, Peru by ❷ Francisco Pizarro in 1531–1534, Chile in 1535, Paraguay in 1536, and Bolivia in 1538. In 1535, the Spanish king, Charles V,

2   Francisco Pizarro, copper engraving, 1673

tively given the legal title of "missionary work," although this concept long remained controversial among theologians.

The ❻ Portuguese, led by Pedro Alvarez Cabral, arrived in Brazil in 1500 and established trading posts there. The Portuguese crown first claimed the country as its property in 1534. From 1549 Brazil was administered by a royal governor-general.

Madrid attempted to control events in the Spanish territories and imposed restrictions on European settlers. The crown considered the trade and resources of the colonies as a source of income for the mother country. ❼ Monastic missionaries converted the Indians to Christianity—sometimes forcibly—but also protected them from the ❽ arbitrary actions of the conquerors. In 1542 they were able to enforce a legal ban on Indian slavery, and in the same year the Dominican father, Bartolomé de Las Casas, the "apostle of the Indians," drew up his *Leyes Nuevas* ("new laws"). These established the equality of the Indians and their liberation from forced labor. However the Church was silent on black slavery, and ❾ Africans were soon transported to work on the plantations of South America and the Caribbean islands. By the time slavery was abolished in 1850, between four million and ten million Africans had been transported to

3

Hernán Cortés, painting, 16th century

5

Antonio de Mendoza, painting, 1786

Brazil alone.

Initially whole tribes of Indians were eradicated by infections carried by the Europeans, but over time the South American-born Europeans (*creoles*), Indians (*mestizos*), and black Africans (*mulattos*) born in the New World mixed. The Europeans, however, continued to form the ruling class.

9

African slaves at a market in Brazil, ca. 1768

6

Battle between the Indians and Portuguese, ca. 1550, colored copper engraving

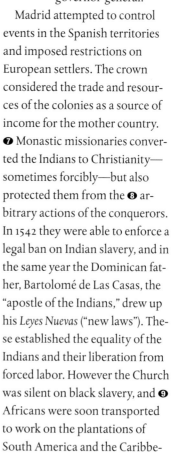

7

A Franciscan monk preaches to the Indians

8

Spanish oppression of the native Indians, colored copper engraving, 1596

appointed ❺ Antonio de Mendoza viceroy of "New Spain," which encompassed present-day Mexico and most of Central America. In 1543 the viceroyalty of Peru was formed, comprising all of Spanish South America and Panama. The conquests were retrospec-

1498 | Columbus lands on the Venezuelan coast   **1519** | Cortés arrives in Mexico   **1535** | Francisco Pizarro founds the city of Lima

1499 | Vespucci lands on the Colombian coast   **1529** | Francisco Pizarro becomes governor of Peru

The Indian Reservations

Under the direction of the Jesuits, autonomous Indian reservations were established during the 17th century. In the 18th century, the Creoles became increasingly politically conscious and sought independence from the motherland.

Under Las Casas, bishop of Chiapas from 1544, the ❿ Dominicans and later the Jesuits began the ⓫ conversion of the Indians. They started in the jungles of Guatemala and founded mission reservations in which the tribal chiefs remained in office with the recognition of the king of Spain. Similar reservations were later set up in Mexico. Protective regulations for the Indians, such as payment for services rendered and prescribed work and rest periods, were often not respected by the local authorities. In 1601 a royal decree gave the rules the force of law—yet they were still routinely disregarded.

In 1604, the Jesuits succeeded in having the province of Paraguay transferred to their control, and in 1609 founded a *reducción* (reservation) for the Guarani as a semi-autonomous Indian settlement. The Indians lived in supervised settlements and cultivated communal lands for two or three days of the week, the yield of which was used to pay Spanish taxes and church construction. The remaining days of the week the Indians worked their own land for their family. All children received an education, a part of which was training in a skilled trade. The Jesuits kept their own ⓬ militia to guard against the raids of slave traders from neighboring Brazil. Similar reservations were set up in Ecuador, northern Bolivia, and northwest Mexico, but they deteriorated after the expulsion of the Jesuits from Paraguay between 1759–1767.

The enlightened government of Charles III of Spain carried out reforms in the second half of the 18th century. These included measures to improve the legal status of Indians and the legal equality of the Creoles and immigrant Spaniards in the appointment to offices. However ownership of the best land and access to office remained the preserve of the Creole elite. This class slowly became acquainted with the concepts of the Enlightenment and the French Revolution. Spanish America saw the Napoleonic occupation and the de facto deposition of the royal house in Spain in 1808 as an opportunity to assume home rule. The hour of the struggle for liberation under Simon Bolívar had come.

10 Dominican monks baptize Indians, ca.1600

11 A Christian sermon in a pictorial script that was developed by the Jesuit missionaries to assist them in converting the Indians of Paraguay, extract written on parchment, 17th century

The Pizarro Brothers

The Pizarro brothers are prime examples of the conquistador spirit. Francisco had himself declared governor of Peru in 1529 and founded Lima in 1535. In 1537–1538, trapped with his brothers in Cuzco, he had a disagreement with the Spanish general, Diego de Almagro, who had hurried to save him. Francisco had Almagro executed in 1538 but was then himself murdered by Almagro's son in 1541. Francisco's brother Gonzalo rebelled against the Spanish viceroy in 1546; he was imprisoned and executed. Their youngest brother, Hernando, went to Spain in 1539 to explain Almagro's execution and was imprisoned until 1560.

The arrest of Gonzalo Pizarro

12 Indians obstruct a Spanish officer from entering their reservation, wood inlay, 17th century

1 Map of North and Central America, colored lithograph, 19th century

NORTH AMERICA TO THE FOUNDING OF CANADA AND THE UNITED STATES 1497–1789

A race began between the British and the French for the colonization of ❶ North America. It ended with the British claiming the area of the later eastern United States and the French pushing north. Canada was eventually divided between the British and the French. In the northeast of the present-day United States, emigrating Puritans and private proprietors and companies founded the New England colonies. In the 17th and 18th centuries, they won cultural independence and political confidence and resisted taxation by the British motherland. The conflict escalated into a war lasting from 1775 to 1783, defined by the United States' Declaration of Independence in 1776, and resulting ultimately in a new constitution for a federal United States of America.

■ The Fight for the Coasts and the First Colonization of North America

On the coasts of America, Great Britain and Spain fought battles for naval supremacy. During the 16th century, the British and the French began the exploration of North America.

While Spain and Portugal were conquering Central and ❺ South America, it was primarily the British and French who established themselves on the coasts of North America. In 1497, just five years after Columbus's first voyage, John Cabot, in the service of the English king, reached the North American coast in Labrador. French exploration began with Jacques Cartier, who sailed through the Gulf of St. Lawrence and up the St. Lawrence River in 1534–1541. The buccaneer Walter Raleigh landed at Cape Hatteras in North Carolina in 1584, claimed the entire Atlantic coast between the 35th and 45th parallels for England, and named the

2 Sir Henry Morgan, privateer and vice-governor of Jamaica, copper engraving

area ❸ Virginia in honor of the "virgin queen" Elizabeth I; in 1607 it officially became a British colony (and in 1624 a Crown colony). Henry Hudson investigated the East Coast of North America for Great Britain in 1609, while the French missionary Jacques Marquette and fur trader Louis Jolliet discovered the Mississippi River Valley from Wisconsin to Arkansas. Louisiana became the center of French colonization in the Mississippi area in

1716–1717, and in 1718 the French founded the city of New Orleans.

In the conflict between the sea powers of England and Spain, English privateers seized many transports of Spanish gold and goods returning to Europe from the Spanish colonies. The ❹ Caribbean islands, the Antilles, and parts of the Central American coasts remained contested areas from which freebooters, independently or under the mandate of the European sea powers, seized ships and set up their own, occasionally highly organized "buccaneer states." The most famous privateer was ❷ Henry

3 First British settlement in Virginia, 1584, copper engraving, 1590

Morgan, who occupied and ransacked trading vessels around Spanish Panama with his British–supported "filibusters," and in 1674 he was knighted before returning to become the British representative governor of Jamaica in the following year.

4 Naval battle of the British fleet against the French fleet near Domenica in the Caribbean, 1782

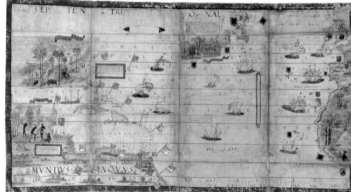

5 Naval map of the South Atlantic with the continents South America and Africa, drawing, ca. 1519

| 1497 | John Cabot lands in Labrador | 1608 | Founding of Quebec | 1623 | Founding of New Hampshire |
| 1607 | Virginia becomes British colony | 1620 | Founding of Plymouth | 1626 | Founding of Salem |

The Establishment of the New England Colonies　17th to 18th century

The earlier British colonies were established and settled either by Puritans driven out of England or by private entrepreneurs. They were soon increasingly prosperous both economically and culturally and developed their own social and political structures.

6 Battle between feuding Indian tribes

At the beginning of the 17th century, North America seemed like the promised land to many groups of English Puritans, who were oppressed by the state church and government in Britain. Their desire to live by the principles of a puritanical Christianity shaped the identity of America and later the United States. In 1620 the ❾ Pilgrim fathers, 102 Puritans who wanted to break with the Church of England because they felt it had not fully carried out the reforms started in the Reformation, sailed to the

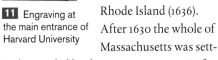

New World in the ⓬ Mayflower. They landed in ❽ New England. As they had the official right to colonize the area, they signed a charter they had drafted themselves, the "Mayflower Compact," in which they vowed to form an autonomous community and subsequently founded the colony of Plymouth. Other, related colonies followed: New Hampshire (1623), Massachusetts Bay (1630), Connecticut (1634), and Rhode Island (1636). After 1630 the whole of Massachusetts was settled by the "Great Migration" of the Puritans. The founding fathers at first tried to live peacefully with the native ❼ Indians, and this was initially successful while the colonies were still small. With time, however, the settlers constantly expanded their territories and began repeatedly interfering in the ❻ feuds between the Indian tribes.

The British government assigned the development of the land both to corporate enterprises and individuals with "free

11 Engraving at the main entrance of Harvard University

7 Indian village in present-day North Carolina

letters," or charters for colonization. Thus the colonies of Maryland (1634) and Carolina (1663), divided into North and South in 1729, arose. The first black slaves were brought to North America in 1619.

The Dutch were also active in colonization on a smaller scale; they settled in present-day ❿ New York, founding the colony of New Netherlands and its capital New Amsterdam in 1624. However, the British took the area from the Dutch in 1664; Charles III assigned it to his brother James, duke of York, after whom it was renamed "New York." The duke sold the area of present-day New Jersey to a private individual. A part of this land was acquired in 1674 by William Penn, the leader of the Quakers, who in addition bought Pennsylvania—named after him—in 1681 and Delaware in 1682. In 1733 the last private colony, named Georgia

8 *Landscape in New England*, painting by Frederick Edwin Church, 1851

9 The pilgrims arrive in America

10 View over the city of New York, copper engraving, 1776

after King George of England, was founded.

After beginnings full of privations, the New England states blossomed by the end of the 17th century, due to the colonists' pioneering spirit and Protestant work ethic. The first American universities were founded, including ⓫ Harvard (1636), Yale (1701), and Princeton (1746).

12 The *Mayflower*'s voyage

William Penn

As a Quaker, William Penn was persecuted in England where he was expelled from Christ Church, an Oxford college, for his beliefs. Yet as the son of Admiral Sir William Penn he also had some influence at court. Penn was able to persuade the government to assign him territories in the New World, where he founded colonies of peaceful Quaker communities. His drafted the first plan to unify all North American colonies (1696) and to found a "league of nations" for Europe (1693).

William Penn

from 1630	"Great Migration"		1634	Maryland colony		1636	Founding of Rhode Island
	1630	Founding of Massachusetts		1634	Founding of Connecticut	1663	Carolina colony, divided in 1729

■ Canada and Resistance to the Crown by the New England Colonies

In the fight for colonial territory, French explorers pushed ever further north into Canada. The New England states united after 1765 in resistance against British paternalism.

The French concentrated in the north of the North American continent. In 1603 the French officer ❶ Samuel de Champlain, who initially set off to Canada as part of a fur trading expedition, began the exploration and settling of Canada. He founded Quebec in 1608. The area around the Gulf of ❸ St. Lawrence was referred to as "New France." The defeat of France in the Spanish War of Succession led in 1713 to the Peace of Utrecht, which transferred Newfoundland, Acadia, and areas of the Hudson Bay to Great Britain.

1

Samuel de Champlain

Paris in 1763, which ended the Seven Years' War, France had to concede the rest of Canada, which later saw an influx of British loyal to the king. The legacy of this maneuvering is seen in the bilingual nature of Canada to this day. The Quebec Act (1774) recognized the validity of both British and French law in the recently acquired area, and the Canada Bill (1791) later split the territory into the predominantly English Upper Canada (later Ontario) and the French Lower Canada (Quebec). In the 1754–1763 war for the

American colonies, known as the French and Indian War, the ❷ New England colonies remained loyal to the British. However, economic power had strengthened their confidence, and the link to the motherland had grown weaker with each new generation of American-born colonists. To pay the debt that had accrued fighting France in North America, King George III attempted—against the advice of leading statesmen—to raise finances through an increase of taxes in the 13 American colonies. The colonies, however, demanded representation by their own delegates in the British parliament in exchange, which London was not prepared to grant. In other areas, too, the colonies saw their freedom being restricted. The high import taxes on all goods from the British motherland were particularly offensive and led to widespread boycotts. As an expression of protest, a group of colonists

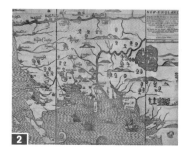

2

Map of New England, wood engraving, 1677

from Boston, Massachusetts. staged the ❻ "Boston Tea Party" in 1773; dressed as Indians, they stormed British ships coming into Boston Harbor and threw their cargo of tea overboard. In response, the crown suspended the constitution of the Massachusetts colony. Armed conflict was not far off.

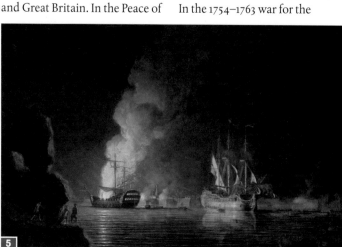

3

The French seafarer Jacques Cartier travels down the St. Lawrence River, 1534–1542

The attempt of the British to expand their control westward into Ohio led in 1754–1763 to a colonial ❹ ❺ war between France and Great Britain. In the Peace of

4

The death of General Wolfe in the battle against the French at Quebec on the September 13, 1759

5

Conquest of the French fortress Louisbourg by the British, 1758

6

"Boston Tea Party" on the December 16, 1773, colored lithograph, 1846

1713	Peace of Utrecht		Sep 13, 1759	Battle of Quebec		1773	"Boston Tea Party"
	1754–63	The French and Indian War		1763	Peace of Paris		1774	Quebec Act

■ The War against the British and American Independence

Friction between London and the colonies led to the American War of Independence in 1775 and a formal declaration of independence in 1776. The Americans won the war in 1783 with French aid.

In September–October 1774, at the Continental Congress in Philadelphia, the delegates of the 13 British-American colonies decided not to accept any taxation without direct representation in Parliament and demanded the reinstatement of the Massachusetts constitution. London responded by sending troops to restore order in the colonies. After the first hostilities, a second congress of colonists decided in May 1775 to establish a combined army, under the supreme command of ❼, ❾ George Washington, later supported by the French ⓫ Marquis de Lafayette and the Prussian Baron von Steuben, who contributed to the professional organization of the army.

In the meantime, independence was implemented politically: on July 4, 1776, the ⓭ 13 colonies (Massachusetts, New Hampshire, Rhode Island, Connecticut, New York, New Jersey, Pennsylvania,

7

Washington crosses the Delaware before the Battle of Trenton, 1776

9

George Washington

10

Benjamin Franklin

Delaware, Maryland, Virginia, North Carolina, South Carolina, and Georgia) adopted the ❽ Declaration of Independence in Philadelphia as an agreement between the people and government, emphasizing the freedom and equality of all humans. After this, the new states ratified republican constitutons.

The badly armed and discordant, yet enthusiastic America troops achieved a major victory in October 1777, forcing the British troops to capitulate at Saratoga. With this, the American ambassador in Paris, ❿ Benjamin Franklin, was able to negotiate an alliance with France in February 1778. With the help of French naval units,

Washington eventually cornered the previously victorious British southern army and in October 1781 forced it to ⓬ surrender. The French brokered the Treaty of Paris, which ended the Revolutionary War with advantageous conditions for the colonists on August 3, 1783. London was forced to recognize the independence of the United States, and the entire territory east of the Mississippi River, south of the Great Lakes, and north of Florida fell to the newly founded nation.

Under the Articles of Confederation, ratified in 1781, the states joined together in a loose league, in which the individual states had great autonomy. This was replaced in 1788 by a constitution that strengthened the federal government, and George Washington was elected the first president of the United States in 1789.

8

Declaration of Independence of the United States of America, July 4, 1776

Virginia Declaration of Rights

Section 1

That all men are by nature equally free and independent and have certain inherent rights, of which, when they enter into a state of society, they cannot, by any compact, deprive or divest their posterity; namely, the enjoyment of life and liberty, with the means of acquiring and possessing property, and pursuing and obtaining happiness and safety.

11

Washington receives Lafayette

12

The surrender at Yorktown on the October 19, 1781

13

Signing of the Declaration of Independence by the 13 colonies of America, 1776

| Jul 4, 1776 | Declaration of Independence | 1777–81 | Articles of Confederation | 1791 | Canada Bill |
| 1777 | British surrender at Saratoga | 1789 | George Washington elected first president | 1812–14 | War for Canada |

OCEANIA AND AUSTRALIA TO THE ARRIVAL OF THE EUROPEANS 16th–18th century

The native inhabitants of Australia, New Zealand, and the ❶ islands of Oceania were able to develop their ancient culture over a long period of time. In the 16th and 17th centuries, the seafaring European nations arrived on the islands and mainland of Australia, but comprehensive European exploration did not occur until the 18th century. The explorers saw the inhabitants of the South Sea Islands as "noble savages" because of their harmonious lifestyle and lack of private property. After the loss of the American colonies, the British used Australia as a penal colony.

1

Moai, monolithic stone statues on Easter Island

◼ Oceania

The diverse cultures of the Pacific islands formed predominantly local communities scattered across large areas. They were encountered by the European nations in the 16th century and gradually colonized.

2

Matavae, a village on the island of Tahiti

Various cultures developed on the islands of New Guinea, Melanesia, Micronesia, and Polynesia. They had in common ❷ village settlements, the use of ❸ stone tools, agriculture, the breeding of animals, and fishing. Most of the societies were based on hierarchy and were led by a king or chief and a priest caste.

Settlement took place over a prolonged period of time in various waves of migration, notably the Austronesian migration that began around 750 B.C., and the Malayo-Polynesian migration that began around 500 B.C. By 700 A.D. Raiatea, one of the Society Islands, was the center of the Polynesian world. Between 900–1000 the ❻ Polynesians reached and settled Easter Island, Hawaii, and New Zealand, establishing the Maori culture.

At the beginning of the 16th century, Spanish and Portuguese seafarers arrived in Oceania,

3 Ceremonial Axehead of the Maori chiefs

initiating two centuries of European exploration. Magellan passed several Pacific islands during his 1519–1521 circumnavigation. In 1526 the Portuguese Jorge de Menezes claimed the island of New Guinea, while in 1524–1564 Spanish voyagers charted the majority of the islands of Micronesia. The Dutchman Abel Tasman, who came to New Zealand in 1642, was the first to make a more exact survey of the Melanesian region. In 1722, his countryman

Jacob Roggeveen named Easter Island after the date of its sighting. On his three voyages between 1764 and 1780, James Cook, commissioned by the British Royal Society, traveled to ❺ Tahiti and circumnavigated New Zealand for the first time. In 1772–1775 he arrived in New Caledonia and mapped the ❹ New Hebrides, the Marquesas, and Tonga.

James Cook

On three voyages to the South Pacific, Captain James Cook, one of the last great seafaring discoverers, explored Oceania, Australia, and New Zealand. In 1773, he became the first navigator to cross the Antarctic Circle, searching for the mysterious Terra Australis ("southern land"). On his third voyage, he looked in vain for a northern passage from the Pacific to the Atlantic. In February 1779, he was killed in Hawaii by a group of islanders.

above: James Cook

4

James Cook in the New Hebrides in 1774, painting by William Hodges

Woman Holding a Fruit, Tahiti-inspired painting by Paul Gauguin, 1893

6

Polynesian woman from the Tonga islands, 1895

| ca. 24,350 B.C. | Evidence of first settlements | 1605 | Willem Jansz sights Australia | 1642 | Tasman gives his name to the island of Tasmania |
| 1526 A.D. | Jorge de Menezes reaches New Guinea | 1642–44 | Abel Tasman's voyage of exploration | 1643 | Tasman reaches New Zealand |

■ Australia up to British Colonization

The Australian native inhabitants, the Aborigines, constitute an independent cultural society. Europeans first arrived in Australia in the 17th century, but colonization by the British only began in the second half of the 18th century.

The Australian ❽ native inhabitants lived as hunter-gatherers and killed wild animals with throwing spears or wooden clubs. They fashioned vessels and tools out of wood, bone, and shells. Their extensive ❿ religio-cultic concepts often revolved around the relationship between the living and totem animals and their ancestors, and are often presented in colorful rock paintings. The oldest settlement finds in Australia have been dated as early as 24,350 B.C. The earliest immigrants probably came through Southeast Asia and Melanesia.

Group of English convicts deported from England to the penal colony, working the land, steel engraving, 1835

Lack of written evidence and the heavily mythological form of the oral histories make a more exact dating extremely difficult. The Aborigines still represent an independent cultural society in Australia today.

The arrival of Europeans in Australia began in 1605 with the Dutch captain Willem Jansz. The ❼ barren, arid land and the often hostile behavior of the Aborigines offered the Dutch little incentive to colonize, though they anchored off the north coast several times. Commissioned by the go-

❽ Portrait of an Aborigine woman

vernor of the Dutch Indies, Anthony van Diemen, ❿ Abel Tasman undertook a voyage of exploration around Australia in 1642–44. He charted the island named after him, Tasmania, in 1642, and the South Island of New Zealand and the Tongan and Fijian islands in 1643. Australia was then called "New Holland," although the Dutch did not pursue their colonial interest.

❶ William Dampier, a British sea captain, reached the northwestern coast of Australia by way

❶ The English discoverer and privateer, William Dampier

of the Marianas and the Moluccas in 1699 and was the first to describe the native inhabitants and their culture. In April 1770, Captain Cook, after crossing the Pacific Ocean, landed on the southeast coast of Australia in Botany Bay, south of modern Sydney, and claimed the land for the British crown, naming it "New South Wales." His companion, the naturalist Joseph Banks, provided the crown with a description of the land, which raised great interest back in Britain, even more so after the loss of the American colonies. London decided to use Australia as a penal colony for ❾ British prisoners, who were to cultivate the land under strict supervision. In January 1788, the first prisoner ship, carrying 730 convicts, anchored north of Botany Bay. There, the New South Wales penal colony was established; Sydney was founded nearby for the colonial officials. Convicted prisoners conti-

❼ The Australian interior or "outback"

nued to be deported to Australia until 1868. The last of the prison colonies, located on the island of Tasmania, was closed in 1877.

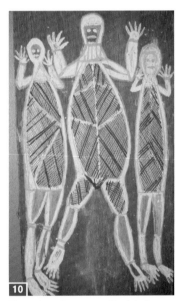

❿ Three ghost figures, an Aboriginal painting on tree bark

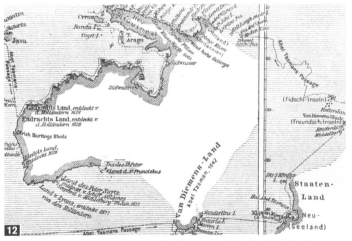

❿ Route traveled by the Dutch explorer Abel Tasman, who in the 17th century searched the Pacific Ocean for new trade routes for the Netherlands

| 1699 | William Dampier reaches Australia | 1770 | James Cook lands in Botany Bay | 1788 | First British convicts arrive in Australia |
| 1722 | Discovery of Easter Island | 1768–71 | First circumnavigation of New Zealand | 1877 | Closure of last penal colony on Tasmania |

Glossary

abdication The renouncing of power, as when a monarch formally relinquishes his or her throne.

absolute sovereignty The undivided rule by a single person.

autonomous Acting independently or having the freedom to do so.

bourgeoisie The middle class.

caliph The chief Muslim civil and religious leader, regarded as the successor of Muhammad.

conclave In the Roman Catholic Church, the assembly of cardinals for the election of a pope.

concordant Harmonious, in agreement.

daimyo In feudal Japan, one of the great lords who were vassals of the shogun.

diet The regular meeting of the states of a confederation; a legislative assembly in certain countries.

dogma A system of doctrines proclaimed true by a religious sect.

ecclesiastic Of or relating to the Christian church or its clergy.

erudition Great or deep learning or knowledge.

estate A class or order regarded as forming part of the body politic, such as the three estates: clergy, the nobility or peerage, and the common people.

excommunicate To officially exclude a person from participation in the sacraments and services of the Christian church.

feudalism The social system in Europe during the Middle Ages, in which the nobility held lands from the crown in exchange for military service, and vassals were in turn tenants of the nobles, whereas peasants were obliged to live on their lord's land and give him homage, labor, and a share of the produce, in exchange for protection.

fief An estate of land that is held on the condition of feudal service.

flagellant A person who subjects him- or herself or others to whipping as a way of a religious discipline.

fraternity A religious society; a group of people sharing a common profession.

giro A service of many European banks that permits authorized direct transfer of funds among accountholders as well as conventional transfers by check.

hemiplegiac Having paralysis of one side of the body.

Holy Roman Empire The empire set up in western Europe after the coronation of Charlemagne as emperor in 800 C.E. It was created by the medieval papacy in an attempt to unite Christianity under one rule.

humanism A cultural movement that turned away from scholasticism and revived interest in ancient Greek and Roman thought.

indulgence In the Catholic Church, the remission, or cancellation, of temporal punishment due for a sin after the guilt has been forgiven.

Interregnum The period of time between the end of a sovereign's reign and the accession of a successor.

investiture The action of formally investing a person with honors or rank; the ceremony at which the honors are conferred on a person.

Levant The eastern part of the Mediterranean with its islands and neighboring countries.

margravate The territory ruled by a margrave (the hereditary title of some princes of the Holy Roman Empire).

maxim A proverb or short statement expressing a general truth or rule of conduct.

mendicant Relating to one of the religious orders that originally relied solely on alms or begging.

ministeriales Royal officeholders.

paternalism The practice on the part of people in positions of authority of restricting the freedom and responsibilities of those subordinate to them in the subordinates' supposed best interest.

pogrom An organized massacre of a specific ethnic group.

raison d'état "Reason of state" in French, meaning a purely political reason for action on the part of a ruler or government.

scholasticism The system of theology and philosophy taught in medieval European universities that was based on Aristotelian logic and the writings of the early Church Fathers and having a strong emphasis on tradition and dogma.

see A place in which a cathedral church stands, identified as the seat of authority of a bishop or archbishop.

shogun A hereditary commander in chief in feudal Japan.

simony The buying or selling of ecclesiastical privileges, for example pardons.

suzerainty A sovereign or state having some control over another state that is internally autonomous; a feudal overlord.

synod An assembly of clergy and sometimes laypeople in a diocese or a division of a particular church.

temporal Relating to worldly or secular matters.

vassal A holder of land by feudal tenure on conditions of homage and allegiance.

For More Information

Asia Society and Museum
725 Park Avenue
New York, NY 10021
(212) 288-6400
Web site: http://asiasociety.org
The museum offers groundbreaking exhibitions on traditional and contemporary Asian and Asian American art.

The British Museum
Great Russell Street
London WC 1B 3DG
England
Web site: http://www.britishmuseum.org
The British Museum has a world-renowned collection of art and human history, from the beginnings to contemporary times. Among its many collections are exhibits of artifacts from medieval Europe, from about 1050 to 1540.

The Cloisters Museum and Gardens
The Metropolitan Museum of Art (MMA)
99 Margaret Corbin Drive
Fort Tryon Park
New York, NY 10040
(212) 923-3700
Web site: http://www.metmuseum.org
The Cloisters Museum and Gardens, a branch of the MMA, is dedicated to the art and architecture of medieval Europe. Its collections include architectural elements and artworks that date from the 12th through the 15th centuries.

Higgins Armory Museum
100 Barber Avenue
Worcester, MA 01606-2444
(508) 853-6015

Web site: http://www.higgins.org
This museum is devoted to the preservation of armor and contains some 4,000 examples of weaponry and armor, including pieces from medieval and Renaissance Europe.

Musée du Louvre
Paris 75058
France
Web site: http://www.louvre.fr
One of the world's largest museums, the Louvre contains nearly 35,000 objects from prehistory to the nineteenth century.

Royal Ontario Museum
100 Queen's Park
Toronto, ON M5S 2C6
Canada
(416) 586-8000
Web site: http://www.rom.on.ca
The collections of this museum, numbering more than six million pieces, include many world cultures and natural history, from the Stone Age to the arms and armor of Europe, the Middle East, and Japan. It also includes exhibits on modern art and design.

Vatican Museums
Viale Vaticano
Rome 00165
Italy
Web site: http://mv.vatican.va
The Vatican Museums includes various art and sculpture collections gathered by popes of the Roman Catholic Church from the 1500s to today.

WEB SITES

Due to the changing nature of Internet links, Rosen Publishing has developed an online list of Web sites related to the subject of this book. This site is updated regularly. Please use this link to access the list:

http://www.rosenlinks.com/wtoh/mid

For Further Reading

Bajou, Valérie. *Versailles*. New York, NY: Abrams Books, 2012.

Bingham, Marjorie Wall. *An Age of Empires, 1200–1750*. New York, NY: Oxford University Press, 2005.

Brown, Nancy Marie. *The Abacus and the Cross: The Story of the Pope Who Brought the Light of Science to the Dark Ages*. New York, NY: Basic Books, 2010.

Corrick, James A. *The Early Middle Ages*. Farmington Hills, MI: Lucent Books, 2005.

Cunningham, Mark E., and Lawrence J. Zwier. *The End of the Shoguns and the Birth of Modern Japan*. Minneapolis, MN: Twenty-First Century Books, 2009.

Davenport, John. *The Age of Feudalism* (World History). Farmington Hills, MI: Lucent, 2007.

Hunt, Norman Bancroft. *Living in the Middle Ages* (Living in the Ancient World). New York, NY: Chelsea House Publishers, 2008.

Johnston, Ruth A. *All Things Medieval: An Encyclopedia of the Medieval World*. 2 vols. Santa Barbara, CA: Greenwood Press, 2011.

Kallen, Stuart A. *Eye on Renaissance Art*. Farmington Hills, MI: Lucent Books, 2008.

Kelley, Donald R., and Bonnie G. Smith. *The Medieval and Early Modern World: Primary Sources and Reference Volume*. New York, NY: Oxford University Press, 2005.

Koestler-Grack, Rachel A. *Eleanor of Aquitaine: Heroine of the Middle Ages* (Makers of the Middle Ages and Renaissance). New York, NY: Chelsea House Publishers, 2006.

Laughton, Timothy. *Exploring the Life, Myth, and Art of the Maya* (Civilizations of the World). New York, NY: Rosen Publishing Group, Inc., 2011.

Morris, Craig, and Adriana von Hagen. *The Incas* (Ancient Peoples and Places). Reprint ed. London, UK: Thames & Hudson, 2012.

Mountjoy, Shane. *The Maya* (Lost Worlds and Mysterious Civilizations). New York, NY: Chelsea House Publishers, 2012.

Nardo, Don, ed. *Medieval Art and Architecture* (Eye on Art). Farmington Hills, MI: Lucent, 2012.

Norwich, John Julius. *Absolute Monarchs: A History of the Papacy*. New York, NY: Random House, 2011.

Riddle, John M. *A History of the Middle Ages, 300–1500*. Lanham, MD: Rowman & Littlefield, 2008.

Roux, Simone. *Paris in the Middle Ages* (The Middle Ages). Philadelphia, PA: University of Pennsylvania, 2011.

Rubenstein, Jay. *Armies of Heaven: The First Crusade and the Quest for Apocalypse*. New York, NY: Basic Books, 2011.

Smith, Michael E. *The Aztecs* (Peoples of America). 2nd ed. Hoboken, NJ: Wiley-Blackwell, 2011.

Streissguth, Tom. *The Greenhaven Encyclopedias of the Renaissance*. Farmington Hills, MI: Greenhaven Press, 2007.

Ullmann, Walter. *A Short History of the Papacy in the Middle Ages*. 2nd ed. New York, NY: Routledge, 2003.

White, Pamela. *Exploration in the World of the Middle Ages, 500–1500* (Discovery & Exploration). Rev. ed. New York, NY: Chelsea House Publishers, 2010.

Index

A

Abbas II, 161, 162
Abbasids, 58, 77, 79, 80–81, 86
Abbas the Great, Shah, 156, 160, 161
Abd al-Latif, 91
Abd al-Rahman I, 82
Aborigines, 191
absolutism/absolute monarchy, 107, 127, 128, 130
Act of Settlement, 128, 132
Afghanistan, 79, 86, 87, 90, 91, 93, 162, 164
Africa
    and colonialism, 137
    in Early Modern Period, 144, 178–179
    East, 101, 178
    North, 158–159, 178
    South, 101
    sub-Saharan in Middle Ages, 100–101
    West, 100, 179
Ahmed III, 157
Akbar the Great, 164, 165, 166
'Alawites, 159
Alba, Duke of, 134, 135
Albert II, 25, 57
Albigensian Wars, 29, 30, 45, 74
Alexius I Comnenus, 63, 70, 71
Alfred the Great, 35
Algeria, 158
Almoravids, 51, 83, 100
Anasazi, 102
Anglicanism, 128, 129
Anglo-Saxons, 12, 34, 35, 36
Anjou, House of, 43, 47, 55, 57
Arabs, 13, 19, 43, 48, 50, 62, 73, 77, 78, 79, 80, 83, 84, 92, 99, 100, 101, 142
Árpáds, 57
Ashikaga shogunate, 172, 173
Asia Minor, 62, 63, 64, 71, 72, 79
Augsburg Confession, 106, 109
Augustus the Strong, 149, 151
Aurangzeb, 92, 164, 166
Australia, 190, 191

Austria, 55, 56, 57, 116, 117, 118, 119, 156, 157
Ayyubids, 72, 73, 85
Aztecs, 103, 180, 181

B

Babur, 91, 93, 164
Baghdad, 80, 81, 82, 84, 86, 87, 88, 89, 90
Baldwin I, 64, 68
Balkans, 66, 68, 69
Bantu tribes, 101
Barbarossa (Khayr ad-Din), 158
Basil I, 62
Basil II, 63, 68
Batu Khan, 89
Bavaria, 15, 16, 18, 19, 22, 111, 115, 116, 119
Becket, Thomas, 29, 37
Berbers, 78, 79, 83, 100
Black Death, 10–11
Bohemia, 24, 25, 54, 55, 56, 57, 74, 111, 112, 113, 119, 148
Boleyn, Anne, 128, 129
Bornu Empire, 179
Bourbon, House of, 122, 123, 126, 141, 146
Brandenburg, 25, 109, 110, 111, 115, 120
Brazil, 144, 145, 184
British East India Company, 129, 133, 167, 169, 171
Buddhism, 93, 94, 96, 98, 99, 172, 177
Bulgaria, 62, 63, 64, 65, 67, 68, 69, 71
Burgundy, 12, 26, 31, 32–33, 134
Burma, 98, 99, 176
Byzantine Empire, 13, 17, 19, 43, 44, 48, 49, 58, 60, 62–65, 66, 68, 69, 70, 72, 79, 84, 154

C

Calukya dynasty, 92
Calvin, John, 27, 110
Calvinism, 108, 110, 111, 120, 123, 130, 134, 142
Canada, 186, 188
Capetians, 28, 29, 30, 32, 39

Carloman, 15, 16

Carolingian Renaissance, 17

Carolingians, 14, 15, 17, 18, 28, 32, 42

Catherine II (the Great) of Russia, 149, 152, 153, 157

Catherine de Médicis, 122, 123, 143

Catherine of Aragon, 128, 129

Catholic League, 112, 143

Celts, 34, 40, 41

Central America
    in Early Modern Period, 180–181
    early settlement and culture in, 102, 103

Central Asia, 87, 90, 163, 170

Charlemagne, 13, 14, 15, 16, 17, 18, 28, 42, 44, 50, 57

Charles I of Anjou, 43

Charles I of England, 130, 131

Charles II (the Bald), 17, 28, 32

Charles II of England, 131

Charles II of Spain, 146

Charles III of Spain, 36, 146, 147, 185, 187

Charles IV (Holy Roman Emperor), 24, 25, 30, 56

Charles V (Holy Roman Emperor), 25, 43, 73, 108, 109, 110,
    122, 128, 134, 135, 138, 140, 141, 142, 158, 184

Charles VII of France, 31, 33, 116

Charles XI of Sweden, 148, 151

Charles XII of Sweden, 151, 157

Charles Martel, 15, 16, 79

Charles the Bold, 31, 33

Chengzu, 168

Children's Crusade, 72

China
    in Early Modern Period, 107, 168–171
    in Middle Ages, 49, 88, 90, 94–95, 96, 98, 99, 101

Christian IV of Denmark, 113, 114, 150

Christianity/Catholicism
    and Anglo-Saxons, 16, 34
    and Byzantines, 63, 64
    and Charlemagne, 16
    in China, 169, 170, 171
    and Counter-Reformation, 111, 139, 142, 143
    and Crusades, 70–75
    in Early Modern Period, 106, 164, 165
    in East Africa, 101, 178
    in Eastern Europe, 54, 56, 57, 179
    in England, 128, 129, 130, 131, 132, 133
    and Enlightenment, 107
    in France, 122–125
    in German Empire, 108–110
    and Great Schism, 42, 45, 47, 63, 70, 152
    Greek Orthodox, 64, 65, 68
    influence/status of, 11, 13, 18, 20, 21
    in Ireland and Scotland, 40, 41
    in Japan, 172, 173, 175
    and Magna Carta, 38
    in Middle Ages, 11, 12, 13, 16, 18, 29, 35, 37, 42, 44–45, 76
    in Netherlands, 134, 136
    in New World, 184, 185, 187
    and Normans, 36
    and Ottoman Empire, 154, 155
    reforms, 20, 21, 26, 27, 37, 44, 45, 70, 106, 108, 139
    and Reformation, 26, 27, 106, 107, 108, 110, 134, 150
    and Renaissance, 106
    in Russia, 58, 59, 60
    in Scandinavia, 52, 53
    Serbian Orthodox, 69
    in southeast Europe, 66, 68, 69
    in Spain and Portugal, 50, 51, 83
    and Thirty Years' War, 112–114

Churchill, John, 132

Clovis I, 13, 14

Cluniac reforms, 20, 44, 70

colonization, 128, 129, 132, 133, 136, 137, 158, 165, 184, 186, 187, 188, 190, 191

Columbus, Christopher, 106, 142, 184, 186

Confucianism, 95, 98, 168, 169, 171, 172

Conrad II, 20

Conrad III, 21, 22, 71

Constantinople, 58, 60, 62, 63, 64, 65, 67, 68, 71, 72, 79, 154, 162

Cook, James, 190, 191

Copernicus, 106, 139

Córdoba, caliphate of, 80, 82

Cortés, Hernán, 181, 184

Cossacks, 60, 61, 152

Council of Trent, 106, 110, 138

Counter-Reformation, 106, 111, 139, 142, 143

Creoles, 184, 185

Cromwell, Oliver, 130, 131

Crusades/Crusaders, 22, 28, 29, 30, 37, 45, 46, 48, 49, 51,
    62, 63, 64, 67, 70–75, 84, 85
    background and causes, 70
    Crusader states, 71
    in Europe, 70, 74
    first and second, 71
    the last and end of, 73, 154
    third and fourth, 72

D

Dagobert I, 14, 15

daimyo, 173, 174, 175

Declaration of Independence, 107, 186, 189
Delhi, sultans of, 93
Denmark
    in Early Modern Period, 112, 113, 150, 151
    in Middle Ages, 34, 35, 36, 52, 53
Domesday Book, 36
Dracula, Count, 67
Drake, Francis, 129
Dutch East India Company, 167, 177

E

East Africa, 101, 178
Eastern Europe
    in Early Modern Period, 148–149
    in Middle Ages, 54–57
Eastern Schism, 44
Edict of Nantes, 123, 125
Edict of Tolerance, 119, 120
Edward I, 38, 41, 75
Edward II, 38
Edward III, 30, 31, 39
Edward IV, 39
Egypt, 81, 82, 85, 89, 158
Einhard, 16
Eleanor of Aquitaine, 28, 29, 37
Elizabeth I, 129, 130, 136, 167, 186
England
    in Early Modern Period, 128–133, 137
    in Middle Ages, 34–39, 40
English Civil War, 40
enlightened absolutism, 116, 117, 140, 145, 147, 151
Enlightenment, 107, 116, 119, 121, 127, 153, 185
Ethiopia, 178, 179
Eugène of Savoy, 118, 149, 157

F

Farnese, Alessandro, 135, 136, 138
Fatamids, 81, 84, 85
Ferdinand I, 50, 57, 109, 110, 148
Ferdinand II, 51, 111, 112, 113, 114
Ferdinand VI, 146, 147
Ferdinand of Aragon, 142
feudalism, 10, 21, 36, 41, 63, 96
Florence, 47, 48, 140

France
    in Early Modern Period, 112, 115, 118, 122–127, 131, 132, 133,
        137, 167, 177, 179
    in Middle Ages, 10, 28–31
    in the New World, 186, 188
    religious wars in, 123, 124
Francis I (Emperor, Francis Stephen of Lorraine), 119, 140, 149
Francis I, 122, 140
Francis II, 117, 119
Franks/Frankish empire, 13, 14–17, 18, 32, 44, 66
Frederick I (Barbarossa), 22, 23, 46, 72
Frederick I of Prussia, 120
Frederick II of Germany, 23, 43, 73, 74
Frederick II the Great, 107, 119, 121, 153
Frederick William I of Prussia, 121
Frederick William, Great Elector, 120
French Revolution, 107, 116, 117, 127, 142, 185

G

Galileo Galilei, 107, 139
Gama, Vasco da, 144, 167, 178
Genoa, 48, 49, 59, 63, 64, 65, 141
George I, 116, 132, 133
George II, 133
George III, 133, 188
George IV, 133
Germany, 54, 56, 71, 74, 75
    German Empire, 108–111, 116, 117
    early tribes, 12–13, 15, 54, 57
Ghaznavids, 93
Genghis Khan, 59, 87, 88, 89, 90, 95, 164
Ghibellines, 46, 47, 48
Ghurids, 93
Glorious Revolution, 40, 128, 131
Godoy, Manuel de, 147
Godunov, Boris, 61
Golden Horde, 89, 90, 91
Great Britain, 128, 132, 164, 167, 179, 190, 191
    in the New World, 186, 187, 188
Great Migration, 12, 32, 54
Great Schism, 42, 45, 47, 63, 70, 152
Greece, 64, 65, 67, 69
Greek Orthodox Church, 64, 65, 68
Gregorian reforms, 21, 44, 70
Gregory VII, Pope, 21, 44, 46, 70
Gregory VIII, Pope, 72
Gunpowder Plot, 131

Gur-e Amir mausoleum, 91
Gustav II Alolph, 114, 124, 148, 150
Gutenberg, Johannes, 106

H

Habsburgs, 24, 25, 26, 31, 32, 33, 43, 47, 48, 51, 56, 57, 66, 108, 109, 110,
    111, 112, 115, 119, 122, 124, 125, 128, 132, 134, 135, 137, 140, 141, 142, 143,
    144, 145, 146, 148, 149, 154, 155
Han dynasty, 94, 98
Hangzhou, 95
Hanover, House of, 116, 128, 132, 133
Hanseatic League, 53, 74
harems, 156
Heian Period, 96, 97
Hengist and Horsa, 12, 34
Henry I Beauclerc of England, 36, 37
Henry I of Saxony, 18
Henry II of Bavaria, 19, 20, 32
Henry II of France, 122
Henry II Plantagenet, 22, 29, 37, 40
Henry III of England, 38
Henry III of France, 123, 148
Henry III of Germany, 20, 21
Henry IV of France, 123, 124
Henry IV of Germany, 20, 21, 44, 46, 75
Henry V of England, 31, 33
Henry V of Germany, 21, 22
Henry VI of England, 31, 39
Henry VI of Germany, 23, 43
Henry VII Tudor, 39, 41, 128, 130
Henry VIII of England, 40, 128, 129, 130
Henry the Lion, 22, 23, 74
Henry the Younger of Brunswick-Wolfenbüttel, 109
Hesychasm, 65
Hideyoshi, Toyotomi, 173, 174, 175
Hindu empires in India, 92, 93
Hinduism, 92, 93, 99, 165, 166
Hohenstaufens, 18, 22, 23, 24, 26, 42, 43, 45, 46, 47, 72
Hohenzollerns, 120
Holy Roman Empire, 14, 28, 32, 33, 38, 42, 43, 45, 47, 49, 56
    beginnings of under Saxons, 18
    end of, 116, 117, 119
    under Enlightened absolutism, 116–121
    in the High and Late Middle Ages, 18–25
    and Thirty Years' War, 112
Huguenots, 120, 122, 123, 124, 125

Hülegü Khan, 89
humanism, 106, 107, 108, 148
human sacrifices, 181
Humayun, 164
Hundred Years' War, 14, 28, 30, 31, 33, 34, 39, 41, 47
Hungary
in Early Modern Period, 148, 149, 156, 157, 173
in Middle Ages, 54, 56, 57, 66, 69, 111, 118, 119
Hung-li, 171
Huns, 12, 57, 67, 68
Hussites, 56, 57, 74

I

Ieyasu, Tokugawa, 173, 174, 175
Inca Empire, 102, 103, 180, 182–183
India
    and colonialism, 133
    in Early Modern Period, 107, 133, 161, 164–167
    in Middle Ages, 86, 91, 92–93, 98, 99
Indian reservations, 185
Indochina, 177
Indonesia, 98, 99, 177
    and colonialism, 137
Inquisition, 11, 29, 51, 145, 147
Interregnum, 24
Iran, 162
Iraq, 81, 85, 87, 90
Ireland, 40
Islam, 10, 43, 48, 50, 51, 63, 64, 76–77, 92, 93, 142
    in Africa, 100, 101, 178, 179
    beginnings of, 76
    centers of Islamic science, 80
    in Central Asia, 163
    and the Crusades, 70–74
    in India, 92, 93
    in Indonesia, 99, 177
    and Mogols, 164, 165, 166
    and Mongols, 88, 89, 90
    and Ottoman Empire, 155, 156
    pan-Arabism and Pan-Islamism, 77
    in Persia, 160, 163
    religious teachings of, 76
    Shia and Sunni, 77, 78, 79, 80, 81, 84, 85, 86, 90, 160, 162
    in Spain, 74, 76, 77, 78, 79, 80, 81, 82, 83, 142
    spread of, 77–87
Ismail I, 160

Italy
    in Early Modern Period, 138–141
    in Middle Ages, 42–49, 62, 63
Ivan I, 59
Ivan III, 60
Ivan IV (the Terrible), 60, 61

J

Jadwiga, 55, 57
Jageillon dynasty, 55, 148
Jahangir, 165
James I of England (James VI of Scotland), 41, 130, 132
James II, 131, 132, 133, 137
Janissaries, 154, 156, 157, 158, 161
Japan
    in Early Modern Period, 168, 169, 172–175
    in Middle Ages, 96–97
Jerusalem, 70, 72, 73, 78, 85
Jesuits, 106, 110, 112, 139, 145, 147, 169, 176, 179, 180, 185
Jewish ghetto, 49
Jews/Judaism, 49, 51, 55, 142, 155, 164
    persecution of in Europe, 70, 71, 75
Joan of Arc, 31, 33
John I Tzimisces, 62, 63
John III Sobieski, 118, 149
John Lackland, 29, 30, 37, 38
John the Fearless, 33
Joseph I, 118, 145, 146
Joseph II, 107, 119, 139

K

Kalmar Union, 52, 53
K'ang-hsi, 170, 171
Khalji dynasty, 93
Khmer Empire, 98, 99, 176
Khwarizm-shahs, 87, 88
Kievan Rus, 55, 58, 59, 68
knights, orders of the, 73
Knights Templar, 30, 73
Kongo Kingdom, 178
Kosovo, Battle of, 68, 69, 154
Kublai Khan, 49, 89, 95, 97
Kurds, 85, 162
Kurfürsten, 24

L

László Posthumus, 25, 57
Leopold I, 118
Leopold II, 119, 140
Lisbon earthquake, 145
Lithuania, 54, 55, 61, 74, 148
Lodi dynasty, 93
Lombards, 13, 16, 19, 42, 43, 46
Lothair I, 17, 32
Lothair II, 22, 32, 42
Louis II, 32
Louis VII, 28, 29, 37, 71
Louis IX, 29, 30, 73
Louis XI, 33
Louis XIII, 124
Louis XIV, 124, 125, 126, 127, 132, 137, 146
Louis XV, 127, 149
Louis XVI, 127
Louis the German, 17, 32
Luther, Martin, 106, 108, 109
Luxembourgs, 24, 25

M

Macedonian dynasty, 62, 63
Machiavelli, Niccolò, 107, 141
Magellan 106, 177, 190
Maghreb, 81, 83, 158, 159
Magna Carta, 38
Magyars, 17, 18, 19, 54, 57, 118
Mahmud of Ghazna, 86, 93
Malcolm III, 41
Malta, siege of, 158
Mamelukes, 73, 85, 89, 155
Manchu dynasty, 107, 168, 169, 170
Mangu Khan, 89
Margaret I, 53
Maria Theresa, 118, 119, 127, 153
Marie Antoinette, 127
Mary I (Bloody Mary), 129
Mary (daughter of Charles the Bold), 25, 31, 33
Mary Stuart, 41, 129, 130
Mathilda of Tuscany, 46
Maya, 103, 180
Maximilian I of Austria, 31, 33, 56, 108, 134, 142, 148

Maximilian of Bavaria, 112, 113
Mazarin, Cardinal, 124, 125
Medicis, 47, 106, 138, 140
Mehmed II, 65, 69, 154, 155
Merovingians, 14, 15, 44
Michael I Romanov, 152
Michael VIII Palaeologus, 64, 65
Middle Ages, 9–103
    culture and spiritual life, 11
    living conditions, 10–11
    social order, 10
    transition to Modern Era, 11
Ming dynasty, 168, 169, 170
ministeriales, 20, 21
Moctezuma II, 181
Modern Period, Early, 105–191
    absolutism and Enlightenment, 107
    humanism and the Renaissance, 106
    inventions and discoveries, 106–107
    Reformation, Counter-Reformation, and Nation-States, 106
    rise of the bourgeoisie, 107
    transition to from Middle Ages, 11
Moguls, 91, 92, 107, 161, 164–167
Mongols, 49, 54, 58, 59, 60, 68, 73, 77, 78, 81, 84, 87, 88–91,
    93, 94, 95, 97, 98, 168, 169
    and Black Death, 10–11
    campaigns of Genghis Khan, 88
    empire of Tamerlane, 90
    rule of the Timurids, 91
    spread of Mongolian rule, 89
Montesquieu, 107, 127, 139
More, Thomas, 129
Morocco, 159
Moscow, 58, 59, 60–61
Muhammad (the Prophet), 76, 77, 78, 79, 159
Münzer, Thomas, 108
Muromachi period, 172
Musa, Mansa, 100

N

Nadir Shah, 160, 162, 163, 166
Napoleon, 27, 66, 73, 116, 117, 137, 139, 142, 145, 147, 151, 185
Nara Period, 96
Native Americans, 102, 185
Netherlands/the Dutch
    in Early Modern Period, 129, 131, 132, 134–137, 142,
        164, 167, 176, 177, 187, 191
    in Middle Ages, 32, 33

New England, 186, 187, 188
New World, discovery of, 106, 144, 184
New Zealand, 190, 191
"Nibelungenlied," 12
Nobunaga, Oda, 173, 174
Normans, 17, 18, 28, 34, 36, 42, 43, 63
North Africa, 158–159, 178
North America
    and colonialism, 129, 133, 136, 144, 186–189
    in Early Modern Period, 129, 133, 136, 142, 143,
        185, 186–189
    early settlement and culture in, 102
northern Europe
    in Early Modern Period, 151
    in Middle Ages, 52–53
Norway, 52, 53, 150
Novgorod, 58, 59, 60, 152

O

Oceania, 190
Ögödei, 89
Olmec, 103
Orange, House of, 134, 135, 136, 137
Ostrogoths, 12, 13
Otto I (the Great), 18, 19, 42
Otto II, 19, 63
Otto III, 19
Otto IV, 29
Ottoman Empire
    in Early Modern Period, 107, 118, 122, 141, 148, 149, 152,
        154–157, 158, 159, 160, 161
    in Middle Ages, 25, 57, 59, 62, 65, 66, 67, 69, 73, 76, 77, 90

P

Pakistan, 78, 79, 86, 93
Palaeologan dynasty, 64, 65
Palestine, 63, 70, 72, 73, 78, 81, 85, 158
papacy/papal states, 13, 16, 138, 42, 43, 44–45, 138
    during Counter-Reformation, 139
    and nobility in northern and central Italy, 140–141
    during Renaissance, 138
Parliament, 38, 128, 130, 131, 132, 133
Peace of Augsburg, 108, 109, 110
Peace of Utrecht, 126, 132, 137, 188

Peace of Westphalia, 115, 116, 124, 125, 150

Peacock Throne, 162

Penn, William, 187

Pépin III, 15, 16

Persia

    in Early Modern Period, 107, 160–163, 164, 166

    in Middle Ages, 78, 79, 80, 81, 84, 86, 88, 89, 91

Peter the Great, 151, 152, 153

Philip II of France, 29, 37, 38, 72

Philip II of Spain, 129, 134, 135, 136, 142, 143, 145, 177

Philip IV of France, 30, 39, 45

Philip V of Spain, 146

Philippines, 177

Philip the Bold, 32, 33

Photius I, 62

Piast dynasty, 54, 55

Picts, 34, 41

Pizarro, Francisco, 183, 184, 185

Plantagenet, House of, 37, 39

Poland

    in Early Modern Period, 148, 149, 151, 152

    in Middle Ages, 54, 55, 61, 74

Polo, Marco, 49, 95

Portugal

    in Early Modern Period, 106, 142, 144–145, 159, 164, 165, 167, 173, 176, 177, 178, 179, 190

    in Middle Ages, 50–51

    and the New World, 184, 186

Potemkin, Prince, 153

Primary Chronicle, 58

printing press, invention of, 106

Protestantism

    in England and Scotland, 128, 129, 130, 131

    in France, 122, 123, 124, 125

    in Germany, 108, 109, 110, 111

    in Ireland, 40

    in Netherlands, 134, 135, 142

    in Sweden and Denmark, 150

    in Switzerland, 27

    and Thirty Years' War, 112, 113, 114, 150

Prussia, 54, 55, 74, 116, 119, 120, 121, 148, 153, 157

Puritans, 186, 187

Q

Qajars, 160, 162

Qarakhanids, 86, 87

R

Raleigh, Sir Walter, 129, 186

Reconquista, Spanish, 48, 50, 51, 72, 74, 75, 142

Reformation, 26, 27, 106, 107, 108, 110, 134, 150

Renaissance, 11, 45, 57, 62, 106, 122, 138, 140, 148

Richard I (the Lion-Hearted), 29, 37, 38, 72, 85

Richard II, 39

Richard III, 39, 128

Richard of York, 39

Richelieu, Cardinal, 114, 115, 124, 125

Romania, 67

Roman Empire, 12, 13, 17, 44, 66

Romanovs, 58, 61, 152

Rousseau, Jean-Jacques, 107, 127

Rurik dynasty, 58, 59, 61

Russia

    in Early Modern Period, 148, 149, 152–153, 163

    in Middle Ages, 55, 58–61, 62, 68, 88, 89

Russian Orthodox Church, 59, 60

S

Sa'did dynasty, 159

Safavids, 155, 156, 160, 161, 162, 163

Saladin, 72, 85

Salians, 18, 20, 22, 44, 46

Samanids, 86, 87

Samarkand, 79, 81, 86, 87, 90, 91, 163, 164

samurai, 96, 97, 172, 173

Savoyards, 26

Saxons, 12, 16, 18, 28, 32, 42, 44, 54

Saxony, 22, 74, 109, 113, 114, 116

Schmalkaldic League, 109

Scotland

    in Early Modern Period, 128, 130, 131, 132, 133

    in Middle Ages, 34, 35, 38, 40, 41

sea voyages, age of, 106, 144, 190

secret societies, Chinese, 171

Selim I, 154, 155, 160

Seljuks, 63, 65, 68, 70, 71, 72, 81, 84, 86, 87

Serbian Orthodox Church, 69

Serbs, 64, 65, 68, 69

Seven Years' War, 119, 121, 127, 133, 147, 153, 188

Shah Jahan, 165, 166

Shah Rokh, 91

Shaybanids, 160, 163

Shir Shah Khan, 164

shoguns, 97

Siam, 176

Siberia, 60, 61

Sigismund, 25, 56, 57, 120

Simeon, 68

slavery, 72, 73, 85, 100, 107, 144, 145, 159, 178, 179, 180, 184, 185, 187

Slavs, 18, 19, 54, 56, 58, 66, 67, 68, 74

Song dynasty, 94, 95

Songhai Empire, 178

South Africa, 101

South America

    in Early Modern Period, 182–184

    early settlement and culture in, 102, 103

    Spanish and Portuguese in, 144, 145

Southeast Asia

    in Early Modern Period, 176–177

    in Middle Ages, 98–99

southeast Europe in the Middle Ages, 66–69

Spain

    in Early Modern Period, 112, 126, 129, 134, 135, 136,
        142–143, 144, 145, 146–147, 158, 177, 190

    Islam in, 74, 76, 77, 78, 79, 80, 81, 82, 83, 142

    in Middle Ages, 50–51, 70, 72

    and the New World, 180, 181, 183, 184, 185, 186

Stuarts, 40, 41, 128, 130, 131, 133

Sufi Order, 160

Suleiman the Magnificent, 154, 155, 156

Sweden

    in Early Modern Period, 112, 114, 124, 149, 150, 151, 152

    in Middle Ages, 52, 53, 59, 112, 114

Swiss Guard, 27

Switzerland/Swiss Confederation, 26–27, 33

Syria, 62, 63, 71, 72, 73, 78, 81, 85, 158

T

Tahmasp I, 160

Taj Mahal, 165

Tamerlane, 65, 88, 90, 91, 93, 164

Tang dynasty, 94, 95, 98

Tasman, Abel, 190, 191

Tell, William, 26

Teutonic Knights, 54, 55, 59, 73, 74, 148

Thais, 98–99

Theodoric the Great, 12, 13

Theophano, 19

The Three Musketeers, 124

Thirty Years' War, 26, 56, 108, 111, 112–115, 116, 118, 120, 124, 136, 143

    Danish war, 113, 150

    Franco-Swedish phase, 115

    Palantine-Bohemian phase, 112

    Peace of Westphalia, 115

    Swedish war, 114, 150

Time of Troubles, Russian, 61, 152

Timurids, 91, 160, 163

Tokugawa shogunate, 172, 175

Toltec, 103, 180

trading companies, European, 129, 133, 164, 167, 169, 171, 176, 177

Tragedy of Karbala, 79

Transoxiana, 81, 84, 86, 87, 88, 90, 91

Tudors, 39, 40, 41, 128, 129, 130

Tulip Era, 157

Tunisia, 158

Turks, 68, 77, 78, 80, 84, 86, 87, 88, 91, 92, 93, 118, 149,
    154, 157, 158, 162

Twelver Shiism, 160

U

Ukraine, 55, 58, 61, 148

Ulugh Beg, 91

Umar I ibn al-Khattab, 78

Umayyads, 50, 77, 78, 79, 80, 82

United States, 186, 187, 188, 189

Uzbeks, 91, 160, 161, 163

V

Valois, House of, 31, 32, 43, 47, 122, 123

Vandals, 12

Varangians, 58

Venice, 42, 48, 49, 59, 63, 64, 65, 66, 67, 141

Versailles, 125

Victoria, 132

Vijayanagar Empire, 92

Vikings, 28, 34, 35, 36, 52, 53, 58

Visigoths, 13, 50, 51, 79

Vladimir I, 58

Vladimir II, 59

Voltaire, 107, 121, 125, 127

W

Wales, 34, 35, 38
Wallace, William, 41
Wallenstein, Albrecht von, 113, 114
Walpole, Robert, 133
Wang Yangming, 168
War of Spanish Succession, 116, 120, 126, 132, 137, 141, 143, 146, 188
War of the Roses, 31, 34, 39, 41, 128
Washington, George, 189
Wattasids, 159
Welfs (Guelfs), 22, 23, 29, 32, 45, 46, 47, 48, 132
Wenceslas IV, 25, 56
West Africa, 100, 179
William I of Orange, 132, 134, 135, 136
William III of Orange, 131, 132, 137

William the Conquerer, 28, 35, 36
witch-trials, 116
Wittelsbach, House of, 24

Y

Yamato dynasty, 96
Yaroslav the Wise, 58, 59
Yung-cheng, 171

Z

Zimbabwe, 100, 101
Zwingli, Ulrich, 27